Intelligent Kindness

Second Edition

The first edition of Intelligent Kindness had a profound effect on me. A very substantial penny dropped. It provided a prism through which the complex decisions of health and social care could be viewed. When I became stuck, I took time to reflect on whether the decisions I was making as a doctor and a human were both intelligent and kind.

The first edition focused largely on healthcare, but this paradigm shift is needed for care wherever it occurs. There are millions of patchwork squares of care, from homeless support to high-tech hospitals, yet many of them are acting in isolation and desperate for support. Intelligent kindness provides a golden thread that weaves these patchwork squares into a connected quilt. It is not a simple book, but then caring is not a simple matter. It delves into a lot of detail and complexity, covering difficult areas of blame, fragmentation and uncertainty to emotional exhaustion. It recognises the burden of caring, how exacting it can be and the fundamental need to care for the carers.

It also emphasises the need to hear the voice of those we are caring for. Our health is our fitness for purpose, but we have to make the effort to discover what that purpose is, and what we wish to do with our wild and precious lives. Rarely do we take the time to ask the people we care for what matters most to them, to pay attention and to act on what we hear. Humans are social animals, and we exist to feel part of something bigger, as if we belong. Our health is relational, not medicational.

The second edition extends beyond health and social care, and into the welfare state. The book argues that it can and must be rekindled. There is a fine chapter on the Politics of Kindness. If MPs embraced a culture of intelligent kindness, and made decisions based on compassion, collaboration and the best flawed science we have, then the progress we make in the public interest would be greatly enhanced, and the toxic culture of blame and fear would diminish. Perhaps we need an Intelligent Kindness Party (anyone for IKIP?). Ultimately, the thread of intelligent kindness needs to weave through and throughout all our lives. Humans are the carers of everything, and we urgently need help. This book is it.

Phil Hammond
NHS doctor, campaigner, comedian and author of *Staying Alive – How to Improve your Health and Your Healthcare*

In our current care system, there is a danger that conscience becomes replaced by compliance and wise, responsive and virtuous practice goes out the window. This timely book shines an insightful, humane and engaging spotlight on this malaise and provides a hopeful, enticing and thoroughly practical blue-print for a better way forward. It is essential reading for anyone who came into social care to make the world a truly better place.

Nick Andrews
Research and Practice Development Officer,
Wales School for Social Care Research

Praise for the First Edition

Ballatt and Campling show how kindness can work to heal individuals, organisations and society

Prof Kate Pickett
Co-author of *The Spirit Level*

A wise and compelling insight into the crisis in compassionate care within the health service, and what can and should be done about it

Paul Gilbert FBPs OBE
Author of *The Compassionate Mind*

A passionate and clear articulation of the issues of kindness within professional caring systems. The message is clear, well argued for and makes a case with conviction beyond rhetoric

Dr Gwen Adshead
Visiting Professor of Psychiatry at Gresham College,
and Jochelson; Visiting Professor at the Yale School
of Law and Psychiatry, and Forensic Psychiatrist

This wonderful book is an urgent plea for kindness as both the driving force and the touchstone of healthcare in the NHS ... more than recommended reading. If I ruled the world, I would arrange for everyone who wields any power in the NHS to be locked in a room until they had read it. But then of course, that is precisely the sort of dictatorial behaviour that the authors see as the antithesis of intelligent kindness, and so I am obliged to fall back on an unrestrained enthusiasm that I hope will prove infectious.

Dr Iona Heath
Past President of the RCGP in a review in the BMJ

Intelligent Kindness

Rehabilitating the Welfare State

Second Edition

John Ballatt
Penelope Campling
Chris Maloney

CAMBRIDGE
UNIVERSITY PRESS

CAMBRIDGE
UNIVERSITY PRESS

University Printing House, Cambridge CB2 8BS, United Kingdom

One Liberty Plaza, 20th Floor, New York, NY 10006, USA

477 Williamstown Road, Port Melbourne, VIC 3207, Australia

314–321, 3rd Floor, Plot 3, Splendor Forum, Jasola District Centre, New Delhi – 110025, India

79 Anson Road, #06–04/06, Singapore 079906

Cambridge University Press is part of the University of Cambridge.

It furthers the University's mission by disseminating knowledge in the pursuit of education, learning, and research at the highest international levels of excellence.

www.cambridge.org
Information on this title: www.cambridge.org/9781911623229
DOI: 10.1017/9781911623236

© The Royal College of Psychiatry 2011, 2020

This publication is in copyright. Subject to statutory exception and to the provisions of relevant collective licensing agreements, no reproduction of any part may take place without the written permission of Cambridge University Press.

This book was previously published by The Royal College of Psychiatrists

First published 2011
The second edition published by Cambridge University Press 2020

Printed in the United Kingdom by TJ International Ltd. Padstow, Cornwall

A catalogue record for this publication is available from the British Library.

Library of Congress Cataloging-in-Publication Data
Names: Campling, Penelope, 1958– author. | Ballatt, John, author. | Maloney, Chris, 1959– author.
Title: Intelligent kindness / Penelope Campling, Leicester Psychotherapy Partnership, John Ballatt, The Openings Consultancy, Chris Maloney, People in Systems.
Description: Second edition. | Cambridge ; New York, NY : Cambridge University Press, [2020] | Includes bibliographical references and index.
Identifiers: LCCN 2019031208 (print) | LCCN 2019031209 (ebook) | ISBN 9781911623229 (paperback) | ISBN 9781911623236 (epub)
Subjects: LCSH: Medical personnel and patient – Great Britain. | Medical personnel – Great Britain – Attitudes. | Medical care – Great Britain – Psychological aspects. | Medical ethics – Great Britain. | Kindness.
Classification: LCC R727.3 .B335 2020 (print) | LCC R727.3 (ebook) | DDC 362.10941–dc23
LC record available at https://lccn.loc.gov/2019031208
LC ebook record available at https://lccn.loc.gov/2019031209

ISBN 978-1-911-62322-9 Paperback

Cambridge University Press has no responsibility for the persistence or accuracy of URLs for external or third-party internet websites referred to in this publication and does not guarantee that any content on such websites is, or will remain, accurate or appropriate.

Every effort has been made in preparing this book to provide accurate and up-to-date information that is in accord with accepted standards and practice at the time of publication. Although case histories are drawn from actual cases, every effort has been made to disguise the identities of the individuals involved. Nevertheless, the authors, editors, and publishers can make no warranties that the information contained herein is totally free from error, not least because clinical standards are constantly changing through research and regulation. The authors, editors, and publishers therefore disclaim all liability for direct or consequential damages resulting from the use of material contained in this book. Readers are strongly advised to pay careful attention to information provided by the manufacturer of any drugs or equipment that they plan to use.

Contents

Foreword

This is a generous book, as befits its subject. It is generous in at least three ways: it explains important ideas in open and understandable language; it explores theories that are actually useful in thinking about how we care for others; and it offers some comfort for those who work at a difficult time for public services and those (all of us in the end) who need these services.

It is also a whistleblower of a book. Not that it makes sensational accusations or revelations about the unintended cruelties of our welfare systems. There has been a succession of surveys, reports and inquiries which have done that for us, if we will only take note. This book does something else: it helps us to listen to what we know – from those reports as well as from our own experience – about the difficulties of responding with ordinary kindness to the distress of others. It helps us to overcome our indifference, to face up to the need to do better according to the demands of our humanity.

The book is very easy to read, and at the same time very difficult. What the authors are saying is important, chronically true and acutely relevant at this time – more so than ever, nine years on from the publication of the first edition. This account of the significance of kindness in our human relations does not flinch from the dark side of not only individual but also group behaviour, where there is disturbing evidence that the ordinarily caring individual may be influenced to act in an unthinking and cruel way. They describe how kind people do unkind things, and how unkind people – the same people – get away with it for so long. They explore the questions 'How do good staff become bad?' and 'How do we prevent that happening?'.

This second edition – reinforcing the arguments of the first – addresses one of the biggest issues of our time. We are more aware than at any time since the founding of the Welfare State that we live in a fragmented society, with great economic inequalities and arguments raging about who belongs or not. Our capacity to care for the other is a test of our humanity, a test that is now challenging us in ways that may seem overwhelming, as the authors describe.

It is difficult to talk about kindness, an ordinary quality caught up in the technological claptrap. Not sentimental. Not clever. Not easy to audit. Being with patients, clients, service-users or benefit claimants can be very hard work. If we deny that as a fact, we are in trouble, because then we build our defences against the difficulty of the work. We try not to feel the pain of the other or our own pain in responding. We have protocols and procedures, form-filling and training days. But this book poses a question for all of us to answer in our own way: how we do things, our practices and systems, are they helpful or are they hindrances to our capacity to show kindness in our relationships?

When we are most vulnerable, the most ordinary acts of kindness have very extra-ordinary effects – the patient or service-user recovers some sense of trust in a world that seems harsh and unforgiving of weakness. An 82-year-old woman, who had been a nurse in her working life, described to me her recent experience of hospital care, how she had found herself suddenly in a state of total dependency on others for basic needs, or as she described it, like a baby but with an adult's internal thoughts. 'For the first time in my life

I found that strangers were treating me with incredible kindness. I was totally charmed by the people. A sub-culture I had not even known existed until I had desperate need of their services.' She had experienced the kindness that this book describes and advocates for all our human services for those who are vulnerable, as all of us are at some time in our lives.

The Welfare State depends for its continued viability on the workforce, itself a reflection of a diverse society. Walk into a hospital and you will be aware of its staff, the women who make up most of its medical, nursing and auxiliary staff, the men and women of different ethnic identities, first and second generation immigrants as well as earlier generations. Some posts are well-paid but the care is delivered largely by those on moderate or low pay scales, many of them, like so many in work, now dependent on benefits to supplement their income. And the same is true of other welfare services, of the social carers supported by local authorities, and the front-line workers in Benefit offices.

This complex workforce is working to the 'common purpose' that Attlee described as the foundation of the Welfare State. A viable system of health and social care should provide a containing function for the wider diversity in our society – a modelling of the capacity to be with the other, which we know in the kinship of family but tend to forget in the disintegrating communities in our wider economy.

The authors show how kindness is eroded by the ethics of consumerism. We are kind because we are all in it together, not because we are looking to exploit our advantage over the other. And in a diverse world we need an ever-expanding vision of kinship.

The individualism that flourishes at the expense of social capital comes at a high cost. Hospitals, like public transport, are shrinking oases of human connectedness, where we still rub up against other people, and not just people like us. Despite under-funding, there is still a public perception of 'our' NHS being worth paying taxes for, while the continuing erosion of funding for social care has become catastrophic. So much for the continuing rhetoric on the need for integration of health and social care.

Multi-disciplinary and multi-organisational work does not depend on designing the perfect system, but on enabling people to work together with shared intentions and a sense of personal and professional agency – not following robotic imperatives, as the authors say. They describe initiatives being implemented to create integrated care networks, and certainly this is the crucial and biggest test of the capacity to cooperate between disparate systems in health and social services. They plead for enlightened leaders, and make the argument also for a facilitated bottom-up approach that takes account of the lived experience of practitioners and patients alike to counter the 'unrealism, rigidity and over-aspiration' of planners – and, I would add, politicians.

Health and social care professionals have learned not to 'love change' – as management gurus might advocate – but to hate the instability brought about by reorganisation fever. The account given here of the manic restlessness of successive reforms is in moderate language but the underlying anger of the authors is palpable. I used to think of these changes like tides that go in and out: mergers and the creation of mega structures in the name of efficiency, then devolution to a smaller scale in the interests of accountability, leading to further mergers, etc. The authors are convincing that these repeated interventions, driven by ideological certainties but with no clear evidence – and no time to collect the evidence before the next wave of reform crashes in – are symptomatic of a deep social anxiety. Such anxiety is unacknowledged but acted out by successive governments, in the face of the inevitable failures of a 'keep death at bay' health service and an underfunded social care system that is increasingly expected to mop-up society's largely unaddressed social issues.

We often want to see the failures of a system as isolated incidents, aberrations in an otherwise well-functioning state of affairs, but there are too many failures for this to be a sustainable argument. The authors make the powerful argument that kinship and kindness, properly understood, can themselves shape the quality, effectiveness and efficiency of care. They undertake a wide-ranging exploration of the conditions that influence the expression of those qualities in individuals, teams and organisations. They know what they are talking about. They dig into their extensive clinical and managerial experience to uncover from below the surface the deeply held concern that what we are doing is actually not good enough.

The authors engage the reader in an intense conversation. They put forward a passionate argument for valuing the Welfare State and how it might be nurtured in our current world. Do not expect to agree with everything the authors say, but be prepared to enter into the argument.

Tim Dartington
(author of Managing Vulnerability: The Underlying Dynamics of Systems of Care, Karnac Books, 2010)

Authors' Note

The enthusiastic reception for the first edition of this book has prompted us to produce a second. We were delighted by the interest from people thinking about and working in public services beyond healthcare, although the book had been unapologetically health focussed.

Eight years have passed, and although the issues we addressed are still very much with us, times have changed. 'Austerity' has bitten hard into the UK's public services, especially social care. Developments in policy, technology, organisation and practice have affected health and social care, separately and together. Mindful of this, we have extended our reach to consider both sectors and, to an extent, the wider world of 'welfare'. Hence our new subtitle: *Rehabilitating the Welfare State*. We have expanded our narratives, case studies and references accordingly, believing that the issues and perspectives in each field illustrate important points for all.

This presents some challenges in our choice of examples, stories and references, and also in our language, especially when we speak of those who need or receive services. Terms such as 'patient', 'client' or 'service-user' carry baggage. In other circumstances one might deconstruct this. Here, though, to keep our central focus we have chosen to alternate between such labels: whilst holding in mind that behind each of them there is always a person, with needs, aspirations, and their own personality and life circumstances.

Our focus is the value and relevance of intelligent kindness to how the public thinks about, how policy shapes, and how organisation and professional practice realise the vision and intentions behind our public services. As a great many factors influence the wellbeing of the Welfare State, we draw on a range of disciplines to place our critique in a wider social and political context.

To maintain the flow, and to avoid excessive detail, we have judged that this is not the place to burden the reader with excessive detail or too much reference to controversy, but rather to create an overarching narrative that stimulates critical thought and exploration. Consequently, we summarise complex ideas and evidence, including those areas where we have our own specialist knowledge and experience. We are aware that this may frustrate readers from various specialisms, who might look for more detail or nuance. To mitigate this, extensive references are used throughout, both to support our argument, and to point to useful and interesting further reading. Ultimately, our argument is grounded in our experience and observations over our working lives.

We have substantially re-written much of the original book. In response to preoccupations in our current world we have added several new chapters, including one on blame, and one on 'the hostile environment'. End of life care, covered in the first edition, is of course still very relevant, but has been covered extensively elsewhere, and has been omitted as part of our change of focus. Our new penultimate chapter, 'Cultivating Intelligent Kindness', offers ideas that may help support and sustain healthy organisational culture and effective, humane practice.

We have cautiously welcomed the appearance of the word 'kindness' in policy, education and practice since the first edition. Many national and local initiatives have promoted compassionate care. This has prompted us to stress a system-wide perspective to help ensure that such focus on kindness and compassion is underpinned by the intelligence without which, we fear, it simply adds to the list of 'musts' so often imposed on people working in challenging circumstances.

Although we are primarily concerned with health and welfare services in the UK, many of the ideas we explore are more broadly applicable – both to other countries, and to other sectors such as education and justice. Fundamentally, we are concerned with culture, with promoting the conditions where relationships flourish, and with bringing out the best in each other as we undertake vital and difficult work.

As we write, British public services are in an even more precarious state than at the time of our first edition. Their staff are under close to intolerable pressure, as they work on our behalf to address daunting suffering, disturbance and need. At the same time, poverty, social division, conflict and preoccupation with excluding others have reached dangerous levels, both nationally and internationally. We believe that our argument addresses these perils, and is, more than ever, important.

Finally, we are now three co-authors, not two. Chris Maloney was a wise adviser on the first edition, and now steps into the team.

Chapter

1 The Heart of the Matter

Real national unity sprang from the things which we had in common; the greater that common interest, the stronger the nation in peace as well as in war.

(Clement Attlee, 1941)

Between 1946 and 1948 the UK's 'social contract' was transformed. A programme of legislation ushered in what has come to be known as our Welfare State. The country was emerging from a long, bloody and destructive war. The population was facing daunting psychological, social and economic challenges and was desperate for change. The new laws were a paradigm shift: a radical change in the funding and organisation of health and social care and the support of those in need.

For centuries, poverty and hardship had been dealt with under the Poor Law. These laws dated back to Tudor times, but had been reinvented in 1834, with the setting-up of the dreaded 'workhouses'. Further reform gathered pace in the early twentieth century, with a range of liberal welfare laws, and the development of friendly societies and trades unions. These reduced the risks of penury, neglect, suffering and death for the poor, disabled, old and sick. But importantly, help was still haphazard and stigmatised. And fear of the workhouse cast a long shadow.

The wartime coalition government of 1941 had set up an inter-departmental committee to review Britain's health, social insurance and allied services, as a way of boosting morale and the war effort. Its report, written by the economist William Beveridge, was probably the most widely read government report of all time and has been referred to by his name ever since. It famously identified five Giant Evils in society: squalor, ignorance, want, idleness and disease (Beveridge, 1942). In 1945 the Labour party won the post-war election on a platform that promised to address these Evils. Clement Attlee's new government then began the work that led to the NHS and the modern Welfare State.

Three laws – the National Insurance Act (1946), the National Health Service Act (1946) and the National Assistance Act (1948) – embodied a radical new approach to organising care. The people of the nation took on formal responsibility for the welfare of each other. We all now *shared* the risks of accident and illness, of unemployment, disability, dependency and poverty. In giving new responsibilities and powers to government, we took on, collectively, the challenges of identifying need, developing strategy, allocating resources within limited budgets, and organising and deploying staff and services to deliver on our behalf.

This was more than an expression of *duty*, more than the embodiment of a moral obligation. True, the aftermath of war, with the death, injury, loss, social disruption, need and expectation of a populace that had in so many ways risen at great cost to do its duty, meant that we owed each other mightily. Those 'in power' embodied – and no doubt many of them felt – that obligation. But perhaps war had reinforced something else. Perhaps we were ready to accept that we needed each other, that the welfare of the one depended on the welfare of all. Perhaps, however dimly, we recognised that investing our resources through taxation and national insurance into the work of promoting universal welfare was in everyone's interests. The introduction of the Welfare State can be seen as a remarkable expression of *kinship*, an idea we will explore in some detail in this book. And it continues to be a project – far from perfect – that invites society to attend to, and value, its deepest interests and connectedness.

There is always a but. This fine idea, this commitment to fostering the health, happiness and wellbeing of the national family, had to be *implemented*. This 'best laid plan' required decisions about how much and whom to tax, how much to invest in national welfare, how much to pay to those in need. We had to decide just how to organise and deliver the financial benefits, healthcare and social services involved. Having a wonderful vision is not enough: the devil lurks in both the overall translation of that vision into reality, and in the complex detail of the systems and practices involved. The arrangements made have time and again been deemed to be failing, insufficient, inefficient or outdated. They have been changed, or 'reformed', with varying degrees of honesty, intelligence and sensitivity, at least as often as governments themselves have changed.

Moreover, the nature of society itself has changed: slowly at first, and then with increasing pace. Longevity has increased, partly as a result of the efforts of the Welfare State itself. Along with this have come previously unimaginable increases in chronic conditions. At the same time, scientific progress has made effective treatment of once thought incurable illness possible. All this means the costs and complexity of care, in all its forms, have escalated.

Social inequality, having initially lessened, has risen massively, between geographical regions, but also within individual communities, along with increased social fragmentation, isolation and division. As the nature of the UK economy has changed, partly through the effects of globalisation, so the nature and availability of work has changed. Economic crises, such as the financial crash of 2008, have disrupted confidence, will and investment. Technical developments, business activity, advertising and consumerism have raised citizens' expectations, and thus the cost of living 'satisfying' lives. Social media, while facilitating connections between people across the globe, have led to fragmented communities of the like-minded, to increased hostility between differing groups, and to overt and covert manipulation of participants.

Partly as a result of these wider changes in society, there have been enormous increases in mental health difficulties, child abuse and family breakdown. The number of children taken into care has risen steeply. Alcohol and drug abuse, and its effects, have steadily escalated. In some parts of the country unemployment and its effects have scarred whole communities for years. At the same time in-work poverty has also become a problem. The Welfare State has become a big part of British family life. In 2013, 20.3 million families were receiving some kind of benefit (64 per cent of all families), about 8.7 million of them pensioners (*The Observer*, 2013). Homelessness – perhaps the most visible barometer of the welfare of a society – grew significantly in the 1980s and 1990s, with significant numbers of women and families living on the streets for the first time in decades. The sharp decrease in public spending during the government's 'austerity' programme from 2010 made a further impact. Homelessness in the second decade of the twenty-first century is so prevalent that some worry it has become institutionalised; a row of people huddled in sleeping bags outside expensive department stores – some of them very young, some of them employed – an unquestioned fact of life.

For a long time, British social attitudes to people in need have been, to say the least, ambivalent. The benign – and, as we will argue, vital – recognition of the importance of investing in the welfare of all has wobbled on rough seas of public opinion, scepticism and political ideology. Certain sections of the press regularly turn out stories about 'scroungers' and 'benefit cheats', feeding the notion of the 'undeserving poor'. Should 'dependency' be encouraged, or people left 'to create their own destinies'? What levels of need justify public help, and what should be expected instead from families, neighbours and communities? Are there indeed 'deserving' and 'undeserving' people?

Should the state deliver all, most, or nothing of what such people need, or should a mixed economy within an allegedly trustworthy and benign ecosystem of market forces be promoted? Is taxation a 'rip off' of 'hardworking individuals', an inhibitor of business creativity, or a civilised way for us all to contribute to what society needs? Should we invest as much per capita in health and social care as other developed nations? How do we guarantee that our money is being spent wisely, efficiently, effectively and safely?

All along the way of course, we have had to contend with other, less appealing, human realities. Greed and competition for resources, the will to possess and dominate, and to reject or exclude, have always disturbed our productive cooperative relationships. People have broken the rules, been lazy, aggressive, and pursued their own interests, at all levels of society.

We need to accept from the start that no approach is perfect. Individuals do have to face limits on what the state, husbanding limited resources on our joint behalf, will and can fund – whether it be new drugs, benefits or more staffing. A universal, comprehensive system requires steering, commissioning, regulating and managing on a grand scale. The system can foster unhelpful dependency and a lack of personal responsibility. Citizens, including public servants, can develop a sense of passive (and sometimes aggressive) entitlement to services or ways of working.

Priorities are often hard to agree upon, and even harder to reconcile locally. They can be skewed by public panic, the interest groups who shout loudest, ideas about most (and least) deserving groups, media campaigns, stigma and denial. Our public investment in health, social care and welfare can be vulnerable to wider events – war, recession, crime and the costs of other public priorities such as leaving the European Community.

Even those in tune with the values underpinning the Welfare State question whether it is possible to adapt the system to the nature of modern society. Critics such as Hilary Cottam argue that its institutions and services reflect the era of mass production in which they were designed and suggest there is a fundamental lack of fit with twenty-first century issues. Like many others, she despairs of the relentless attempts to 'fix' the Welfare State, believing that it is the underlying philosophy of the system that is the problem.

> *While we focus narrowly on how to patch and mend our post-war welfare institutions our attention is diverted from the bigger social shifts and transitions that are taking place. The world that surrounds our welfare systems is very different. When we ask our questions and start our innovations from within – standing inside the institution and wondering how they can be fixed – we miss the mismatch between what is on offer and what help is required. And crucially, we also overlook the potential that surrounds us: the new ideas, resources, inventions and energy that we could bring to the problems at hand.* (Cottam, 2018, p. 28)

Where Now?

The approach in this book is both practical and pragmatic. We are where we are, and, to be frank, the problems being so immense, it is not where we would want to start from. Nonetheless, we believe that the NHS is the best way of providing professional healthcare for all, and that collectively investing in financial support and social care for those in difficulty is in everyone's interests. Whilst we would concur with many of the criticisms of the Welfare State from Cottam and others, we also know – and indeed have experience of – centres of excellence, and services within state-funded health and social care that encourage constant improvement, welcome new ideas, inspire creativity and energise both staff and service-users.

In short, we believe that the Welfare State, despite its many flaws, is the best and most practical way to go about securing the health of a civilised society: and that making this model work well should be a priority for us all. Politicians should be articulating this clearly and powerfully to the people, and we the people should in turn be campaigning for it.

Facing and struggling with the inevitable complexities and shortcomings in its delivery has to be worth it. The NHS, in particular, despite it being commonly agreed to be at crisis point, was still, in 2018, the most valued institution in the UK, a prime element of our social capital, with 61 per cent of us happy to increase our taxes to pay for it (National Centre for Social Research, 2018).

It is, however, of concern that so little attention has been given to understanding and promoting what we see as central to the Welfare State: its embodiment of kinship. There seems to be a failure to understand and value it, a paucity of positive rhetoric, a lack of pride, a loss of historical narrative. This becomes more pressing as the generation who are old enough to remember the hardships and anxiety before the Welfare State was part of our landscape are no longer with us. Programmes of reform are more likely to be effective if we are able, as a society, to reconnect to, and so rehabilitate, the idea that pooling resources and sharing responsibility for each other can be good for everyone.

One important aspect of this kinship is its expression in the compassionate relationship between skilled practitioners and the people they are trying to help. To fail to attend to the promotion of kinship, connectedness and kindness between staff and those they assist is to fail to address a key dimension of what makes people do well for others. Such failures can sometimes be no more than minor irritations, but they can also lead to appalling systemic abuses, neglect and maltreatment.

This dark reality is evidenced in the reports of a succession of inquiries. These have covered shortcomings and abuse in the care of the elderly, people with intellectual disabilities, and in several acute healthcare trusts, child protection and residential care. Such scandals raise disturbing questions in the public mind about how compassion can fail. But, disappointingly, these questions receive far less attention than they deserve when subsequent corrective action is taken.

As well as prompting concern about the nature of care, sagas of abuse and neglect trigger doubts about the whole enterprise of the Welfare State. Of course, abuse and neglect can, and do, occur in all health and social care systems, both public and private, and in all parts of the world. Our exploration in this book seeks to shed light on some of the factors leading to such failures, in our particular time and place. More importantly, we hope to illustrate how such failures may be minimised, and how services can be helped to achieve what our commitment to them deserves.

Ideas to Guide Us

The dictionary definition of 'rehabilitation' includes both 'the action of restoring to health' and 'the action of restoring someone to former privilege or reputation after a period of disfavour'. Both are needed. Since the 1970s, the very idea of the Welfare State has been denigrated, with its champions easily appearing apologetic and defensive, and impractically idealistic. Meanwhile, those ideologically opposed to the underlying concept of socially funded health and welfare simply cut funding and disparage the services. As neglect becomes more common, services deteriorate and highly trained staff choose to leave.

As to kindness: kindness is generated by a thought and felt understanding that self-interest and the interests of others are bound together. In professional roles, we have a range of knowledge, skills and tools. When we work with intelligent kindness, we intervene with an understanding of the likely meaning, effects and value of what we do for the other as a person.

When the way we relate to the other is shaped by such intelligent kindness, the quality of their experience, the effectiveness of our intervention and the efficiency of our efforts are all improved. We will lay out evidence for this argument, examining ideas relating to the challenges for the individual, the team, the wider system and society when they try to make this real.

If we were to apply this understanding to the way things are run, we believe that our public hopes and expectations for the service would be far more likely to be met. It may be unavoidable that we have, some of the time, to consider and frame what we do in a transactional, commodified, industrial and value-for-money perspective. But we will argue that it is dangerous to undervalue attention to ways in which the work is a commitment to the skilled and effective expression of fellow feeling and kindness. Neglecting this will lead to waste and poor performance, to low morale and poor service-user satisfaction, to continued shameful abuses. The loss of valuable staff will continue.

The great majority of people who choose to train and practice in health professions, social work and wider social care do so with at least some such fellow feeling. Everyone has received help from another. Everyone knows, on some level, that the value and effectiveness of such help, however technical or practical, has depended on the capacity of the helper to connect with the other personally. Everyone knows that help, whatever else it involves, is fundamentally *relational* and that good results emerge from the quality of the *collaboration* between the helpers and the people helped.

Intelligent kindness begins with deliberately directing our attention to connecting with the other person. It then involves allowing their needs, experience and personality to influence us, to prompt our imagination and knowledge to shape a response that will help and reduce suffering. To undertake this task, we must be alert to, and manage, feelings that distract us, that push us away from responding kindly, even that tend towards unkindness or cruelty. We must also look after ourselves and our colleagues.

Perhaps reassuringly, many readers will see what we have to say as just common sense. Conductors and theatre directors, sports managers, coaches and psychologists all recognise the crucial 'edge' given by addressing the psychology of the individual and the group. They practise, rehearse, analyse their players' collaboration, and work to promote confidence and intuitive teamwork. More broadly, sports pages, theatre and music reviews all recognise as crucial the issues of attitude, commitment, morale and the mutual attunement of players. When the 'giant killers' in football, Leicester City, rose to win the Premiership in 2016, Leicester developed into a city of excited football analysts. The success of the team became the focus of conversation in pubs and corner shops. Everyone competed to explain how the club led the field in committing resources and skill to the health, fitness and psychology of their team. Where are the conversations that show similar understanding and passion when it comes to the services that meet our deepest needs?

During the men's football World Cup in 2018, Gareth Southgate, England's new manager, rapidly became a hero, admired for his emotional intelligence and his understanding of his team, both as individuals and as a unit. One of the many stories around was his decision that they spend a week with a group of Royal Marines, knowing that the training of our armed forces is particularly focussed on fostering strong relationships. The team spoke warmly of what they had learnt from this experience, even the fact that mobile phones were expected to be turned off at meal-times, and conversation encouraged! If only the same amount of attention was paid to these matters across health and social care.

Human beings have great capacity for kindness, but also for destructiveness and violence. This book is not about sentimental 'niceness' or simple altruism. When we speak of people acting with intelligent kindness, we expressly do not mean that they feel only warmth and goodwill towards another. Life is, of course, a great deal easier when we feel nothing but kindness for another person. But all of us can be tired, selfish or impatient. We all have competing and conflicting motives and priorities. All of us have darker feelings. Any politician or other leader who strives to create a vision of national wellbeing, whether it be the 'Big Society', the 'Good Society' or a rejuvenated Welfare State, will need to apply their intelligence, and adequate resources, to managing potentially destructive feelings and processes, at the same time as encouraging enthusiasm for the idea.

Particularly when undertaking complex, emotionally-laden human work, simply requiring people to be compassionate and effective will have little effect unless the systems, and the culture, within which they work, are organised and managed in ways that support the humanity of their members, their relationships with each other and the people they aim to help. Staff at the front-line work within teams, institutions and cultures that will either support or undermine them as human beings, as intelligent practitioners.

At times we will talk about 'genuine' or 'authentic' kindness. By this, we mean, a spontaneous, informed, improvisation arising from the particular nature and circumstances of the person one is with. This is not the same as the barista in the coffee shop automatically asking everyone she serves if they've had a nice day, because that's what the firm have taught, indeed ordered her to do, with 'mystery shoppers' ensuring she complies. True kindness involves a sense of agency.

Nevertheless, the difference between authentic and inauthentic kindness is far from clear-cut. Acting kindly while feeling reluctant or resentful is no bad thing in itself – indeed, it can be valuable hard work. But if it becomes mechanical or habitual rather than guided by an awareness of the other person, this is another matter.

There is a substantial body of knowledge to illuminate what kindness is, and what managing to be kind is about. This knowledge relates to the attitudes and behaviour of individuals, to teams and groups, to organisations and to society. It also illuminates our understanding of why things go wrong, of why people behave unkindly; and also what conditions promote kindness and effective action to restore wellbeing. It shows direct links between kindness, effectiveness and positive outcomes. It suggests virtuous circles that affect the recipient of help, the worker and the organisation.

The Task in Hand

Let's say we put a fraction of the effort that has gone into organising, regulating and industrialising public services into cultivating what helps and hinders this sort of way of working. It would have enormous impact on effectiveness and efficiency as well as on staff morale and the experience of the people receiving services.

We are not suggesting yet another evangelistic 'national programme'. Nor are we proposing some sentimental crusade. We do not advocate a 'technology of kindness'. But what if this body of knowledge were to be used to develop our understanding about how to reform, improve and ensure the quality and value for money of our services? What if we understood better how to bring out, nurture and protect kindness and its related attentiveness to what others need? What if people were educated, trained and supported in bringing this understanding into practice, whether as policy makers, managers or practitioners? And here's a radical thought: what if all aspects of the Welfare State – skills, technologies, procedures, research, where money is spent, how people are recruited and managed – were considered through the lens of intelligent kindness?

This book is an experiment with this approach. We hope to help those who work in the Welfare State to consider how to manage themselves, as they labour on society's behalf in stressful, anxious, often traumatic situations. We will offer ideas to help them think about how to integrate the technical aspects of their task with sensitive and skilled relational practice. The book addresses and attempts to help policy and opinion makers, leaders and educators come to grips with what will genuinely improve services. People who are patients or service-users, especially those active in trying to influence the system, may find some or all of our observations helpful. However, all of us who live in, and rely upon, the Welfare State need to think about and reconsider its value, and how we can nurture it. This book is for everyone who cares about that.

We, the authors, have worked in the NHS and in social care for many years. We have cared for people, supervised and trained staff, managed budgets, delivered savings and reshaped services. We have developed strategy and managed change. We have made mistakes in our work, and also done things we are proud of. We have been patients, needing care from many parts of the healthcare system at different times in our lives. We have supported children, friends and elderly relatives through health and social care at times of vulnerability, illness and dying. These experiences have been of variable quality – sometimes apparently due to 'the system' and sometimes because of the attitudes and skills of staff. It has often been difficult to tell the difference.

We have found the work gruelling and gratifying, enriching and draining; deeply satisfying but raising profound questions about our humanity; a treasured privilege that comes at a cost. Like millions of others, we have tired of the frequent 'reforms' and ever-increasing entanglement with bureaucracy. Like thousands of others we have had to struggle with disillusion and cynicism whilst also being aware of the dangers of idealising the past. As our frustration has grown, so has our conviction that there must be a better way of organising things, a way that brings out the best in people, a way that connects us to each other and to the inspired vision that prompted the formation of the Welfare State.

There have been times in history when kinship could be taken for granted. At other times it has been under threat, and needed attending to. Often it has only reasserted itself after traumatic disruption: it is as if, without such disruption, people may have grown complacent. There are enough indicators that the Welfare State – indeed the UK's broader social contract – is currently under serious threat, for us to want to put forward arguments that might contribute to its rescue, its 'rehabilitation'. We hope that all readers, whoever you may be, will be prompted to think more about what is really needed to ensure the vision of 1948 is realised in the face of new and increasing challenges, and how we can all re-discover a sense of kinship. This is the heart of the matter. Now we need to think more about kindness.

References

Attlee, C. (1941) Speech in Chesterfield (13 June, 1941), quoted in *The Times* (14 June, 1941), p. 2.

Beveridge, W. H. B. (1942) Social Insurance and Allied Services: Report by Sir William Beveridge. HMSO.

Cottam, H. (2018) Radical Help: how we can remake the relationships between us and revolutionise the Welfare State. Virago.

National Centre for Social Research (2018) British Social Attitudes Survey 35. Available at: www.bsa.natcen.ac.uk/media/39285/bsa35_key-findings.pdf [last accessed 14 August, 2019].

The Observer (2013). Benefits in Britain: separating the facts from the fiction. *The Observer*, 6 April, 2013. Available at: www.theguardian.com/politics/ 192013/apr/06/welfare-britain-facts-myths [last accessed 14 August, 2019].

Chapter 2 Rescuing Kindness

Yet do I fear thy nature; it is too full o' the milk of human kindness.

(William Shakespeare, Macbeth*)*

Kindness and Kinship

The word 'kindness' evokes mixed feelings in the modern world. To begin this exploration of its importance and the value of making it central to improving health and social care, it is important to bring into focus what it is we are discussing. This means attempting a definition. More importantly, it means rescuing the concept (and what it indicates) from the grip of a range of social and cultural forces that obscure, warp and denigrate what kindness is, marginalise it in the debate about what matters, and make it more difficult to be kind.

As an adjective, *kind* means being of a sympathetic, helpful or forbearing nature and, importantly for our argument, being inclined to act to bring pleasure or relief. It is important to keep the word rooted in its deeper meanings, though. It can easily become a mere synonym for individual acts of generosity, sentiment and affection, for a general, fuzzy 'kindliness'. The origins and derivation of the word 'kind', in English evolving from Old, through Middle, to Modern English, suggest a much deeper collective, ethical meaning.

The roots of the adjective lie with the noun – also 'kind' and, when applied to human beings, cognate with 'kin'. It indicates that we are 'of a kind', who we are, that we are linked together, in the present and across time, with natural responses and responsibilities towards each other. Tracing the word to its roots helps us recapture these deeper meanings, with resonances that are central to our argument. For those interested in the origin of language, the linguistic history of kindness is outlined in Box 2.1 below.

The word 'kindness' indicates the quality or state of being kind. It describes a condition in which people recognise their nature, know and feel that this is essentially one with that of their kin, understand and feel their interdependence, feel responsibility for their successors and express all this in attitudes and actions towards each other. Kindness is both an obligation to our kin born of an understanding of our connectedness, and the natural expression of our attitudes and feelings arising from this connectedness.

Box 2.1 The Roots of Kinship

Old English
Cynde or cynn,
Noun: family; race; kind; sort; nature; kin
(ge)cynde
Adjective: natural, native, innate

Midde English
Kende, or kunde, or kinde,
Noun: kind; nature; race; kin
Adjective: natural, native, innate; originally 'with feeling of relatives for each other'

Modern English
Kind
Noun: a group of people or things having similar characteristics
Adjective: having or showing a friendly, generous, and considerate nature

Genuine acts of kindness emerge from this state. Kindness challenges us to be self-aware and takes us to the heart of relationships, where things can be messy, difficult and painful. It is closely linked with the concept of compassion (literally, suffering with), sympathy (fellow feeling) and the biblical word 'agape' (neighbourly or 'brotherly' love). People who are rooted in a sense of kinship with each other are inclined to attentiveness to the other, to gentleness, warmth and creativity on their behalf. Kindness is kinship felt and expressed.

Kindness is natural – we see it all around us. It motivates people to pay attention to each other, to try to understand what they enjoy, what they need, and to act accordingly. It emerges from a sense of common humanity, promotes sharing, effort on others' behalf, sacrifice for the good of the other. It drives imagination, resourcefulness and creativity in interpersonal, family, community and international life. When people are kind, they want to do well for others.

Understanding the roots of kindness in kinship can help us grasp some of the challenges involved in its expression. There is, and always has been, a drive to define ourselves *against others*, to narrow down our sense of kinship to immediate family, social group, race or nation. On the other hand, much of what is civilized about humanity has grown through extending kinship to *include* others, to share, cooperate, and to develop a wider sense of common identity and common interest. Julian Tudor Hart, in 'The Political Economy of Health Care' (Tudor Hart, 2010) puts it another way:

> *Solidarity, a belief that humans are all of one species, that we are social animals who stand or fall together, whose survival depends on helping one another, and whose genetic diversity is a strength rather than a weakness, has sound foundations in human biology.*

The challenge to broaden our sense of belonging from self, to 'our family', to 'the human family' (and beyond) is ever-present. When we use the word kinship throughout this book, it is with the constant recognition of this perennial struggle to expand our sense of 'kin', to include 'the other' in our sympathies.

So kindness is difficult, involving overcoming narrow self-interest, anxiety, conflict, distaste and limited resources. It involves cost, and the risk of getting things wrong, maybe of being hurt somehow in the process.

Kindness is most effective when directed by intelligence. It really is no good fixing the boiler for the elderly lady next door if you are not qualified in gas engineering, however good she or you feel about your apparent generosity. Knowing not to feed a hungry newborn with pasta can be a help.

A classic illustration of how kindness can miss its target or even make things worse is the relief of Belsen concentration camp in 1945 where the initial attempt to save lives led to more deaths because of ill-informed attempts to feed the starving.

Box 2.2 The Importance of Intelligence

Memoirs of the soldiers and medical teams liberating Belsen concentration camp recount the mixture of shock, pity and a passionate desire to reach out to the starving and very ill.

This prompted compassionate soldiers to hand over their beef rations to the starving prisoners, tragically unaware that many would die faster from this sudden unaccustomed protein.

When the outcome of this ill-informed kindness came to light, the Army sent for a tinned formula that had been used to relieve famine in India. Sadly, the unfamiliar smell and taste was received by the sufferers with revulsion.

It was only when the tinned formula was tailored to the particular needs of the Belsen inmates – in this case, mixed with paprika – that the sufferers' bodies and minds were able to accept the nourishment and deaths were averted.

This story teaches us about the importance of applying intelligence to kindness and some of the ways uninformed kindness can go wrong. We will explore later in the book, for example, how over-identifying another person's needs with one's own (the well-meaning Belsen soldiers handing over their rations) can lead to problems; and look at the tendency across the Welfare State to standardise interventions (those in charge at Belsen, failing to realise that what worked in India would not be stomached – literally – in Eastern Europe) as if everyone's needs are the same.

Kindness can be general and intuitive in many situations, but there are other situations where it is necessary to be more informed and specific if it is to be effective.

Most decorated service personnel directly ascribe their heroism to strong, intimate fellow feeling and kinship with their comrades – as individuals and as groups. They know and feel that they are 'kin', 'of a kind', and act accordingly. Such inspiring connectedness is also required when a parent cleans the faeces and vomit of the infant or when the care worker sees through frightening, distasteful evidence of illness, inadequacy, addiction or chaos to care for the person suffering. The armed services, along with their emphasis on drill, discipline and chain of command, put enormous effort and attention into promoting connectedness, loyalty and kinship. This fellow feeling helps those in the services to overcome fear, focus on their frightening task, and work together – even in the face of death.

It cannot be said that the same attention is given to the promotion of fellow feeling and kinship in those working across the Welfare State, and this is alarming. It is particularly worrying because staff need not only to develop solidarity among themselves but must work together to meet others (service-users and their families), to connect with them, ascertain their needs (which is frequently difficult), treat and care for them and help them stay well.

There is something rather distasteful about the current vogue for the metaphor of 'war' in health – the 'war' on cancer is a common trope, for example. However, staff and those they care for occupy a field full of dangers, uncertainties and choices that frequently demands courage, teamwork in crisis situations, and intense relationships. The daily work is full of routine, procedures and resources that need to be brought to life and marshalled to address real needs and dangers for real human beings. Though the risk to the clinician or social worker is far less lethal than that to the soldier, there are frequently high risks of mistakes, of things going wrong, of illness killing the patient, of suicide, of damaged parents murdering their infant. Small errors can have enormous consequences. To fail to attend to promoting kinship, connectedness and kindness between staff and with those they serve is to fail to address a key dimension of what makes people do well for others in such circumstances.

For centuries, kindness was seen as a primary virtue. Crucially, that does not mean it was simply regarded as 'a good thing'. A virtue has to be worked at, because achieving it is, however 'natural', difficult. All major religions, and the cultures they have influenced, promote compassion, hospitality to the stranger, treating other people as one would wish to be treated oneself, indeed 'loving kindness', whilst recognising that much of human nature pushes against it (Armstrong, 2009).

Many thinkers have criticised the way, as human beings in the modern world, we are increasingly short-termist in our thinking. We are encouraged to assume that solving the problem immediately in front of us is what matters. We forget that patterns of sociability and ethical standards have evolved over millennia. The problem with this is that it is easy to lose sight of the larger questions about, for example, the meaning and purpose of our social institutions in the long term. Rowan Williams, philosopher, author and the ex-Archbishop of Canterbury, wrote the following in response to evidence of the 'thinning out' of historical knowledge.

> *But if we don't know how we got here, we will tend to assume that where we are is obvious. If we assume that where we are is obvious, we are less likely to ask critical questions about it. The less likely we are to ask critical questions about it, the more resistant we will be to other people's challenges to it. In other words, not understanding how we learned to be the people we now are has an immediate and highly dangerous effect on the society we are and might seek to be, just as it might have a dangerous effect on any individual who tries to block out the memory of the experiences that have, as a matter of fact, made them who they are.*
> (Williams, 2018, p. 56–7)

It is often religious leaders that draw attention to the importance, not only of individually working at virtues such as kindness, but understanding the historical development of such values within the human race. However, kindness as we have defined it is not just asserted as a virtue in religion. It has also had a central place in secular – indeed materialist – movements.

Political concepts such as the brotherhood of 'man', the 'fraternité' that goes with liberté and egalité, are direct expressions of kinship and kindness. Socialism, and projects such as anti-slavery, women's suffrage and anti-racism are all centred on the idea of overcoming apparent differences, removing conditions of inequality, disadvantage and suffering, restoring kinship. Right-wing movements are also characterised by an idea of kinship – of a 'volk', a family, a race, a nation. Here, though, we usually see 'kinship' being defined against or at the expense of, rather than in the interests of, others. A similar position is readily identifiable in the more fundamentalist religious movements, which set themselves and their kin against those of other religions and of none. In left-wing thinking, too, especially revolutionary socialism, a principle that we are all equal and interdependent, a commitment to serving the common interest ('from each according to their ability; to each according to their need') has nevertheless frequently split 'the human family' into insiders and outsiders. Thinking about these trends may help us grapple intelligently with some of the problems inherent in the 'project' of kindness at a societal level.

Within the family, of course, the problems of kinship are all too frequently revealed. The vast majority of child sexual abuse and, by definition, all domestic violence, happens there. Such perversions of kinship demonstrate just how vulnerable it is to the toxic invasion of the worst forms of 'selfishness', to the dark side of intimacy, and to abuses of power. Kindness can be eclipsed even within the bounds of 'blood kinship'. As we build our arguments throughout this book, we will pay close attention to the factors that pervert healthy kinship and kindness: intelligent kindness requires such understanding.

One of the more problematic aspects of kinship, then, is whom we include as kin, and how we understand and manage the difficulties in our relationships and obligations 'within the family' and 'with the other'. How we behave within and on this boundary determines how much kinship is expressed as kindness beyond narrow self-interest.

A philosophical attachment to kinship and kindness, therefore, is not enough. The espousal of the 'virtue' has been used to justify all sorts of actions, ranging from the inspired to the barbaric, in both religious and secular life. Kindness implies an attitude of openheartedness and generosity, but also a practice that can be challenging and risky and that requires skill. The inconsistency in the application of the virtue has not just been because it is hard to fight unkindness in the world: it is also because it can be very hard to be kind, individually or in groups. That, in turn, is difficult to admit.

Kindness Disparaged

A consequence of this difficulty has been a growing tendency to suspect any person, movement or institution promoting kindness of being naïve, hopelessly idealistic and ineffectual, or even sinister, hypocritical and dangerous. We have learned to suspect assertions of values like kindness and kinship, to suspect 'virtue signalling', and to put our faith in more selfish, more technical, more 'privatised' things. In modern Western society this retreat from kinship has been accelerated by a wide range of powerful influences, many of them explored in later chapters.

The warping and obscuring of what kindness is about is extensively discussed by psychoanalyst Adam Phillips and historian Barbara Taylor in their book *On Kindness* (2009). They explore the way in which a philosophy and culture of competitive individualism and the pursuance of self-interest have challenged the value, and negatively influenced the meaning, of kindness. Kindness, they say, is not a temptation to sacrifice ourselves, but to include ourselves with others – kindness is being in solidarity with human need. They describe a process in which what had been a core moral value, with a subversive edge, at centre stage in the political battles of the Enlightenment, became something sentimentalised, marginalised and denigrated through the nineteenth and into the early twentieth century:

> *Kindness was steadily downgraded from a universal imperative to the prerogative of specific social constituencies: romantic poets, clergymen, charity-workers and above all, women, whose presumed tender-heartedness somehow survived the egoist onslaught. By the end of the Victorian period, kindness had been largely feminized, ghetto-ized into a womanly sphere of feeling and behaviour where it has remained, with some notable exceptions, ever since.* (Phillips and Taylor, 2009, p. 41)

Gradually, the value and pertinence of kindness was edged into this periphery by a spirit of 'manly' rugged individualism and competitive enterprise. This movement was closely associated with the Industrial Revolution, with its valuing of scientific progress, technology and entrepreneurship, reinforced by the attitudes and wars of Empire. A split developed between (empty-headed, unrealistic, amateur, female) kindness and (knowing, clear-sighted, professional, male) competitive enterprise and the pursuit of self-interest. A range of other cultural crowbars widened this split. One of the key influences was that of mass production and the associated market. This shifted the emphasis in people's lives to being consumers rather than sharers, to acquisition and to the competitiveness that used quaintly to be referred to as 'keeping up with the Jones's' and might today be expressed as keeping up with the Americans or Chinese.

Increasingly, the quest for security and wellbeing through acquisitiveness and material goods has centred on technology and industry. Possessions, that which makes and secures them, and that which communicates and displays them become signs of worth and identity. Such competitiveness is not reserved for such wealth and possessions but extends into all aspects of social life. This is most vivid in celebrity culture and the myriad 'reality television' shows that tout the popularity of 'a to d listers' with the public, and that offer 'wannabes' the chance to join the celebrity family. To return to Phillips and Taylor:

> *A culture of 'hardness' and cynicism grows, fed by envious admiration of those who seem to thrive – the rich and famous: our modern priesthood – in this tooth-and-claw environment.* (p. 108)

An individualistic, competitive society, is, then, whatever its achievements, prone to breed unkindness.

Kindness and Survival

A strong driver of the imbalance towards competitiveness and self-interest has been a widespread misapplication – and misrepresentation – of social Darwinism, which has had increasing influence in economics, politics and most aspects of social life. Competition, based on self-interest, has been reinforced by ideas derived from simplistic readings of Darwinism itself – the skewed reading of nature as 'red in tooth and claw'. Later work, such as Richard Dawkins' *The Selfish Gene* (Dawkins, 1976), has fed such a rhetoric and been claimed as an 'evidence base' for justifying the promotion of competition and individualism in politics and economics, as well as in social and personal life. Nowhere is this influence more evident than in the way 'free market forces' (the unregulated competitive interaction of enterprises bent on the profit motive) have been regarded, until very recently, as benign, creative and even natural – indeed, as the only road to human wellbeing.

In fact, Dawkins is clear that reciprocity based on a sense of human kinship is an evolutionary reality. Action directed even by the most 'selfish' of genes is expressly characterised by the fact that its interests lie in connecting with, cooperating with and caring for others who carry that same gene – kinship. Dawkins is also passionate about our unique (evolved) capacity as human beings to transcend the purely determined and to transform civilisation using our intelligence and moral consciousness (Dawkins, 2009). Other students of evolution have recognised that Darwin himself described an important role for cooperation and interdependence in *The Origin of Species* (1859). Many scientists, including Lynn Margulis, have described a remarkably powerful place for cooperation within and between species in evolution itself (Margulis, 1998). Kinship and its expression in kindness can, then, be seen not just as a psychosocial concept, but as the representation in human psychology and social life of a primary evolutionary process.

When apes descended from the trees and began to evolve into us, competitive tool-making helped, but cooperation and kinship transformed and combined the invention and ingenuity of individuals into a social evolutionary force of unimaginable power. Cooperation actually creates 'the fittest' who 'survive'. Reproductive success may have been dependent on having the most impressive tools, but it was through sharing them that the conditions emerged for accelerated development towards safety and comfort. At least at the level of higher animals and primates, this sharing is clearly driven by recognition of the other, and their wellbeing, as being connected to one's own, and requiring attentive response. This idea, and the kindness involved at a human level, needs to be restored to its rightful place.

Enterprise, self-confidence and self-reliance, individualism and science and technology are all of value. It is the split between these qualities and those of kinship and interdependency that is disturbing. Without the recognition, and balancing influence, of common destiny and connectedness inherent in kindness, these things can become toxic. The unregulated financial market, the fetishism of the body as a commodity or building site for 'beauty', and unrestrained polluting industry are various forms of this toxicity. Social wellbeing degenerates as these products of the split multiply. Without applying our knowledge of the power of cooperation, inspired by kinship and expressed through kindness, we will fail to create the thriving society most would look for. We are all, more than ever, interdependent at a planetary level, and our future depends on our being able to cooperate – and better than we have ever done before. Moreover, global issues, such as climate change, challenge us to be imaginative enough to extend our sense of kinship to generations as yet unborn, as well as to other countries, such as Bangladesh, parts of Africa and the USA, where the crisis is already extreme.

The Trouble with Kindness

Apart from universal human struggles to overcome self-centredness, bad temper and greed (daunting in themselves) there is a deeper problem associated with kindness. As Phillips and Taylor (2009) put it:

> *Real kindness changes people in the doing of it, often in unpredictable ways. Real kindness is an exchange with essentially unpredictable consequences. It is a risk precisely because it mingles our needs and desires with the needs and desires of others, in a way that so-called self-interest never can.* (p. 12)

Kindness, then, may be, deep down, frightening and hazardous.

In the modern world, this problem with kindness is particularly challenging. The risks to health and wellbeing from genetics, lifestyle, relationships, society, environment and international affairs are, more than ever, preoccupations for all of us. There is clear evidence that anxiety levels (or their twin, attitudes of denial) are consequently higher. Education and the media also expose us to the vulnerability, suffering and dangerousness of humankind, close to home and afar. We are daily confronted with evidence of just how perilous it is to link ourselves with the destiny of others. This all goes to amplify the sense of danger inherent in kindness and cooperation. It takes courage to link one's fate with others in the context of such apparently vast and frightening problems.

Phillips and Taylor, quoted above, speak of kindness being *'ghetto-ized into a ... sphere of feeling and behaviour where it has remained, with some notable exceptions, ever since'* (p. 41). The foundation of the Welfare State was one of those notable exceptions – as well as being an optimistic project to eradicate ill-health and ill-being, it was an expression of kinship, a commitment to kindness.

In the Second World War, British men and women had laboured for each other, fought, been wounded, bereaved and died for the sake of the common good. The founding of the Welfare State after the war saw a peacetime expression of this commitment. At one and the same time it was an act of appreciation and recognition by the people to the people. It was a contract and understanding between us that we would continue to share our resources to face our common risks and improve our common destiny. It was an expression of kinship. We took our vulnerability, woundedness and loss, our courage, self-sacrifice and fellow feeling, and invested them, along with our resources and our ingenuity, in a peacetime 'family enterprise'. Like war, this common pursuit would bring us, individually and collectively, victories and defeats, costs and advantages, miracles and tragedies.

Phillips and Taylor argue that this commitment to communal wellbeing was, in fact, short-lived. They suggest that the individualism, independence and 'enterprise culture' that has emerged over the past 30 years or so has been a very poor soil for the growth of kindness. On the other hand, signs of the founding values of the Welfare State can still be detected and it is central to our argument that the NHS, social care and benefits system should be valued as core components of our public good. Take a look at the 2009 NHS Constitution for England:

> *The NHS belongs to the people. It is there to improve our health and well-being, supporting us to keep mentally and physically well, to get better when we are ill, and, when we cannot fully recover, to stay as well as we can to the end of our lives.*
>
> *... It touches our lives at times of basic human need, when care and compassion are what matters most. ... The NHS is founded on a common set of principles and values that bind together the community and the people it serves – patients and public – and the staff who work for it.* (Department of Health, 2009, p. 2)

This document commits the NHS to work in partnership to prevent ill health, to provide care that is personal, effective and safe. The policy also sets down the latest expression of values of the NHS: respect and dignity, commitment to quality of care, compassion, improving lives, working together for patients and 'everyone counting'. Would that the same unambiguous assertion of the value of social care and social security was offered to the public. It is evident that the NHS, at least, is still seen as having a responsibility to deliver on the public compact of communal kindness that was entered into at its foundation. There are, however, problems in translating that view into action.

Given the sustained onslaught on the value and power of kindness, the untrammelled growth of the culture of self-interest and the deep fears kindness evokes, it is unsurprising that many of us – from citizen to government – lose our nerve. At times of stretched resources – such as during the years of 'austerity' – this loss of nerve is more likely. Instead of valuing and reinforcing the core commitment to kinship and kindness involved in the Welfare State, we turn our minds to setting rules for and to policing people we seem not to trust. At best, we increasingly prefer to think of this enterprise mainly in terms of technology, industrial systems, processes, survival statistics, financial efficiency and 'rights'.

Could it be that we have lost confidence? Could it be that we have succumbed to anxiety and embarrassment about focussing on the central vision of kinship, the reciprocity and the values it requires? Have we lost faith in the idea that keeping connected to that vision can make a difference?

We may have lost our nerve in this way; that is, except when we or our loved ones are patients or in need of social care. Then the importance of kindness comes to the centre of things. Patients and people receiving care realise how kindness makes them feel. Just as important, they seem to know how closely it is connected to effectiveness.

Kindness and the Common Good

Kindness, then, is not a soft, sentimental feeling or action that is beside the point in the challenging, clever, technical business of managing and delivering health and social care. It is a binding, creative and problem-solving force that inspires and focuses the imagination and goodwill. It inspires and directs the attention and efforts of people and organisations towards building relationships with those they care for, recognising their needs and treating them well. Kindness is not a 'nice' side issue in the project of competitive progress. It is the 'glue' of cooperation required for such progress to be of most benefit to most people.

The mistrust that has been evoked in society relating to the motives and behaviours of those professing to be kind was highlighted earlier. The concept of kindness in this book assumes authenticity, where emotional response and behaviour are in tune with and spring from generosity, empathy and openheartedness. This rules out those whose seemingly kind bedside manner masks sadistic motives and behaviour – Harold Shipman being the most extreme example – and those who preach kindness as a duty but are unable to connect genuinely with the living humanity of another person. It also rules out those who gush with sentiment; and the self-righteously pious, whose primary motivation is to be saintly. A twenty-first century version of this is the superficial kindness that is required of employees, taught and monitored by the organisation within which they work. Of course, it is in an organisation's interest to have the staff 'on side' with its core values, but there are ways of doing this that deepen our humanity and others that cheapen it.

A concept within the discourse about emotional labour that has gained traction in the corporate world, is that of 'surface acting'. Research has found surface acting, involving a performative process through which outward expressions are altered without attempting to modify the employee's actual emotional experience, to be problematic for employee wellbeing (Grandey, 2003; Hülsheger and Schewe, 2011). We would argue too, that such a lack of authenticity is unlikely to inspire trust in those that need health and social care. It is certainly not what we mean by intelligent kindness.

There is no doubt that true kindness, though it makes us all feel better, is difficult. Later chapters will discuss the nature of this difficulty and consider some of the ways in which it can be overcome. However, from the start, we need to make sure we are comfortable with, and properly understand, the concept of kindness itself. The renowned academic historian Tony Judt wrote passionately about collective welfare and the values of community (Judt, 2010a). In an interview just before he died, he spoke movingly about the need for a language that binds us all together:

> *We need to rediscover a language of dissent. It can't be an economic language since part of the problem is that we have for too long spoken about politics in an economic language where everything has been about growth, efficiency, productivity and wealth, and not enough has been about collective ideals around which we can gather, around which we can get angry together, around which we can be motivated collectively, whether on the issue of justice, inequality, cruelty or unethical behaviour. We have thrown away the language with which to do that. And until we rediscover that language how could we possibly bind ourselves together?* (Judt, 2010b)

Questions about kindness are fundamental to this project: whether we dare rescue the enlightenment concept of kindness, with its depth and political potency; whether we can find a way to use it to edge us towards a society based on the common good; and whether we can unashamedly re-own the language of kinship and the simplicity with which it asserts our common humanity. Nowhere is this more important than in health and social care, in the enterprise of the Welfare State.

References

Armstrong, K. (2009) Charter for Compassion. See http://charterforcompassion.org [last accessed 5 August, 2019].

Darwin, C. (1859) *On the Origin of Species*. John Murray.

Dawkins, R. (1976) *The Selfish Gene*. Oxford University Press.

Dawkins, R. (2009) *The Genius of Charles Darwin* (DVD). Channel 4.

Department of Health (2009) The NHS Constitution for England: The NHS Belongs To Us All. HMSO.

Grandey, A. A. (2003) When 'the show must go on': Surface acting and deep acting as determinants of emotional exhaustion and peer-rated service delivery. Academy of Management Journal. 46 (1): 86–96.

Hülsheger, U. R., Schewe, A. F. (2011) On the costs and benefits of emotional labor: A meta-analysis of three decades of research. Journal of Occupational Health Psychology. 16 (3): 361–89.

Judt, T. (2010a) *Ill Fares the Land: A Treatise on Our Present Discontents*. Allen Lane.

Judt, T. (2010b) Interviewed in London Review of Books, 25 March, 2010.

Margulis, L. (1998) *Symbiotic Planet: A New Look At Evolution*. Orion Books.

Phillips, A. and Taylor, P. (2009) *On Kindness*. Penguin.

Tudor Hart, J. (2010) *The Political Economy of Health Care: A Clinical Perspective*. Policy Press.

Williams, R. (2018) *Being Human*. SPCK Publishing.

Chapter

3 A Politics of Kindness

The notion that ethics, altruism and fellow-feeling are scarce resources, whose supply is fixed once and for all and depleted with use, this idea seems to me outlandish – outlandish but deeply influential. My aim in these lectures has been to call this idea into question. I've tried to suggest that the virtues of democratic life – community, solidarity, trust, civic friendship – these virtues are not like commodities that are depleted with use. They are rather like muscles that develop and grow stronger with exercise.

(Michael Sandel, Reith Lecture 2009)

To dare to look at the Welfare State through the lens of what we know about kindness requires, of course, strong justification. In short, our argument is that focussing on kinship, expressed through kindness, will both improve health and wellbeing, and make our systems of care more effective and efficient. Some of the evidence for this is found before we even open the door to the consulting room or the hospital, or follow the community nurse or social worker into a person's home. It relates to the dynamics of kinship at a societal and political level.

Poverty and Health

Improvements in the health and wellbeing of a nation are due to many things other than the way it chooses to organise the delivery of care. While there is no doubt that public wellbeing improved during the early years of the Welfare State, the reasons for this were many. Much of the progress was the continuation of a process of sanitary reform and infrastructure improvement that began in the nineteenth century. Medical advances such as the use of antibiotics and vaccination programmes made a radical difference. The early decades of the NHS coincided with a period known by public health specialists as the 'epidemiological transition', when infectious diseases lost their hold as the major cause of death in the industrialised world. Chronic diseases such as heart disease and cancer replaced infections as the main cause of mortality. Though the toll of these diseases is serious, the general level of health in higher-income countries continued to rise throughout the twentieth and into the first decade of the twenty-first century. Socioeconomic factors have also played a significant role in improvements in general health, particularly the lessening of absolute poverty, which, in the UK in the last century, was addressed through the financial safety nets and benefits of the Welfare State.

The link between poverty and poor health is well known; the fact that people at the bottom of society have shorter lives and suffer more illness is no surprise (Department of Health, 2009). The World Health Organization's Commission on Social Determinants of Health published a hard-hitting report in 2008 with the stark message that, on a global perspective, social injustice was killing people on a grand scale (WHO, 2008). In Britain, health disparities have been a major item on the public health agenda for years, with at least a seven-year difference in life expectancy between the lowest and highest socio-economic groups. The Marmot review, Fair Society: Healthy Lives (Marmot, 2010), advocated reducing health inequalities through putting social justice, health and sustainability at the heart of all policies. The report was critical of the poor record of policy in tackling health inequalities in the UK and placed an emphasis on delivery systems and leadership. Sadly, it confirmed that the health gap between the average and worst-off areas was wider than it was in 1997. Moreover, it is not simply a matter of the poor having worse health than everyone else: in richer countries, higher income leads to a lower death rate at every level of society.

If we look a little deeper into what was going on in Britain in the years preceding the foundation of the NHS, some interesting issues emerge. In the two decades that contained the First World War and the Second World War, the increase in life expectancy for civilians was six-to-seven years for men and women. This is roughly twice that seen throughout the rest of the twentieth century in the eight decades before, between and after the wars, where the increase in life expectancy was between one and four years (Wilkinson, 1996). This is surprising given the fact that material living standards declined during both wars. It is true that nutritional status improved with rationing in the 1940s, but rationing continued into the 1950s and did not happen during the First World War. Both periods of war were characterised, however, by full employment and narrower income differences, and rates of relative poverty were halved. Could it be that the encouragement to cooperate with the war effort, the reduction in inequality, and the resulting sense of mutuality, camaraderie and kindness contributed in some way to better health?

Inequality and Health and Social Outcomes

Income inequality appears to have a dramatic effect on the health of a nation. In Japan after the Second World War, the huge redistribution of wealth and power led to an egalitarian economy with unrivalled improvement in population health (Subramanian and Kawachi, 2004). In contrast, Russia has experienced significant decreases in life expectancy since the early 1990s as it has moved from a centrally planned to a market economy, accompanied by a rapid rise in income inequality (Walberg et al, 1998). Perhaps the best-known example of the linkage between inequality and health is that of impoverished but egalitarian Cuba, which has maintained lower infant mortality rates than its rich neighbour, the USA, and a similar life expectancy to the UK (Hertzman et al, 2010; World Bank, 2018). This is worrying: in the 1970s the UK was the second most equal country in Europe: by 2015 we were the most unequal. Between 1990 and 2015, the UK slipped from seventh to nineteenth out of 28 European nations in terms of neonatal mortality (Dorling, 2018).

Public health, it seems, is improved not only by reductions in absolute poverty, but also by the degree of income equality. This has been referred to as 'the big idea', and while it is an idea that attracts emotional and ideological opposition, the evidence supporting it continues to accumulate (British Medical Journal, 1996; Pickett and Wilkinson, 2009; 2015).

In their books *The Spirit Level* and *The Inner Level*, Richard Wilkinson and Kate Pickett (2009, 2015) collate the evidence that inequalities are as crucial as absolute poverty in predicting the condition of a society, including the health of the population. Using 30 years of research data, they demonstrate that almost every modern social and environmental problem is more likely to occur in a less equal society and has little correlation with average income. In their first book, they cited evidence showing the correlation of inequality with ill health, breakdown of community life, violence, drug addiction, teenage births, obesity, mental illness, big prison populations and lack of social mobility. A decade later, in *The Inner Level*, they showed that inequality correlates with a dizzying range of health and social problems. For example, depression, schizophrenia, narcissism, problem gambling, child ill-being, bullying, poor educational attainment, low social mobility, and household debt are all worse the more unequal a nation is.

These correlations appear to hold across all societies. Inequality is bad for poor countries because a significant proportion of the population will not have their basic needs met – access to clean water, food and shelter – whilst others live in luxury. In rich countries, where meeting such basic needs can more generally be taken for granted and levels of absolute poverty are low, the effects of inequality are more complicated. Examination of the relationship between life expectancy and national income per person shows life expectancy increasing rapidly with stages of economic development among poorer countries but this slows down and then levels off completely across the richest 30 or so countries (Wilkinson and Pickett, 2009, p. 7). Rates of economic growth are no longer linked to improving the general health of the population, which is now more to do with influencing lifestyle choices and managing risk. Among richer countries, the more unequal ones do worse even if they are richer overall, so that per capita GDP turns out to be much less significant for general wellbeing than the size of the gap between the richest and poorest 20 per cent of the population (the basic measure of inequality Wilkinson and Pickett use).

What matters is the scale of material differences between people. In a country where that difference is low, the average life expectancy is likely to be higher and infant mortality rates lower than in a country where the gradient of material inequality is steeper. Comparisons between states in the USA show this pattern, with unequal states clustering together regardless of income. Utah (relatively poor and equal) does as well as New Hampshire (relatively rich and equal) on a range of measures, while California (relatively rich and unequal) scores badly, like Mississippi (relatively poor and unequal) (Wilkinson and Pickett, 2009, pp. 22, 83).

The links between health and social problems and income inequality have been becoming clear since the 1970s, and by 2019 the case was supported by hundreds of published peer-reviewed studies looking at a range of health and social measures as well as life expectancy (Kondo et al, 2009; Wilkinson and Pickett, 2018, p. xviii). It is not, though, simply the case that inequality means bad outcomes for those at the bottom of the social ladder. The link between inequality and poor health outcome is distributed across the social scale: it affects nearly everyone, rich and poor. What seems to matter is where you sit on the socioeconomic gradient in relation to other people within the same country, as well as the steepness of this gradient compared with the steepness of the gradient in other countries. How could this be? And does it have any link with kindness?

Chronic Stress, Inequality and Health

Many have hypothesised that the link between equality and health is mediated through psychosocial mechanisms. In other words, material inequalities have a detrimental influence on social relations, which in turn affect people's psychological state, and physiological balance, particularly through the effects of chronic stress.

As affluent countries have grown richer, rates of anxiety and depression have risen, presumably as a result of the psychological and social effects of wealth inequality and consumerism. Once a country has reached the level where a rise in average income makes no significant improvement to health and wellbeing, purchases become used as signifiers of status and identity. Citizens are then caught in a stressful play of desire, uncertainty and choice. There is a growing literature about the tyranny of consumerism, the problematic nature of excessive choice, and the stress this causes in relatively wealthy societies. The American psychologist Barry Schwartz has explored this issue in such books as *The Paradox of Choice: Why More Is Less* (Schwartz, 2004).

Schwartz suggests (and uses research to demonstrate) that excessive choice can evoke paralysis: too much choice makes choosing harder, promotes procrastination, and lessens the likelihood of any choice being made. The enormous pressure put on the consumer by marketing on the basis of what goods say about you, combined with the technological complexity of those goods, promotes high anxiety. Choice increases that anxiety. Schwarz goes on to suggest that excessive choice evokes dissatisfaction. Choosing one thing from too wide a range of choices, finding any (inevitable) shortcoming, or later hearing (or dreaming) about some superior benefits of other options, leads to regret and reduced satisfaction with one's choice. This dissatisfaction fuels the anxiety that the choices you make close off other options, and that these alternatives would somehow have been better. Next, Schwartz argues that too much choice provokes an escalation of expectations: the quest for perfection is aroused, which, inevitably, amplifies dissatisfaction with both the choice you make and the range of choices available.

This combination of paralysis, anxiety, dissatisfaction, disappointment and perfectionism is a fertile breeding ground for depression. Rich and poor alike are vulnerable to its effects. The severity of this stress, though, and the degree to which it leads to depression (which is itself highly correlated with many physical conditions and social problems), appears to be very significantly influenced by relative inequality.

It may well be that the stress Schwartz describes is amplified by inequality because people are preoccupied with status, image and possessions, and constantly driven to compare themselves to those around them. Even those with high incomes are likely to be more fearful of the repercussions of dropping down the social ladder than their counterparts in more egalitarian societies. Those 'beneath' them will be more preoccupied with their relative deprivation compared with the group above. There is a rise in 'status anxiety' (Layte and Whelan, 2014). As the economist Richard Layard put it, 'the consumption of the rich reduces everyone's satisfaction with what they have' (Layard, 2005, p. 53).

Modern life is stressful in so many ways – competitiveness (as gauged by longer working hours, higher debts, a greater percentage of GDP spent on advertising), uncertainty about the future, isolation and loneliness, worries about identity, lack of trust, too much choice, a risk-averse and high-blame culture. All these stresses are amplified where there are big differences between the 'haves' and 'have-nots', or 'have-lesses'.

Money, of course, buys power and influence, so another factor which overlaps with material wealth is social status. Numerous studies over the past 30 years have confirmed that social status affects both physical and mental health. The most well-known of these is the Whitehall study of civil servants, summarised in Box 3.1. It suggests that it is not just inequalities in wealth, but differences in social identity, power and control over one's life, that affect our wellbeing. Those in low-status jobs who feel they have little control over their working lives are more likely to suffer from poor health.

Box 3.1 The Whitehall Studies

- Longitudinal prospective cohort study of British civil servants of all ranks;
- Started in 1967 with women included in a new cohort from 1985;
- Investigated the relationship between work, stress and health;
- Found a strong association between grade levels of civil servant employment and mortality rate: the lower the grade, the higher the mortality rate;
- Low job status is related to higher risks of heart disease, some cancers, chronic lung disease, gastrointestinal disease, back pain, depression, suicide, sickness absence from work and self-reported ill health (Bosma et al, 1997);
- This link holds up even when the influence of lifestyle differences is accounted for;
- A crucial factor seems to be the degree of agency an individual enjoys at work.

Social Divisions

A consequence of inequality is the increase in social divisions in society. One explanation for the link between inequality and poor health and wellbeing outcomes is the social gulf that tends to exist between people in different socioeconomic groups.

There is a reduction in civic participation in more unequal societies (Lancee et al, 2012). In the 2009 BBC Reith lectures on citizenship, Michael Sandel, Harvard Professor of Government, addressed this issue in his final lecture. Part of the problem is that we tend to talk about inequality as if the problem were how to redistribute access to private consumption. But the real problem with inequality, Sandel argues, lies in the damage it does to the civic project, to the common good:

> *Here's why. Too great a gap between rich and poor undermines the solidarity that democratic citizenship requires. As inequality deepens, rich and poor live increasingly separate lives. The affluent send their children to private schools in wealthy suburbs, leaving urban state schools to the children who have no alternative. A similar trend leads to the withdrawal by the privileged from other public institutions and facilities. Private health clubs replace municipal recreation centres and swimming pools. Affluent residential communities are frequently gated, hire private security guards and rely less on public police protection. A second or third car removes the need to rely on public transportation. And so on.* (Sandel, 2009)

Sandel describes how large material differences can hollow out the public realm, diminish what we think of as common space, and damage our social relations. The trend is to spend our leisure time, whether face-to-face or on social media, with people from similar socioeconomic groups – 'people like us'. Meanwhile, people from other social groups become less familiar and we find it increasingly hard to put ourselves in their shoes. Mistrust grows and easily escalates to fear and prejudice. There is increasing concentration of poverty in neglected neighbourhoods, whether it be inner-city Baltimore or a 'sink' estate in Leicester. In these areas, poor people have to cope not only with their own poverty, but also with the consequences of their neighbours' deprivation. With greater inequality, people are more frightened of losing what they have, and there is more pressure to fend for themselves and see other people as a threat. Social barriers are erected, and tensions break out on the edges between different social groups.

People at the bottom feel stuck and powerless – with good reason, as the relationship between income inequality and low intergenerational social mobility is strong (Blanden et al, 2005). After the heyday of the socially mobile 1960s, intergenerational social mobility in the UK and the USA from the 1980s onwards (perhaps surprisingly, given the mythology of the 'American dream') has been much lower than in Canada and the Scandinavian countries, where there is greater equality. This links to educational opportunities, where the picture confirms Sandel's sense that in societies where the better off are encouraged to opt out of public provision, lives are set on different trajectories that tend not to cross.

Such separation leads to less mutuality in relationships across social divisions and less caring about one another, and the absence of what Hilary Cottam, in her book *Radical Help*, calls 'bridging relationships' (Cottam, 2018). These are relationships that connect us to people and experiences different from ourselves. For Cottam, the fostering of such relationships can offer alternative life paths for the disadvantaged and disempowered – and opportunities for personal growth, 'remoralisation' and development for all involved.

Instead, social groups have become more suspicious and frightened of each other, and more competitive. They exhibit various manifestations of envy, and defences against it, such as hostility, greed, violence, and crime in general. At this societal level, kinship – the recognition of likeness and interrelatedness, and the subsequent impetus to generosity – is severely undermined.

In a modern, relatively affluent, consumerist society, then, income inequality is a toxic influence on individuals across the social and socioeconomic spectrum, and on the structure of, and relationships within, society: it is bad for everybody's health and wellbeing. Inequality, through the mechanisms explored thus far, also has a direct and negative influence on another key aspect of society closely related to kinship: the quality and degree of 'social capital'.

Social Capital and Health

It is well established that having friends is good for you and even increases your life expectancy. The Harvard Professor of Public Policy, Robert Putnam, author of *Bowling Alone: The Collapse and Revival of American Community*, claims that 'Joining and participating in just one group cuts in half your odds of dying next year!' (see www.bowlingalone.com).

There is also evidence that people in rich countries have fewer friends than in the past. To quote Putnam again; 'People watch Friends on TV – they don't have them!' (Putnam, 2000, p. 108). The extent and quality of relations between people are essential to our social fabric, and as such have become a major focus of study. This is what social scientists refer to as social capital – the range and quality of positive connections between individuals, and the social networks that embody people's involvement in community life.

In *Bowling Alone*, Putnam shows how Americans have become increasingly disconnected from one another, and how social structures have disintegrated, impoverishing the lives of both individuals and communities. He describes three main areas of social change over the last 30 years of the twentieth century: first, a reduction in political and civic engagement; second, a reduction in informal social ties; and third, a reduction in trust of each other. Using comparative studies of different communities with different levels of social engagement, he argues that stronger social capital (the sum total of people's involvement in community life) is linked to better health and other positive social outcomes.

Box 3.2 summarises some of the evidence for a link between social capital and wellbeing.

Box 3.2 Social Capital, Health and Wellbeing

In the 1990s, epidemiologists did a comparative study looking at death rates across states in the USA using data from the General Social Surveys and counted how many people from each state were members of organisations such as church groups and trades unions. In short, the higher the group membership within a state, the lower was the death rate. This held true for all causes combined, as well as deaths from coronary heart disease, cancers and infant deaths.

A decade later, Putnam looked at social capital in the different states in relation to an 'index of health' that included such factors as percentage of babies categorised as low birth weight, the number of people with AIDS and cancer, and death rates from different causes. He found a close link between high levels of social capital and high scores (reflecting good health) on the index. States such as Minnesota and Vermont scored high on both accounts, while states such as Louisiana and Nevada scored badly.

There was also a positive correlation between social capital and measures of healthcare such as expenditure on health, numbers of hospital beds, immunisation rates and percentage of mothers receiving antenatal care (Kawachi et al, 1997). Perhaps unsurprisingly, people who are strongly linked together invest more in caring for each other's health.

Putnam also demonstrated a strong connection between social capital and child development, again by comparing states in America and showing a correlation between their differing social capital index and measures of child wellbeing. In addition to mortality and morbidity statistics, there was close correlation with school drop-outs, teenage birth rates, juvenile violent crime and child poverty.

Social capital, with its implication of connectedness and civic engagement, can be seen as a measure of a society's success in expressing kinship and kindness. Social capital knits society together and affects the quality of public life. It is based on, and contributes to, a sense of trust and reciprocity. It is also linked to equality, in a mutually reinforcing way.

Social capital can be measured using 'social network analysis', a methodology for exploring the relationships between people, outlined in Box 3.3.

Box 3.3 Social Network Analysis

By asking study participants to list the people they know, and which acquaintances know each other, researchers seek to represent visually and quantitatively the web of relationships around and among people.

Social networks consist of two elements: individuals (nodes) and the relationships (social ties) between them.

Once all the nodes and ties are known, one can draw pictures of the network and discern every person's position within it.

Within a network, researchers analyse clustering and the distance between two people (also known as the degree of separation).

Research in a number of academic fields, including sociology, community psychology and public health, has shown that social networks operate on many levels, from families up to nations. They play a critical role in determining the ways in which problems are solved and organisations are run, in addition to their effect on the health and wellbeing of individuals.

A team at Harvard Medical School, for example, has shown that obesity and smoking behaviour cluster, and that this association holds up to three degrees removed in the social network (Christakis and Fowler, 2007, 2008; Fowler and Christakis, 2009). One is more likely to smoke if one's friends' friends' friends smoke. More importantly, for the argument in this chapter, they have shown that networks of the right kind are also powerful positive forces.

Happiness, Health and Kindness

Fowler and Christakis' research on the spread of happiness is pertinent to kindness. Their data suggests that people at the core of their local networks are more likely to be happy, while those on the periphery are more likely to be unhappy. The authors discount the influence of similar socioeconomic status on the clustering of happy people: next-door neighbours had a much stronger influence than neighbours who lived a few doors away, and who had similar housing, wealth and environmental exposures. Moreover, the geographical distribution of happiness in the study was not systematically related to local levels of either income or education. In short, happiness spreads from person to person and is influenced particularly by first-degree relatives, close friends, neighbours and co-workers. The authors suggest:

> *Happiness is not merely a function of individual experience or individual choice but is also a property of groups of people. Indeed changes in individual happiness can ripple through*

> *social networks and generate large scale structure in the network, giving rise to clusters of happy and unhappy individuals.* (Fowler and Christakis, 2009, p. 338)

Happiness is not everything, and it is worth stressing that one can be unhappy and still be a valued friend and productive citizen. Happiness does, however, have a positive effect on health and wellbeing, and has been used as a measure of the overall quality of human lives, as an alternative to economic measures such as GDP (Layard, 2005). Moreover, there is evidence that people who care about the happiness of others, and the relief of misery, will themselves be happier. In other words, happiness is in dynamic relation to how we treat each other – it is promoted through offering and receiving kindness.

Political Implications

Social, psychological and physical health and wellbeing are, then, highly influenced by levels of absolute poverty, by inequality and stress, and by the quality and closeness of the connections in society. Societies and communities that embody kinship to the extent that there is common purpose, active recognition of interdependence and responsibility for each other, greater equality and warm, positive interpersonal and group bonds are, very simply, healthier. These societies are overcoming the fear and anxiety involved in recognising and expressing collective kinship – and the social forces working against it. More importantly, consciously or otherwise, they realise that it pays to be kind – and are willing to invest in it, emotionally, practically and financially.

If improved health and wellbeing for society is your goal, then, it is pretty clear what you must do. Policies across government departments must be directed towards:

- eradicating poverty;
- energetically reducing income inequality;
- promoting common identity and purpose;
- communicating the value of, and supporting, combined effort and shared risk;
- reducing isolation and social divisions;
- supporting positive connections between people.

This is a politics of kinship and kindness. Clearly, health promotion, lifestyle advice and heath and social care will make some difference. However, whether people pay for their care through taxes, private insurance or in cash, they will get poorer outcomes and value, the less these wider social and economic factors are collectively addressed. Currently, UK politics fails to take this integrated radical approach. Reduced income inequality and reinforcement of strong social capital correlate with lower drug misuse, reduced levels of crime, and less illness and family breakdown. However, society continues to address these symptoms with a complex and disconnected mixture of legal, remedial and financial weapons, rather than positively and vigorously addressing deeper causal factors.

The UK has long failed to address inequality and build social connectedness. Research by the National Equality Panel (NEP) (Hills, 2010) and the National Centre for Social Research (NCSR, 2010) showed that the divide between rich and poor in the UK was greater than at any time since the Second World War, and among the highest in the world. Social mobility was low, whether measured by income or profession. But the problem is deeper: it begins in the underlying public commitment to collective national life – to kinship in action.

In the British Social Attitudes Survey the NCSR reported the public commitment to collective investment in the common good as being lower than it had been for many years, and the decline had been severe in the years up to 2010. Only 56 per cent of the general public believed there was an obligation to vote (68 per cent in 1991). Only 38 per cent felt that government should strive to create a more equal society (51 per cent in 1994). The number who supported increased taxation to fund health, education and social services (38 per cent) was the lowest since 1983. Although this was mitigated by a small rise in those believing that tax should stay the same, the number who felt it should fall was at its highest for over 20 years (8 per cent in 2010, with an average over the preceding 20 years of 5 per cent, and a steep rise between 2001 and 2010).

Perhaps encouragingly, the NCSR Survey of 2018 showed an increase in social trust, and in the recognition of the need to invest more in public services. However, it revealed quite strong contrasts between the views on these matters held by those with higher incomes and educational attainment and those who were less well-off, or less qualified. Younger, better-off, better-educated adults held such views more than the over 55s. The report suggested that

> *... it will be a major social cohesion challenge to bridge the views of young and more formally-educated people with those of older people and those with few qualifications.* (NCSR, 2018)

These surveys showed that there was still a clear majority in support of pooling resources and responsibility in public services, but the social divisions on the subject, and the alarming degree of drift away from such commitment in the years up to 2010, suggest real vulnerability in that social contract.

Subsequently, a 'YouGov' survey in 2018 reported a dramatic increase in public support for raising taxes to support the NHS – 54 per cent, up 12 percentage points in one year. In contrast to the NCSR surveys, they found that this support was higher amongst the older generations than among the young (Smith, 2018). However encouraging such findings might seem, as well as being complex, such rapid swings of opinion only go to underline the fundamental fragility of public commitment to investment in the common good. It is also worth noting that the question posed did not address public services as a whole – both the investigators and those they surveyed are 'single issue' focussed, rather than considering the wider social contract. Attitudes to 'benefits', for example, might be quite different.

The trends towards social fragmentation and increased inequality remain. Failure to restore confidence, to engage the public in the politics of kinship and communality, is likely to have far-reaching consequences for the health and wellbeing of the nation. The fact that the more encouraging shifts in public opinion, at least in attitudes towards the NHS, have occurred during the years of 'austerity' following the financial crisis also presents a conundrum: must people suffer to generate understanding of the need for investment in themselves and each other, or are there ways to assert its value, and engage the public, more positively in this enterprise?

Successive governments have failed to embrace a genuinely integrated politics of kinship – either philosophically, or in how their vision is implemented. The Labour governments from 1997 to 2010 were ideologically committed to reducing social exclusion, and espoused many ideas relating to strengthening communities and the redistribution of wealth, whilst also giving out mixed messages. Inequality rose and social fragmentation appears to have increased in many ways, if the findings of the NCSR and many other reports are to be trusted.

The 2010 Conservative–Liberal coalition government introduced the idea of the 'Big Society', which advocated increased voluntarism and philanthropy, public services reform – promoting voluntary, private and social enterprise – and community empowerment. This three-point strategy proposed increased connectedness and involvement across society, but it had profound weaknesses. Behind the laudable wish to remove bureaucracy and waste, and to generate innovation, diversity and responsiveness, lay a clear antipathy to, and denigration of, large-scale state-run services. There are many things that could change for the better in publicly run services, but uncritically starving them of resources risks fragmentation, inconsistency, diluted expertise and lack of coordination. Removing unnecessary bureaucracy and waste is not the same as removing vital systems that ensure that the needs of the many and of the few are addressed. Encouraging a multitude of innovative projects and organisations, whatever its merits, is not the same as ensuring a comprehensive system of services.

Theresa May, in her words to the public on becoming UK Prime Minister in 2016, seemed fleetingly to understand the importance of kinship, the importance of a sense of connection and belonging:

> *. . . we believe in a union not just between the nations of the United Kingdom but between all of our citizens, every one of us, whoever we are and wherever we're from.*
>
> *That means fighting against the burning injustice that, if you're born poor, you will die on average 9 years earlier than others.*
>
> *If you're black, you're treated more harshly by the criminal justice system than if you're white.*
>
> *If you're a white, working-class boy, you're less likely than anybody else in Britain to go to university.*
>
> *If you're at a state school, you're less likely to reach the top professions than if you're educated privately.*
>
> *If you're a woman, you will earn less than a man. If you suffer from mental health problems, there's not enough help to hand.*
>
> *If you're young, you'll find it harder than ever before to own your own home.* (May, 2016)

Fine words, but they were not connected to policy. The realities of how to promote commitment, capacity and capability, and how to resource and support an increasingly atomised public sphere for the good of all, were neglected. Whatever the rhetoric, whatever the very limited action, policy was focused on symptoms rather than causes. The Big Society idea, with its vision of social commitment and philanthropy, and May's virtuous statement may promote some helpful social initiatives, or make gestures towards reducing inequality, but it is the wider picture that is of concern. They neglect the fact that society faces large-scale, collective problems that require systematic and comprehensive attention, and the expert deployment of resources. This task is well beyond the capacity and influence of individuals and local groups, or under-funded, fragmented, out-sourced services, many driven by the profit motive, many facing 'payment by results'. Dislike of the manifold weaknesses of the 'big state' does not, in itself, prove that there is any other vehicle than the state (at a national, regional or local level) able to address these challenges.

Between 2010 and 2018 central investment in local government fell by 49 per cent. In 2017, the Local Government Association announced that they would suffer a 77 per cent cut in their core funding between 2015 and 2020. It estimated a £5.8 billion shortfall in funds by 2020 'even if councils stopped filling in potholes, maintaining parks and open spaces, closed all children's centres, libraries, museums, leisure centres, turned off every street light and shut all discretionary bus routes' (Bounds, 2017 reporting in the *Financial Times*).

This disastrous description does not even reflect the parlous state of social care. For example, in May 2017, the Guardian reported that 75 companies running care homes had become insolvent in 2016 (Ruddick, 2017 in the *Guardian*). A thousand care homes had closed by early 2018 (Donelly, 2018 reporting in the *Daily Telegraph*, on a report by LaingBuisson, a healthcare business intelligence consultancy). In 2017, 14,490 children were taken into care – just under twice the number in 2008, placing ever more demands on shrinking budgets. The £20bn rise in investment in the NHS announced in 2018 did no more than fill some of the resource gap that resulted from the previous eight years of austerity funding, under which a 'protected' NHS budget fell disastrously behind the rise in need, as obesity, diabetes, alcohol related illness and the multiple needs of an ageing population steadily escalated – to say nothing of the massively expanding costs of litigation. Such budget and 'demand' issues affect the whole system – and inevitably threaten social capital and services from whatever sector.

Underlying these risks to the social fabric is the reality, spelt out by the Institute for Fiscal Studies (Browne and Levell, 2010) and many others, that the poor bear a disproportionate burden of cuts to the public sector. Inequality, then, continues, and threatens to worsen. Just how serious this reality is was underlined in November 2018 by the UN's rapporteur on extreme poverty and human rights, Philip Alston. He found that a fifth of the UK population lived in poverty, and that child poverty was predicted to rise to as much as 40 per cent by 2022. He stated that compassion had been abandoned during the period of 'austerity' policies from 2010 onwards, policies that had swept away many elements of the social contract underpinning the Welfare State (Alston, 2018). In December 2018 the Joseph Rowntree Foundation reported that 40 per cent of people in work lived in poverty (JRF, 2018).

The poor and vulnerable suffer most, but all of society faces the cost of the disruption and destruction of vital services that have taken years to develop. Alston pointed out, for example, that the middle classes would 'find themselves living in an increasingly hostile and unwelcoming society because community roots are being broken'.

The crucial issue of gaining support for equality, and investment through taxes, needs framing in the ethic and the vital impulse of kinship. Nowhere is there the clear, unembarrassed assertion that sharing resources more equally and paying taxes for health, education, social and wider public services are good things, and that we all benefit enormously from doing so. Instead, income inequality has been at best tentatively discussed, and the anxiety to reassure voters that taxation will be proportionate to levels of wealth and income has all but silenced any voice actively promoting the ethical argument for and collective benefits of paying taxes. To reassure the people that taxation will be fair and manageable is only good sense. But it is close to tragic to fail to communicate its value, to fail to engage the public in the vision of the good society, and to fail to argue positively for pooling resources and efforts to achieve it.

The British people seem to have inexorably fallen for the idea that 'the state' is something different from the community – that 'they' take our money away from us, rather than organise valuable things on our behalf, to meet our needs. As important as the rational perspective is the emotional. There is resistance to the unashamed promotion of equality and collective investment, accompanied by a fundamental failure to reconcile the risks of binding ourselves together with the need for, and benefits of, our doing so. The Labour Party's headline slogan for its 2017 General Election manifesto – 'For the many not the few' – suggested a more collective national project, but still, unfortunately, signalled a division in society. People with rare diseases, or immigrants, are the few, not just the rich. And a slogan is just that, and though there were elements in that manifesto that sought to embrace diversity, the big challenge remains – how can the nation be convinced and inspired to turn back to and re-assert the power and value of kinship, and to invest in it?

The Politics of Ambivalence: Lessons from the United States

The 2009 US presidential election was interesting in that Barack Obama appeared to appeal directly and powerfully to the collective kinship of the American people. Domestically, he communicated a vision of black and white, rich and poor, city dwellers and country people, being of equal value, and a vision of a nation with rifts and divisions healed. He also stressed that success in addressing problems depended on the commitment, generosity and ingenuity of all. Internationally, he communicated a recognition of common interest, and the value of talking, of working together to solve problems, and of sharing resources and resourcefulness.

It was striking how deeply this message seemed to influence the balance in America, and how much it seemed to find a resonance among many sections of society. Vox pop interviews in the mainstream media following his election demonstrated how many people in the USA had taken to heart his three-word election slogan 'Yes we can'. In a radio interview, a young, poor, black woman involved in an urban welfare project sketched out the three principles in interplay: 'yes' = positive attitude and commitment, 'we' = collective interdependency and effort, and 'can' = resourcefulness and capability.

It was no coincidence that Obama expressed his values of inclusivity and interdependence and his appeal to the generosity of spirit of the people most explicitly in his healthcare policy. Some of the resistance he encountered amongst voters seems to have been an expression of a mixture of the fear of interdependency and kinship, and the mistaken belief that unrestrained competitive individualism is the prerogative of the citizen and better for society. On the right in US politics, in particular, there has always been a strong narrative generated by that fear: that individual liberty and wellbeing are mortally threatened by state-sponsored communality, by sharing risk and limits to resources. This view proposes that the good of the individual lies in facing his (for this is a very male doctrine at heart) and his close kin's circumstances alone. The individual secures his wellbeing by buying assistance for difficulties with his own hard-earned cash, in a creative struggle to overcome hardship, push ahead and rise. This cherished idea in the American dream – the land of opportunity – is challenged by the evidence on social mobility. Nonetheless, the right's fixation with individualism and the 'privatised family' has endured.

The fragility of Obama's collective vision of kinship was demonstrated by the election of Donald Trump, who managed to 'inspire' nationalist populism while also provoking racial and other divides, promising to wind back Obama's healthcare reforms, and to cut back many other investments in the common good.

There is much to be admired and valued in the optimism and vigour of US individualism, indeed of positive individualism anywhere. It is not the pluralist, the courageous, the creative aspects of US culture that need questioning. It is the phobic, even hysterical, reaction to interdependency and communality that raises concern. The evidence we have cited shows that 'hitching our wagons together', mutual support, curbing our own desires in favour of greater equality and investing our resources in our common destiny improves everyone's lot. The American right says no: the liberty to choose whether or not to buy any care one needs is paramount.

The political drama in the USA can be seen, then, as a struggle between two responses to the value and danger of kinship. Obama was publicly asserting the value of kinship at a whole-community level and advocating the generous sharing of risks and resources. Trump and the right narrowed the concept down, and asserted the necessity of freedom from the restrictions and compromises of such interdependence. In the 2016 election, 'swing voters' in the USA appeared to have retreated from being profoundly moved and inspired by an appeal to mutuality, to a loss of nerve in the enterprise. The understandable anxieties aroused by collectively facing the nation's problems appear to have been a fertile ground for sowing doubt and asserting individualism – even for suggesting that Obama's appeal to solidarity and kinship was actively evil. Of course, this is only one perspective on extremely complicated political circumstances, and there are other ways to tell this story. Nevertheless, it does seem to illustrate something important about the politics of kinship.

Obama's vision and invitation – if not his concrete policies or capacity to implement them – were supported by evidence. The emergence of strong voices to champion a similar vision in the UK is urgent in the light of the ever-present danger of a drift away from it. But the lesson from the USA is not just that offering such a vision is possible, but that we must understand and address the profound ambivalence we have towards kinship and kindness if it is to be sustained. That ambivalence is as evident in the UK as it is elsewhere. It is interesting in this respect that Wilkinson and Pickett's books triggered a volley of criticism, with pieces appearing under emotive titles such as 'Beware false prophets' (Saunders, 2010) and 'The spirit level delusion' (Snowdon, 2010), despite accumulating evidence from meta-analyses in peer-reviewed journals (Kondo et al, 2009). Given the controversy the first book attracted, Professor Michael Sargent of the National Institute for Medical Research, London, writing in the prestigious multi-disciplinary science journal *Nature*, felt the need to reassure readers that 'the statistics are from reputable independent sources' (Sargent, 2010). But there is the danger that mud sticks. Such vehement and ideological attacks may undermine confidence in a strongly argued case for equality. Whatever the technical debates about the use and presentation of statistics, it is clear that the politics of equality and kinship, the idea that the country would be a better place for us all if we were less divided, attracts highly anxious opposition and denigration.

Why should the creative vitality of independence and individuality have to be pitted against kinship and collective kindness? How can we keep our nerve and trust that they can be realised together? How can such a vision be turned into effective policy and action? It was cheering that by the time the second book appeared in 2018 these issues were beginning to be addressed more widely in public policy debate in the UK. For example, Carnegie Fellow Julia Unwin CBE, former Chief Executive of the Joseph Rowntree Foundation, published a report 'Kindness, emotions and human relationships: The blind spot in public policy'. In it, she asserts the principles of social solidarity and kindness as crucial components of policy making (Unwin, 2018). Also in 2018, a movement, Compassion in Politics, was launched in the UK, supported by a wide range of academics, writers, MPs and social activists (www.compassioninpolitics.com). Such developments were welcome, but much work is required to develop the detailed arguments for kindness as a core shaper of the many strands of policy and of the detail of their implementation.

In the next chapter, we explore the meaning and place of kindness in the delivery of health and social care, and outline the case for it being valued and understood as a legitimate, and powerful, force for improvement and efficiency.

References

Alston, P. (2018) Statement on visit to the UK, by Professor Philip Alston, United Nations Special Rapporteur on Extreme Poverty and Human Rights. Available at: www.ohchr.org/en/NewsEvents/Pages/DisplayNews.aspx?NewsID=23881&LangID=E [last accessed 6 August, 2019].

Blanden, J., Gregg, P., and Machin, S. (2005) Intergenerational Mobility in Europe and North America. Centre for Economic Performance, London School of Economics.

British Medical Journal (1996) The big idea (Editor's choice). British Medical Journal, 312, 20 April. Available at: www.bmj.com/content/312/7037/0.full [last accessed 6 August, 2019].

Bosma, H., Marmot, M. G., Hemingway, H., et al (1997) Low job control and risk of coronary heart disease in Whitehall II (prospective cohort) study. British Medical Journal. 314: 558–65.

Bounds, A. (2017) Local government to see 77% cuts by 2020. *Financial Times*, 4 July, 2017. Available at: www.ft.com/content/9c6b5284-6000-11e7-91a7-502f7ee26895 [last accessed 6 August, 2019].

Browne, J. and Levell, P. (2010) The Distributional Effect of Tax and Benefit Reforms to be introduced between June 2010 and April 2014: A Revised Assessment. Institute for Fiscal Studies.

Christakis, N. A. and Fowler, J. H. (2007) The spread of obesity in a large social network over 32 years. New England Journal of Medicine. 357: 370–9.

Christakis, N. A. and Fowler, J. H. (2008) The collective dynamics of smoking in a large social network over 32 years. New England Journal of Medicine. 358: 2249–58.

Department of Health (2000) The National Health Service Plan. HMSO.

Department of Health (2009) Tackling Health Inequalities: 10 Years On. HMSO.

Donnelly, L. (2018) NHS Crisis fuelled by closure of 1,000 care homes. *Daily Telegraph*, 13 January, 2018. Available at: www.telegraph.co.uk/news/2018/01/13/nhs-crisis-fuelled-closure-1000-care-homes-housing-30000-pensioners/ [last accessed 6 August, 2019].

Dorling, D. (2018) *Peak Inequality: Britain's Ticking Time Bomb*. Policy Press.

Fowler, J. H. and Christakis, N. A. (2009) Dynamic spread of happiness in a large social network: longitudinal study of the Framingham Heart Study social network. British Medical Journal. 338: 23–7.

Hertzman, C., Siddiqi, A. A., Hertzman, E., et al (2010) Tackling inequality: get them while they're young. British Medical Journal. 340: 346–8.

Hills, J. (2010) An Anatomy of Economic Inequality in the UK. National Equality Panel Report. HMSO.

Joseph Rowntree Foundation (2018) Annual Report: UK Poverty 2018. Available at: www.jrf.org.uk/report/uk-poverty-2018 [last accessed 6 August, 2019].

Kawachi, I., Kennedy, B. P., Lochner, K., et al (1997) Social capital, income inequality, and mortality. American Journal of Public Health. 87: 1491–8.

Kondo, N., Sembajwe, G., Kawachi, I., et al (2009) Income inequality, mortality and self-rated health: meta-analysis of multilevel studies. British Medical Journal. 339: b4471.

Lancee, B. and Van de Werfhorst, H. G. (2012) Income inequality and participation: a comparison of 24 European countries. Social Science Research. 41(5): 1166–78.

Layard, R. (2005) *Happiness: Lessons From a New Science*. Penguin.

Layte, R. and Whelan, C. (2014) Who feels inferior? A test of the status anxiety hypothesis of social inequalities in *health*. European Sociological Review. 30: 525–35.

Marmot, M. (2010) Fair Society, Healthy Lives. The Marmot Review. Available at:www.instituteofhealthequity.org/resources-reports/fair-society-healthy-lives-the-marmot-review [last accessed 26 August, 2019].

Marmot, M. (2016) *The Health Gap: The Challenge of an Unequal World*. Bloomsbury Paperbacks.

May, T. (2016) Statement from the new Prime Minister Theresa May. Available at: www.gov.uk/government/speeches/statement-from-the-new-prime-minister-theresa-may [last accessed 6 August, 2019].

National Centre for Social Research (2010) British Social Attitudes Survey 2010. HMSO.

National Centre for Social Research (2018) British Social Attitudes Survey 2018. HMSO.

Pickett, K. E. and Wilkinson, R. (2009) Greater equality and better health. British Medical Journal. 339: b4320.

Pickett, K. E. and Wilkinson, R. (2015) Income inequality and health: a causal review. Social Science & Medicine. 128: 316–26.

Putnam, R. D. (2000) *Bowling Alone: The Collapse and Revival of American Community*. Simon and Schuster Paperbacks.

Ruddick, G. (2017) Record number of UK care homes declared insolvent. *The Guardian*, 5 May, 2017. Available at: www.theguardian.com/society/2017/may/05/social-care-crisis-record-number-of-uk-homes-declared-insolvent [last accessed 20 August, 2019].

Sandel, M. (2009) Reith lectures 2009, lecture 4: 'Politics of the Common Good', broadcast 30 June, Radio 4.

Sargent, M. (2010) Why inequality is fatal. Nature. 458: 1109–10.

Saunders, P. (2010) Beware false prophets. Policy Exchange.

Schwartz, B. (2004) *The Paradox of Choice: Why More is Less*. HarperCollins.

Smith, M. (2018) A majority of Brits now support increasing income tax to fund the NHS. YouGov (2018). Available at: www.yougov.co.uk/topics/politics/articles-reports/2018/07/03/majority-brits-now-support-increasing-income-tax-f) [last accessed 6 August, 2019].

Snowdon, C. (2010) The Spirit Level Delusion: Fact-Checking the Left's New Theory on Everything. Democracy Institute/Little Dice.

Subramanian, S. V. and Kawachi, I. (2004) Income inequality and health: what we have learned so far? Epidemiologic Review. 26: 78–91.

Unwin, J. (2018) Kindness, emotions and human relationships: The blind spot in public policy. Carnegie Trust.

Walberg, P., McKee, M., Shkolnikov, V., et al (1998) Economic change, crime and mortality crisis in Russia: regional analysis. British Medical Journal. 317: 312–18.

Wilkinson, R. G. (1996) *Unhealthy Societies: The Affliction of Inequality*. Routledge.

Wilkinson, R. G. and Pickett, K. (2009) *The Spirit Level. Why More Equal Societies Almost Always Do Better*. Allen Lane.

Wilkinson, R. G. and Pickett, K. (2018) *The Inner Level*. Allen Lane.

World Bank (2018) Available at: https://data.worldbank.org/indicator/SP.DYN.IMRT.IN [last accessed 6 August, 2019].

World Health Organisation (2008) Commission on Social Determinants of Health (2008) Closing the Gap in a Generation: Health Equity Through Action on the Social Determinants of Health. Available at: www.who.int/social_determinants/thecommission/finalreport/closethegap_how/en/index1.html [last accessed 20 August, 2019].

Chapter

4 Building the Case for Kindness

Ability is what you're capable of.
Motivation determines what you do.
Attitude determines how well you do it.
(Variously attributed to Raymond Chandler and Lou Holtz)

In the previous chapter, we argued the case for valuing kinship, positive connections and kindness as key determinants of the health and wellbeing of societies. The more people have in common, the more equal they are, the more links between them, and the more they invest in each other, the healthier the society, in physical, mental and social terms. We suggested that politicians and other leaders have a responsibility to articulate and champion emotional, social and financial investment in strengthening kinship, and to challenge individualistic preoccupations and ambivalence about the 'common good'. We would argue that to take on this challenge is the political expression of intelligent kindness.

There is a similar case to be made for bringing such intelligent kindness into its proper place in the practice and organisation of health and social care. Here we must engage with a pervasive and problematic split. Too often, the attention of educators, managers and staff is directed to the technical, the performative elements of the clinical or caring task, rather than to the relational. Whatever the rhetoric, kindness can often be relegated to a 'nice but secondary' aspect of the work of busy people who should be focussing on delivering their specified task rigorously and effectively.

There is no doubt that people using services recognise and appreciate kindness – and are understandably upset by the too-frequent occasions when it is missing. Is there, though, anything other than a sentimental argument to support the assertion that intelligent kindness will improve not just the emotional experience of those receiving care, but also effectiveness, outcomes, even efficiency? Is there evidence that care that integrates the quality of the 'doing' with the quality of the relationship makes a difference?

To consider these questions, we want to begin by exploring the light shed on how people engage with each other by what is known as 'attachment theory'. This model considers how individuals are shaped by infant experiences of bonding with those upon whom they depend, especially, but not only, their parents. It has much to say about the nature and effects of relationships throughout life, and has particular relevance to our understanding of 'helping relationships'.

Attachment theory was pioneered and developed over several decades by the British paediatrician and psychoanalyst John Bowlby, from the late 1950s onwards. His work was informed by an interest in ethology, and his central role in a World Health Organization study looking at the physical and psychological health of the many thousands of children orphaned during the Second World War. Many other researchers and theorists have since contributed to the work, especially Mary Ainsworth, the US developmental psychologist. Over the years it has been informed and enriched by ideas and evidence from evolutionary biology, ethology and object relations psychoanalysis. The model has been subject to a wide range of empirical research.

Lessons from Attachment Theory

Bowlby defined attachment as a 'lasting psychological connectedness between human beings' (Bowlby, 1969). He recognised it as a fundamental, evolved instinct in infant animals, which maintains their safe proximity to adult 'attachment figures', thereby improving their chances of survival. Healthy attachment not only keeps the infant safe, but also provides a 'secure base' for them to venture out into the world, to explore, and to manage uncertainty, anxiety and distress. Research and exploration into the nature of infant attachment and of care-giving has laid the foundations for thinking about the ways adults experience themselves and others, how they manage their feelings and relationships.

Human infants are helpless for much longer than other animals, so the period in which attachment behaviour predominates is also longer A strong bond needs to be forged between the infant and its main care-giver(s), allowing for several years of nurtured development. At its best, this bond evokes a sense of warmth, safety, security and trust, especially confidence that anxiety or distress will be contained, soothed, or averted by the response of an attentive care-giver. The care-giver offers a safe haven and a secure base, by being near enough and available for the infant to find them when they need them ('proximity-seeking') and to soothe the anxiety caused by their absence ('separation-distress').

Proximity seeking is at its height between the ages of six months and two years, although this period of sensitivity varies from person to person. Separation from the primary care-giver at this time results in anxiety and anger, and, if prolonged, will lead to sadness and despair. However, there is evidence that the quality of the carer's attunement to the infant is more important than the amount of time they spend together. An emotionally inaccessible or unresponsive care-giver will trigger anxious attachment behaviour in the infant, regardless of the amount of time they have in each other's company. This is highly relevant when we consider the busy routines of staff in health and social care who often feel they can never be available enough for those in their care.

Threats to the infant's sense of security include prolonged absence, communication breakdown, emotional unavailability, signs of rejection or abandonment, and outright hostility, neglect or abuse. Such factors will continue to trigger insecurity in adult life and can lead to distress, problems with dependency and fear of change. Positive qualities in the care-giver, in infancy and beyond, include consistency, emotional attunement and a repertoire of soothing behaviours, including sensitive touching.

Research and observation suggest that the child's early experience with care-givers gradually gives rise to an internal working model of social relationships that they carry into adulthood. As a result, they develop a system of thoughts, memories, beliefs and expectations about the self and others, which continues to develop throughout life. This internalised model can be modified through subsequent experience, but is heavily influenced by the patterns established during this sensitive period in infancy. Attachment theorists speak of 'styles' of attachment, that characterise the ways individuals tend to meet the world and relate to others: a kind of 'default position' to which they return. Bowlby summarises the influences upon these styles as follows:

> *Confidence that an attachment figure is, apart from being accessible, likely to be responsive can be seen to turn on at least two variables: (a) whether or not the attachment figure is judged to be the sort of person who in general responds to calls for support and protection; (b) whether or not the self is judged to be the sort of person towards whom anyone, and the attachment figure in particular, is likely to respond in a helpful way. Logically, these variables are independent. In practice they are apt to be confounded. As a result, the model of the attachment figure and the model of the self are likely to develop so as to be complementary and mutually confirming.* (Bowlby, 1973, p. 238)

Attachment styles have attracted slightly different labels from different theorists, but Box 4.1 offers our own summary.

Box 4.1 Attachment Styles

1. Secure
Individuals with a secure attachment style have a positive expectation of relationship with another. The internal model they have developed means they anticipate that relationship will offer nurture, safety, goodwill, concern and a positive experience. They also have positive expectations about what they themselves will bring to relationship with others. They can manage dependency and independence.

2. Insecure: Anxious-preoccupied
In this style, individuals are plagued by doubts about the goodwill of the other, their concern for and readiness to respond to them, with a parallel doubt about their own value. They seek constant contact with, approval from and reassurance about the other's goodwill, and about their own worth. They frequently make excessive demands on others, and can become anxious and clingy when they are not met.

3. Insecure: Dismissive-avoidant
People with this style avoid closeness to or dependency on others. They often deny their need for others, assert their independence, frequently appearing to value themselves more than other people. This 'style' can be simply expressed as tending to have a positive view of oneself and a negative view of others, and often leads to compulsive self-reliance.

4. Insecure: Fearful-avoidant
Often as a result of infant trauma or abuse, people with this style are highly ambivalent about intimacy with or dependency on others. They crave, but feel uncomfortable with, closeness, with conscious or unconscious fears and negative expectations about themselves and the other that heighten anxiety, mistrust, doubt or even hatred, of self or other. Neither self nor other feel dependable or trustworthy.

Research studies have explored the determinants of secure and insecure attachment, observing and categorising attachment behaviour in infants (Ainsworth, 1989), as well as developing tools to analyse adult attachment styles and care-giver behaviour (Main, 1995).

Throughout life, for all of us, whatever our 'style', our attachment systems will be triggered by anxiety, fear, illness, extreme tiredness and separation, and will usually respond positively to expression of caring and kindness. An understanding that different people, in different circumstances, will find such kindness more or less easy to trust can help clinicians and social care staff shape their responses to make the most difference. In the extremity of serious illness, or when one's life is in chaos, or fills one with shame, anyone may be pushed towards the insecure modalities, even the 'fearful-avoidant' stance. As a consequence, the power of sensitive, consistent and unambiguous kindness in such circumstances is all the more important.

Attachment theory sheds light on the profound effects of intelligent kindness on the development of the personality: but there is also clear evidence that the impact of the quality of such care-giving goes further. It shapes the development of the neurological systems that regulate stress responses and self-soothing. Research has confirmed not only that warm, attuned caring in early life can turn genes on and off, and influence the way our brains develop (Depue and Morrone-Strupinsky, 2005), but also that throughout life the experience of kindness actually nourishes our brains by triggering the release of endorphins (naturally produced opiate-like substances) and oxytocin (a hormone produced in large quantities during breast-feeding and implicated in the feeling of emotional closeness) (Carter, 1998). Put more simply, neurobiologists have identified an emotion regulatory system where millions of coordinated brain cells are programmed to be activated by kind, soothing, affectionate behaviour to produce a subjective mental state of peaceful contentment and safety.

In case there is any confusion, nurturing such a state is not the same as 'positive thinking'. The onus in 'positive thinking' is on the individual rather than the interpersonal and, when taken to extremes, can be felt as persecutory or guilt inducing. The American writer Barbara Ehrenreich, for example, in her book *Smile or Die* (2010), describes her experience of being diagnosed with breast cancer and, while expecting to discover some sort of supportive sisterhood, was surprised to encounter a tidal wave of injunctions to be positive and even grateful for the experience. Her complaints about the debilitating effects of the treatment were criticised as bad attitude, and expressions of horror and dread were taboo. Despite a poor evidence base to support the claim that positive thinking affects outcome in cancer patients, it seems that many American patients experience their failure to think positively as deeply troubling (Ehrenreich, 2010). This 'positive thinking' is far from the sense of safety that can be nourished by kindness, and that has a neurobiological basis.

The Direct Effects of Kindness on Wellbeing and Healing

The experience of kindness, then, profoundly affects the development of a person's sense of self and others, and their continued sense of security and ability to cope in the world. There is a range of evidence that suggests more: that, at any stage in the human life cycle, it can have a restorative, therapeutic, even physical healing effect. For example, the famous Harvard Grant Study followed up a cohort of young American men born around 1920 through to the early 2000s. A key finding was that those who were better at forging warm, intimate relationships did better – in a nutshell, they lived longer, healthier, happier lives (Vaillant, 2012).

The placebo effect is well recognised in medicine. A placebo is anything that seems to be a 'real' or specific medical treatment – but isn't. It could be a pill, an injection, or some other type of 'treatment' that does not contain an active substance, or otherwise cannot impact directly upon health. Time and again, in clinical trials, placebos are shown to have a positive effect well above that of no treatment at all – and at times comparable with 'genuine', rationally designed treatments. Hypotheses abound as to why this might be so, but presumably the instillation of hope contributes. It also seems likely that the quality of the therapeutic relationship is a key element. This was borne out by a literature review of research on the placebo effect (Turner et al, 1994), which concluded that 'the quality of the interaction between physician and patient can be extremely influential in patient outcomes'.

There appear to be no studies of healthcare outcomes where kindness itself is the explicitly defined focus of exploration. Kindness is a broad, inclusive concept and may mean slightly different things to different people. There are, though, studies that reinforce our argument. Whether they relate to 'physical' or to 'mental health' care, they underline the inextricable link between the felt quality of the relationship between service-user and professional, and the outcomes of intervention. This evidence is relevant, we believe, across all 'helping relationships' in health and social care. We will summarise some of this work, before telling several human stories that demonstrate the importance of intelligent kindness, not simply to 'service-user experience', but to the effectiveness and efficiency of services.

One study demonstrated that patients give more useful information about their symptoms and concerns when the staff member shows empathy (Epstein et al, 2005), and that this leads to greater diagnostic accuracy. Another study compared 'compassionate care' against 'normal care' in a group of frequent attenders at an accident and emergency department and showed that people assigned to 'compassionate care' had fewer repeat visits and were more satisfied with their care (Rendelmeir et al, 1995). After considering more than 1,000 scientific abstracts and 250 research papers, Trzeciak and Mazzarelli, of Cooper University in New Jersey, found compelling evidence of a link between compassion and health outcomes. For example, they report that the odds of people with diabetes having optimal blood sugar levels are 80 per cent higher if they receive compassionate care, with 41 per cent lower odds of them having serious complications (Trzeciak and Mazzerelli, 2019).

The clear implication of such studies is that skilfully expressed kindness improves trust, openness and communication, which in turn lead to decisions about need, care and treatment that are effective, reassuring and satisfying for those seeking help. Beyond these relational factors, there is some evidence that such kindness can have a directly physical effect. A number of studies make the link between high levels of anxiety and delayed healing (e.g. Cole-King and Harding, 2001; Weinman et al, 2008), and as we have seen, treating people kindly helps to reduce anxiety levels.

Research in the field of mental health, especially psychotherapy, offers a great deal more evidence to support our argument. There are comparative outcome studies that assess – and confirm – the effects of important constituents of kindness such as empathy and warmth, and associated qualities such as attunement and unconditional positive regard.

The term 'therapeutic alliance' describes the quality and strength of the relationship between a psychotherapist and their client. It links to the concept of trust, which, as we have seen, is affected, in any relationship, both by the baggage each party brings in terms of experiences from the past, and by what happens in the here and now. Simply put, a good therapeutic alliance is a relationship where the client believes that the therapist has their best interests at heart, that their interest in them is benign. This concept is relevant to any helping relationship.

Thousands of publications have been written on this subject, and dozens of different rating scales developed to measure it. While the degree to which the therapeutic alliance contributes to the variance in outcome is debated, there is consistent evidence and agreement that a good outcome is more likely where a good therapeutic alliance has been established (Cooper, 2008; Wampold and Imel, 2015).

The research suggests that certain qualities and behaviours in a therapist will foster a strong therapeutic alliance. These include warmth, friendliness, genuineness, openness (as in wisely judged self-disclosure), empathy (entering the private perceptual world of the other and having an accurate, felt understanding of the person's experience) and positive regard (a warm, non-judgemental acceptance of the other and their experience). Many of these relational factors are highly inter-correlated, with some authors suggesting that, from the clients' perspective, there is really just one main relational variable: experiencing the therapist as caring/involved (Williams and Chambless, 1990).

Research also shows that where a strong therapeutic alliance has been established, clients tend to respond better to challenges, are less likely to drop out of treatment, and recover more quickly when the therapist is perceived as making a mistake. A similar finding has been established in group therapy. People will feel safer, and therefore more able to make constructive and therapeutic use of a group setting, where there is a strong sense of group cohesion, which, in turn, is fostered by the therapist modelling a transparent, inclusive, non-judgemental, accepting style of intervention (Burlingame et al, 2002; Minkulince et al, 2005).

There is also evidence that interpersonal contact boosts the efficacy of 'non-relational' approaches such as self-help manuals and web-based therapeutic programmes which aim to help with behavioural problems such as smoking (van Boeijen et al, 2005).

Interestingly, there seems to be evidence that even psychotherapists can underestimate the importance of relational factors, preferring to believe their efficacy derives from their particular modality of treatment, and/or professional mastery, when to a large extent it may come from helping to create an atmosphere of warmth and tolerance (Feifel and Eells, 1963). Their clients, on the other hand, consistently ascribe most importance to relational factors, such as having someone care, listen and understand, and provide encouragement and reassurance (Bohart and Tallman, 1999) or offer calm, sympathetic listening, support and approval (Ryan and Gizynski, 1971).

Whilst much of the work of psychotherapy services is with people who are highly anxious, with a deep-seated tendency to be mistrustful, the same states of mind can be triggered in all of us by family crisis, accident, physical illness, pain, fear and uncertainty. It seems that kindness can mitigate this by building trust, which, in turn, underpins a good therapeutic alliance. This will directly improve service-users' sense of wellbeing, but also promotes communication and cooperation which stands people in good stead when things are particularly difficult. A strong therapeutic alliance, in whatever field of care, helps a service-user take in complex information, manage bad news, respond to challenges about their behaviour, or cope with dependency and vulnerability.

Applying the Lessons

The argument for recognising kindness as fundamental to the practice of any method, technique or model of intervention is persuasive. If staff apply an understanding of what influences, and what will reduce, anxiety, and what will promote trust, openness and cooperation in those in their care, this will make a difference to the effectiveness of their work, and to the satisfaction of their client or patient. Understanding the difficulties people can have in forming a 'secure attachment', especially in times of distress, can help staff tailor their way of relating to the person in their care. Whatever the sophistication of such understanding, the headline messages are clear. People receiving care, whether physically ill, mentally troubled, dependent, or struggling to be good partners or parents need to be helped:

- to know that someone is there for them;
- to feel that they are noticed, that they are held in mind;
- to believe that they matter, that they have worth;
- to trust in the goodwill and concern of those who work with them;
- to feel safe;
- to have their distress, anxiety and pain soothed;
- to have a sense of consistency and continuity in the care and attention they are offered;
- to develop an 'alliance' with those working with them to address the difficulties they face.

It is also important to remember that it is the quality, not just the quantity, of the attention paid to the person that matters.

In everyday practice, applying these truths can vary from individual 'small acts of kindness' to more complex, systemic arrangements. We will begin with an example of the latter. It is the true story of a boy going through a rather frightening experience. Only his name has been changed. As it happens, this story relates to an NHS intervention, but it is to be hoped that it is not hard to catch the lessons for any form of care (see Box 4.2 below).

Box 4.2 Timo's Story

When Timo went to hospital for a circumcision he was seven. He'd had increasing trouble peeing and an inflamed, itchy, sore penis for months. He'd been anxious and restless, and his behaviour at home and school had not been good. After a long wait for the operation he and his mum were very anxious.

He found himself walking into a side ward under a huge 'Welcome Timo' sign with a smiley face. A delightful Spanish nurse introduced himself as Andreas, and showed him pictures of the surgeon and anaesthetist who would be helping him. Then, chatting happily about superheroes and Pokemon, Timo proudly received a 'tattoo' on his hand (his pre-anaesthetic).

Timo then met the anaesthetist who got down to Timo's level (literally) and went through a form, explaining everything in language that a seven-year-old could understand. Timo was then told the most exciting news. There were five different types of (charity-funded) electric cars on the ward and he could choose one and drive it to the operating theatre. Timo was over the moon with excitement and set off down the corridor to the operating theatre, having chosen – surprise! surprise! - the cool red sportscar.

In the anaesthetics room, Andreas produced a 'Where's Wally' book and Timo and his Mum were absorbed with this whilst the anaesthetist busied himself and Timo fell asleep. He woke from his operation, suitably pain-relieved, a new boy, soon proud enough of his new willy to show it off to his friends. His behaviour with his mum and at school improved rapidly.

Timo's story is rich in humanity. Just in case it is necessary, let us note that the paediatric surgery department involved ensured that he was treated in ways that met each of the needs we have summarised above. It may be tempting to think that this department must be lucky, with the charitable donations, the apparent wealth of time and facilities involved. However, what if Timo had thrown a tantrum on arrival in an impersonal reception area? What costs, in terms of time and intervention would that have caused? What if he had not been offered the chance to bring to mind the people who would be caring for him, and panicked at each stage of the journey? What if his pre-anaesthetic had been an invasion by a terrifying surgical tool, rather than a 'tattoo'? What if his anxiety had led to problems with receiving his anaesthetic? What if he'd experienced the whole process as traumatic? It can be argued that the costs to the hospital, in terms of time, human resources, and delays for other patients, would have been significant, not to mention the likely problems back at school, or the next time Timo needed healthcare.

An example from social care underlines the gradual, cumulative effects of repeated acts of kindness as part of care for a young person. Jenny Molloy, once in care, and now a writer, reflects on her journey from difficult beginnings (Box 4.3 below).

Box 4.3 The Kindness of Social Workers and Carers Helped Me to Overcome Childhood Trauma

As a child living in a chaotic home, and later in care, any act of perceived kindness was welcomed. As an adult, however, I realised that I had set a very low bar as a child for what constituted kindness.

I would believe that someone speaking to me without anger, without shouting or without aggression was kind. As a teenager, I thought it was kind when an adult, sometimes my parents, offered to buy me alcohol – and an adult buying me drugs or hiding me when I was missing was the ultimate act of kindness.

I realise now, though, that these acts were far away from what kindness should look like. You see, when a child has such low expectations and self-worth, anything which doesn't hurt your heart can appear like a light in an otherwise dark world. Social workers and carers are in the honoured position to alter this belief and create a space for us to learn what we, as precious children, should receive as acts of kindness.

Memories from my time in care spring into my mind immediately:

A pre-arranged visit to my parents with my care worker. My parents do not turn up. My care worker treats me to a strawberry milkshake.
Being unwell as a child in care and the cook makes me hot Ribena, and brings me in a magazine.
Hot sugary donuts waiting for us when we get home from school.
A hot water bottle on cold nights.
I tell the staff that I am going to have a posh corner bath when I leave care. My care worker applies to take me home for the weekend where she has a corner bath of her own.

What I wanted was a normal life – my life had been anything but normal – and I got a glimpse of this through being in their home.

Jenny Molloy, 2016

Jenny Molloy's story suggests that her sense of self-worth, her 'safe' trust in others and the healthiness of her engagement with the world around her, were built up partly through the combined effects of repeated ordinary, but empathic, acts of kindness. The power of such ordinariness, and the easiness of these acts should also be reassuring to busy, over-worked staff. Integrating kindness into good practice does not require a revolution – mainly just recognition of its value.

All the evidence from the people who use our health and social care services is that they want to be seen and known as the people they are, not just as a list of risks or problems. In among the (too many) complaints and squalid detail of poor practice in child protection, care homes, hospitals and general practice, the encouraging message in the emergent narratives is that ordinary kind behaviour makes a real difference. Something as seemingly small as making the effort to pronounce a name properly, explaining and sympathising with a delay, helping to re-fit a hearing aid, or taking the time to help someone brush their hair, can significantly affect a person's experience and engagement with care. The effects, in turn, help those doing the caring.

The simple story below (Box 4.4) demonstrates this. The storyteller, Jane, is a thoughtful, intelligent woman who faced years of aggressive treatment for cancer, including radical, high-risk surgery. It is the link between the tiny gesture she remembers and the effects on her relationship with her doctor that speaks volumes.

Box 4.4 A Personal Communication

The consultant who has been treating me does not fit my stereotype of the cold, distant, arrogant surgeon at all. After any examination, he always offers me a hand to help me get up from the examination table. This small gesture of kindness I have found very significant. It has helped me feel able to communicate with him in an open and honest way as a person, not just another ill patient.

I have had complete trust in both the surgeon and the oncologist who have been treating me for cancer. When I have had decisions to make about the choices open to me in the next steps of treatment, each of them, while discussing the possible options, has also offered a more personal opinion. In the case of the male surgeon, what he would recommend if his wife were in this situation, and in the case of the female oncologist what she herself would do given this choice of options. Because of the trust I have in both of them, this has made the decision about what to do next very easy for me. I have not felt the need to examine statistics, or trawl the internet for information. I have felt confident in making my decision given that my doctors, whilst being experts in their fields and having my best interests at heart, were also able and willing to empathise with me and with my situation.

Personal communication

Whatever reservations readers may have about staff making personal recommendations about difficult choices, Jane's story is one of the development of trust through the experience of humanity and kindness. It meant she went through painful, frightening times with more peace of mind than she might have, preserving her sense of self-worth, and collaborating with those caring for her with confidence, and a great deal less anxiety than she might have had.

A Virtuous Circle

We have highlighted the effectiveness of felt and expressed kindness, which both promotes and is informed by attentiveness. It is possible to follow this linkage further. Attentive kindness promotes the attunement of staff actions to the felt and real experience of the person with whom they are working. Such attuned actions help a person feel recognised, so that anxiety is reduced, trust is increased, and an effective therapeutic alliance is enabled. This alliance promotes better communication, understanding, assessment and diagnosis, and cooperation with treatment, intervention or advice. This combines with the direct experience of kindness to improve outcomes, wellbeing and satisfaction.

There is a further, interesting dimension to this argument: the potential for the powerful and continuous reinforcement of kind, attentive behaviour. A reduction in anxiety, improved satisfaction (for staff and service-user), less defensiveness; all improve the conditions for intelligent kindness to emerge. The suggestion is that, as staff practise more kindly, a virtuous circle is set in motion, as illustrated in Figure 4.1.

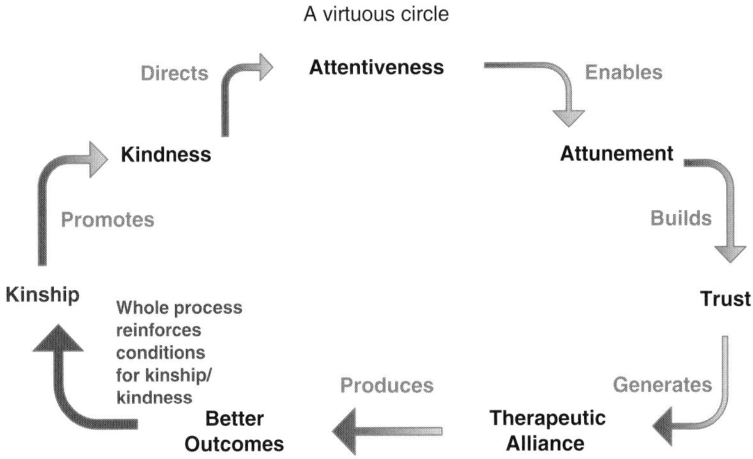

Figure 4.1 A Virtuous Circle

Of course, this is a simplification: the benefits and dynamics of this virtuous circle are more complex and potentially creative than our figure can convey. It can work to bring staff and patients or clients together to review services, and to improve them; it can be considered as a driver for improving staff morale, lowering stress levels and consequent sickness rates. Each linkage in the cycle can be seen as a 'reinforcing cycle' in itself. Kindness breeds attentiveness, which in turn inspires kindness. Similarly, a stronger therapeutic alliance does not just produce better outcomes: it also reinforces trust, which, in turn, strengthens the alliance, and so on.

These powerful dynamic processes also look as if they can contribute to productivity and efficiency – a key challenge for all services and, in particular, for the NHS and social care in the light of the likely state of public finances in the foreseeable future. A useful concept in the management of organisations is that of 'getting it right first time' as a key driver for eliminating waste – of time, resources, and so on. All stages of, and the combined effect of, the virtuous circle contribute to such effective activity. The more work is founded on kinship, motivated by kindness and expressed through attentiveness and attunement to the patient's or service-user's needs, the more it is likely to be timely and 'right first time'.

Helpful Initiatives

'Seeing the person in the patient' is an expression taken from a 2008 review paper by the King's Fund, an independent health charity founded in London in 1897. When the NHS was created in 1948, the Fund became a policy 'think tank', with a national reach, and has continued as a well-respected and provocative contributor to the health debate since then. The philosophy of 'seeing the person' is relevant to all aspects of health and social care. Its aim resonates with definitions of kindness that focus on the shared root with kinship and kindred (see Chapter 2).

From 2007–2013 the Fund ran the 'Point of Care Programme' with the aim of improving patients' and families' experience of care in the NHS: 'to help staff deliver the sort of care they would like for themselves and their own families' (Goodrich and Cornwell, 2008). The project was a good example of work that tried to translate concepts such as personalisation and person-centred care into real change in hospital practice. It was subsequently continued through the 'Point of Care Foundation', established by Jocelyn Cornwell, a medical sociologist, one-time NHS Community Services manager and a founding director of the Commission for Health Improvement (CHI).

The Point of Care Foundation's 'Sweeney Programme' was set up to promote the idea that staff can provide the best care by stepping back and seeing the experience through the patients' eyes. This training programme was named in honour of Kieran Sweeney, a General Practitioner and academic who campaigned for more compassion-based care after he was diagnosed with untreatable cancer. In an article in the British Medical Journal, he described eloquently how he felt the clinical staff hid behind science. He did not fault the clinical care – 'the transactions have been timely and technically impeccable' but he felt staff fell short when it came to relational aspects of care, where their actions often worsened the fear, anxiety and confusion he felt. He observed that it would not take much to move from insensitive communication to communication that puts someone more at their ease (Sweeney, 2009). Kieran Sweeney described the clinicians caring for him as well-meaning but 'displaying a hesitation to be brave'. In Sweeney's case, respecting his dignity would have involved sharing the truth with him, having the courage to talk honestly about his diagnosis and what was likely to happen to him. Putting oneself in the shoes of people approaching the end of their life is not easy, particularly in a society uncomfortable with the reality of death.

Staff across the Welfare State are challenged at times to empathise with situations of extreme human misery, dependency and disturbance. So, it is good to see words like compassion appearing in policy, and in initiatives such as the King's Fund and Point of Care Foundation projects and the 'Compassion in Practice' strategy that ran in the NHS from 2012 to 2016 (Serrant, 2016). In social work, initiatives such as 'Reclaiming Social

Work' and 'Restorative Practice' have placed the relationship with service-users at the centre of practice, the way it is conceived, supported and organised (Forrester, Westlake et al, 2013; Vanderheeren, 2018).

In such practice, a form of brave kindness different from Sweeney's example is required. Even when having to make difficult judgements, a child protection social worker can dare to 'see the person' in the potentially neglectful or abusive parent, understand their experience and attempt to make a constructive bond that helps moves them on to less damaging behaviour. They will work on the assumption that the experience of being attended to, valued, understood and treated kindly can help a client face difficult realities about themselves and improve the way they live with and relate to other people.

Such initiatives and approaches will be discussed more in subsequent chapters. At this stage, we will simply comment that there are clues in many of their titles that something important is being reasserted, rescued. All health and social care professionals work within disciplines which have historically known and valued the importance of intelligent kindness, expressed within a relationship, in their dealings with their clients or patients. A range of circumstances, explored later, have tended to devalue or obscure such knowledge: so now, it appears, 'innovation' and 'initiatives' are needed to restore it!

In any case, it is crucial that, even where policy or institutional initiatives do recognise and champion kindness, some realities are faced squarely. Making things into standards or 'must dos' is not enough – in fact it can have a deleterious effect, as we will see later in this book. Delivering more compassionate care is only possible if staff are genuinely encouraged to value intelligent kindness as a core element of their practice, not as something, however important, added on. Staff need practical and emotional support to open themselves to the experience of the vulnerable people in their care, and to think about how to be more responsive to their needs. They need teams and organisations around them that support such practice. Day-to-day, they need to experience the same virtuous circle in their interactions with each other.

None of this work will bear fruit unless the very difficult realities that society is asking health and social care practitioners to work with are held in mind. The following chapter will explore their practice and experience from this perspective.

References

Ainsworth, M. (1989) Attachments beyond infancy. American Psychologist. 44: 706–16.

Bohart, A. C. and Tallman, K. (1999) How Clients Make Therapy Work: The Process of Active Self-Healing. American Psychological Association.

Bostock, L., Forrester, D., Patrizo, L., Godfrey, T., Zanouzish, M., Antonopoupou, V., Bird, M., Moreslesing, T., Goldberg, T. (2017) Scaling and developing the Reclaiming Social Work model. Department of Education. Children's Social Care Innovation Programme Evaluation Report 45.

Bowlby, J. (1969) *Attachment, Volume 1 of Attachment and Loss*. Hogarth Press.

Bowlby, J. (1973). *Separation: Anxiety & Anger, Volume 2 of Attachment and Loss*. Hogarth Press.

Burlingame, G. M., Fuhriman, A. and Johnson, J. E. (2002) Cohesion in group psychotherapy. In *Psychotherapy Relationships That Work: Therapist Contributions and Responsiveness to Patients* (ed. J. C. Norcross), pp. 71–87. Oxford University Press.

Carter, C. S. (1998) Neuroendocrine perspectives on social attachment and love. Psychoneuroendocrinology. 23: 819–35.

Cole-King, A. and Harding, K. G. (2001) Psychological factors and delayed healing in chronic wounds. Psychosomatic Medicine. 63: 216–20.

Cooper, M. (2008) *Essential Research Findings in Counselling and Psychotherapy*. Sage.

Depue, R. A. and Morrone-Strupinsky, J. V. (2005) A neurobehavioural model of affiliative bonding. Behaviour and Brain Sciences. 28: 313–50.

Ehrenreich, B. (2010) *Smile or Die: How Positive Thinking Fooled America and the World*. Granta.

Epstein, R. M., Franks, P., Sheilds, C. G., et al (2005) Patient-centred communication and diagnostic testing. Annals of Family Medicine. 3: 415–21.

Feifel, H. and Eells, J. (1963) Patients and therapists assess the same psychotherapy. Journal of Consulting Psychology. 27: 310–18.

Firth-Cozens, J. and Cornwell, J. (2009) The Point of Care. Enabling Compassionate Care in Acute Hospital Settings. King's Fund.

Forrester, D., Westlake, D., McCann, M., Thurnham, A., Shefer, G., Glynn, G. and Killian, M. (2013) Reclaiming Social Work? An Evaluation of Systemic Units as an Approach to Delivering Children's Services. University of Bedfordshire. Available at: https://core.ac.uk/download/pdf/30322069.pdf [last accessed 26 August, 2019].

Goodrich, J. and Cornwell, J. (2008) Seeing the Person in the Patient. The Point of Care Review Paper. King's Fund.

Main, M. (1995) Interview based adult attachment classifications: related to infant–mother and infant–father attachment. Developmental Psychology. 19: 227–39.

McMillan, M. and McLeod, J. (2006) Letting go: the client's experience of relational depth. Person-Centred and Experiential Psychotherapies. 5: 277–92.

Minkulince, M., Shauer, P. R., Gillath, O., et al (2005) Attachment, caregiving and altruism: boosting attachment security increases compassion and helping. Journal of Personality and Social Psychology. 89: 817–39.

Molloy, J. (2016) The kindness of social workers and carers helped me to overcome childhood trauma. Available at: www.communitycare.co.uk/2016/03/15/kindness-social-workers-carers-helped-overcome-childhood-trauma/ [last accessed 7 August, 2019].

Oliver, M. and Young, J. (1939) 'Tain't What You Do (It's the Way That You Do It). First recorded by Jimmie Lunceford, Harry James and Ella Fitzgerald.

Rendelmeir, D. A., Molin, J. and Tibshirani, R. J. (1995) A randomised trial of compassionate care for the homeless in an emergency department. Lancet. 345: 1131–4.

Rix, J. (2011) How Hackney Reclaimed Child Protection Work report in *The Guardian*, 8 November, 2011. Available at: www.theguardian.com/society/2011/nov/08/reclaiming-social-work-hackney-breakaway-success [last accessed 26 August, 2019].

Ryan, V. L. and Gizynski, M. N. (1971) Behavior therapy in retrospect – patients' feelings about their behavior therapies. Journal of Consulting and Clinical Psychology. 37: 1–9.

Serrant, L. (2016) Compassion in Practice: Evidencing the impact. NHS England. Available at: www.england.nhs.uk/wp-content/uploads/2016/05/cip-yr-3.pdf [last accessed 7 August, 2019].

Sweeney, K. (2009) Mesothelioma. British Medical Journal. 339: b2862.

Teale, K. (2007) What's wrong with the wards? British Medical Journal. 334: 97.

Trzeciak, S. and Mazzerelli, A. (2019) Compassionomics. The Revolutionary Scientific Evidence that Caring Makes a Difference. Studer Group.

Turner, J. A., Deyo, R. A., Loeser, J. D., et al (1994) The importance of the placebo effects in pain treatment and research. Journal of the American Medical Association. 271: 1609–14.

Vaillant, G. E. (2012) *Triumphs of Experience. The Men of the Harvard Grant Study*. Harvard University Press.

Van Boeijen, C. A., van Balkom, A., van Oppen, P., et al (2005) Efficacy of self-help manuals for anxiety disorders in primary care: a systematic review. Family Practice. 22: 192–6.

Vanderheeren I. (2018) Walsall: Restorative Practice – a common-sense approach. Available at: www.scie.org.uk/strengths-based-approaches/blogs/right-for-children-walsall [last accessed 7 August, 2019].

Wampold, B. E. and Imel, Z. E. (2015) *The Great Psychotherapy Debate: The Evidence for What Makes Psychotherapy Work* (2nd ed.). Routledge.

Weinman, J., Ebrecht, M., Scott, S., et al (2008) Enhanced wound healing after emotional disclosure intervention. British Journal of Health Psychology. 13: 95–102.

Williams, K. E. and Chambless, D. L. (1990) The relationship between therapist characteristics and outcome of in vivo exposure treatment for agoraphobia. Behaviour Therapy. 21: 111–16.

Chapter

5 Managing Feelings of Love and Hate

There is nothing heavier than compassion. Not even one's own pain weighs so heavy as the pain one feels for someone [else] . . . pain intensified by the imagination and prolonged by a hundred echoes.

(Milan Kundera, The Unbearable Lightness of Being, *1984)*

The Pull Away from Kindness

Why do seemingly caring people behave unkindly? As one author put it, 'how do good staff become bad?' (Farquharson, 2004, p. 12). There are many dimensions to this question. There is always a systemic component which will be considered later, but in this chapter we focus on the processes at work at the individual level.

First, it seems appropriate to remind or acquaint ourselves with some of the most notorious scenarios that have occurred in supposedly caring institutions. We start with a description of a ward in Mid-Staffordshire NHS Trust, in the English Midlands, between 2005 and 2009 taken from the executive summary of the report of the inquiry (Francis, 2010, p. 10):

> *Requests for assistance to use a bedpan or to get to and from the toilet were not responded to. Patients were often left on commodes or in the toilet for far too long. They were also left in sheets soaked with urine and faeces for considerable periods of time, which was especially distressing for those whose incontinence was caused by Clostridium difficile. Considerable suffering and embarrassment were caused to patients as a result.*

Although the main focus of the recommendations following the inquiry was on the systemic failings, the evidence given by patients and their relatives describes in grim detail some glaring indifference and cruelty on the part of individuals. Similar themes were apparent in reports of the Patients Association around the same time.

Examples also abound in social care. There have been repeated reports warning of the shocking abuse and neglect in residential care of the elderly (Cooper et al, 2018) with descriptions of elderly persons forced to wear other people's clothes, denied help eating, drinking and dressing, and left bruised after rough handling. Scandals in institutions such as Winterbourne View, supposedly caring for people with learning disabilities, reflect a widespread problem with the inappropriate use of physical restraint and seclusion (Bubb, 2014). Over-medication, including the use of anti-psychotics, has been common in settings for the vulnerable elderly and for people with learning difficulties.

How do we begin to make sense of the more extreme cases of abuse and neglect? And is there any link between these extremes and how the rest of us practise?

An important key is understanding that motivation is almost always mixed and more complex than it at first appears. The fundamental ambivalence towards kindness based on the risk it exposes people to through sharing the vulnerability and needs of others has been discussed in Chapter 1. But ambivalence may also arise for other reasons. Why do workers in health and social care choose the jobs they do? The profession? The specialty? The patient group? Individuals may well offer a quick, ready, 'off-the-peg' response, but altruism, vocation and commitment are very likely mixed with other motives relating to what they (and all of us!) seek through status, role identity and community. It might be important to look deeper, explore motivations that may go back to early experiences of death and illness and styles of caring – or lack of caring. Sometimes people find new light is thrown on this question many years into their careers, when they are disturbed by a particular situation, or feelings arise in relation to a particular patient or client, that require some introspection to sort out.

Choice of profession or of a particular patient or client group often reflects personal history: for example, an individual might choose a career in intellectual disabilities because a sibling has Downs syndrome; become interested in medicine because of personal experience as a diabetic; choose to work in child protection because of their own experience of abuse; or want to work in public health because a heavy-smoking parent died of lung cancer. Such personal links can be a driving force and source of compassion and commitment – both the health service and social services are full of such people and benefit enormously. But there is a danger: where the links are not fully conscious and understood, this drive can tip over into the type of demanding zeal that can alienate others – service-users and colleagues – and lead too easily to overwork, burnout and a sense of grievance.

The Wounded Healer

Psychoanalytic thinking suggests that people are driven, often without being aware, to seek ways in the present to deal with problematic or unresolved hopes, hurts and fears from the past, especially infancy and childhood. The choice of profession or of client group often reflects and offers a theatre for people to play out wounded, unresolved, even aggressive or sadistic elements of their personalities. In these cases the unconscious motivation may, for example, be to heal a sick, or dead, family member and the guilt and fear of facing failure can become channeled into a relentless drive to work ever harder – a phenomenon that has been referred to as the unassigned impossible task (Zagier Roberts, 2019).

Unfortunately, the choice of work brings not only the opportunity for reparation and healing, but also potentially repeats the experience of failing the incurable, which, in turn, further feeds the associated emotional drive to apply oneself to this impossible task. This can become a vicious circle. People caught up in this may make harsh, unforgiving task masters, not just for themselves but for their colleagues, and even sometimes their patients or clients, who they may unconsciously blame for not responding positively to their heroic efforts. The potential for depression and burnout is obvious and this in turn can eat into the capacity for careful attention to those in their care, or worse, nourish resentment and mistreatment.

Many people learn through painful experience that their greatest strengths can also be weaknesses. For example, someone much loved as a charismatic teacher can also be narcissistic and greedy for attention; someone whose obsessional traits mean they have an admirable eye for detail in one area of their work may otherwise be an ultra-critical and controlling colleague. It is important to be curious about oneself, to recognise the shadow side to the declared motivation for choosing the job that one does, and to be aware of resonances between the work and one's own life experiences. The importance of self-awareness and insight is succinctly stated in the much quoted words, 'physician, heal thyself'.

Intrinsic Horrors and Anxieties

The relationship with the work that one does is not fixed and there is the potential for many types of experience along the way to push one to behave in an unkind manner or get stuck in an unkind state of mind. Studies confirm that the majority of healthcare students are motivated by the wish to make things better but during training and the early years of their career, there is a tendency for empathy to wane and they become more distanced from patients (Lowenstein, 2008; Maben, 2007; Wear and Zarconi, 2008). Many a clinician will be conscious of something they found particularly painful and distressing and able to see how this caused them to withdraw emotionally from patients and colleagues for a while.

It is worth trying to stand back and consider the sort of things people working in care services actually have to do. It is easy to forget the appalling nature of some of the jobs carried out by NHS and social-care staff day in, day out – the damage, the pain, the mess they encounter, the sheer stench of diseased human flesh and its waste products.

> *The smell makes my eyes water. You get used to all sorts of smells as a nurse. But having spent most of my time as a children's nurse, I've never got used to the violence with which adults vomit and shit and bleed. I have had to leave the room on one occasion and felt terrible about it for evermore, when, due to an abdominal blockage, a man vomited his own faeces. Sick people have colostomy bags that need changing; and ileostomies (a stoma in the small intestine) and spew thick green secretions from their tracheostomies; have yellow penile or grey vaginal discharge; pass melaena from their rectums, the foulest-smelling thing of all from a bleed in the stomach.* (Watson, 2018, p. 199–200)

It takes energy and concentration to be in the right state of mind so as not to physically recoil and express disgust. It is common to say that this state of mind involves professional detachment, but it also takes courage and human kindness as Christine Watson continues to describe in her aptly entitled book, *The Language of Kindness.*

> *But for all that I've seen and touched and smelled, and as difficult as it is at the time, there is a patient at the centre of it, afraid and embarrassed. Nurses make good poker players, understanding the importance of not breathing in; of breath-holding so subtly that the patient does not realise, and does not see any expression other than a matter-of-fact-one. The horror of our bodies – our humanity, our flesh and blood – is something nurses must bear, lest the patient think too deeply, remember the lack of dignity that makes us all vulnerable.* (Watson, 2018, p. 200)

The detail in the reports of the Mid-Staffordshire inquiry reminds us of the shocking extremes of unkindness when failure of bodily functions are not managed sensitively and efficiently. For example, one woman told of finding her mother-in-law, a 96-year-old woman with dementia, in a cubicle in the emergency admissions unit, having soiled herself.

> *We got there about 10 o'clock and I could not believe my eyes. The door was wide open. There were people walking past. Mum was in bed with the cot sides up and she hadn't got a stitch of clothing on. I mean, she would have been horrified. She was completely naked and if I said covered in faeces, she was. It was everywhere. It was in her hair, her eyes, her nails, her hands and on all the cot sides, so she had obviously been trying to lift herself up or move about, because the bed was covered and it was literally everywhere and it was dried. It would have been there a long time. It wasn't new.* (Francis, 2010, p. 57)

As separation from, and denial of, bodily failure and squalor become forever easier in the squeaky clean environments many of us in higher-income countries in the twenty-first century enjoy, it is easy to deny the inhumanity of nature. Most of us simply have little acquaintance with it. A generation of young adults have grown up who recoil from blood (post-HIV), change their clothes so often they do not know what body odour is, never come into contact with babies' nappies and have certainly never seen a dead body. As George Orwell wrote:

> *People talk about the horror of war, but what weapon has man invented that even approaches in cruelty some of the commoner diseases? 'Natural death' almost by definition means something slow, smelly and painful.* (Orwell, 1946)

While many of the diseases Orwell was referring to have been eradicated in countries like the UK, there is no escaping the vicissitudes of the flesh. Raymond Tallis, British philosopher and retired professor of geriatric medicine, comments on the enormity in the history of civilisation of the imaginative and moral step involved in engaging with the realities of illness. He describes a challenging process of cognitive self-overcoming on the part of humanity and reminds us that humans found it easier to assume an objective attitude towards the stars than towards their own inner organs (Tallis, 2005, p. 13). This self-overcoming – surely one of humanity's greatest achievements – has to be done on an individual level by thousands of NHS and social-care staff every day as they muster the will, the necessary balance of kindness and professional detachment, to perform the most intimate tasks imaginable. No wonder they struggle sometimes to manage and process their feelings – and no wonder that they can fall short of attentive, kind and attuned care.

Contact with emotional distress and disturbance can be equally, if not more, harrowing. Many social workers and mental health staff will recognise Christine Watson's description of the poker player expression and the necessity to control one's breathing as they uncover or listen to accounts of child abuse, virtually unimaginable.

Existential questions about identity, suffering, insanity and death are raised and may put people in touch with extreme feelings of pain, confusion and loss. The struggle with feelings of helplessness and hopelessness in the face of suffering cannot be avoided, although different people cope in very different ways. A workshop participant quoted by Firth-Cozens and Cornwell (2009, p. 6) commented as follows:

> *I went to work on an elderly ward where patients died daily and there was great pressure on beds. At first I did all I could to make the lead up to death have some meaning and to feel something when one of them died. But gradually the number of deaths and the need to strip down beds and get another patient in as fast as you can got to me and I became numb to the patients; it became just about the rate of turnover, nothing else.*

Social workers, too, can become weighed down by their encounters with suffering and may find it difficult, for example, to manage feelings of hatred towards an inadequate mother who sends her children to school in dirty clothes smelling of urine. The phrase, 'burn-out or numb-out' is common parlance. Like the nurse for the elderly quoted above, social workers have described the system in which they work as like a conveyor belt, with huge individual case-loads and little support or time to reflect (Jones, 2014).

Engaging with Ill-being

Staying open to the needs and experience of the people one is trying to help in the face of one's own motivations and reactions to illness and social disturbance is essentially a psychological task. Modern health and social care policy and guidance make frequent reference to the notion of wellbeing. It is worth considering the opposite concept: that of ill-being. Ill-being is more than symptoms and disease, and it is what health and social-care workers meet most of the time. It is important to understand what this encounter is like, how it impinges on the work and how it might influence a sense of kinship and the expression of kindness.

Health and social care workers have to engage with and 'read through' the many dimensions of ill-being. They must connect to the person in this uneasy and uncertain state in order to empathise, to evaluate and to respond. The process of diagnosis or formulation, frequently complex and uncertain, is compounded and coloured by the complex psycho-social nature of ill-being. To offer continued empathic attention and response can be challenging. Often the person's ill-being will evoke difficult feelings in the worker: sometimes in very obvious ways, like felt disapproval, overprotectiveness, anger or fear; and sometimes more obscurely, with subtler disturbances to engagement, empathy or response. Being intelligently kind in these circumstances requires self-awareness and the capacity to manage oneself in one's role.

Having a sense of the type of relationship one is aiming for, can be helpful. The 'Restorative Practice' philosophy of care (Ife, 2012) emphasises the importance of working *with* people, not doing things for them or doing things to them. This way of working was piloted in a number of local authorities (for example Leeds, Walsall, and Gloucestershire). The focus is not on a particular 'model' or 'tool', but on building, maintaining and restoring relationships through challenge and support. It is described as a 'way of being' and aims to create a new social contract between the state and citizens (Ife, 2012).

Psychological Defence Mechanisms

One of the important themes in this book is that we need to think more about how to help people process disturbing feelings generated by health and social care work. The concept of psychological defence mechanisms is helpful here. This is a model for understanding how an individual mind protects itself from being overwhelmed. The fundamental process is that of repression, whereby thoughts and feelings that threaten our equilibrium because of their disturbing nature are shut out of consciousness. This shutting-out happens without our awareness, and is achieved through using defence mechanisms. Some of the more common defence mechanisms are briefly summarised in Box 5.1.

Box 5.1 Common Psychological Defence Mechanisms

- **Displacement** involves the redirection of our feelings towards people or things that are not the cause of them, but which are easier to deal with – the 'kicking the cat' phenomenon.
- In **projection** we ascribe our feelings to others instead of struggling with them ourselves – through such processes as scapegoating or infantilising other people, we get the chance to deal with bad or dependent feelings by ascribing them elsewhere.
- **Rationalisation** leads to us inventing reasons for our feelings and behaviour more comfortable to us than the real ones – an example would be 'I did it for your own good' – and can be closely related to minimisation – 'it was only a little punch'.
- In **reaction formation**, anxiety-provoking or unacceptable emotions and impulses are mastered by exaggeration of the directly opposing tendency – hence our discomfort with showy, sentimental, ingratiating expressions of 'love', and the often used quote from Hamlet – 'the lady doth protest too much, methinks'.
- **Sublimation** is when the energy attached to an unacceptable or destructive impulse is converted into a creative or more acceptable activity – the sublimation of aggression into, for example, positive promotion of professional interests and perspectives, such as union activity, or, in personal life, into a sporting activity.

These and other defence mechanisms evoke intuitive recognition in most of us, even in people who do not subscribe to the full psychoanalytic view of the world. Some of these mechanisms are illustrated in what follows. The point, though, is that they are happening, to some extent or the other, all the time: life is an ongoing drama, with complicated subplots involving combinations of these ways of defending ourselves from its complexity and pain and our baser instincts. Sometimes we can recognise that these things are happening – in ourselves or others – but at other times we are quite unaware.

We all use defence mechanisms and of course they do not in themselves indicate pathology. Indeed, like the inflammatory response, they can be understood as a defence system that in many situations protects and promotes survival. But just as smoking and overeating are examples of coping mechanisms that have become problems in themselves, so mental defence mechanisms, if overused or extreme, will become rigid shells which narrow our personality and capacity to relate to others. In extreme cases, the behaviours driven by the defence mechanism take over as the focus of the problem and become part of a vicious circle from which it is hard to escape.

Because health and social care work is so emotionally demanding, defence mechanisms will be triggered frequently. Individuals will protect themselves in different ways, depending on their personality and past experience, from the emotionally traumatic environment.

A group of doctors and nurses working in an emergency department, for example, involved in managing the casualties of a severe road traffic accident, will manage the feelings engendered in a variety of ways. One might cope with her feeling of helplessness by being unnecessarily bossy; another will go straight off to the library and bury himself in academic work; another will go partying and tell over-the-top jokes all night; yet another will take her anger out on her husband, arguing over something trivial. While these are all legitimate and understandably human ways of coping in the short term with a virtually unbearable experience, problems can arise if staff are exposed to frequent emotional trauma, without space to process their feelings. Defensive styles of coping then become entrenched. As walls build up, feelings of vulnerability and sadness become more deeply buried. Kindness suffers as the capacity for fellow feeling recedes.

Over-identification

Even emotionally well-supported staff used to managing traumatising situations may find that a particular incident or patient gets under their skin and throws them, beyond sadness, into turmoil. This may be because the situation resonates with their own experiences in a way that might not even be conscious at the time. Peter Speck, a hospital chaplain, experienced at working with death and the dying, described the tragic death of a 13-year-old boy who had run in front of a lorry because he was late for school (Speck, 2019). Speck describes candidly how the level of his own distress prevented him being of much support to the parents and his over-identification was such that he even mixed up the name of the dying boy, John, with his own son, David. Once Speck had been helped to reflect on the level of his upset and work out what was going on in his mind, he was able to resume his role and be emotionally available to the suffering parents.

> *Then I remembered how that morning, as I was leaving for work, I had heard my wife shouting up to our son 'you're late! Get out of bed, now!' When Mrs Brown had used exactly these words in telling me her story, she momentarily became my own wife, telling me that our son was dying.* (Speck, 2019, p. 120)

Kindness is rooted in fellow feeling, a sense of the other as kith and kin, yet here is an example of over-identification being unhelpful. In health and social care, we are bound to encounter people who resemble ourselves or those close to us. This brings the work 'closer to home' and can cut through the defences we have built up. Sometimes it can feel a relief to be more connected; at other times, the experience can feel unbearable. In the story told by Speck, the important point is that he was able to become consciously aware of how his mind was working and understand why he was behaving in the way he did. This psychological work enabled him to untangle the muddle between his own family situation and the Brown family, which was interfering with his capacity to help them. It is easy to imagine how another person might have reacted to an experience like this by distancing themselves in an attempt to prevent similar situations in the future from touching them in the same way.

Linked to the concept of empathy is the idea that there is an optimal emotional distance from the work that can both help sustain one's own wellbeing and allow one to be emotionally helpful to patients. Of course, this is an ideal, best envisaged as a rough line which needs to be kept in mind as we swing above and below it and struggle to return to it. Problems arise if we become fixed too far from this line and unable to get back.

Sexual Feelings

Every year a small but significant number of health and social care staff are discovered to have transgressed sexual boundaries with their patients, and lose their registration. There may be more who remain undetected. Staff who regularly work on their own are particularly vulnerable, but scandals in hospitals and in care homes are not as rare as one might expect.

Extraordinarily, given that doctors and other health professionals work so intimately with the human body, the subject of sexual feelings is hardly mentioned during training. In her book *Also Human* (Elton, 2018), Caroline Elton, a chartered psychologist who has spent a large part of her career working with unhappy or failing doctors, describes many examples of doctors being left alone to struggle with their sexual feelings and is highly critical of medical education for being 'in denial about doctors being sexual beings' (Elton, 2018, p. 124).

She sensibly suggests that sexual feelings are common and would feel much safer if they were normalised in training and could be talked about before they get out of control. The only examples she found where this could safely take place was in Balint Groups – reflective practice groups attended by certain GPs committed to this approach.

Elton is also critical of the General Medical Council whose guidelines contain no mention of the possibility that a doctor could ever feel attracted to a patient (GMC, 2013) despite the fact that a national research project concluded that brushing these issues under the carpet increases the risk of sexual boundaries being breached (CHRE, 2007). She contrasts the GMC guidelines to parallel guidance for Australian and New Zealand doctors which includes the following:

> *It is important to remember that doctors and patients have the same emotions and feelings as any other people. It is not uncommon for two people who meet in a professional setting to feel attracted to each other. Judgement on your behaviour is not based on the attraction you feel towards a patient but how you respond to this attraction.* (Medical Board of Australia, 2018)

Dependency and Loneliness

While scandals involving a few clinicians and their improper relations with patients are the cause of many of the inquiries conducted by the General Medical Council and Nursing and Midwifery Council, these sexual liaisons point to a wider issue, relating to the need for comfort and closeness, and the management of boundaries. However much we speak of empowerment, health and social care have, at their heart, the issue of dependency. The patient or client depends on the worker's goodwill, kindness and skill; and the worker may well be unconsciously depending on the patient/client, through getting better, or being grateful, to make them feel good and well in return. The experience can feel very lonely for all involved. In this mutual loneliness either or both in the relationship may begin to see in the other someone to meet personal emotional needs that go beyond the terms of the working relationship. The most dramatic form of this response may be sexual, but there are other ways in which too close, and too dependent, a relationship can express itself. Each party may idealise the other, and the wish not to disappoint the other may skew communication, honesty and the interactions between care-giver and the recipient of care. Any disappointment arising from such feelings may, of course, tip over into anger and hostility.

Dependency and vulnerability are frightening states of mind. One response can be to denigrate such feelings, to regard them as 'demeaning', 'pathetic' or worse. Many health and social care workers are loath to acknowledge these emotions or motivations in themselves. They may deny them, and begin to work in isolated anxiety and exhaustion. Another reaction is to collapse into self-pity when the feelings finally break through. Rather more sinister, though, can be the phenomenon of holding the sick and vulnerable in contempt for their neediness, even to hate them for it. Many patently kind people will admit to the occasional intrusion of such feelings – especially those who care for people with long-term debilitating conditions. Others will not feel it safe to voice such feelings, a situation that is likely, in the longer term, to harm them and those they try to help.

Anger and Hatred

Having feelings of anger towards, or strong dislike or even hatred of the people they directly work with is, of course, a normal part of professional emotional life. There are many reasons to dislike a patient or client, some more understandable than others. Patients and clients can be rude and demanding, particularly when they are frightened, confused, in pain, or feel powerless. When hostility arises, for whatever reason, staff may occasionally be physically hurt (or, very rarely indeed, the victim of a homicide), but, much more often they are left emotionally traumatised and mistrustful. Many feel that their altruism has been betrayed and make efforts, consciously or unconsciously, to protect themselves better in the future.

It is all too easy to feel furious with people who appear to be undermining all efforts to help them. Some patient groups are seen as undeserving, such as people who have harmed themselves or fallen over in a drunken stupor. Staff on a medical ward or in a frantically busy emergency department may find it difficult to feel kindly towards a teenager who has overdosed at the same time as they are caring for an acutely ill patient with heart failure. Carers will find it harder to attend to a belligerent patient who grunts and complains, than the sweet grateful old lady two streets away. Even within psychiatry, there is often a kind of unacknowledged hierarchy, with some patient groups seen as less deserving than others with a more clear-cut illness, such as schizophrenia.

Importantly, staff in A&E report feeling more compassionate towards difficult people if they have had some input to help them reflect on what might be causing them to behave in this manner, and have a safe forum to express their feelings, including frustration and anger, and sometimes simple dislike. Similarly, social workers who are helped to think about family dynamics, and have adequate reflective supervision, are more likely to have empathy towards the families with which they work (Munro, 2011; Bunn, 2013).

Individual staff are particularly prone to suffer from guilt and depression if their hateful feelings towards a patient are not shared by the rest of the team or feel so unacceptable that they are kept from conscious awareness. It may be that the individual is in touch with a hateful part of the patient that others in the team are not being exposed to. Or it may be that the patient's situation or personality reminds the staff member of something they find hard to manage in their own life – their mother's tendency to helplessness perhaps, or their father's cold manner. These types of resonances are inevitable but often feel unacceptable, particularly to nursing staff driven by the idea of themselves as angelic carers.

Donald Winnicott, a paediatrician and psychoanalyst, recognising that basically good parents could have feelings towards their children that were not always nice, wrote a classic paper listing eighteen reasons why a mother might hate her baby, drawing parallels with how psychoanalysts might feel at times towards their patients (Winnicott, 1949). In doing so, he was trying to normalise such feelings, giving us permission to recognise them as inevitable, and by being more conscious of them, make them seem safer, easier to integrate and more under our control. Caroline Elton draws up a similar list of reasons why doctors might sometimes resent or hate their patients (Box 5.2). Although she has doctors in mind, much of her list will be recognisable to other workers in health and social care.

Box 5.2 Reasons Why Doctors Might Hate Their Patients (after Winnicott)

- Fear of making a significant mistake;
- Time pressures; too many patients to see in too short a time;
- Uncertainty about the diagnosis or treatment plan;
- Professional impotence when the patient's illness can't be cured;
- Patients' unrealistic expectations about what modern medicine can achieve;
- Patients challenging your professional knowledge;
- Fear of being the subject of a complaint or a legal claim;
- Exhaustion caused by working through the night;
- Hunger and thirst through working a whole shift without a break;
- Being on the receiving end of derogatory comments from patients;
- Disgust at physical decay or deformity;
- Fear of contagion;
- Contempt at injuries caused by the patient's own behaviour;
- Having to work in a part of the country where one is separated from family and friends;
- Missing out on a special family celebration because one has to work.

From Caroline Elton, *Also Human*, p. 313

At the end of her list, Elton continues:

> *And above all else, the reason why patients have always had, and will always have, the potential to evoke difficult feelings in the doctor is that inevitably they remind doctors that they, and those they love, are mortal.* (p. 313/314)

Hateful feelings driven by fear of disease and suffering, the physical disgust described above, and a sense of being way out of one's depth can be difficult to face. The emergence of communal rage in the cases of two high profile cases involving babies, 'Baby P' and 'Baby Alfie' (both discussed in Chapter 11) gives us a glimpse of how being in touch with extreme vulnerability and helplessness can so easily turn into hatred (Jones, 2014).

Being Good Enough Rather Than Perfect

The majority of health and social care staff suffer from anxiety on and off throughout their career, sometimes at a level which makes life difficult. Stress, depression and anxiety are common among health and social care workers: 2,080 cases per 100,000 workers, as compared to an average of 1,320 per 100,000 workers in all jobs. Within human health and social-work activities, nurses and midwives are significantly high – 2,760; and welfare professionals are the highest of all occupations – 4,080 (Health and Safety Executive, 2018).

Feelings of helplessness in the face of suffering and a sense of inadequacy predominate. Self-blame, a sense of guilt, and the growing fear of making a mistake and being publicly humiliated, will be discussed in more detail in Chapter 11.

Self-absorption (often linked with self-protection) is a feature of depression and very obviously affects the capacity for attentive kindness. A sense of profound disconnection with the environment, including psychological withdrawal from relationships, is referred to as 'depersonalisation' and is also a component of severe stress and depression. It can lead to the development of a negative, cynical and callous attitude and will again limit kindness or even, at the extreme, produce cruelty. While some staff end up having to take significant periods of sick leave or retire, others keep working, often for years.

The idea of being 'good enough' can feel like a lifeline. This is an expression first coined by Donald Winnicott (1965), in a series of popular radio talks he delivered to mothers in the kindly, rather paternalistic fashion of the day. Winnicott reassured mothers not only that they did not need to be perfect and that being merely good enough was all right, but that in fact their babies' mental development depended on them not trying to fulfil their babies' every need. In other words, experiencing minimal frustration – ideally in manageable rather than traumatising chunks – is important for psychological development.

This idea is particularly helpful in the field of mental health and social work, where some staff have a tendency to think that unconditional love will cure all, unwittingly infantilising the patients or clients in the process. More generally, being 'good enough' is the only realistic aspiration for staff who want to avoid burnout. Being 'good enough' is not about shrugging one's shoulders in an offhand manner when standards are not met; it is more about letting go of the idea that everything is down to oneself as an individual. Being good enough depends on good teamwork. It also links to the important idea that adopting a kind and compassionate attitude to oneself is a prerequisite for being kind to others.

We need to put in a proviso here: the most common reason staff have been giving for leaving health and social care posts in the first two decades of the twenty-first century is that they simply feel they cannot do their job properly given the settings they are working in. In many cases, this is a realistic appraisal, not a symptom of neurosis.

> *On a care of the elderly ward there can be 30 beds and two qualified nurses. The staffing levels are so bad this week that the nurses often don't take a single break the entire day. A nurse I know who works on the ward carries glucose tablets in her pocket, in case her blood sugar drops dangerously low; she has fainted at work a few times when there hasn't been enough time for lunch or dinner breaks. Another nurse has repeated cystitis and has been told it was because she didn't go to the toilet when she needed to. There are times when you literally don't have time to go to the toilet; days when you purposefully don't drink water, as you know you won't have time.* (Watson, 2018, p. 284)

A recent British Medical Association survey concluded that patient care was at risk because of a 'mental health crisis' among doctors dealing with overwork, red tape and a lack of camaraderie. Its poll of 4,300 staff found that eight in ten doctors were in danger of burning-out because they felt exhausted, emotionally drained or were doing their job 'mechanically'. 27 per cent of respondents reported being formally diagnosed with a mental health condition at some time in their life, 7 per cent in the last year. Four in ten of the respondents reported suffering from depression, anxiety, emotional distress, burnout, stress or a mental health condition that is impacting on their work. 90 per cent stated that their current working environment contributed to their mental condition (BMA, 2019).

Compassionate Mind and Mindfulness Training

A positive development in the twenty-first century, has been a renewed scientific interest in 'mindfulness', the psychological process of bringing one's attention to bear on experience occurring in the present moment, rather than the mass of other thoughts, feelings, fears and wishes that preoccupy us as we go through the day. This has accompanied a growing understanding of the role of positive emotions in sustaining mental health and wellbeing. A specific application of this is 'compassionate mind training' (CMT), an intervention that has attracted interest within the field of mental health (Gilbert, 2009). The principles behind this are drawn from a wide range of fields, including evolutionary psychology, neuroscience and models of emotion, cognition and behaviour – some of which will be explored in later chapters of this book.

CMT refers to the specific techniques that can be used to help us experience compassion and to develop various aspects of compassion towards ourselves and others. It includes attributes and skills and is best understood as a pattern of organising various components of the mind involved with compassion. If you are feeling under threat, for example, it is likely that the compassionate components of your mind are turned off and instead your mind has a pattern of motivation and ways of feeling that are about protecting yourself from danger. In CMT, one practises activating the components of compassion so that they organise and pattern the mind in certain ways. The idea is to change one's relationship to emerging thoughts and feelings rather than to change the thoughts themselves. Empathy for one's own distress, for example, and the link to wider suffering, is fundamental.

Of course, the aspiration to develop a more compassionate state of mind is not new: the techniques are adapted from Buddhism and link to the practice of meditative prayer in other religions. It is not easy or straightforward and for some people will involve working with a lot of anxious ambivalence towards suffering and compassion – particularly self-compassion, which can feel frighteningly unfamiliar in our frenetic, acquisitive, twenty-first-century environment.

Michael Sandel, Harvard Professor of Government, argues that virtues such as altruism and fellow feeling are 'like muscles that develop and grow stronger with exercise' (Sandel, 2009). If we accept that prioritising kindness and kinship is important, we need to find ways of facilitating this 'exercise'.

Mindfulness is a rather over-inclusive term with practice and trainings varying enormously. However, there is no doubt that mindfulness techniques can help with attentiveness towards the other. Both mindfulness training and CMT are accessible and relatively easily taught. Some professional trainings (for example at Leicester medical school) have encouraged their students and staff to take up training in mindfulness in an attempt to improve their general sense of wellbeing, and their quality of attentiveness. It would not be impractical to include this type of training in more professional curricula or to give everyone the opportunity to do this training as part of continuing professional development. Pilot studies could be evaluated from various perspectives, looking, for example, at the effects on the individual staff member, patient experience, team morale and organisational efficiency.

But again a proviso: although training staff in CMT or mindfulness clearly has the potential to make a positive impact on the virtuous circle described in Chapter 4, it will only really make a difference if there are parallel changes in the culture within which people work. To escalate the demands on already frantically busy staff and then suggest they train in mindfulness in order that they don't become too stressed, is understandably seen as disingenuous. It also risks promoting an inauthentic 'going through the motions' in order to tick boxes.

Rachel Clarke, in her book about being a junior doctor (Clarke, 2017), describes how the offer of a 'stress-busting Zumba class' was the last straw that broke down a previously uncomplaining stalwart senior nurse: *"You know what's really done it?" she said to me. "It's the bloody Zumba. I mean, for Christ's sake! Zumba!"*

Clarke goes on to explain, a touch sarcastically:

> *... lunchtime Zumba classes were predicated on the notion that we could stroll along for a relaxing dance during our notional 'lunch hour'. Book groups and lunchtime walks were also on offer for all those doctors and nurses with an hour to spare in their day, equating to no one I knew in the hospital. That they were offered felt like an insult. We needed more staff, not a token gesture towards our 'wellbeing'. Sod yoga, sod book groups and sod sodding Zumba.* (Clarke, 2017, p. 105–6)

No surprise that staff offered the chance to do Mindfulness Training, but working in the kind of conditions Clarke describes so vividly in her book, would probably respond with cynicism. This chapter is about the emotional struggle of the individual staff member but it needs to be recognised that there are limits to how much an individual can do in the face of overwhelming systemic dysfunction.

The interplay between the individual, the team and the organisation is vital to the theme of this book. For if, as a society, we want a workforce who feel secure enough to invest deeply in the work, to put patients before self-interest, to be sufficiently in touch with their own vulnerability to show compassion towards the suffering of others, then we need to think about the type of culture we wish to create. We need constantly to look for ways to make it more secure, consistent and affirming. One dimension of this is a clear commitment to actively nurture kindness and compassion, for kindnesses to staff will find their way to patients and service-users.

Contrast this with the reports from staff in the Mid-Staffordshire inquiry of the prevalent bullying, the rudeness and hostility, the lack of support and general climate of fear – for example, the words of a medical consultant about how he saw the nurses being treated:

> *I got no sense that the nurses had any protection whatsoever. I felt that nurses were hung out within the department. They were definitely not supported.* (Francis, 2010, p. 188)

It is really very simple: the safer people feel in their role, the more they will be able to look with curiosity at their own attitudes and prejudices and be more open to the emotional experience of those with whom they work.

References

British Medical Association (2019) Supporting the mental health of doctors and medical students. Available at: www.bma.org.uk/collective-voice/policy-and-research/education-training-and-workforce/supporting-the-mental-health-of-doctors-in-the-workforce [last accessed 20 August, 2019].

Bubb, S. (2014) Winterbourne View - Time for Change. Transforming the commissioning of services for people with Learning Disabilities and/or Autism. NHS England. Available at: www.england.nhs.uk/wp-content/uploads/2014/11/transforming-commissioning-services.pdf [last accessed 20 August, 2019].

Bunn, A. (2013) Signs of Safety in England. NSPCC Report. Available at: www.signsofsafety.net/new-report-signs-of-safety-in-england/ [last accessed 8 August, 2019].

CHRE (2008) Clear sexual boundaries between healthcare professionals and patients: responsibilities of healthcare professionals. Available at: www.professionalstandards.org.uk/docs/default-source/publications/policy-advice/sexual-boundaries-responsibilities-of-healthcare-professionals-2008.pdf [last accessed 20 August, 2019].

Clarke, R. (2017) *Your Life in My Hands*: A Junior Doctor's Story. John Blake Publishing Ltd.

Cooper C., Marston L., Barber J., Livingstone D., Rapaport P., Higgs P. and Livingstone G. (2018) Do care homes deliver person-centred care? A cross-sectional survey of staff-reported abusive and positive behaviours towards residents from the MARQUE (Managing Agitation and Raising Quality of Life) English national care home survey. Available at: https://journals.plos.org/plosone/article?id=10.1371/journal.pone.0193399 [last accessed 26 August, 2019].

Elton, C. (2018) *Also Human*. William Heinemann.

Farquharson, G. (2004) How good staff become bad. In *From Toxic Institutions to Therapeutic Environments* (eds P. Campling, S. Davies and G. Farquharson), pp. 12–19. Gaskell Publications.

Firth-Cozens, J. and Cornwell, J. (2009) The Point of Care. Enabling Compassionate Care in Acute Hospital Settings. King's Fund.

Francis, R. (2010) The Independent Inquiry into Care Provided by Mid-Staffordshire NHS Foundation Trust, January 2005–March 2009. HMSO.

Francis R. (2013) The Public Inquiry into the Mid-Staffordshire Foundation Trust, Jan 2005–March 2009. HMSO

General Medical Council (2013) Maintaining a professional relationship between you and your patient. Available at: www.gmc-uk.org/ethical-guidance/ethical-guidance-for-doctors/maintaining-a-professional-boundary-between-you-and-your-patient/maintaining-a-professional-boundary-between-you-and-your-patient [last accessed 26 August, 2019].

Gilbert, P. (2009) *The Compassionate Mind: A New Approach to Life's Challenges*. Constable and Robinson.

Health and Safety Executive (2018) Work related stress depression or anxiety statistics in Great Britain, 2018. Available at: www.hse.gov.uk/statistics/causdis/stress.pdf [last accessed 26 August, 2019].

Ife, J. (2012) *Human Rights and Social Work. Towards Rights-based Practice*. 3rd Edition. Cambridge University Press.

Jones, R. (2014) *The Story of Baby P*. Polity Press.

Lowenstein, J. (2008) *The Midnight Meal and Other Essays About Doctors, Patients and Medicine*. Yale University Press.

Maben, J., Latter, S. and Macleod Clark, J. (2007) The sustainability of ideals, values and the nursing mandate: evidence from a longitudinal qualitative study. Nursing Inquiry. 14: 99–111.

Medical Board of Australia (2018) Sexual boundaries in the doctor-patient relationship: A resource for doctors. Availale at: www.medicalboard.gov.au/Codes-Guidelines-Policies/Sexual-boundaries-guidelines.aspx [last accessed 26 August, 2019].

Munro, E. (2011) The Munro Review of Child Support: A Child Centred System. HMSO.

Orwell, G. (1946) How the poor die. In *The Collected Essays, Journalism and Letters of George Orwell. Vol. 4: In Front of Your Nose, 1945–50* (eds S. Orwell and I. Angus), 1970, pp. 261–72. Penguin.

Sandel, M. (2009) Reith Lectures 2009, Lecture 4: 'Politics of the common good', broadcast 30 June, Radio 4.

Speck, P. (2019) Working with dying people. In *The Unconscious at Work* (eds A. Obholzer and V. Zagier Roberts), pp. 119–26. Routledge.

Tallis, R. (2005) *Hippocratic Oaths: Medicine and Its Discontents.* Atlantic Books.

Watson C. (2018) *The Language of Kindness.* A Nurse's Story. Chatto & Windus.

Wear, D. and Zarconi, J. (2008) Can compassion be taught? Let's ask the students. Journal of General Internal Medicine. 23: 948–53.

Winnicott, D. W. (1949) Hate in the countertransference. International Journal of Psychoanalysis. 30: 69–74.

Winnicott, D. W. (1965) *The Maturational Processes and the Facilitating Environment.* International Universities Press.

Zagier-Roberts, V. (2019) The self-assigned impossible task, in *The Unconscious at Work* (eds Obholzer and Zagier Roberts), pp. 127–35. Routledge.

Chapter

6 The Emotional Life of Teams

Insanity in individuals is something rare; in nations, groups, parties and epochs it is the rule.

(Nietzsche, 1886)

The Team Dynamic

Ideally, the work people do should bring out the best in them. This does not always happen. The previous chapter explored some of the reasons why individuals can find it hard to provide compassionate health and social care. This chapter is about group dynamics: how people behave in teams and how healthy team working can be supported, but also how teams behave in relation to other teams and how good team working can be replicated.

Most of us have some awareness that our behaviour can be affected by the group of people we are with, that working in a 'good' team is a very different experience from working in a 'bad' team. We may even have caught ourselves behaving out of character in a particular group situation, or celebrated having the 'best brought out of us' in another. Being part of a group or team can also provoke anxiety. We want to feel accepted and liked but retain our sense of individuality. We prefer to see ourselves as autonomous and the agents of control in our lives but have some awareness that our thoughts and feelings are heavily influenced, often to a surprising degree. We are most conscious of this anxiety when we are new to a particular team. Then we may catch ourselves sizing up the other members, wondering how we will fit in, looking for similarities and differences, trying to work out the official hierarchies and professional divisions as well as where the real power lies and the informal subgroupings that might form around things such as age, culture or outside interests.

Health and social care teams tend to draw from a wide spectrum of society in terms of race, religion, age, socioeconomic status, educational achievement and personality types – with all the richness that such diversity brings. But such diversity can also lead to tensions around difference, which can be amplified when everyone is under pressure. Underneath all this, we may be vaguely conscious of stirrings of trust and mistrust, sexual attraction and repulsion, fear, competitiveness and shadowy resonances with other people and situations, particularly teams we have worked with in the past. If these develop into rivalries, romances, subgroupings and so on, the potential for being emotionally available for the task in hand will be affected.

In the main, there is a tendency to underestimate the effect of the group and a poor understanding of how group dynamics can influence behaviour. This is an area where centuries of accumulated wisdom and decades of research and theoretical understanding have made little impact on the general consciousness. In the Western world, where personal autonomy is valued so highly, it is uncomfortable to think of behaviour – often unconsciously – being driven by group forces.

If we are serious about the importance of kindness, there is a need to understand how it can be facilitated or undermined by the group dynamic. In the aftermath of the Second World War, people were asking a much more extreme version of this question as they tried to come to terms with the atrocities committed – the industrial scale of the death systems in place and the widespread collusion. The human capacity for treating others cruelly has much preoccupied thinkers in the years since, but hardly gets a mention in professional curricula.

To begin with, a number of instructive classic experiments from social science and psychology have demonstrated how easy it is to impair an individual's capacity for independent thought and moral judgement, and illustrate the universality of the problem.

Group Pressure

The first experiment, by Solomon Asch (1951), a Polish Jewish refugee, gestalt psychologist and pioneer of social psychology in the USA, showed the powerful capacity of the group to undermine individuals' belief in the information that they are receiving from their senses, and the overwhelming inclination of most of us to conform to the group. His study involved groups of nine people, only one of whom was a real volunteer participant: the rest were confederates of the experimenter. Groups were asked to make judgements in a series of questions comparing different lines in a diagram. Once the experiment got going, the eight confederates would give wrong answers and the effect that this had on the responses of the genuine participants was monitored. Overall, 76 per cent made at least one error, compared with 99 per cent accuracy in pre-tests where no-one had been planted to give deliberately wrong answers.

Many of the participants stressed afterwards that they conformed only because they did not want to stand out from the group (i.e. they claimed to know they were giving the wrong answer) but even when this possibility was eliminated by changing the experiment so that other group members were unable to see the answers of the participant and judge them, the error rate was significant. This suggests that beliefs, even perceptions themselves, were influenced by simply being in the presence of others with seemingly different beliefs as well as there being strong overt pressures to conform. Very few of the participants in this study were able to stand up against the prevailing group opinion, despite the evidence of their own eyes. This experiment has been repeated in numerous studies since, with similar results (Bond and Smith, 1996).

Such research has direct relevance to our understanding of institutions and the sometimes inhumane behaviour of those who work in them. Although 'closed' institutions, such as secure psychiatric units and prisons are particularly vulnerable, all health and social care workers are susceptible to the process of institutionalisation, where the capacity to think independently becomes weakened by group pressure. With a scandal such as that in the Gosport Memorial Hospital where over 450 people had their lives shortened by administration of inappropriate drugs such as diamorphine, one of the obvious questions is why those present allowed the situation to continue for so long (Jones, 2018). The fact that, in some cases, protest by staff was supressed by those in authority, only partially answers a question about a situation that continued for 20 years.

This was also one of the themes of the report of the Mid-Staffordshire inquiry: '*there was an acceptance of standards of care, probably through habituation, that should not have been tolerated*' (Francis, 2010, p. 86).

An interesting phenomenon in the Mid-Staffordshire inquiry was how 'disappointingly few' staff were willing to give independent evidence (p. 31). This would be partly down to a sense of loyalty or fear, but there is a suggestion that individuals were also confused about what they thought.

> *I also held a series of meetings for staff at the hospital. ... Some of these were attended by a very small number. It was clear to me that some of those, in particular nursing staff, were very hesitant to express views which they feared might be considered disloyal to their employer, if those views came to the Trust's attention. A phrase commonly used was 'I cannot believe I am saying this.'* (p. 34)

Our Relationship to Authority

In another major series of (now widely considered rather distasteful) experiments, by Stanley Milgram (1963), the participants – all lay people – were told that the experimenters were exploring the effects of punishment on learning. They were instructed to apply increasingly powerful electric shocks, rising to 450 volts, to apparent 'students' in response to a failure to learn a task. Despite seeing the physical distress caused by the electric shocks (in fact feigned by the 'students' but seen as real by the participants), most of the participants continued to do as they were told, when, despite their questions, and in some cases their upset and protest, they were sternly instructed to continue. The physical distress observed escalated from the apparent victims of this regime banging on the walls, to complaining about their heart condition and eventually to collapsing completely. The experiment is frequently cited as an example of how easily we succumb to the power of malignant authority. Details of the methodology have been challenged in recent years suggesting that the interpretation of the findings may be more complex than originally thought (Haslam et al, 2014): but it is difficult to dismiss the overall phenomenon.

Variations on the experiment have been carried out in many different countries and cultures, with the percentage of participants who are prepared to inflict fatal voltages remaining remarkably constant, at 61–66 per cent, according to a meta-analysis (Blass, 2000). In general, where the victim's physical immediacy was increased, the participants' compliance decreased. The participants' compliance also decreased when the authority's physical immediacy decreased, for example if contact was over the telephone. The highest compliance was in experiments where the task of implementing the shocks was divided up and each participant presumably felt they were only a small 'cog' in the system. In 2009, a version of the experiment was repeated as part of a television documentary entitled 'How violent are you?' (Horizon, BBC2). Of the 12 participants, only three refused to continue to the end of the experiment.

Conforming to Role Expectations

An experiment by Philip Zimbardo in the 1970s developed these themes. In the 'Stanford Prison Experiment' (Haney, Banks and Zimbardo, 1973) he and his team devised an extended prison simulation where 24 students were randomly allocated to play the role of prisoner or guard. Despite being given no further instruction, the students took up stereotypical roles and ended up with the guards adopting overtly sadistic behaviours while the prisoners became progressively passive and depressed. So extreme was the distress experienced by some of the 'prisoners' that the experiment had to be stopped after six days rather than running for the planned two weeks. Moreover, some of the 'guards' were so gratified by the roles they were playing that they wanted to carry on for longer (Haney et al, 1973).

While the Milgram and Zimbardo series of experiments are of their time and have since been criticised on a number of counts, particularly ethical ones, they illustrate how easily ordinary people can be pulled into situations where they collude with or actively instigate not just unkind but frankly cruel and abusive behaviour. Interestingly, a version of Zimbardo's experiment was repeated more recently on the BBC in a documentary programme, 'The Experiment' (Reicher and Haslam, 2006). Perhaps in line with the way attitudes to authority and power have shifted over the intervening 30 years, the 'guards' were more lenient, but a group of 'prisoners' staged a coup and set up a regime where some of the others were badly treated and humiliated. Reicher and Haslam criticise many of the generalisations in the conclusion from the original Zimbardo experiment and specifically draw attention to the importance of leadership in the generation of institutional abuse.

These social psychology experiments seem to illustrate: first, a tendency for the individual to conform to the group – to the degree that the group 'norm' is likely to override information from the individual's own sensory system; second, a tendency to obey authority figures – however dangerous; and third, a tendency to act into the roles expected of one – even if these involve cruelty.

Interestingly, Zimbardo himself served as an expert witness for an Abu Ghraib defendant. The Abu Ghraib prison made international headlines in 2004 when photographs of US military personnel abusing Iraqi prisoners were published. Much of the court proceedings focused on the general conditions in the prison, which were understood as contributing to the behaviour of the individuals on trial. Whilst being clear that people are always accountable for their behaviour, Zimbardo believes that certain situations – and in this respect Abu Ghraib represented '*a perfect storm of conditions*' – can be sufficiently powerful to undercut empathy, altruism and morality and make ordinary people commit horrendous acts (Zimbardo, 2007).

These insights cannot be dismissed. The capacity for groups of staff – be they in prisons, children's homes or hospitals – to participate in cruel and abusive regimes is ever evident. It is well to remember that these staff often have to face and process distress and disturbance that is not encountered elsewhere in personal or community life.

Our Hunter-Gatherer Heritage

An understanding of evolutionary history gives us another perspective on group behaviours. An understanding of how human minds have evolved, and what they have evolved for, can offer valuable insights into the challenges of living and working together. Our psyches are the result of millions of years of evolution, and one way of understanding the psychological problems integral to modern life is to reflect on our adaptive strategies as these reflect the range of emotions and social behaviours that are shared with our distant ancestors and many other animals. As the psychologist Paul Gilbert puts it, *'the passions and fears of the "old brain/mind" were designed to be very powerful and not easily over-ruled'* (Gilbert, 2009, p. 36).

The hunter-gatherer lifestyle that existed for thousands of years made very different demands on the brain to those presented by life today. Our brains are threat-focussed with a fast-acting system for alerting and protecting us from danger. This involves the hormone cortisol, which causes a generalised rise of anxiety and a rush of energy that can activate us to escape or fight or sometimes to freeze – the fright–fight–flight response. In hunter-gatherer times this response was geared to infrequent, sudden and often severe threats.

In modern life, rather than living in forests or wildernesses, wary of dangerous animals, we inhabit a world where the sense of threat is prevalent but tends to be of a different kind and more chronic. The response that was well-adapted in our ancestors is often inappropriate and has to be inhibited. The fear and aggression experienced are unwelcome and potentially destabilising. They may be perceived as so threatening and dysfunctional that every effort is made not to think about them, a process known as *suppression*; or in some cases, the feelings are pushed out of conscious awareness completely, through what is called *repression*. This conscious or unconscious inhibition can lead to an overload of somatic symptoms, which in some cases lead to problems such as panic attacks, obsessive–compulsive symptoms and depression. While a neurophysiological system for soothing and comforting ourselves and each other has also evolved, the threat response – predominantly anger and fear – was designed to override these positive emotions in order to ensure survival. This is part of our evolutionary legacy.

One reading of problematic human social behaviour is to see it as driven by adaptive strategies to a primitive lifestyle that are not such a good fit with life in the twenty-first century. The tendency to compete for food and sex and to define ourselves as part of tightly demarcated groups – ideal for hunter-gatherers – can be seen as driving our relationships to a far greater extent than we are usually happy to acknowledge. This need to belong to small groups and feel connected can lead people to conform to rigid group norms, split the world into 'insiders' and 'outsiders', and institute social ranks and hierarchies, all of which can result in tribalism and hatred quite unhelpful to people leading modern lives as global citizens.

A different and perhaps more positive perspective is provided by the American cultural anthropologist Christopher Boehm in his book entitled *Moral Origins* (2012). Boehm is interested in the evolution of human generosity and cooperation and traces the development of altruism and group social control over six million years, eventually leading to the more developed sense of virtue and shame that we know today. He argues that our moral sense is a sophisticated mechanism that enables individuals to survive and thrive in groups. Getting by requires getting along, and this social type of selection singles out altruists for survival, or more accurately, disadvantages those who cannot control their aggression.

Boehm is particularly interested in our ancestors living some 45,000 years ago as he believes this was a crucial period in our psychosocial development. These ancestors did not store food, so their survival depended on them sharing their big meat carcasses in a reasonably equitable fashion. Much of Boehm's research is based on independent, nomadic and egalitarian hunter-gatherer societies in existence now – the Inuits of Greenland or the 'bushmen' from the Kalahari Desert, for example – as models for humans of the earlier epoch, with connections made between today's ethnography and yesterday's archaeology.

These foraging bands that Boehm believes were so vital to the development of human conscience tended to live in groups of about 30–40, and shared a core of moral beliefs with an egalitarian emphasis on every hunter being a political equal. They managed behaviour that threatened their cooperation through a system of group-sanctioned punishment that involved banishment, ostracism and, very rarely, capital punishment. All these punishments disadvantaged the reproductive prospects of individuals prone to social deviance, individuals who challenged the egalitarian philosophy by not controlling their sexuality, greed or hunger for power. At another level, the powerful bonding habit of gossip, particularly amongst women choosing their mates, was important. It was also sometime during this epoch that human blushing is thought to have evolved, all part of the development of self-consciousness, the emergence of social reputation and the evolution of empathy, shame and virtue.

Importantly, from an evolutionary point of view, the climate at this time is thought to have changed rapidly and dramatically, and these challenges would have speeded up social selection – it was a time when human brains were getting bigger very quickly. Pertinent to this chapter and the importance we put on team working, there is agreement amongst scholars that this type of living, in smallish cooperative groups, was particularly adaptive and socio-ecologically flexible. The modern world, with its complexities of role, status and culture, and the pressures and identity challenges of mass communication, especially through social media, is a different and more difficult place. It may well be that strengthening and securing how we operate at team level is now crucial for our ongoing creative adaptation and success.

The Unconscious Life of Groups

It is in groups that human beings have to manage and express their urges, passions and fears, and it is these sometimes very primitive emotional states that form the basic material of group dynamics.

Psychoanalytic thinking suggests that unconscious processes influence many of the things that happen in groups, including how well or badly they function. People bring conflicting needs and desires into groups. How these things are played out and managed influences much of how the group feels and behaves.

Groups – teams – struggle with several sources of conflict. Individuals both want autonomy and to be dependent on others. There is a tension between attending to the needs of the group for the group's sake, and to meeting the needs of its individual members. The team can be torn between investing collective effort or sitting back and expecting intense, often polarised work between a powerful pair of individuals within the group, to relieve everyone else of responsibility for working with the complexity of the real world.

Wilfrid Bion, the pioneering and influential group psychoanalyst, suggests (Bion, 1961) that how these conflicts are managed at any time leads the group to fall into one of three modes in which group feeling and behaviour appear to be based on an unconscious 'basic assumption':

- When the unconscious assumption is that the group's primary task is to meet people's dependency needs, its behaviour is typified by passivity, self-gratification and reliance on authority.
- When the assumption is that fight–(or)–flight is required to preserve autonomy, meet needs and escape difficulties, the group is characterised by conflict, especially with authority, by self-protection, by 'fleeing' from challenges in the task.
- When the assumption is that the pairing of powerful individuals will resolve group problems and needs, the group tends to sit back and invest their hope in magical solutions emerging in the future, rather than whole-group, 'adult' application to the challenges of the task in the present.

Bion thought that whilst groups and teams may be capable of functioning in a fully engaged and creative 'work group' mode, they also have a tendency to move in and out of one or other of these basic assumption states for short or long periods of time.

Reflection on our experience of being in teams may well prompt recognition of some of the ways Bion describes group psychology and behaviour – such patterns are also often vividly present in the relationship between a team and its wider environment. As important here as the specifics of the theory is Bion's highlighting of the contrast between a well-functioning task-focussed group, and group behaviour that can, without conscious intention, fall into less than creative states.

Ideas like Bion's prompt team members, and their leaders, to be attentive to the climate and culture of teams – 'how are we going about things?' – and to think about how best to move into effective 'work group' mode. They prompt team members to think about how they and their colleagues are collectively managing anxiety, their own needs, authority and the challenges of the task itself. When teams are in modes where self-gratification, passivity, conflict and evasion, or unrealistic expectation undermine attention to their task, they become vulnerable to poor functioning. Depending on the personalities of their members, the anxieties and pressures of the task, and the broader system within which they are operating, this under-functioning can veer from understandable temporary distraction to more extreme states, where colleagues and patients/clients are not met as persons.

Primitive Defence Mechanisms

We are all subject to group dynamics, even at the best of times, but some team settings evoke more extreme processes. The combination of an inherently traumatic and conflictual primary task, the close and complex working relationships that characterise a health or social care team, and worries about external threats and change, means that anxiety levels within individuals and in the team can be overwhelming. At this point, primitive defence mechanisms are likely to be triggered, and an understanding of these concepts can be helpful in understanding the behaviour of both the individual and the group. Like the psychological defence mechanisms described in the previous chapter, primitive defence mechanisms are an attempt to process anxiety but, because of the nature and degree of the anxiety, they characteristically distort reality and therefore amplify dysfunction. See Figure 6.1.

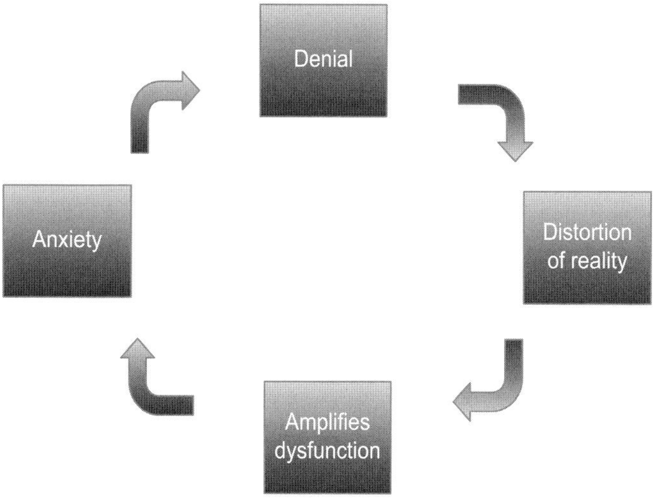

Figure 6.1 Anxiety and the Distortion of Reality

The concept of such mental defence mechanisms sheds light on how individuals protect themselves from extreme anxiety by denial and unconscious attempts to rid themselves of feeling. An important premise is that highly disturbing emotions and thoughts – those that are so anxiety-provoking that they cannot be thought about and put into words – spill over into other people.

This idea provides a model for understanding the unconscious transactions between people; how feelings are communicated when they are outside conscious awareness. It can help us think about how disturbed feelings and the cognitions that accompany them can spread in teams, almost like an infection. Just as primitive defences, when they are firmly established in an individual, affect functioning and distort the sense of identity and relationships of the person concerned, so it is in teams and wider organisations when primitive defences have become the main mode of processing emotion.

This perspective helps explain some of the processes at work in extreme situations such as Abu Ghraib, abusive children's homes, residential care homes and mental health units. It also throws light on the more everyday dynamics in health and social care teams overloaded with anxiety. Such understanding takes us on from the psychology experiments described earlier, which demonstrated how cruelly and unkindly many ordinary people will behave in specifically manipulated group circumstances, to a growing knowledge of what is going on within and between people in ordinary life.

Primitive defences are thought to originate in earliest infancy when the infant is totally dependent on others for its very survival. Before the development of language, feelings have to be expressed and communicated non-verbally and reactions are elicited in others as a result – often 'gut-to-gut', as it were. Similar means of communication may recur in adult life in situations of extreme anxiety, where painful reality cannot be faced in full. For some unlucky individuals, scarred by trauma and neglect, such mechanisms can dominate their personality and make everyday living and relating an enormous struggle, not just for themselves, but for those around them.

What makes these emotional communications so powerful is that people do not know what they are doing: they become active when we cannot bear to acknowledge what we face, and are consequently unaware of the processes we are using to evade it. When these defences predominate in the mental life of a team, conflicts, poor communication and distraction are amplified and the focus on the core care task is severely undermined. Teams may suffer debilitating conflict and poor leadership. Staff are more likely to go off sick or leave the job, and there is an increased likelihood that mistakes will be made. Inevitably, attention to those in their care suffers.

The Power of Denial

Primitive defences are all founded upon denial. This is common in health and social care situations, where the reality that needs to be faced or, as we are suggesting, denied, is often one involving enormous risk. Sometimes in acute medicine, survival of a patient depends on both individuals and the team ignoring the dreadful statistic and determinedly latching on to the small chance of hope. The line between such optimism and denial is fine, but important.

Denial is a step on from repression. It involves active distortion of the truth. Denial frequently involves omnipotence, grandiosity and triumphalism, in claiming that reality is other than it might appear, or be expected. Some professional groups are particularly prone to these traits and, in some teams, they become institutionalised – in other words, they become the norm and are unquestioned. There is evidence that this was happening in the Mid-Staffordshire Trust, which was criticised for its disregard of its high mortality statistics and where it was noted that:

> *in spite of the criticism[s] the Trust had received recently, there is an unfortunate tendency for some staff and management to discount these by relying on the view that there is much good practice and that the reports are unfair.* (Francis, 2010, p. 16)

In another trust in the Midlands, the low returns and negative views expressed in the annual staff survey are repeatedly attributed to failures on the part of the staff responsible for administering the survey. The undue acceptance of such procedural explanations is a common way of denying bad news.

Another common pattern of behaviour driven by denial is where a group of staff invest considerable energies into a new treatment or way of working, so much so that they see their identities as linked with the success or otherwise of the particular approach. The reality of disappointing outcomes perhaps accompanied by poor immediate effect on patients or clients, who may be in danger of being over-treated, or even wrongly treated, is ignored or rationalised away.

A further example often seen is the team that ignores the realities of major change in the outside world (such as a change in commissioning arrangements or the development of a new competitor), denies the threat involved, and rather than consider adaptations to their service, carries on as usual – almost as if they have a right to exist unchanged.

These examples may be extremes, but such dynamics are clearly recognisable to a greater or lesser extent in teams both inside and outside the public sector. The denial at their heart is a powerful force in interpersonal and team life.

Denial prevents healthy adaptation and distorts relationships, both within a team and between the team and the outside world, as well as, critically, with service-users and patients. Two psychoanalytic concepts, splitting and projective identification, help us to think in more detail about how this happens. These two concepts will now be described in some detail as they have considerable practical value for those working across health and social care.

The Theatre of Love and Hate

Psychoanalysts have a particular model for understanding how infants organise their experiences as emotions and how relationships develop. This is based on the idea that very young infants feel love when all is well with them, and hate when all is not well; but, existing, as they do, totally in the present, these feelings are experienced separate from one another – an 'either/or' mode of functioning. Gradually, as the brain evolves and neural pathways open up, the infant develops the capacity to remember and to think about experiences in an increasingly complex, integrated and realistic fashion. As time moves on, the young child begins to be able to contemplate the reality that the same person can make them feel love and hate, and cope with that ambiguity. With this maturation comes the capacity both to face and cope with distress and to maintain sufficient optimism to move on.

For some people, however, and for everyone at times of extreme anxiety, some experiences and memories are 'unthinkable', too full of horror and fear to be borne in mind. The pressure of illness or hospitalisation, or of working with needs and suffering that are hard to face, may well push an individual back on to infantile forms of splitting the world into either good or bad, the 'good' being idealised and the 'bad' denigrated. The effect of this splitting may be seen in relations between team members – and between the team and the people the team are trying to help, as described in the healthcare example in Box 6.1 below.

Box 6.1 An Example of 'Splitting'

Sally, who has cancer, puts all her hope into complementary therapies while being negative about and uncooperative with the treatment the specialist at the hospital is offering.

Clues that her response is driven by an unconscious process rather than thoughtful opinion are her vehemence and inflexibility. The consultant, for example, tries to discuss the possibility of using acupuncture for pain relief, but Sally dismisses this straightaway in the same manner that she has dismissed other suggestions.

Her behaviour is driven by her need to keep the 'good' and 'bad' separate in her mind. In this way, she can invest hope, uncontaminated by doubts, in the alternative therapist, while blaming the consultant for her deteriorating health.

Now imagine the potential effects on the team dynamic if Sally splits instead between nurses and doctors, or projects all her contempt onto one nurse while idealising the others (a particular form of group splitting known as scapegoating) or becomes fixed on the idea that the surgical team can do nothing wrong while the oncology team can do nothing right.

This brings us to the second key concept: projective identification. Basic projection, discussed in the previous chapter, is relatively straightforward, and often easily recognised. As an example, someone may be angry and hostile but this does not fit with their need to see themselves as kind and generous. People being what they are, however, their anger and hostility will come out unconsciously. As any problems due to negative feelings can't be of their making, as they see it, it must be the other person who is angry. The feeling is thus 'projected', and the other person is viewed as the angry one. This is regardless of how that person actually feels: they may be oblivious of what's been attributed to them, and surprised if they suffer accusations accordingly.

This only goes so far in avoiding disowned feelings however, particularly if the other person doesn't 'rise to the bait'. Here a more complicated process may come into play – 'projective identification'.

Most of us can find ourselves responding strangely readily to other people's feelings and expectations. If someone believes and expects you to be clumsy, you may find yourself being clumsy in their presence. A wide range of other subtle cues from people can elicit emotions in us, often without either party being aware that a communication has taken place.

If a feeling is projected, the process is much more effective if the person it's projected into actually has that feeling. Thus, with the example of anger, if the anger is projected into another person, and that person becomes angry, then it's obvious that they're the angry one, not you. The anger has been much more successfully disowned, by virtue of being projected into the other person, and that person then identifying with the feeling: this is projective identification. The process is mediated by a variety of interactions that produce the feeling in the other; always unconscious (if it's done consciously, it's a different phenomenon) and in ways learnt and developed from infancy onwards.

Sometimes this process can exploit and perpetuate racial or gender stereotypes with the person that is 'identifying' with projected feelings having been drawn into responding in such ways. Sometimes it will hook on to existing personality traits: in our example, the process of getting another to be the angry one instead of you goes so much more smoothly if the recipient is usually an angry person themselves. Sometimes, however, there will be little to hook it on, and the projected feelings will sit rather oddly with the recipient, who may be surprised to find themselves having uncharacteristic feelings.

It is important to bear in mind that both parties are unconscious of this dynamic and the feelings are projected in the first place only because the original person was unable to face them. It is as if the unwanted feelings are being pushed into the other person.

The recipients of projective identification, experiencing the feelings as their own, may well act upon them. At this point, in a group, things may become even more complicated and difficult to disentangle, as staff members start acting on feelings of, say, incompetence, depression or anger that do not fully belong to them in the first place. These feelings may come from patients or clients, from colleagues or from leaders. Individual members of staff, or groups of staff, may unconsciously (or part consciously) resort to the splitting and displacement of inconvenient or threatening realities onto colleagues within a team, or in another team.

In teams where projection and projective identification, together with the 'basic assumptions' described by Bion (see above), are at work – which is all teams some of the time, and some teams all of the time – individual and collective feeling and behaviour are profoundly influenced. Box 6.2 attempts to summarise the impact of disowned anxiety on teams.

Box 6.2 Disowned Anxiety in Teams Can . . .

- Cause communication breakdown, where different perspectives can't be talked about;
- Prevent the reality of a situation being properly faced;
- Be projected into other people, including service-users, who end up more anxious than the situation warrants;
- Lead to scapegoating where one person or subgroup is blamed unfairly;
- Cause 'splitting' in the team, where one's own subgroup is seen to hold all the virtue, wisdom and rationality and the rest of the team are to blame for everything that goes wrong;
- Be projected onto other teams in a way that prevents scrutiny of the problems in one's own team, and damages effective collaboration;
- Make team members ill.

Where leaders and team members lack a mental model of what is at work in groups, and are unable to pay attention to how the team as a whole and its members are behaving, the team is vulnerable to dysfunction and distortion of its relationships and work. Moreover, where the wider organisation is characterised by extreme forms of processes such as denial and projection, individual teams within the umbrella organisation are more vulnerable to them.

Team Resilience

From this point of view, it seems right that the recommendations in the report of the inquiry into the Mid-Staffordshire Trust mainly addressed failures in the system, rather than individual staff at the front-line (Francis, 2010, pp. 398–418). Interestingly, though, there were areas of good practice within the trust described in some of the accounts given by patients and their representatives. One contrasted the 'excellent' care on the coronary care unit with that on some of the wards, which should have brought *'shame to the nurses' uniform'*; another comparing the care on ward six with that on ward seven, likened them to two *'different lands'* (p. 159). Whilst there may have been an element of splitting going on, it would seem that even within a dysfunctional umbrella organisation, there are opportunities to create islands of good team working, where attention to the needs of those they care for is paramount. Research into team functioning demonstrates that thoughtful, well-managed teamwork can 'buffer' the effects of a wider dysfunctional organisation (Borrill et al, 2000).

This may be largely due to the quality of team leadership. The Frontline charity was given a mission to transform the lives of vulnerable children by recruiting and developing outstanding individuals to enter social work. Commissioned by the Department of Education, it extensively researched what makes a good team leader. Their 'Firstline' programme focussed particularly on such leadership, i.e. those who directly work with and lead those practising on the front-line. Not surprisingly, the research affirmed both how vital this role is to the functioning and outcome of a team, and also how challenging the role can be. In fact, interviews with staff higher up the organisations revealed that they thought First Line leadership roles were the most demanding in their careers. Good leaders at this level require: high intellect to make considered judgements in difficult situations; emotional intelligence to contain emotion and inspire confidence in teams; and strong leadership capability. In their words: *Enabling excellent children's social-work in a high risk, resource stretched, pressured and politicised context requires not just good managers but outstanding leaders* (Frontline, 2017, p. 4). The same could be said for hands-on clinical management roles in the health service.

Unhelpful Structures

It is frustrating that so little of this sort of knowledge is applied more widely. Health and social care teams in the UK are not generally highly evolved in their functioning as teams and little sustained effort goes into enabling outstanding leadership at this level. The quality of meetings is often poor and team objectives unclear (Borrill et al, 2000).

Health service teams tend to be large, much larger than the ideal of six to ten that is thought to promote a sense of cohesiveness and belonging, good communication and participation in decision-making (Firth-Cozens and Cornwell, 2009, p. 7). They also tend to have unclear boundaries and sometimes conflicting objectives, with different professions approaching the task from different perspectives and tensions sometimes arising between professional and organisational hierarchies. In addition, many healthcare staff, particularly senior staff, have a peripatetic role and belong in several different teams, or, as some have described them, 'pseudo-teams'.

Added to this, many staff are on rapid training rotations: junior doctors, for example, move every few months. Nurses are frequently moved without consultation to cover shortages in other teams. One unwanted effect of the European Working Time Directive (which set a legal maximum shift length and working week) has been the breakdown of close-knit medical 'firms', which were made up of a consultant and several junior doctors of varying degrees of experience, working together as a unit in clinics, on the wards and when 'on call', with responsibility for a specific group of patients identified as exclusively under their care. Patients have subsequently complained that they see a series of junior doctors and do not know the name of their consultant, whilst junior doctors complain of feeling isolated and unsupported, having exchanged the small, exclusive team for a wider, and more diffuse, peer group.

The social care sector, in particular domiciliary care, is widely challenged by the absence of any real supportive team environment. Frequently, domiciliary workers travel alone from client to client and have almost no team identity, exchange or support. Care homes can fall into fragmented shift systems, with agency staff coming and going. In such circumstances, the need for support, the need for help managing feelings, and the need for sharing, thinking about and learning from experience, are all poorly met.

Team Boundaries

One important aspect of teams is how they manage their boundaries: their relationships with the world outside. There are two aspects to this: how a team manages its relationship with clients or patients, for example how easy it is for them to access the service; and how its members communicate and cooperate with other teams and services. These boundary relationships will include issues relating to membership, space, time, task and role. How a team manages such factors will affect the safety, appropriateness and effectiveness of the work. Thinking about such boundary management can be helped by four categories of question:

- How open is the team to welcoming and including *'outsiders'* in work with the patient/client, and how ready to think about their perspective and concerns?
- How flexible is the team about *where it operates* – where it will meet others, where it will deliver its service?
- How flexible is the team about *when it does its work* – opening hours, sessions and clinics, visits and contacts, waiting lists, duty systems, and so on?
- How rigid or flexible is the team about *what its task should be* and about the *roles* it is ready to take on in partnership with others?

In each case there is always a pull between being too 'tight' and too 'loose' in managing the boundary: too tight, and the team will be hard to work with, inaccessible and rigid, pursuing its own agenda at the expense of a system-wide approach focussed on the needs of the service-users; too loose, and clarity and cohesiveness will suffer and the team might be distracted from its primary task. Building good relationships between teams will lead to a more comprehensive consideration of the issues. A less fragmented picture of the patient or client in the minds of the staff will lead to that person having a greater sense of being met and held in mind as a person.

Boundary management is not a simple matter of procedure and operational policy. It is a complex two-way process. Feelings belonging within the team can be transferred to people outside – especially managers, referrers and other colleagues – who can then begin to be seen as persecutory, uncooperative, withholding or incompetent. Even where a team needs to protect itself from genuinely unhealthy realities outside, this kind of externally focussed aggression or defensiveness is unhelpful. The less cooperative and responsive a team is within the wider system, the more likely the receiver of care is to suffer from discontinuity and errors. In general, it has been shown that the culture of a team and, in particular, the nature and intensity of the defence mechanisms at work will determine how the team manages its boundaries (Zagier Roberts, 1994).

Healthy Teamwork

The perspectives on teams that can be gained from applying the psychological models described in this chapter are summarised in Box 6.3 below.

Effective teamwork manages to minimise the playing out of those team dramas that undermine people's sense of themselves and instead enables them to connect with their goodwill, capability and responsibilities.

Research clearly establishes the importance of well-functioning healthcare teams, and Carol Borrill and her colleagues at Lancaster University (2000) even established a link between the proportion of staff working in teams in a particular hospital and patient

Box 6.3 **A Well-Managed Team Has to Contain and Manage the Following . . .**

- Anxiety – conscious and unconscious;
- Evasion, unrealistic expectations, denial of reality;
- Passivity and conformism;
- Neediness, pairing;
- Conflict, aggression and acquisitiveness;
- Sub-groupings and scapegoating;
- Over-rigid or too loose boundaries with the 'outside world'.

mortality – where more employees work in teams, the death rate is lower. The same authors found those working in teams had better mental health than those working in looser groups or individually, and that well-functioning teams have better retention and lower turnover rates.

Similar findings have emerged from the new wave of social-work initiatives. The quality of team working is related to effectiveness in terms of clearer team objectives, better peer support, a higher level of participation by team members, greater commitment to quality and more support for innovation.

A well-established team tradition and school of thought within the field of social care and mental health concerns the 'therapeutic environment' or 'therapeutic milieu'. Here, healthy functioning of the staff team is seen as an essential therapeutic agent of change. Alongside and supporting this recognition that the social environment is a key aspect of treatment, conceptual and technical ways of measuring the therapeutic environment have developed, through instruments such as the Ward Atmosphere Scale (Timko and Moos, 2004). Such instruments can be used to describe and compare different types of treatment setting, and to evaluate different components of the social climate including which aspects of a therapeutic programme are most likely to facilitate good outcomes. This type of action research allows an ongoing study of therapeutic environments, with everybody being involved as both an object and an agent of enquiry. The findings, implications and indeed some of the research techniques could usefully be extended beyond the field of mental health. There is an increasing range of tools that may be used by teams to help them consider, evaluate and work to improve team relationships and functioning, including the Team Climate Assessment Measure (TCAM) and the Team Self Review (TSR). Both these are health focussed, but can readily be adjusted for teams in both health and social care (TCAM: www.npsa.nhs.uk/nrls/improvingpatientsafety/ teamworking/tcam; TSR: www.npsa.nhs.uk/nrls/improvingpatientsafety/teamworking/tsr).

Making the Team Dynamic a Priority

This chapter has brought together strands of thinking from diverse theoretical backgrounds in an attempt to throw light on the reasons why people behave as they do – often irrationally and destructively – when they are part of a group, in this case a health or social care team. There is little doubt that pressures on teams of staff addressing the health and socials needs of our society in the twenty-first century continue to increase. It cannot be assumed that even generally kind and sensible people will behave well when they are part of a team coping badly under pressure. Indeed, there is a great deal of evidence that many of us have the potential to be unthinkingly neglectful and even abusive.

In a paper on supporting staff teams, Rex Haigh, a psychiatrist and group analyst, describes a model that addresses the needs of staff in health and social care settings. The model is based on the idea that staff all have irreducible emotional needs that will be stirred by their work. Consistent attention to these factors can be as much help as the tools referred to above. Haigh sees these needs as coloured by early experience and frames them in a developmental sequence, summarised in Box 6.4.

Box 6.4 **Five Qualities of a Therapeutic Environment, Presented as a Developmental Sequence**

Quality	Expression in a Therapeutic Environment
Attachment	A culture of belonging, in which attention is given to joining and leaving, and staff are encouraged to feel part of things.
Containment	A culture of safety, in which there is a secure organisational structure and staff feel supported, looked after and cared about within the team.
Communication	A culture of openness, in which difficulties and conflict can be voiced, and staff have a reflective, questioning attitude to the work.
Involvement	A 'living–learning' culture, in which team members appreciate each other's contributions and have a sense that their work and perspective are valued.
Agency	A culture of empowerment, in which all members of the team have a say in the running of the place and play a part in decision-making.

From Haigh (2004, p. 120).

As infants, our emotional journey can be seen as a series of relational steps, the solidity of each one laying the foundation for the next. How we face the demands of being ill or vulnerable, or working with ill-being as adults, will draw on strengths accumulated through this process and hook into weaknesses. If our emotional labour as adults is well facilitated, there is opportunity for reparation, affirmation and further development.

Sadly, many health and social care teams are not well structured to fulfil these needs although there are some exceptions. Haigh's model, however, by focussing on underlying principles rather than prescriptive formulae, provides a framework that we can all use to reflect on and contribute to improving the social climate in the team so that individual staff members and the team itself can function well.

An understanding of what can undermine relationships within small human groups, a grasp of what makes it so difficult to work effectively together under pressure, and some ideas about how to address and contain such dynamics is ever helpful.

References

Asch, S. E. (1951) Effects of group pressure upon the modification and distortion of judgment. In *Groups, Leadership and Men* (ed. H. Guetzkow), pp. 177–190. Carnegie Press.

Bion, W. R. (1961) Experiences in Groups. Tavistock.

Blass, T. (ed.) (2000) Obedience to Authority: Current Perspectives on the Milgram Paradigm. Lawrence Erlbaum Associates.

Boehm C. (2012) *Moral Origins: The Evolution of Virtue, Altruism and Shame.* Basic Books.

Bond, R. and Smith, P. (1996) Culture and conformity: a meta-analysis of studies using Asch's (1952b, 1956) line judgement task. Psychological Bulletin. 119: 111–37.

Borrill, C., West, M., Shapiro, D., et al (2000) Team working and effectiveness in healthcare. British Journal of Health Care Management. 6: 364–71.

Firth-Cozens, J. and Cornwell, J. (2009) The Point of Care. Enabling Compassionate Care in Acute Hospital Settings. King's Fund.

Francis, R. (2010) The Independent Inquiry into Care Provided by Mid-Staffordshire NHS Foundation Trust, January 2005–March 2009. HMSO.

Francis, R. (2013) The Public Inquiry into the Mid-Staffordshire Foundation Trust, January 2005–March 2009. HMSO

Frontline (2017) Developing Outstanding Social Workers. What Makes Great First Line Leadership? Department of Education, HMSO.

Gilbert, P. (2009) *The Compassionate Mind.* Constable and Robinson.

Haigh, R. (2004) The quintessence of an effective team: some developmental dynamics for staff groups. In *From Toxic Institutions to Therapeutic Environments* (ed. P. Campling and R. Haigh), pp. 119–30. Royal College of Psychiatrists.

Haney, C., Bank, W. C. and Zimbardo, P. G. (1973) Interpersonal dynamics in a simulated prison. International Journal of Criminology and Penology. 1: 69–97.

Haslam, A., Miller, A., Reicher S. (2014) The Journal of Social Issues Special Milgram Themed Edition, September 2014.

Jones, J. (2018) The Report of the Gosport Independent Panel. Available at: https://www.gosportpanel.independent.gov.uk/panel-report/ [last accessed 9 August, 2019].

Milgram, S. (1963) Behavioural study of obedience. Journal of Abnormal and Social Psychology. 67: 371–8.

Nietzsche, F. (1886) *Jenseits von Gut und Bose (Beyond Good and Evil)*. Druck und Verlag von C G Neumann, Chapter 4.

Reicher, S. and Haslam, S. (2006) Rethinking the psychology of tyranny: the BBC Prison Study. British Journal of Social Psychology. 45: 1–40.

Timko, C. and Moos, R. H. (2004) Measuring the therapeutic environment. In *From Toxic Institutions to Therapeutic Environments* (ed. P. Campling and R. Haigh), pp. 143–56. Royal College of Psychiatrists.

Zagier Roberts, V. (1994) The organisation of work: contributions from open systems theory. In *The Unconscious At Work* (eds. A. Obholzer and V. Roberts), pp. 28–38. Brunner-Routledge.

Zimbardo, P. (2007) *The Lucifer Effect: Why Good People Turn Evil.* Rider & Co.

Chapter 7 Cooperation and Fragmentation

The only thing that will redeem mankind is cooperation.

(Bertrand Russell)

When individual practitioners work to connect with those they care for, and with each other, through the 'virtuous circle', and manage the inevitable difficult and ambivalent feelings involved in their task, their practice will be enormously improved. When the teams they work in manage their internal relationships, and those with other teams and services, well, individual and collective intelligent kindness can be sustained. However, in the modern world, the sheer complexity of health and social difficulties, and of the range of services people may need, presents an ever-present challenge. Consider the story in Box 7.1.

Box 7.1 A Family in Need

The two Croft children are raising concerns at their primary school. Teachers and the school nurse worry that their parents are neglecting them. A teaching assistant wonders whether one of them has a learning disability. The staff know that their father is being supported with drug and alcohol problems by Turning Point, a voluntary sector provider. They aren't yet aware that the police have been called to the parental home on several occasions when neighbours have worried that he has been violent to his wife, who is being treated by her GP for depression. Since the father recently missed signing on for his benefits, he has been sanctioned, and the family are, not for the first time, in financial straits.

Mrs Croft's mother, an important carer for the children, is in pain and very weary. A GP refers her to orthopaedics, who, after a six week wait, do some tests and find nothing. They send her back to the GP practice for referral to rheumatology. She waits three weeks, after which another GP makes the referral. After a three month wait, rheumatology assess her and again find nothing. Again, she is sent back to the practice, where, after a wait, during which the pain worsens, a third GP considers a recommendation to refer to the pain clinic . . . Meanwhile, grandfather is diagnosed with the early stages of dementia by yet another GP in the same practice, and referred to older people's mental health services.

This narrative will be immediately recognisable to staff working across public services. It points to several challenging truths:

- As has been highlighted before, services encounter many human problems that cannot be understood simply as 'health' or 'social care' issues.
- Staff in any service will always have a *partial* view of an individual's or family's circumstances, needs and risks.
- Many individuals require a range of assessments and services, even for 'single', let alone 'multiple' needs – needs that can also change, as time passes, depending on circumstances.
- The services required may be from one organisation, or from several. Organisations involved will very frequently span health, social care, education, benefits, the criminal justice system, the statutory and non-statutory, public, private and voluntary sectors. All have their own cultures, priorities, targets and challenges.
- Each service has its own routines and procedures, that people – staff and service-users alike – will be subject to. Waiting lists, protocols and priorities, staff rotas, resource management etc., all influence the timeliness of intervention, consistency, understanding, and 'holding in mind' of the service-user.
- Staff must refer, or direct, the service-user out into the wider system, meaning that continuity can be broken, and that circumstances may change without them knowing. Their connection with, and role in supporting, a person may become, at best, tenuous.
- Individual needs sit within a wider, family, context, and they, and associated risks, may be inter-related – but frequently there is no-one with the perspective, or the explicit responsibility, to assess this.
- The nature, and the timing of, interventions by any single service may influence not just the wellbeing of the individual, but those of others in the family – but just how will always be difficult to judge.
- If everybody with a perspective shared their views, effective understanding and intervention would be more likely. But it is hard to know definitively who to involve at any given time, or, indeed, when and how to invest the time and effort in bringing them together.
- Improved information systems across and between organisations would no doubt help: but which information, about whom, and as part of what service to whom? Who should decide what to share and when? What would be the legal and ethical implications of sharing such personal data, and how would it fit with the person's right to privacy?

These inescapable challenges face anyone attempting to promote cooperation or integration of services, and to make the journey through the system more humane and effective for a patient or client.

Why do we stress 'inescapable'? Because to make the mistake of believing that *any* way of organising services can entirely remedy or remove these problems will be to fail both the staff who have to work with complex needs in a complex system, and those who need their help. Systems must be designed and, vitally, led, in ways that recognise both the value *and* the limitations of agreements, structure and specification if they are to enable the best possible care. Partnerships are required within and between services, which promote and enable *cooperation* by intelligent, curious people, with the permission to act upon what they find, or understand, in response to the needs of those they are caring for. How people's circumstances and needs are understood is almost always provisional, changeable and incremental. Individual staff members and the systems within which they work need to be able to respond accordingly.

A central idea from Complexity Theory may help us keep in mind what has to be fostered as attempts are made to organise care systems. Paul Plsek, author, consultant, researcher and chair for innovation at the Virginia Mason Medical Center in Seattle, suggests that a complex adaptive system – for that is what is involved – is:

> *a collection of individual agents who are free to act in ways that are not totally predictable and whose actions are interconnected, such that one agent's actions change the context for other agents.* (Plsek, 2016)

In his chapter in *Dialogic Organization Development: The Theory and Practice of Transformational Change* (Bushe and Marshak, 2015), Ralph Stacey, a pioneer in the field of complexity in organisations, uses an even more pertinent term to describe this system: '*organizations as complex responsive processes of relating*'.

Of course, in the real world, the quest to enable such systems will always have to be married with the more 'engineered' approach of structural organisation. Too disorganised a system will mean inefficiency, chaos and failure to bring the right services to bear on need. A system that is too rigidly organised will prevent intelligent work to shape intervention around people's individual circumstances. A balance must be found. It is such a balance – and the difficulty of finding and maintaining it – that presents a continuing challenge for all, from 'front-line' practitioners to leaders, managers, planners and commissioners.

With this in mind, we will explore approaches to organising and structuring multi-professional, multi-agency and 'multi-sector' activities to promote their integration, and to facilitate service-users' journeys through them. Such approaches include the creation of multi-disciplinary teams, integrated care systems, care protocols and pathways, and other ways of organising the care of individual patients or clients.

As we consider these ways of promoting effective collaboration in the interest of service-users, it is important that the factors that influence the collaboration of individuals, teams and services are borne in mind. Historically, it can be argued that good intentions about cooperation in the interests of patients and clients have repeatedly failed to make the difference hoped for because such dynamics have been insufficiently recognised and addressed.

The Dynamics of the Multi-disciplinary Team

We explored earlier how the way individuals manage the difficult feelings involved in addressing ill-being, and challenging needs, can influence their relationship with those they are caring for, and with their colleagues. If the working relationships within a team are fostered effectively, with sufficient support for its members, and attention to the group dynamics discussed in Chapter 6, individual effectiveness, and creative collaboration, will be improved. Such work needs determined attention, even in teams of people of the same profession: in the multi-disciplinary team there are additional, sometimes complicated, factors to manage.

Into a multi-disciplinary team come the mind-sets and politics of the professions represented. Members bring, to varying degrees, their 'self-identification' as members of professional groups. The social worker, doctor, nurse or allied health professional carries with them the values, ways of thinking, language and working models of their discipline. This is, of course, what the multi-disciplinary team aims to bring together: to blend the various perspectives into a cooperative enterprise; to ensure as broad an understanding of the client or patient as possible; to bring a coordinated range of interventions to bear on helping them. What can happen when these different mind-sets are brought together needs to be understood.

The first challenge is to manage potential divided loyalties: who do you see as kin – your fellow professionals or your multi-disciplinary colleagues? Team members carry into the team the interests of their professional group, their collective attitudes and expectations about their work, and views about the organisations in which they work. Many bring the agendas and cultures of the professional organisations, trades unions, and the various local uni-disciplinary, formal and informal groups and committees, established in their organisations. The hierarchies within each profession are very different. Members often have professional supervision from beyond the team. Practitioners are held, or feel, responsible for their practice in different ways, some explicit, some implicit, within their professions and organisations. The social worker or doctor will have a different sense of 'carrying the can' than the psychologist, the nurse or the care assistant. All these factors can influence personal and professional identity, and ways of approaching collaboration.

This professional identity can be as strong as, or stronger than, members' sense of themselves as belonging to the multi-disciplinary team. When the team is also multi-agency, this potential to be 'pulled both ways' can be amplified. The people 'seconded' to such a multi-disciplinary team bring their identities as members of their 'home' organisations, their experience and preoccupations in them, and their duties as they are understood and prioritised by them.

The second challenge is to recognise that relationships in a multi-disciplinary team will also be influenced by differences in status, salary and influence between the professions represented. Along with, and complicating, such factors, there are often gender, race and cultural imbalances and interactions at play within professional groups, and, of course, between them.

If healthy, cooperative and collaborative multi-disciplinary teamwork is to be achieved, individuals, and the team as a whole, need to pay attention to and work to manage the effects of these factors on their relationships. Unattended to, they can amplify the dynamics that work against good teamwork that were explored in Chapter 6. Teams can become passive and dependent, dominated by one professional voice, or suffused by avoidance, envy or conflict. Members can, to various degrees, detach themselves from the group. Communication, sharing of ideas, commitment and 'co-construction' of routines and ways of working can consequently suffer. Decisions, whether about need, risk or intervention, are likely to be impaired. Important elements of creative and safe teamwork, such as healthy challenge, questioning and disagreement, become more difficult. The multi-disciplinary team can fail to develop the inter-disciplinary and inter-personal identity, dialogue and working culture that is their purpose. The potential for such under- or mal-functioning to undermine connection with, understanding of, and effective help for, service-users, is obvious.

It is vital that all team members routinely commit to the work needed to address and manage the dynamics of inter-disciplinary relationships. Consideration of these dynamics needs to be integrated *explicitly* into individual and team reflective practice. It is essential that team leaders or coordinators are encouraged, authorised and able to take a lead in this work. It is by no means always very complicated or difficult: if promoting the quality of the human relationships between team members is given the attention it deserves, managing inter-disciplinary dynamics becomes much easier. And addressing these dynamics is frequently a way of maintaining or improving the morale and effectiveness of already well-functioning teams, not just dealing with under-functioning or failure.

So, building cooperative multi-disciplinary practice is not simply a matter of deciding what pieces of a machine to put together: understanding how they may interact for good or ill is crucial. The 'pieces' themselves are not mechanical, but human beings, with their own personalities, professional pride, identities, anxieties and convictions. Given that multi-disciplinary work is nowadays ubiquitous in professional practice, it is crucial that professional education, and leadership, prepares and supports practitioners to participate with awareness, commitment and responsibility in both formal and informal inter-disciplinary exchange. Staff need to understand how to contribute the value of their professional paradigms, evidence and language in a diverse environment, and, crucially, how to make space for, listen to and cooperate with other disciplines. They need to join teams with the recognition of the likely dynamics and power relationships involved. These are not 'side issues', but necessary aspects of building good cooperative practice in the interests of service-users or patients.

The Dynamics of the Multi-service System

For many years, attempts have been made to organise or integrate diverse services so that they can better collaborate to meet complex needs. This work may focus on integrating the activities of various departments in one organisation – such as a hospital, an NHS trust, or a social services department. It may aim to bring together hospital and community services, primary and secondary 'tiers' of healthcare, or to integrate the work of several organisations. Typically, this will involve trying to align the strategies and work of the statutory and voluntary or private sector providers, or bringing together the activities of police, education, housing, health and social care services. Such work may be based on promoting collaboration through building joint vision and planning. It may be underpinned by agreements, protocols, procedures, or structural organisation, creating formal managed networks of services. Often there are elements of all these approaches. These projects have attempted to improve services in areas such as cancer care, working with vulnerable older people, children and young people in need, diabetes, obesity, mental health, and learning disabilities, etc. A predominant concern has been to find ways of 'integrating' the work of health and social care services. Box 7.2 summarises the position across the UK as of 2019.

Box 7.2 Policy on Health and Social Care

Health and social care services have been formally integrated in **Northern Ireland** since 1973. The Health and Social Care (Reform) Act (Northern Ireland) in 2009 re-structured the system to integrate hospital care with community services.

In **Scotland**, in 2016, legislation was passed to integrate health and social care services for adults (see www2.gov.scot/Topics/Health/Policy/Health-Social-Care-Integration). This built upon previous work to align the work of health and social care towards common outcomes (see www.gov.scot/Publications/2015/02/9966/downloads).

In **Wales**, in 2016, the Government took a less structural approach, following up legislation over a number of years with guidance to align the work of health and social care towards common outcomes (see www.gov.wales/docs/dhss/publications/160405summaryen.pdf). In 2018, its plan 'A Healthier Wales' committed to 'joined-up work between health and social care' (see www.gweddill.gov.wales/docs/dhss/publications/180608healthier-wales-mainen.pdf).

In **England**, Health and Wellbeing Boards, bringing together the leadership in the social care and health sectors, with other players, were established following the Health and Social Care Act 2012. In 2016, 44 'Sustainability and Transformation Partnerships' were established to promote collaborative planning and service delivery, with the development of 'Integrated Care Systems' a priority (see www.england.nhs.uk/integratedcare/integrated-care-systems/).

In all four countries of the UK, a range of local strategic and delivery partnership arrangements have been introduced over the years. These have included pilots, locally designed partnerships, or statutory arrangements.

It is beyond the scope of this book to undertake a comprehensive review of such developments. Our purpose is to consider what is involved in sustaining cooperative practice directed by intelligent kindness. Just as the multi-disciplinary team involves dynamics that, unattended to, are likely to undermine such work, so inter-departmental, service and organisational collaboration is complicated by similar, and potentially problematic, factors. Historically, attempts formally to organise and structure have dominated the quest to integrate work across the system, with less attention to the dynamics involved. As Chris Ham and his colleagues commented in their report on the lessons for England of integrated care in Northern Ireland, Scotland and Wales:

> *To use a medical analogy, the focus now needs to be on ensuring that the physiology of health and social care is fit for purpose rather than seeking to alter the anatomy. To be sure, anatomical changes may be needed at some point in the future but the clear message of this report is that on their own they are unlikely to be sufficient . . .* (King's Fund, 2013)

It is this 'physiology' that we want to explore. It is a concept relevant, not just to integrating health and social care, but to all attempts to promote collaboration by multiple organisations towards common outcomes. In Chapter 6 we discussed the way teams manage their boundaries. The inter-agency care system is made up of teams, departments and organisations, all of which may manage their own boundaries well or badly, who may bring openness and cooperation or negative, self-protective, attitudes and feelings to partnership work. The consequent 'landscape' through which staff – and service-users – must move will involve encounters with these boundaries. How they experience this landscape profoundly affects the emotional climate, the conditions for kindness, and the effectiveness of services.

Narrowing Down the Primary Task

Where boundary management in teams within a wider system is too much infected by defensiveness, that system can become seriously dysfunctional. There is often no real collective agreement about, and alignment with, what should be the collective primary task, or the central *purpose* – bringing all of the required resources from across the system intelligently and kindly together to help the person whose well-being they are working to support. At worst, we get the ugly sight of teams accusing each other of 'dumping' clients or patients on them, or otherwise denigrating each other, with a consequent resentful colouring of relationships with each other and those they serve.

The problem of embattled teams fragmenting the system of care needed by an individual or family can be found in all areas of health and social care. But it seems to be at its worst when the task is to work with a condition that is chronic rather than acute, where interventions are low on technology, reliant on people, and mainly provided in the community – elderly patients with dementia being an obvious example. Staff teams working in such areas will usually acknowledge that needs are high and that resources are far from adequate. This can lead to a tendency for teams to manage their own part within the system by narrowing the definition of their 'primary task'. They tell themselves they are doing – or being asked to do – much more than is expected, and at the same time project their sense of inadequacy onto other teams. Management of task boundaries is infected by defence mechanisms.

In his book, *Managing Vulnerability*, Tim Dartington, a researcher and consultant in health and social care, previously of the Tavistock Institute of Human Relations in London, explores this phenomenon, with a particular focus on the split between health and social services in the care of the elderly. He is interested in why the split seems so intractable and notes:

> *there appears to be an unconscious wish to act out the insolubility of an intractable problem – that people get older and weaker – by taking sides, even when this becomes dysfunctional.* (Dartington, 2010, p. 93)

He sees the 'defining down' of the task, as in the examples above, as a symptom of stress, leading services increasingly to be out of touch with reality (p. 96). In the face of overwhelming vulnerability and helplessness in the people they are caring for, teams like to see themselves as in control of their working environment and end up behaving as if there are no other stakeholders and no wider system within which to negotiate compromises. The normative task (what we ought to do) is defined down, as within a closed system, as if it is not subject to vagaries of the environment. The existential task (what we think we are doing) is experienced as ever broadening, with a sense that the system is being flooded by the environment. *In the perception of those that live and work in them, care systems are inadequate to meet the challenges that face them, but it is not their fault* (p. 97).

A classic example from mental healthcare is that of someone who suffers from schizophrenia and also misuses illegal drugs. There is a general sense that such people pose complex clinical management problems that tend to overwhelm the available resources and therapeutic skills. Staff on acute general psychiatry wards often tell themselves their 'task' is to work with people who are mentally ill, so having to care for people with drug problems is going over and above what they are there to do. The drug teams usually define their primary task as working with drug users, the priority depending on the class of drug as defined by the Home Office. In other words, both teams are sure they are doing more than they should when they work with people with the dual diagnosis, and they tend to blame the other team for doing a lot less than they should. Their definitions of the primary task are a way of keeping complexity, guilt and a sense of failure at bay.

Of course, there are probably areas of the country where care for those with a dual diagnosis is exemplary. In general, however, despite various policy initiatives, unhelpful splitting of the task between teams with different backgrounds and perspectives tends to be difficult to change. Most staff will be able to relate to similar situations and recognise such stock phrases as 'we are not really supposed to ... ', 'it's not really our responsibility ... ', 'we're not set up to deal with incontinence ... ', 'I wasn't trained to do this ... '.

The way processes like this colour how teams manage their boundaries and relationships requires attention if the patient or client as a person is to find real recognition and cooperative compassion in the care system. To create the conditions for such healthy cooperation requires work at individual team level, to develop a mature culture internally, and to attend constructively to boundaries and relationships with the wider system.

How the wider care system is structured, organised and led, and the contracts and specifications that shape it, is, of course, important. Attending to these 'business' factors can create conditions within which healthier relationships are more likely, but without attention to team and system dynamics and their effects on cooperation, they will be of limited effectiveness, and may even do real damage to compassionate care.

The Dynamics of Partnership Work

It will, we hope, be becoming obvious that there is an emerging theme here. There are similar dynamics at play, whether it is individual practitioners or teams that are attempting to work collaboratively with others. This is just as true when we consider the attempts of organisations to align their activities.

Consider what arrives around the table when senior managers from across the system come together to develop joint vision or to plan joint work. The aim may be, for example, to develop an Integrated Care System, collective plans to work with vulnerable children, or to address 'joined up' care between hospital and community services for vulnerable older people. There is always a substantial tension between a predominant culture in which individual, hierarchical organisations ply their trades as separately accountable, often competitive, providers, and a model involving horizontal collaboration, pooled resources and risks. There will, inevitably, be imbalances of power, resources and readiness, or ability, to change around the table.

The relationship between those 'holding the purse strings' – commissioners and those who 'contract out' services – and those who provide services, will always colour the dialogue, and affect the realism of any plans. This may simply influence power relationships around the table, but is likely also to involve mismatches between aspirations for, approaches to, and competence in, commissioning actual services. Commissioners may have apparent commitment to, and understanding of, integrated or 'whole system' services, but this can very frequently dissipate as fragmented contracts are developed and implemented with individual providers in the system.

The organisations represented at our imagined meeting are subject to various inspection, performance, and contract management regimes, with targets and priorities that preoccupy them. All this may or may not align well as collaboration is addressed. Each organisation is working within financial constraints, that will always influence how they are able to commit to the joint enterprise, whether through simply creating anxious distraction, or driving preoccupation with internal re-organisation, cost savings or actual cuts to services. The larger organisations may have more resource flexibility than smaller providers, but are likely to have even more complex distractions. The flexibility in thinking or readiness to take risks with new ways of working of providers governed by 'payment by results', or highly specified contract specifications, will inevitably be affected. This will often be despite an enthusiastic in-principle readiness to change. Very often, such providers are highly dependent on referral of potential clients by other agencies: another factor that creates power imbalances. Each participant around the table is also accountable within their home organisation, working within a climate of priorities, challenges and internal systems that all influence the way they can commit to joint work.

Even when representatives put such preoccupations to one side, and participate creatively in developing joint vision or plans, a yawning gap can emerge between what is agreed and designed, and what each organisation is willing, or able, actually to do. Often, this is because of the sheer complexity of the tasks facing partner organisations if they are to adjust their ways of working to fit within new collaborative models. Just as frequently, it is the product of a failure to recognise and manage the dynamics we are describing, which can lead to unrealistic agreements, as variously well-meaning, passive, disengaged or anxious participants sign up to ambitious visions, without being able to bring these complex challenges to implementation into the conversation.

These realities influence high level, 'whole system', planning and more specific attempts to integrate services. They, or their symptoms, have been identified in reviews of such work. In 2006, the Royal College of Paediatrics and Child Health reported on the learning from several years of work to develop Managed Clinical Networks, which began in Scotland with cancer care (Scottish Office, 1999; Kunkler, 2002). Without directly naming many of the dynamics that we have suggested are in play in joint work, their findings illustrate the challenges (see Box 7.3 below).

As we have said, many systemic factors can undermine the collaborative efforts of individuals working together to envision and design networks. The effects of these factors can be even more toxic when attempts are made to implement plans in the real world.

In 2018, the Social Care Institute for Excellence (SCIE) prepared a report for the NHS Leadership Academy on the development of Integrated Care Systems (ICS). SCIE quoted NHS England as saying that ICS represented 'the biggest national move to integrating care of any major western country'. Their report into what leadership was required to

Box 7.3 Challenges for Managed Clinical Networks

- The sheer complexity of provision;
- Varying structures which do not map onto one another;
- Incompatible systems and policies across agencies (e.g. information technology systems, inspection methods, commonly used terminology);
- Contrary policy directions;
- Different approaches to quality improvement;
- Concern about information-sharing across agencies;
- Lack of commissioning capacity;
- Fragmented commissioning practice;
- Variable quality of commissioning;
- Policies such as payment by results and practice-based commissioning;
- A shortage of high-quality information on which to base decisions;
- Organisational inertia, bureaucracy and unwillingness to change;
- Preoccupation in organisations with challenges such as meeting the demands of the European Working Time Directive, targets and existing overspends;
- Imbalance of power between consumers and providers.

Royal College of Paediatrics and Child Health, 2006

enable such a move is eminently sensible, if daunting in how much needs to be done. A summary of their key findings appears in Box 7.4 below.

It is an exhaustive, and exhausting, list, and not one, it is to be hoped, that will be simply turned into yet another bureaucratic initiative. Readers will bring their own areas of interest or concern to bear as they survey it. SCIE's findings are relevant here because of their comprehensiveness, their explicit recognition of the scale of the task involved, and of the radical cultural changes required, in service integration. They suggest that the leaders involved in their programme were encountering many of the dynamics we have discussed. The prominence given to the need for skills in relationship building, promoting mutual learning, creative engagement and involvement of people across a wide and complex system is particularly telling.

Among SCIE's findings were some key challenges that are particularly relevant to our theme. How do we promote the 'willingness to work together' in the light of the factors that, we have argued, will colour collaboration between organisations? How can we facilitate the relationships between leaders, and create the 'safe spaces' to share problems and solutions? How can they engage staff across their organisations, both in multi-disciplinary teams, and as members of the 'whole system'? How can the eyes of individual leaders and their networks, with which they need to survey and learn from the system, be kept open? How can they begin to work, with their staff, to face the sheer complexity of aligning governance and quality assurance arrangements, information systems etc., across partner agencies in very different sectors?

Working with Reality

A clue may lie in the words 'skilled external facilitation'. Too often, vision is directly translated into a list of changes, structures and arrangements without real recognition of the complexities of their implementation. Leaders need help to bring realism about these

Box 7.4 Leadership of Integrated Care Systems

- With no basis in law, ICSs are entirely dependent on a collaborative approach to leadership, and willingness on the part of the organisations involved to work together.
- Leadership in ICSs is very much a form of systems leadership, but with new and unique challenges, such as the need to exert influence across an even larger range of organisations and co-produce services with people who use them.
- Effective systems leadership relies on a composite set of capabilities and behaviours, which can be grouped under the following four domains (NHS Leadership Academy Systems Leadership Framework):
  - innovation and improvement
  - relationships and connectivity
  - individual effectiveness
  - learning and capacity-building.
- Leaders in ICSs need to be skilled at:
  - identifying and scaling innovation (e.g. from pilots);
  - having a strong focus on outcomes and population health;
  - building strong relationships with other leaders, and often working with them informally to develop joint priorities and plans;
  - establishing governance structures which drive faster change, often going where the commitment and energy is strongest;
  - setting the overall outcomes and expectations on behaviours, but handing day-to-day decision-making to others;
  - supporting the development of multi-disciplinary teams (MDTs);
  - designing and facilitating whole-systems events and workshops to build consensus and deliver change;
  - understanding and leading cultural change;
  - building system-wide learning and evaluation frameworks;
  - fostering a learning culture across the whole system.
- Leaders told us that they would welcome support in the following areas:
  - skilled external facilitation, to help deliver complex programmes;
  - the creation of 'safe spaces' for leaders to meet with peers and share problems and solutions;
  - more opportunities to learn from other professions and sectors;
  - systems leadership development for middle managers across the system;
  - masterclasses on:
    - co-production theory and practice;
    - finance and risk-sharing;
    - scaling innovation;
    - understanding local government and social care;
    - large-scale and large-group facilitation;
    - working and influencing across multiple layers of governance.

Social Care Institute for Excellence, 2018

factors, both to their planning, and to their approach to subsequent action. A neutral outside perspective may be vital, one that can, without negativity, help them hold the system in mind, confront avoidance or denial, and address complexities and potential damaging factors, while they plan their work, engage and lead their staff. A core task is to build relationships between partners: relationships that promote cooperation and trust, that can face the difficulties of collaboration, and create alliances committed to joint work, and to engaging practitioners in the collective venture.

Just as the various professionals involved in a multi-disciplinary team must learn to manage potential divided loyalties, so leaders who are given the task of managing integrated multi-agency services face a similar predicament. The routines and preoccupations, risks and priorities of their 'home' organisation can all too easily pull them away from the needs of the care system they are charged with leading. Leaders can be caught between two cultures. Even as they work to build a culture of inter-agency and inter-professional cooperation, they can default to that of their own profession or employing agency. In addition, such roles, and the arrangements for engagement, consultation and day-to-day management required in the integrated care system, can simply add to their workload. The necessary meetings and duties, inside the integrated system, are simply grafted on to their duties within the routines in their home organisation. This will threaten to overwhelm them, and, at the very least, mean they are able to give less attention than is required to any one aspect of their task. Leaders of inter-agency care systems need the full, and genuine, support of their own bosses, with an understanding of these risks, and associated action taken to free them up and help them focus on their task. It is also vital that leaders in services that are nominally 'outside' the integrated system have an understanding of what their colleagues inside that system are undertaking, and are supportive of their work.

It will be of great value if leaders have the facilitative, developmental and engagement skills that SCIE referred to. These should be recognised, and properly valued, as core aspects of good management. At times, though, they also need to be part of the reflective system, and that is where judicious use of neutral external help can be of great value.

There is another, probably more important, issue to address. Too often, skilled practitioners 'on the front-line' of practice are brought together to hear their leaders' vision and plans, and to consider how to implement them. This is very different from being invited to educate their leaders as to the realities of practice, and practitioners' perspectives on what collaboration might, and should, mean, in the interests of their clients and patients. If this happens, it can show leaders what their efforts should focus on, to bring *practice* to the centre of their thinking. When Eileen Munro and colleagues reported on the multi-site Signs of Safety English Innovations Project in 2016, they highlighted the need to do this (Munro, Turnell and Murphy, 2014). This learning is relevant to all practice in modern care organisations, but is particularly relevant to attempts at cross-boundary networking and cooperation.

> *The problems with so much past reform work, from national reviews and local strategies, is that they have addressed structures and professional development without addressing the questions of how the work actually occurs with families. The corollary of this has been that organisational development has not been built to support how front-line work is actually practiced.* (p. 56)

> *In the face of relentless demands on leadership – financial, organisational and political – the focus on practice requires sustained deliberate effort.* (p. 56)

At the very least, staff should be able to bring their own experience of practice into planning and review processes. This will help to direct thinking and planning, to test and evaluate proposed models of organising and delivering care. It will ensure that monitoring and review of the effectiveness of collaboration is based in reality. This input can be immeasurably strengthened when patients or service-users are able to bring their own complex stories to the table. Only then will there be the real possibility that the system will have the characteristics we have highlighted as necessary: sufficient organisation and structure to facilitate the deployment of the interventions required, and sufficient flexibility for individual practitioners to act intelligently upon their own perceptions of, and commitments to, the needs of their clients and patients.

Whatever apparent success is achieved in this enterprise, the proof of its value will lie in the experience of practitioners, and, most importantly, service-users. A joined-up, or integrated system of care will, fundamentally, promise access to, and intervention by, the right professional or service, equipped with the right information, in response to various needs, in a timely fashion. For each organisation involved in a system of integrated care, the core task is to organise and enable their staff to do that. To close this chapter, we will now consider some of the issues to be faced when designing care pathways or protocols to shape the patient's or client's journey to, and through, the care that they need.

Maps and Guides

'We ran out of walls', a director of children's services told us. He was describing what happened when he and colleagues tried to map all the services and organisations that they thought should be involved in implementing 'Every Child Matters' (discussed later in Chapter 11). Such an approach is no doubt necessary. But it can be more helpful to start from the needs of the service-user: to try to design the most effective and timely journey for an individual to, and through, the services and interventions they need. That work can then be used as the basis for organising services. This is more like creating a travel guide or programming a Satnav or GoogleMaps, thereby avoiding the overwhelming nature of a complete atlas. The system requires attention to both types of mapping, of course. Care pathways and clinical/care protocols are versions of the second kind, and can be key elements of the design of collaborative health and social care systems.

Commissioning, designing and delivering integrated care pathways that shape the work of clinical/care networks across multiple services or agencies can contribute to helping disparate parts of the system work together. Care pathways tend to be developed to support people with named conditions like cancer, depression, or dementia, or people with more complex needs, such as a combination of intellectual disability with physical disabilities or chronic illness. Pathways can be designed to organise the responses and interventions of staff in various agencies to service-user need.

For a particular kind of need, a care pathway may specify such elements as:

- assessment tools and processes;
- eligibility criteria or risk categories prompting intervention;
- interventions and their intended outcome;
- the roles and responsibilities of different professionals;
- the timing and sequencing of elements of care;
- recording and sharing information.

The approach aims to guarantee a standard of care, based on evidence and, where relevant, legal and ethical factors. Care pathways can help both to clarify what a person's journey through care will look like, and to secure effective deployment of the right interventions and services to make it happen. They can help to foster healthy and person-focussed collaboration across and between teams and services. They are most effective when the clinical or practice dimension of the pathway is supported by clear intra- and inter-organisational commitment to, and systems to support, collaboration that will make care available in the way a pathway indicates.

There is a danger, though, that pathways can become mechanical, mere manuals for menu-based interventions. They can encourage practitioners to see those they care for solely through the lens of fragmented 'conditions', assessing them as eligible or ineligible for services providing only a specified intervention. Care pathways can over-emphasise the outcomes or progress a service-user 'should' make, so that, too often, if they don't do so, they are left in limbo. The pathway can veer towards being coercive. 'Recovery pathways' in mental health or in acute hospital care can make the 'unrecovered' patient or client into an inconvenience, with no more options.

The very plethora of pathways, or associated clinical or care protocols that are likely to be in place where someone has complex needs can become overwhelming and distracting, despite their good intentions. Jane Carthey, a consultant in 'human factors' in healthcare, and her clinical co-workers considered a typical 'patient journey' for an elderly person admitted for emergency surgery on a fractured neck of femur in 2011. They estimated that there were 75 different clinical guidelines and trust-wide policies covering the different stages of her management (Carthey et al, 2011). In such an environment, the working routines and culture around care pathways, and similar approaches can become over-dominated by too complex a bureaucracy. Staff time, and their attention, can become dominated by the tasks of registering and monitoring decisions and plans, following procedure, and justifying departures from specified practice. Leaders, and practitioners, need to recognise the potential for the consequent distraction from the lived experience, and needs, of patients and service-users. Work to simplify procedures wherever possible, and, at the very least, to build in the time they require, is vital.

It is important to get the right balance between prescription and flexibility in care pathway work, to ensure that staff are able to attend and respond to the ill-being or difficulties of service-users, and work towards desired outcomes. Too much prescription, too many checklists, and staff become mechanical in their efforts – too little, and vital services are unready, or poorly organised, to respond to need. Staff who feel like cogs in a machine, or who are frustrated by the gap between intentions and reality, are unlikely to be able to bring kind attention to the person they serve.

Another challenge is to make pathway development comprehensive and genuinely inclusive. Pathways are, of course, much easier to design and implement where there is a relatively clear and boundaried process – the journey into hospital and through cardiac surgery, for example – and where there is a relatively defined group of staff or services involved. Pathways that indicate what will be offered to people as they 'travel through' a particular ward, team or service, or that embody agreements only about roles and systems in one organisation, are relatively easy to design. But in reality, the 'journey' for the person in need often requires the cooperation of more than one organisation, and the coordination of staff from several teams, with their own duty and referral systems, waiting lists, working hours and so on. Where a person has multiple needs, this challenge is all the greater. Services and interventions have got to be there, and be delivered, as the pathway specifies. This cannot happen by specification, through communications protocols and procedures, alone.

To borrow Chris Ham's expression cited earlier, the 'physiology' of a complex cooperative system involves the interplay of individuals, professions, teams and services as they manage the pressures and limits they face, and the responsibilities with which they are charged. The 'anatomy' – structures, procedures, pathways and processes – has a part to play, but as vital 'landscapes' and navigation guides for staff with *agency*, not as robotic imperatives. Across the system of services involved, work is required to build and sustain a sense of common purpose and identity. This work must prioritise the need to facilitate *relationships* between people who are responsible for cooperating, for responding to each other, and for combining their efforts in the interests of the service-user. Individually and collectively, they must have a central voice in the design and review of systems and procedures. It is in everyone's interest that 'front-line' practitioners can bring their lived experience of their work to the planning and management tables.

We began this chapter with the story of a family, and used it to introduce our examination of the complexities of system-wide planning and integration of services. Such stories, brought by practitioners, or, even better, by service-users themselves, need to be heard, and thought about, when commissioners and leaders try to shape and sustain effective integrated care. They are a powerful counter to unrealism, rigidity and over-aspiration on the part of well-meaning planners and managers. Such stories from life can be invaluable pointers to the challenges and opportunities involved in creatively bringing together the work of disparate organisations.

References

Bushe, G. and Marshak, R. (eds.) (2015) *Dialogic Organization Development: The Theory and Practice of Transformational Change.* Berrett-Koehler.

Carthey, J. et al (2011) Breaking the rules: understanding non-compliance with policies and guidelines. British Medical Journal. 2011: 343: d5283

Dartington, T. (2010) *Managing Vulnerability.* Karnac Books.

Ham, C., Heenan, D., Longley, M., Steel, D. (2013) Integrated Care in Northern Ireland, Scotland and Wales: Lessons for England. King's Fund.

Kunkler, I. H. (2002) Managed clinical networks: a new paradigm for clinical medicine. Journal of the Royal College of Physicians. 34: 320–3.

Munro, E., Turnell, A., and Murphy, T. (2014) 'You Can't Grow Roses In Concrete.' Organisational reform to support high quality Signs of Safety practice. Available at: www.basw.co.uk/system/files/resources/basw_102921-2_0.pdf [last accessed 26 August, 2019].

Plsek, P. (2016) Complexity Science. AQuA. Available at: www.aquanw.nhs.uk/resources/complexity-science-paul-plsek/21238 [last accessed 9 August, 2019].

Royal College of Paediatrics and Child Health (2006) A Guide to Understanding and

Implementing Networks. Available at: www.rcpch.ac.uk/sites/default/files/Bringing_Networks_to_Life.pdf [last accessed 26 August, 2019].

Social Care Institute for Excellence (2018) Leadership in Integrated Care Systems. Available at: www.scie.org.uk/integrated-care/leadership/systems [last accessed 9 August, 2019].

Scottish Office (1999) Cancer. Introduction of Managed Clinical Networks in Scotland. Scottish Office.

Chapter

8 On the Edges of Kinship

We each hold the power in our words and in our actions, in our daily acts of kindness. We are not immune to the viruses of hate, of fear, of other. We never have been. But we can be the nation that discovers the cure . . . Humanity. That's it. Simple.

(Jacinda Ardern, at the Remembrance Service for the victims of the Al Noor Mosque massacre in Christchurch, New Zealand. 2019)

Powerful political and psychosocial processes influence the extent to which society recognises and responds to its members as kin. There are difficult 'edges' at which goodwill and rejection compete for dominance in the public mind. Health and social care staff are frequently working at these edges. This can overlap with, complicate and amplify the powerful emotions and relationships that are described in Chapter 5. Sometimes the dilemma is pretty obvious – the violent drunk haemorrhaging in an accident and emergency department inevitably arouses conflicting responses; the mother who continues to get herself pregnant despite all her previous infants being taken into care. The continued, often dangerously fluctuating, needs of old people with long-term conditions persist in frustrating our wish to remove suffering and can wear us down. Our generosity competes with our instinct to turn away, to recoil, even to punish.

In this chapter, we focus particularly on how and why the sense of profound difference or 'otherness' emerges. And the consequences for those we see as outsiders and for ourselves. This may involve attitudes to people who come from 'outside' our geographical and social boundary – such as migrants and asylum seekers; or other such 'edges' – such as people with profound intellectual disabilities, mental health problems, the old and the dying, even the very poor.

Whilst such groups can arouse inclusive, generous and compassionate responses, there is also the potential to evoke feelings of fear, and the wish to reject or deny things about them, or, at the deepest level, about ourselves. The refugee evokes 'indigent' anxiety and competitive feelings about possessions, security, work, identity, culture. The dying person evokes helplessness in the healthy, and profound fear and rage about an inescapable and frightening reality; a poor family, a sense of the precarious nature of our social and material wellbeing; the person with an intellectual disability, a fear of dependency and difference; the psychotic individual, a fear of their disturbance and of our own incipient madness.

These feelings, of course, reflect wider social uncertainty, complexity of feelings, division and discrimination. They reflect profound anxieties about the extent of our resources, material and emotional, and where they should be invested. They confront us all with the limits to our generosity and fellow feeling. At worst, our own underlying fear is denied and we use people on these edges to evacuate our hatred. Through the splitting process described in Chapters 5 and 6, we project our anxiety and anger into the 'other' so they become the problem and we don't have to deal with it – except by trying to get rid of them or distancing ourselves.

Such feelings not only affect our attitude to the Welfare State, but also influence its very essence. In the beginning, the vision driving the enterprise was of a shared project to build a better country for everyone. Over the years, increasing demand and shortage of resources, means, like it or not, the whole Welfare State has become obsessed with rationing and gatekeeping. Huge amounts of time and money go into devising and maintaining systems for *keeping people out*. To this end, we devise labyrinthine systems, narrow down the categories of need, and allow an impersonal bureaucracy to apply inflexible rules. Not only do the edges become more rigid, but an increasing number of us find ourselves, at times of need, on the wrong side of them.

Of course, even in the early days of the Welfare State, society's ambivalent, reluctant or even hostile feelings about including 'the other' as kin, infiltrated national policy, consciously or unconsciously undermining the principle of equitable access to and delivery of services. In the second decade of the twenty-first century, however, such hostility started to be expressed more overtly: for example, in 2015, it became policy that only official residents of the country should access free secondary healthcare such as cancer treatment. This policy has caused direct harm to the health of vulnerable people and been criticised from a medical ethics and human rights perspective. It puts healthcare professionals in a conflicted position, requires complex and expensive administration and is feared to have a knock-on negative effect on public health (Keith and Van Ginneken, 2015).

Equally damaging is the hostile rhetoric that can so easily invade our thinking and make us look at sub-groups of the population in a more negative and fearful way. The policy above was supposedly to 'crack down on healthcare tourism'. This leaves an unhelpful division in our minds between the deserving and undeserving patient, despite the fact that so called 'tourists' accounted for a tiny percentage of the health budget and the new discriminatory policy may well end up costing more.

A similar polarised view has emerged regarding the recipients of benefit payments. Despite the fact that most benefit recipients are now employed, we are encouraged to view claimants as either in true need or 'scroungers'. The problem is the system then treats everyone as a potential scrounger. The same can be said of the system that processes claims for asylum, where every claimant is treated as likely to be bogus. It is interesting how words such as 'asylum' (a place of safety) and 'benefit' (something that promotes good) become denigrated and start to take on a different meaning. This is captured in the following quote:

> *We have an asylum system that purports to provide sanctuary, and yet the public have little understanding of what 'asylum' means, associate it – indelibly – with a range of negative and unrelated issues, and have little confidence in the asylum system itself. There is a profound disconnection in the public mind between the sanctuary they want the UK to provide and their perception of the asylum system.* (Independent Asylum Commission, 2008, p. 6)

There is an argument for rehabilitating the words asylum and benefit just as this book is trying to rehabilitate the concepts of kindness and welfare.

A common feature of many of the groups at the edges of kinship is that discrimination and abuses in the care of their members are frequently reported. Such occurrences result, often repetitively, in policies and programmes to address stigma, provide education and specify corrective action. There is a danger, however, that these abuses will continue if the complexity of what underpins neglect and brutality is not recognised more thoroughly. Indeed, updating this chapter for the second edition of the book, our overall sense is of reports and policies gathering dust whilst conditions for those living on the edges has got worse under the pressures of austerity, inequality and hardening attitudes.

There are a number of overlapping themes that emerge when working on the edges of kinship. These themes, summarised in Box 8.1, operate both at the level of the staff member working with the individual and at the level of society addressing the challenges raised by particular vulnerable groups within the population.

Box 8.1 Emerging Themes on the Edge of Kinship

- Feeling overwhelmed by frightening need and anxious about our capacity to respond;
- Extreme feelings, ranging from compassion to repulsion;
- A profound struggle between the urge to include and exclude;
- Polarised thinking, involving extremes of idealisation and denigration;
- Muddled thinking and contradictory policy initiatives.

Overwhelming Need

Dick Blackwell, a psychotherapist, describes the following encounter in his book about working with victims of torture.

> *One colleague described the look some of her clients gave her which made her feel she was the only person left in the world who could help them. It was a look she had not previously encountered in many years working as a psychiatric social worker. This look is not unlike that of the totally dependent infant. It can induce powerful feelings of responsibility and protectiveness or, conversely, a wish to disengage in order to escape the weight of so much need . . . However, there is another look which seems like that of someone returned from the dead: the haunted look of eyes that have seen unspeakable horrors, perhaps horrors that the mind can no longer remember.* (Blackwell, 2005, p. 72)

The story captures an extreme experience, but many staff, working with a variety of needs, will recognise the mixture of feelings he describes. His description captures the disturbing tension that can be aroused in us all, as we face extreme need. The mixture of powerful feelings of compassion and responsibility, anxiety about how much such people need, the disturbing nature of their suffering and the urge to turn away can be overwhelming. This experience can be acute – in a particular encounter on a particular day – or chronic – evoked by working with profound needs, risks and vulnerabilities that do not go away over long periods of time, if at all. Work with the dependency and vulnerability of many people with intellectual disabilities, with the suffering and fragile lives of people with severe mental health difficulties, with the decline and decay that can characterise ageing, all confront staff with versions of these feelings.

The trouble with profound need is that it confronts us with the fear that we are not equipped to meet it – in terms of managing to face it, doing anything helpful about it, perhaps even surviving the encounter intact.

On one level, the worker is pitched into these experiences by the nature of the needs of the particular individual. The experience can be amplified, however, by processes at work in the wider community. These processes influence not only the attitudes and feelings of the worker but also the resources offered to particular kinds of need, the policies that frame the work and the outcomes for patients – and staff. Staff working with people from groups on the edge of kinship have not only to manage disturbing feelings aroused in themselves but also to encounter others who may react in extreme ways, and to work in a system that may be overwhelmed.

The Dangerous Impact of Projection on Problem Solving

There is an inevitable struggle with intense feelings, ranging from compassion through anxiety to overt anger and hostility. Such negative feelings can arise because we cannot bear the demand that need makes on us – so we end up hating the needy for it, and sometimes ourselves for feeling like that. The antipathy can extend to hating the other for the demands they make on material resources, blaming them for those demands, and finding ways to challenge their rights to make them. People in need can remind the rest of us of things we do not wish to acknowledge, about life, other people, ourselves – and we hate them for these reminders. Such hatred sits very uncomfortably alongside feelings of duty, compassion and concern.

The brutal end of the spectrum is vividly expressed with dismaying frequency in the case of people with physical and intellectual disabilities. For years, journalists have chronicled experiences of violence, harassment or neglectful indifference in the community. As one carer of a person with intellectual disabilities put it:

> *Care in the community was brought in so people are not locked away; they are cared for in the community and have normal lives. But they don't have normal lives. They are bullied and terrified, and the law is not protecting them.* (*Sticks and Stones*, Channel 4, 2010)

Though brutality is by no means the only experience for people with intellectual disabilities and other vulnerable groups, the reality is that the mixture of responses they evoke includes such very unpalatable feelings, as well as generosity and concern. Citizens in general, and health and social care staff, in particular, resort to various mechanisms to deal with this discomfort – with the need to manage, to justify or to avoid the feelings involved.

These 'strategies' may apparently be conscious, but they will almost always be accompanied and coloured by an unconscious element. They become dangerous when they are dominated by processes like the projection of dangerous, untrustworthy or malignant characteristics onto those in need. Such projections stop us seeing and thinking clearly.

The case of asylum seekers illustrates this vividly. The prospect of an uncontrolled invasion of people with the kind of needs described in Blackwell's vignette invokes fear and hostility – evidenced in our politics, throughout the media and on the streets of many of our cities. Importantly, such feelings undermine our attempts as a society to manage the problem to the best of our ability as numerous reports attest.

For example, in her report 'Fast and Fair?' the Parliamentary Ombudsman (2010, pp. 7–8) addressed the question of what kind of service should be provided by the UK Border Agency:

> *What should we expect from an effective system for the assessment of asylum applications? That applicants are told what to expect: that they are safe and properly supported while awaiting a decision, and that they receive a 'fast and fair' decision on their application. For those who are unsuccessful the expectation must be that, unless there is some other reason why they should be allowed to stay in the UK, they should promptly leave the country, or be removed as soon as is practicable.*
>
> *In our experience the Agency are a very long way from achieving this.*

Her investigation of complaints shows a system that was slow, unresponsive, intimidating and made errors about people's status. The very process of assessing eligibility appeared to alienate, frighten and demean.

The Independent Asylum Commission also picked up on the extreme and conflicting feelings that confuse and seem to get in the way of effective problem solving:

> *It denies sanctuary to some who genuinely need it and ought to be entitled to it, is not firm enough in returning those whose claims are refused and is marred by inhumanity in its treatment of the vulnerable.* (2008)

Clinicians working with asylum seekers estimate that up to 30 per cent of those turned down for asylum have, in fact, been tortured (Ashton and Moore, 2009). It is unsurprising that traumatised people are less than comfortable 'qualifying' themselves for asylum by describing experiences of torture. Shame, and the effects of post-traumatic stress, are likely to inhibit such communication, even in the most humane of circumstances. The system does not appear to offer such humane circumstances, either in its processes or in the skills and sensitivity of its staff. A necessary procedure has become imbued with hostile and even brutal feelings that override compassion and justice.

Reports paint a depressing picture of the dysfunctional situation described above becoming stuck and chronic, as for example in this 2015 report on Yarl's Wood Immigration Centre.

> *While there have been instances of unacceptable individual behaviour, most staff work hard to mitigate the worst effects of detention and women told us they appreciated this. These are issues that need to be addressed at a policy and strategic management level. We have raised many of the concerns in this report before. Decisive action is needed to ensure that women are only detained as a last resort. Other well-respected bodies have recently called for time limits on administrative detention, and the concerns we have identified provide strong support for these calls.* (Hardwick, 2015)

Exclusion and Scapegoating

In the face of extreme feelings, society is torn between recognising the other as kin, and offering kindness and support, or rejecting their otherness, and punishing or ejecting them. Policies to promote the social inclusion of people from vulnerable groups tend to underestimate the degree to which this urge to hurt and eject is operating. The concept of stigma is often emptied of the sheer urge to obliterate that can be part of the response to difference. This urge can be expressed directly through violence, but is no less powerful when it is expressed in less obvious ways.

One mechanism at work is the process of scapegoating, where we project unwanted aspects of ourselves onto another person or group and then reject, hate or fear them (see Chapter 6). This is an irrational, unconscious process, a process that allows us the illusion of ridding ourselves of things that we are frightened to face – our vulnerability, our neediness, our violent feelings.

The term 'scapegoat' originates from the Old Testament. The story takes place on the Day of Atonement, when the prophet Aaron confessed all the sins of the children of Israel and ritually transferred them to a live goat, then sent the goat into the wilderness, bearing all these sins. The goat is literally excluded from the community, banished to the inhospitable environment of the wilderness. The community is, in turn, freed from its responsibilities and moral discomforts. Exclusion does not simply try to remove difficult people from among us but also seeks to banish unpalatable aspects of ourselves.

Society has traditionally responded to the challenging needs and dependency of vulnerable groups by putting people into institutions, often as far away from the rest of us as possible – out of sight and out of mind. This included placing them in asylums and workhouses, but also involved imprisonment of very vulnerable people – as continues to this day. Although people with intellectual disabilities make up 2 per cent of the UK population, estimates suggest that 7 per cent of people in prison have an IQ of less than 70 and 20–30 per cent of offenders have intellectual disabilities or learning difficulties that interfere with their ability to cope within the criminal justice system (Jacobson, 2008; Hellenbach, 2017). Similarly, the best estimates suggest that 7 per cent of sentenced male prisoners suffer from psychosis. The figure rises to 10 per cent for males on remand and 14 per cent for women, with many more having difficulties such as depression, anxiety and substance misuse (Appleby, 2010). A report by the National Audit Office (2017) on mental health in prisons reported a significant rise in rates of self-inflicted deaths and self-harm.

Disturbing trends of neglect and abuse in asylums and similar residential settings have been reported for decades, and described and analysed in detail by sociologists such as Irving Goffman (1961). It seems that the dynamics of institutional life conspire with the concentration of people with challenging needs to provoke neglectful and abusive behaviour, amplifying the tendency to rejection in society at large. Goffman and others showed that even those who were not overtly abused by the system were significantly damaged, losing their sense of psychological autonomy along with practical skills of daily living.

Through the 1970s and 1980s, a number of scandals involving asylums in the UK were uncovered and the conditions in some of these institutions became public knowledge. This was one of the driving rationales for 'community care' and led to the closure of a number of large institutions for the mentally ill and for those with intellectual disabilities.

The move to community care may have brought benefits to many people, but the problems did not go away. The toxic nature of psychiatric wards in many parts of the UK – now mostly on a smaller scale and attached to general hospitals – attracts ongoing concern despite a number of policy initiatives that have addressed the issue (Mental Health Act Commission, 2009). Likewise, ill-treatment in residential homes for those with intellectual disabilities or the elderly continues to emerge. What's more, drastic bed closures as a result of financial pressures mean that psychiatric patients are being sent to hospitals in different parts of the country, far from their social networks and so making them more vulnerable to institutionalisation (Keown et al, 2008; Wise, 2017).

Institutionalisation expresses both benign concerns to protect and care, and impulses to eject difficult people from the public sphere. The difficulty of including people with complex needs, the feelings aroused, and the challenges involved in consistently meeting those needs humanely in society at large are transferred into these institutions. It is as if the institution itself becomes the scapegoat, bearing society's sins, absolving us of responsibility and making it easy to locate where any blame for our nastiness and limits lies. It (unsuccessfully, of course) carries the problems 'outside' society. Such institutions can become places where, all too frequently, our darker responses, our 'sins', continue to find expression, conveniently hidden, and frequently amplified, behind closed doors.

Nowhere is this more in evidence than in the history of Yarl's Wood Immigration Removal Centre. Yarl's Wood can be seen as a concrete 'edge of kinship', a place where society deposits its overwhelmed and disturbed feelings about this particular human kinship issue. As such it makes an educative case study. See Box 8.2 below.

But there are many kinds of wilderness. Beyond the walls of the immigration centre, many unsuccessful applicants for asylum continue to live in the community. Because of the slowness and inefficiency of the state processes for appeal against the decision to remove someone, they enter a state of limbo that can last for years, deprived of benefits and other rights – including specialist healthcare – and unable to legally work or engage in higher education.

The lesson is clear: the emotional challenges of inclusion, and the negative feelings it evokes, do not go away. They seep into our attempts to establish systems to determine deservedness, as in the case of asylum seekers and those claiming benefits; and they seep into our institutions. Extremities of difference and of need inevitably evoke both compassionate and cruel feelings – in the same person, in groups, in institutions and in society. This reality becomes toxic if it is not managed through acknowledgement and support for workers.

Just as important, there is a need for policy and inspection systems that drive remedies to, rather than just describe, ill-practice.

Polarised Thinking and 'Splitting'

Being in two minds about how to respond to otherness and need often expresses itself in splitting: the attempt to deny and remove the discomfort of having very mixed, conflicting feelings by simplistically seeing people as either deserving unambiguous love or unambiguous hate (see Chapter 6). A crucial truth about splitting is that it distorts reality. As a defence against anxiety, it may afford a bit of respite in the heat of the moment, but beyond that, it simply doesn't work.

The splitting process can be seen, for example, in mental healthcare, where the complexity of mental distress can evoke sharp and oversimplifying distinctions. These splits and contradictions find their way into mental health practice and policy when the

Box 8.2 Case Study: 'A Place of National Concern'

When it was opened in 2001, Yarl's Wood Immigration Removal Centre was the largest immigration centre in Europe. Set in the middle of fields with no other habitation in view, it is easy to forget about despite serious inhumane incidents being catalogued in numerous reports in the public domain.

The centre lurches from crisis to crisis. Shortly after being opened, the building was described as 'not safe' following a fire where detainees were injured (Morris, 2003; Prisons and Probation Ombudsman, 2004). Evidence of racist and sexual incidents and a lack of legal representation are documented in report after report by the Chief Inspector of Prisons at the time (e.g. 2003, 2008, 2015). In a 2010 report, the Children's Commissioner, Sir Al Aynsley-Green, described how the 1,000 children detained in the centre each year often faced 'extremely distressing' arrest and transportation procedures, and were subject to prolonged and sometimes repeated periods of detention. This report received a lot of media coverage and eventually led to a High Court ruling that continued detention of children was unlawful. This was of little comfort, however, to the many women who are now separated from their children when detained.

In 2018, 90 per cent of the 400 detainees were women. They were not there because they have committed criminal offences and many are victims themselves of violent sexual crimes. The supposed reason for them being there is to establish their identities or facilitate immigration claims. However, a number of reports have highlighted the dubious grounds on which many of them are held (Amnesty International, 2018; Home Office/Shaw, 2016).

Hunger strikes are a very desperate way of trying to draw people's attention. There have been hunger strikes at Yarl's Wood in 2001, 2005, 2007, 2010, 2015 and 2018. As one hunger striker said in 2018, *'We feel voiceless, forgotten, ignored . . .'*

In 2014, the UN's Special Rapporteur on Violence Against Women, Rashida Manjoo, was barred from Yarl's Wood by the Home Office (Sherwood, 2014). Such a scenario, which Manjoo likened to the Bangladeshi government refusing her access to one of its most notorious mental asylums (Townsend, 2015) confirms a sense that 'voiceless, forgotten, ignored' is deliberate government policy.

A year later, the Chief Inspector of Prisons, Nick Hardwick, described the centre as 'a place of national concern' and expressed his frustration with the chronicity of the problems. A joint inquiry by two All Party Parliamentary Groups found that *'the UK detains too many people for too long a time and that in far too many cases people are detained completely unnecessarily'* (HMIP, 2016). Even a review commissioned by the Home Office (Home Office/Shaw, 2016) argued that immigration detention should be reduced considerably and called for a *'smaller, more focused, strategically planned immigration detention estate'.*

In 2017, a further report described improvement at Yarl's Wood, but repeated hunger strikes in 2018 suggest there are still significant problems. In particular, it is clear that the recommendation to use Yarl's Wood only as a 'last resort' is very far from the reality, with an Amnesty International report highlighting the fact that undocumented people are routinely detained on questionable grounds (2018) and for some of them, indefinite detainment continues.

question of balancing the promotion of a socially inclusive response to vulnerability with the management of risk and dangerousness is considered.

Despite, or perhaps because of, the fact that around 25 per cent of the population will experience some form of mental health difficulty in their lifetime, mental ill health continues to arouse profound fears in the general population. These fears are expressed both as fear of madness and as fear of those who are mentally ill. In that mental ill health is profoundly distressing, the first fear is rational, even if it often leads people to turn away from sufferers. It can, of course, enable empathy, and strengthen people's resolve to help. The second, which attributes dangerousness, is rarely justified, despite press and public alarmism about the relatively few cases where people with mental illness harm others.

Despite the substantial increase in homicides committed in the UK over the last 50 years of the twentieth century, those attributable to people who were mentally ill remained stable, despite the closure of the asylums and a reduction in bed numbers (Taylor and Gunn, 1999). That truth does not seem to make much difference. An Edinburgh study looking at media coverage of psychiatric illness in 2000 (Lawrie, 2000) was repeated in 2017 (Chen and Lawrie, 2017). Despite several prominent government-led and charity campaigns in the intervening years, the linking of mental illness and violence was still pervasive, being part of about a fifth of all articles on mental health. The later study also found that people with mental disorders are twice as likely to be portrayed as a perpetrator of crime rather than as the victim, again giving an erroneous and misleading impression.

Mental health staff must, of course, always work in a manner that includes an assessment of risk. They must reconcile their care-giving responsibilities with their duty to intervene to restrict liberty. This has and will always be a tension. However, when resources are tight, the anxiety is intensified as staff are forced to ration their efforts. There is an inevitable pull towards risk assessments and coercive control, towards rationing and withholding resources from those who do not arouse such anxiety, and away from open and welcoming kinship and compassionate practice.

This is not just something that happens as a result of staff anxieties. Wider public anxiety infects inspection, management and governance, so that mental health workers are operating in a system that is preoccupied with the view of people as dangerous. This pressure can be felt as very much at odds with being part of a service that promotes recovery and social inclusion. If policy makers and managers do not manage the tendency towards anxious splitting, then the work of staff drifts from imaginative compassion to a split between caution and control on the one hand, and underestimation of need and complexity on the other.

Such a drift is suggested by a look at some mental health statistics between 1996 and 2018. As bed numbers fall, involuntary admissions to acute mental healthcare increase (Keown et al, 2008; Wise, 2017). In the ten years between 2005/2006 and 2015/2016, the number of involuntary admissions increased by 40 per cent (Care Quality Commission, 2016). Perhaps most shocking is the rise in numbers of patients with mental disorders in England sent out of their own area, sometimes hundreds of miles away from home. In 2016–2017 alone, 5,876 adults and 1,365 children were sent out of area for mental health treatment (Wise, 2017). At a time when the focus across healthcare – but especially in mental health – was care in the community, recourse to locking people away miles from their homes and families increased. So much for integrated care. Such a system is neither humane, nor economically efficient.

Problematic Idealisation

Splitting always involves polarising between idealisation and denigration. Such splitting is frequently highly unstable – with individuals and society, through policy or preoccupation, swinging between contradictory positions as in the mental health example above. Whenever these processes are at work, genuine attentiveness to people, as well as creative responses to their needs and aspirations, are undermined.

Intellectual disability is another subgroup vulnerable to this phenomenon. The aim to look after more such people outside of institutions has been official policy for many years (e.g. Department of Health, 2009a) and is laudable. But as with any ideology, there is a temptation to simplify reality, which in this case can lead to serious underestimation of the difficulties in community life for service-users and for those close to them. The woman quoted in the documentary earlier vividly expresses one aspect of this minimisation, the denial of cruelty that can be part of community life. Even without such extremes, life in the community is complicated and challenging for everyone, and it is easy to underestimate the difficulties involved, not just for people with intellectual disabilities, but also for frail older people and people with severe mental health difficulties.

Idealisation of the capabilities and potential of vulnerable people for coping in the community, and a parallel idealisation of that community, can lead to a dangerous underestimation of the difficulties. Idealisation of community care and denigration of residential care can also be cynically used by policy makers and commissioners to save money.

Dramas involving idealisation and denigration can also be played out between different parts of the caring network. For example, specialist staff may be understandably anxious about the challenges for their patients in the community. In some cases, this can lead to them seeing themselves as the only ones capable of understanding and responding sensitively to the vulnerable individual. This can involve mistrust of, even contempt for, the capabilities of others. Realism about the limits of people and services is, of course, vital, but this dynamic can lead to a sort of default mistrust. This can undermine and restrict positive work between health and social care colleagues to improve practice and secure their service-users' wellbeing.

Similarly, families, dedicated to a relative with a disability, and aware of a less than easy wider world, can fall into the same position, leading to mistrust of the community and professionals. The idealisation and denigration involved in both these cases can lead to overprotectiveness, diminished opportunities, and reduced access to services and the world for the person in need.

These processes of splitting can be at work whether the group involved has intellectual difficulties, mental health problems or any other category of need that seriously challenges society's inclusiveness. The danger is that simplistic idealisation leads to people living materially, socially and emotionally impoverished lives. Just as seriously, idealisation makes it hard, or impossible, for society or services to recognise or admit it. The complex task of engaging with real people, assessing their needs, evaluating risk, orchestrating resources, monitoring and responding, is undermined.

Box 8.3 outlines the tensions that have to be intelligently balanced by commissioners, planners and providers to guide the right mix of priorities and resources.

Box 8.3 An Intelligently Kind Balance

- Work both to remove barriers to mainstream services and provide an adequate range of specialist services;
- Minimise risk but be prepared to take therapeutic risks;
- Facilitate community support but protect from public neglect or abuse;
- Manage dependency whilst promoting independence.

When discussions and plans are influenced by urges to idealise or denigrate any element of this mix, or to minimise inconvenient truths, the danger is that the resulting service systems will be ill equipped to respond to vulnerable people's needs. It is dangerous, for example, to base 'efficiency' plans for specialist healthcare services on idealistic assumptions that social care supports and opportunities for inclusion will be there, when resource limits and public sector cuts mean they will be scarce. Sadly, such lack of realism is common.

The resulting services are difficult environments in which to work. It is hard to maintain open attentiveness, empathy and responsive, responsible, kindness if services are affected by powerful splitting and polarising processes that encourage the denial of key aspects of the personhood and needs of people in vulnerable groups. The fact that these splits are played out at a policy level means staff also find themselves trying to reconcile the contradictions in organisational objectives, performance targets and scrutiny from seniors.

Denial

More aspects of denial and its consequences are illustrated vividly when the care of older people is considered. One of the benefits of the improvements in living conditions and healthcare in the UK has been the survival of more and more people into old age. The fastest population increase has been in the number of the 'oldest old'. In 1983, there were just over 600,000 people in the UK aged 85 and over. Twenty-five years later there were 1.3 million. By 2033 this group is projected to more than double again, to reach 3.2 million, or 5 per cent of the total population. There is a gap, though, between life expectancy and how much of that is disability-free, for large numbers of people. Dementia, for example, affects 4 per cent of those between 71 and 79, but the risk rises sharply, so that, between the ages of 95 and 99, one-in-four women and one-in-five men will be disabled by the disease.

Society is faced, then, with the prospect of having to care for an increasing number of people with dementia and for increased demands for cancer care and treatment for long-term conditions such as diabetes, chronic obstructive pulmonary disease and heart disease. These trends have been known for years. Despite that knowledge, there has been a consistent failure to address the scale of need. Politicians, for example, have continued to fail to resolve the question of how personal care (vital for a life in the community) will be funded.

Sometimes this failure has been accompanied by vivid signs of just how anxious and angry society is about this rising need. In the course of multi-party dialogue about this issue in February 2010, the Conservatives withdrew and began a poster campaign, caricaturing one option put on the table by Labour as a '£20,000 Death Tax'. Almost a mirror image of this was played out in 2017 when the Conservatives proposed to increase the number of pensioners contributing to the cost of their care by allowing them to borrow money from their estate and pay it back after their death. Jeremy Corbyn, leader of the opposition, responded with derision, labelling it the 'Dementia tax' and forcing the Conservatives to do a U-turn. Both campaigns neatly stirred up contempt and fear of taxation while playing on public fear of and wish to avoid the reality, and the costs, of ageing and dying.

Discrimination

The inability to provide or sustain compassionate care for older people has been vividly illustrated in a variety of reports over the last 25 years. AgeUK reports (e.g. 2016, 2017) for example, described active and direct age discrimination – across a wide range of conditions and care delivery – in terms of access to or adequate funding for services needed by older people. A similar situation is faced by those with a physical disability. For example, a large study in 2017 (Floud et al, 2017) found disabled women are a third less likely to participate in screenings for breast cancer than non-disabled women. Regardless of the controversies around the effectiveness of such screening, many of the reasons given such as lack of accessible transport or the fact wheelchairs can't reach the traditional mammogram machines, suggest that the issues affecting the disabled need to be given more thought in the design of services.

Disabled women also complain that it can be hard to get contraception from their GPs. This is partly because cultural prejudice means some medical staff assume that disabled women do not have sexual relationships (Ryan, 2018). Likewise, Carruthers and Ormondroyd's 2009 report for the Department of Health showed that much of the discrimination against the elderly is based on ageist assumptions about the value of intervention into the illnesses of older people, about the comparative worth of the lives of younger and older people, and about how older people feel.

Discrimination is part of everyday life for many people. Sadly, racism continues to be prevalent in society and there is no reason to think that health and social care staff are immune to this particular form of conscious and unconscious prejudice, either as individuals or within their institutional systems. The 2018 Independent Review of the Mental Health Act, for example, highlighted the fact that rates of detention were over four times higher for black people compared with white people, and around twice as high in the entire Black and Asian minority ethnic (BAME) population. Reasons for this are complex. As highlighted by the Equality and Human Rights Commission, BAME people are more likely to experience poverty, have poorer educational outcomes, be unemployed and come into contact with the criminal justice system – all of which are risk factors in developing mental illness. Children from the BAME population are also more likely to be taken into the care of their local authority.

Sometimes racism can work in paradoxical ways. At a psychological level, the amplification of perceived difference to the point of seeing someone as 'other' rather than kin and the false assumptions that can follow from this, restricts our vision and undermines our capacity to face the truth. In Oldham and Rochdale, between 2008 and 2009, police and social services were unable to comprehend what was being told them: that a criminal group of British Pakistani men were routinely grooming, drugging and raping vulnerable children – most of them white (Erelowitz et al, 2013). In the six years since these men were prosecuted and found guilty in 2012, similar paedophile trafficking rings have been uncovered across Lancashire, Yorkshire and the East Midlands, the crimes persisting for years with literally hundreds of victims. In all these locations, anxiety about race seemed to adversely affect professional judgement and behaviour and paralyse the system from acting to prevent such atrocity.

Sadly, some staff are themselves victims of racist prejudice. One uncomfortable question raised by the case of Dr Bawa-Garba (discussed later in Chapter 11) is whether she would have attracted such vitriol if she had been white. Certainly there are reports that black and minority ethnic staff working for social services and the NHS experience higher rates of bullying, harassment, and abuse from both clients/patients and their colleagues than white staff (NHS England, 2016).

Indirect Discrimination

Carruthers and Ormondroyd also described an indirect form of discrimination, which they define as the disproportionate negative effect of policies, practices and management of care on older people. Unpicking this indirect discrimination sheds light not only on the predicament of older people themselves, but also on the circumstances of people with intellectual disabilities or mental health problems.

A number of reports by The Centre for Policy in Ageing (2009) show how the pressure to discharge people from hospital can be at the expense of the right pace and detail of planning for life after the ward. As people age, the capacity for compensation, the resilience and the ability to restore functioning in the face of illness, trauma or stress, decreases, in degree and in pace. This slowed, or impaired capacity for recovery in older people makes them particularly vulnerable to the effects of drives for efficiency, for speeding up and systematising the journey through care. Older people will generally be more affected than others by the reduction of staffing levels on wards, the pace at which staff are passing by, the fragmentation of care delivery in acute services, the speed of discharge processes, the shortness of primary care consultations. It takes time for the older patient and staff alike to establish the sense of attunement and trust described in Chapter 4.

Experience of in-patient care can be very bad, too, for people with intellectual disabilities and their carers. The Michael report (Michael, 2008) identified failures of acute healthcare for six people across the UK, whose deaths were highlighted in the Mencap report 'Death by Indifference' (Mencap, 2007). Again, assumptions about the value and needs of the patients were seen to influence neglectful care. Although requirements for staff training and new systems and procedures followed the report, there has been little sign of progress. The stark title of the follow-up report, 'Death by Indifference: 74 Deaths and Counting' (Mencap, 2012) suggests that well-meaning policy directives will not make much difference unless the focus changes. A crucial underlying issue needs to be addressed: namely the provision of sufficient time and staffing to enable unrushed, attentive and sensitive dialogue with patients.

Time, and the attention and quality of communication it allows, is in increasingly short supply across the whole of the modern Welfare State, not just the NHS. The whole system is characterised by the drive to speed up processes and to save money by providing the minimum numbers of staff. Time and human resource pressures frequently conspire to direct attention to procedures, to fragmented targets and tasks, and away from genuine engagement with the person. The specialisation of functions in the NHS makes it even more difficult to ensure continuity of relationships within which the person is known and understood. Often, neither the task nor the sympathetic relationship is even half-adequately addressed. In reality, vulnerable groups, with problems affecting communication, understanding and mobility, are experiencing indirect discrimination across the whole social and healthcare system, because of its very culture of 'efficiency' and engineered processes.

This glaring paradox suggests a fundamental denial is at work. It seems impossible to acknowledge that, even when fear, prejudice and hostility are managed, even with well-meaning directives and models, these people and their complex needs just do not seem to fit into our way of going about things. This is frightening, to say the least, particularly when we consider the fact that approximately 65 per cent of hospital beds are occupied by people over the age of 65 and that 25 per cent of the population will experience mental health problems in their lifetime. Even if only a proportion find the system poorly geared to meet their needs, this is a lot of people not to fit in.

A consequence of this denial is to consistently underestimate the resources required to properly attend to the needs of the aged and other vulnerable groups. Indeed, the very concept of 'efficiency' is distorted. Inconveniently for both staff and patients, the needs of people in vulnerable groups on the edge of kinship require a lot of what the system has increasingly less of: time, unprejudiced attitudes, kindly concern, and high levels of interpersonal skill. What is needed is a system that adjusts to their needs, rather than the other way round.

Promoting Kinship at the Edges

Members of groups on the edge of kinship, however much they inspire love, compassion, conscientiousness and concern, can be at the same time inconvenient and unwanted, even feared and hated. This reality is hard to face, and to address, especially as it is not going to go away, however much stigma and discrimination are challenged.

A core challenge for staff is to remain open to them and their needs, to bear them in mind, despite anxiety and discomfort. Staff must then somehow manage to resist the temptation to split – to idealise or denigrate, to swing between trust and suspicion, to overestimate or underestimate both the person and community resources. This temptation is personal, but it is also powerfully built into how society as a whole responds, and the pressures this puts on the worker.

Fundamentally, though, staff have constantly to deal with the lack of fit between the needs of their patients and the wider health and social care system. Often this will involve an encounter with under-funding and frank discrimination, and almost always it will entail an engagement with culture and processes. The system frequently does not make available the resources patients need, and in fact too often goes about its business in ways that actually work against meeting their needs.

Somehow, the time and space to build relationships with, and to develop and share understanding about vulnerable people need to be found. Ways of strengthening the continuity of their care and supporting them as they encounter the many sharp edges in wait for them in the community, and in the health and social care systems, are vital. Recognition of the dynamics at work at the edges of kinship may free up staff, may 'clear their heads', so that they can engage more compassionately with the real needs and aspirations of those they are trying to help. Managers can help, by resisting the urge to minimise the difficulties of the caring task; the urge to idealise partial solutions; the urge unreflectingly to demand contradictory priorities; and the urge to deny the shortcomings and limits that staff will encounter as they try to serve the most vulnerable people in society.

References

Age UK (2016) Hidden in plain sight. The unmet mental health needs of older people.

Age UK (2017) Briefing: Health and Care of Older People in England.

Amnesty International (2018) A Matter of Routine. The Use of Immigration Detention in the UK.

Appleby, L. (2010) Offender health: the next frontier. The Psychiatrist. 34: 409–10.

Ardern, Jacinda (2019) Remembrance Service for the victims of Al Noor Mosque massacre, quoted in 'The leader who spoke for a nation and moved the world', an article by Toby Manhire, *The Guardian Weekend*, 6 April, 2019.

Ashton, L. and Moore, J. (2009) Guide to Providing Mental Health Care Support to Asylum Seekers in Primary Care. Royal College of General Practitioners.

Aynsley-Green, A. (2010) Follow-Up Report to 'The Arrest and Detention of Children Subject to Immigration Control'. HMSO.

Blackwell, D. (2005) *Counselling and Psychotherapy with Refugees*. Jessica Kingsley.

Care Quality Commission (2016) Mental Health Act. The rise in the use of the MHA to detain people in England. Available at: www.cqc.org.uk/publications/themed-work/mental-health-act-rise-mha-detain-england [last accessed 26 August, 2019].

Carruthers, I. and Ormondroyd, J. (2009) Achieving Age Equality in Health and Social Care. HMSO.

Centre for Policy in Ageing (2009) Ageism and Age Discrimination in Secondary Health Care in the United Kingdom. HMSO.

Chen, M. and Lawrie, S. (2017) Media coverage of mental illness. British Journal of Psychology Bulletin. 41: 308–13.

Department of Health (2009a) Valuing People Now. HMSO.

Department of Health (2009b) Dementia Strategy. HMSO.

Erelowitz, S., Clifton, J., Firimin, C., Gulyurtlu, S., and Edwards, G. (2013) "If only someone had listened": Office of the Children's Commissioner's Inquiry into Child Sexual Exploitation in Gangs and Groups: final report. Office of the Children's Commissioner. Available at: www.thebromleytrust.org.uk/files/chidrens-commission.pdf [last accessed 26 August, 2019].

Floud, S., Barnes, I., Verfurden, M., Kuper, H., Gathani T., Blanks, R. G., Alison, R., Patnick, J., Beral, V., Green, J., and Reeves, G. K. for the Million Women Study Collaborators5 (2017) Disability and participation in breast and bowel cancer screening in England: a large prospective study. British Journal of Cancer. 117: 1711–14. Available at: www.nature.com/articles/bjc2017331 [last accessed 26 August, 2019].

Goffman, E. (1961) *Asylums: Essays on the Condition of the Social Situation of Mental Patients and Other Inmates*. Penguin.

HMIP (2016) Report on an unannounced inspection of Yarl's Wood Immigration Removal Centre by HM Chief Inspector of Prisons. Available at: www.justiceinspectorates.gov.uk/hmiprisons/wp-content/uploads/sites/4/2015/08/Yarls-Wood-web-20151.pdf [last accessed 26 August, 2019].

Hellenbach, M. (2017) Intellectual disabilities among prisoners: prevalence and mental and physical health comorbidities. Journal of Applied Research in Intellectual Disabilites. 30(2): 230–41. Available at: www.ncbi.nlm.nih.gov/pubmed/26775928 [last accessed 9 August, 2019].

HM Chief Inspector of Prisons (2002, 2008, 2015) Annual Reports. Available at: www.gov.uk/search/transparency-and-freedom-of-information-releases?organisations%5B%5D=hm-inspectorate-of-prisons&parent=hm-inspectorate-of-prisons [last accessed 26 August, 2019].

Home Office/Stephen Shaw (2016) Review into the Welfare in Detention of Vulnerable Persons. Reports available here: www.justiceinspectorates.gov.uk/hmiprisons/inspections?s&location=yarls-wood [last accessed 9 August, 2019].

Independent Asylum Commission (2008) Saving Sanctuary: The First Report of Conclusions and Recommendations. IAC.

Independent Review of the Mental Health Act. Interim Report (2018) Available at: www.gov.uk/government/publications/independent-review-of-the-mental-health-act-interim-report [last accessed 26 August, 2019].

Jacobson, J. (2008) No-One Knows. Prison Reform Trust.

Keith, L. and Van Ginneken, E. (2015) Restricting access to the NHS for undocumented migrants is bad policy at high cost. British Medical Journal. 350: h3056.

Keown, P., Mercer, G. and Scott, J. (2008) Retrospective analysis of hospital episode statistics, involuntary admissions under the MHA 1983, and number of psychiatric beds in England 1996–2006. British Medical Journal. 337: a1837.

Lawrie, S. M. (2000) Newspaper coverage of psychiatric and physical illness. Psychiatric Bulletin. 24: 104–6.

Mencap (2007) Death by Indifference. Mencap.

Mencap (2012) Death by Indifference: 74 Deaths and Counting. Mencap.

Mental Health Act Commission (2009) The Mental Health Act Commission Annual Report. HMSO.

Michael, J. (2008) Healthcare for All. HMSO.

Morris, S. (2003). Asylum seekers 'were locked in during fire'. *The Guardian*. Available at: www.theguardian.com/uk/2003/jul/23/immigration.immigrationandpublicservices [last accessed 9 August, 2019].

National Audit Office (2017) Mental Health in Prisons.

NHS England (2016) NHS Workforce Race Equality Standard – WRES.

Parliamentary Ombudsman (2010) Fast and Fair? Report by the Parliamentary Ombudsman on the UK Border Agency. HMSO.

Prisons and Probation Ombudsman (2004) Annual Reports. Available at: www.ppo.gov.uk/document/annual-reports/ [last accessed 9 August, 2019].

Ryan, F. (2018) 'Disability', in *Can We All Be Feminists* (ed. June Eric-Udorie). Penguin Random House.

Shaw, S. (2004) Report of the inquiry into the disturbance and fire at Yarl's Wood Removal Centre. Available at: www.ppo.gov.uk/app/uploads/2015/11/special-yarls-wood-fire-021.pdf [last accessed 9 August, 2019].

Sherwood, H. (2014). UN special rapporteur criticises Britain's 'in-your-face' sexist culture. *The Guardian*. Available at: www.theguardian.com/world/2014/apr/15/un-special-rapporteur-manjoo-yarls-wood-home-office [last accessed 9 August, 2019].

Taylor, P. and Gunn, J. (1999) Homicides by people with mental illness: myth and reality. British Journal of Psychiatry. 174: 9–14.

Townsend, M. (2015). Yarl's Wood: UN special rapporteur to censure UK government. *The Guardian*. Available here: www.theguardian.com/uk-news/2015/jan/03/yarls-wood-un-special-rapporteur-censure [last accessed 9 August, 2019].

Wise, J. (2017) Sending mental health patients out of area for treatment is 'endemic'. British Medical Journal. 357: j3087.

Chapter

9 Unsettling Times

. . . there was a Chinese curse which took the form of saying, "May you live in interesting times". There is no doubt that the curse has fallen on us.

(Sir Austen Chamberlain, as reported in The Yorkshire Post, *March 1936)*

The attitudes, emotions and actions of staff are powerfully influenced by the culture within which their work takes place. In turn, the culture of an organisation arises from the ways in which tasks, priorities, values, anxieties and relationships are viewed and managed in the system as a whole. This matrix of influences is internalised by all involved, as the context for the individual's reactions to experience.

Larry Hirschhorn, former President of the International Society for the Psychoanalytic Study of Organizations, has termed this 'the workplace within' (Hirschhorn, 1988) whilst David Armstrong, a principal consultant at the Tavistock Consultancy Service, London, uses the term 'the organisation in the mind' (Armstrong, 2005). The core concept is that staff members have an internal working model of the organisation, part conscious, part unconscious. This colours their experience, how they understand their tasks, and how they manage themselves both in their own roles, and in their work with others.

A positive therapeutic culture, which promotes a positive 'workplace within', will reinforce the virtuous circle shown in Figure 4.1. It takes hard work, over a long time, to build such a culture. This work includes constant attention to a wide range of pressures, the management of difficult feelings, and the development of agreements, norms and understandings between staff at all levels in the system. All this has to occur against the background of how the workplace is organised and experienced as a whole, and how this is translated into the specific settings in which people work. If stresses, tensions, disagreements and disaffection are poorly managed and unmitigated, they will instead feed into a vicious circle that pulls daily practice away from effective kindness, and undermines the culture that sustains such kindness.

A number of factors have had powerful effects on the culture of care and welfare in contemporary Britain. We will now explore their influence on the delivery of services. In this chapter, our focus turns to the political approach taken to systemic and structural change.

As a starting point, it is helpful to understand what may need to be attended to in preserving kinship and mutuality in human groups, and just how fragile these 'civic virtues' might be.

A Lesson from Ethology

In his book *Social Fabrics of the Mind* (1988) Michael Chance, the pioneering social ethologist, makes some pertinent observations about how we organise ourselves. Chance was interested in the behaviours we have in common with monkeys and apes – all of us being the so-called 'higher primates' – and also in those behaviours that set us apart from them: 'what drags us back and what potentially sets us free, by setting free our intelligence' (Chance, 1988, p. 1). He described how it has become clear from studying our zoological relatives that they tend to function in one or other of two 'modes' in their group relations, the 'agonic' and the 'hedonic'.

In the agonic mode, individuals are primarily concerned with their own security, warding off potential threats from other group members, and maintaining their status in the hierarchy. In the hedonic mode, much more time is spent nurturing social relations, with rituals of affiliation, reconciliation and reassurance between mutually dependent individuals reducing tension and arousal. This frees up attention to further the aims of the group. Characteristics of these two modes are outlined in more detail in Box 9.1. This is of necessity a simplification of complex work, but the broad principles offer a helpful evolutionary perspective on the function of kindness.

Box 9.1 Two Modes of Social Functioning

In the **agonic mode**, characteristic of hierarchical groups such as African savannah baboons, individuals are primarily concerned with self-security, warding off potential threats from other group members, and maintaining their status in the hierarchy. Rank is all-important, as are channels of command and control. Members of the group become either authoritarian or subservient. They are preoccupied with inhibiting overt expressions of aggressive conflict, which means tension and arousal remain at a characteristically high level. The result is a social culture that inhibits individual development and restricts expressions of intelligence.

In the **hedonic mode**, typical of some wild chimpanzees and gorillas, much time is spent nurturing social relations. This includes competitive play, often followed by displays of tenderness, gentle touching, grooming and kissing. The hedonic mode deploys such rituals of affiliation, reconciliation and reassurance between mutually dependent individuals to free up attention to further the aims of the group. Such behaviour is rewarding because it reduces tension and arousal. Apart from short-lived bursts of excitement, levels of tension and arousal in the hedonic mode are characteristically low. Amongst other things, this enables the transitions between one generation and the next to be smoothly integrated.

Members of groups in the hedonic mode are not all of equal status: nor is there an absence of conflict, but the low arousal leaves individuals more able to form a network of personal relationships that offer mutual support, freeing up attention from self-protective needs within the group, and so allowing expression of intelligence and creativity, and a virtuous circle of reciprocity.

Hedonic social interaction promotes self-confidence, empathic cooperation and reality-based intelligence. The hedonic mode seems to capture the virtuous circle of kind and attentive behaviours outlined in Chapter 4, but can be vulnerable under pressure.

Chance also described a third form of relating, notable especially among those primates who spend much of their time in hedonic mode, when subject to such pressures as competition for territory, food or sex: the **agonistic mode**, where individuals simply 'fight it out' among themselves. The violence can be chaotic, shocking and devastating, possibly fatal to individuals, and consuming important group resources – all disadvantageous to group survival.

Summarised from Chance (1988), *Social Fabrics of the Mind*

Extrapolating from what he had seen in the groups of primates, Chance hypothesised that human groups and subgroups may function in either the agonic or hedonic mode, or move back and forth between them. Each mode predisposes individuals and groups to deploy their attention in distinct ways, influencing whether or not they can develop their intelligence and creativity.

Chance was particularly interested in how cultures may shift rapidly from the hedonic to the agonistic – open conflict. He was fascinated by events at Jane Goodall's Gombe Stream Reserve in Tanzania (Goodall, 1965), where something tipped a generally happy hedonic society of chimps into a murderous civil war. Human researchers had begun to provide bananas to engage the chimps. Chance hypothesised that it was the competition for these bananas that had provoked the change: it had distracted their attention, squeezing out the expression of reciprocity and the mutual soothing so essential to keeping tension down and sustaining benign relationships.

The type of attention that characterised the chimpanzees' relationships had changed from 'awareness of', into 'reaction to', each other (Power, 1988). When the opportunity to practise mutually reassuring rituals was reduced through a critical period of prolonged competitive provocation, the network of social attention underlying the social relations collapsed.

Hedonic groups seem to be more prone to sudden collapse than the agonic – hence hedonic functioning does not confer an unequivocal evolutionary advantage. The members of a hedonic group may not have learnt to directly inhibit their violent and aggressive impulses as effectively as the tense and highly aroused agonic individuals. In addition, the rigid in-built structure of agonic groups can more readily reassert itself after some form of civil war temporarily breaks the social links.

Have Chance's conclusions withstood the test of time? Subsequent researchers have argued that there may have been other reasons for the heightened competition and deteriorating relationships that eventually led to chimpanzees hounding and killing members of rival groups. However, the original data has also been reviewed (Feldblum et al, 2018), confirming that, in the preceding two years, intermingling and affiliative rituals had become gradually less frequent between males in the two groups that eventually fought it out.

Meanwhile, chimp life has moved on. Whereas ethologists in the 1970s were shocked at the outbreak of violence in the previously calm chimpanzees of the Gombe reserve, twenty-first century chimpanzees have become notorious for their intra-species violence: no surprise perhaps, given the ongoing destruction of their natural habitats. The 2018 David Attenborough BBC series, *Dynasties*, featured a group of about 30 chimpanzees in Senegal in West Africa, where gold mining, human encroachment, poaching and forest fires were taking their toll. It was estimated that the total number of chimpanzees in West Africa had fallen by 80 per cent in 25 years (BBC, 2018). However, despite the hardship, the heightened fight for survival and a violent male dominance struggle, the importance of affiliative ritual and returning to the hedonic mind-set remained clear.

This is an important lesson: hedonic relations, although they may liberate creative intelligence, are vulnerable; particularly in the context of an overcrowded world with limited resources. A kind and attentive society of primates is dependent on an ongoing reward cycle of active reciprocal kindnesses. The infrastructure of mutually dependent hedonic social relations has to be constantly maintained by reassurance and tender appeasement, reducing arousal.

The ideas of Chance and his colleagues offer a frame for further understanding of the alarming findings of the social experiments summarised in Chapter 6. These experiments spoke eloquently of how authority, conformism, threat and risk can drive behaviour towards brutality, and how anxiety and limited resources can provoke division and unproductive disputes between people and teams. The lessons from non-human primates emphasise the potential vulnerability of a culture of kindness and illustrate some of the dynamics that can fatally undermine it. At the heart of the issue is how (hedonic) attentiveness to, and nurture of, the other can be so easily subverted, even replaced, by uncontrolled (agonic) self-protective or status-driven anxieties, either as a stage in, or as protection against, further slippage into (agonistic) brutality.

'Re-disorganisation'

Earlier in the book, we explored the conflicting pressures that beset individuals and teams, and the importance of people being helped to focus on their role. Probably the most frequent topic of discontent among staff across the public sector is the climate of constant change, sometimes referred to scathingly as 're-disorganisation' (Smith et al, 2001) or 'recidivist major change' (Jones, 2016). For the NHS, the scale of the change in culture over the first years of the new century was summed up in an editorial in the British Medical Journal in 2010:

> *Over the past 30 years, governments have reached repeatedly for structural reorganisations of both the NHS and the Department of Health. They have created, merged and abolished health bodies, and distributed service, functional and geographical, responsibilities in different ways. Reorganisation has often been cyclical, with new governments or ministers reinventing structural arrangements that their predecessors abolished, seemingly unaware of or uninterested in past reorganisations. Reorganisation has happened frequently – with at least 15 identifiable major structural changes in three decades, or one every two years or so. And reorganisation has been rapid, with changes often being initiated in advance of formal legislative approval, the details of reforms being worked out as they are implemented, and the timetable for hasty consultation being a matter of weeks or months.* (Walshe, 2010)

This scenario will be familiar to people working across the whole of the 'Welfare State'. In the NHS, especially in England, in addition to the major reorganisations, there have been changes in commissioning arrangements, merging and demerging of trusts, the breaking and formation of working partnerships, and sundry other restructurings. Health and social care staff have also been close to overwhelmed by the mushrooming of top-down policies, guidelines and audits and major strategic changes that significantly influence the way they practise. Those working in management roles have had little, if any, occupational stability. They have faced repeated disruption to professional career planning and ways of working, changes that have not always been well led or well managed. Stability and consistency have been further undermined by multiple changes at service level, including 're-engineering' of teams, changes to contracts, service reductions and cuts and shifts of resources.

It is not that far-reaching changes should not be made. However, few if any successful businesses or industries outside the public sector have been in such a state of permanent disequilibrium, or subject (almost without exception) to so many unfinished processes of change for so long. How can a stable, compassionate, task- and relationship-focussed culture survive in the face of such disturbance? The lessons from primates indicate that calm and stability are required to nurture and sustain kindness and creativity. Calm and stability are not the same as stagnation and complacency. Change management that conflates the two requires rethinking.

Top-Down Change

Experience in public services has repeatedly been that change is rushed through, with poor planning, and little thought about its likely effect on what is good about existing systems. Ensuing difficulties are then used as a justification for more change: it has been said that few politicians try to build a reputation by making their predecessor's reforms work.

The coalition programme for government in 2010 committed to 'stop the top-down reorganisations of the NHS that have got in the way of patient care' (HM Government, 2010). Despite this, a white paper, 'Equity and Excellence: Liberating the NHS' (Department of Health, 2010) was produced at speed, only seven weeks after the formation of the coalition, proposing the most radical changes in the organisation of the NHS for decades. Widespread protest by professional groups and academic experts in health policy and management produced a brief respite, but in the end the Health and Social Care Act 2012 for England and Wales implemented most of the changes that had been proposed.

For England, these changes included the 'any willing provider' policy allowing outside businesses to tender for the provision of health and social services, and the abolition of previous commissioning arrangements through 'Primary Care Trusts', transferring the responsibilities to 'consortia' of GPs. Crucially, in what was passed off as a minor semantic detail, the responsibility of the Secretary of State (and thus the Department of Health) was changed from having to 'provide' a comprehensive health service, to having to 'promote' it. Critics were given reassurance that the two terms were equivalent: but it was not explained why, in that case, there needed to be a change.

These reforms were widely seen as opening the door to privatisation (Peedell, 2011 amongst many others), albeit as a logical development of policy over previous decades. Critics were not easily won over. Six years into the new regime, in 2018, delegates at the BMA's annual representative meeting passed an unopposed motion noting that it was 'wasting significant sums of monies in procurement processes, fragmenting care and destabilising NHS providers through accelerating private sector provision' (Moberly, 2018).

It has been estimated (Walshe, 2010) that every major restructuring puts the NHS back three years. It does not achieve the (repeatedly) stated objectives of increasing efficiency, reducing management costs and channelling a greater proportion of resources to the front-line. Transition costs are always underestimated and intended savings rarely realised (National Audit Office, 2010). Management costs have grown steadily over the past 30 years regardless of, and perhaps as a result of, repeated reorganisations.

Why do politicians, and those in power beneath them, feel a need to overwhelm the system with repeated changes of direction and structure, rather than putting their energy and the country's resources into improving the systems already in place? This is not even about the government changing hands. The Labour government in 2000, for example, set out a 'road map' for the next ten years in 'The NHS Plan', with a strengthened approach to targets and performance management (Department of Health, 2000). Only 12 months later, before the approach had had a chance to deliver improvements, the emphasis changed to promoting 'choice' and competition (Ham, 2009).

There is evidence that large-scale change programmes are never linear, and are often characterised by the so-called 'J curve', in which there is a dip in performance before any improvements occur. Constant revolution, then, may also mean a constant sense of failure, reacted to in a 'knee jerk' way by plotting more revolution. Politicians, apparently unable to learn from history, seem equally unable to allow time for the changes to become embedded – let alone properly evaluated – before disrupting the system again. The persistence of this pattern, despite its irrationality, suggests that there may be some 'pay off', over and above the politician's reputational need to be seen to be doing something. Is some psychological defence mechanism thus in operation? Might the continual change be a means of avoiding some reality that cannot be faced by the system, and its members?

Social Defences

In previous chapters we considered how individuals and teams have a tendency to act and organise in ways that minimise the conscious experience of anxiety. The behaviour of large organisations can be explored from a similar perspective. The work of Isabel Menzies Lyth, a psychoanalyst and pioneering organisational consultant, has made an influential contribution to such a way of thinking. Her work, 'The Functioning of Social Systems as a Defence against Anxiety' (Menzies Lyth, 1959) explored the organisational dynamics affecting nurses. She sought to understand why so many nurses were resigning from the profession: something that was happening even then. Her work is relevant to all systems where the task is to engage with, and respond to, complex human vulnerability and need.

Menzies Lyth thought that the work of nursing, because it involves physical and emotional contact with the inevitability of illness, pain, suffering and death, arouses feelings and thoughts associated with the 'deepest and most primitive levels of the mind' (1959; 1988, p. 47). She suggested that the organisation of a hospital could be seen as consciously and unconsciously structured round the evasion of this anxiety. A range of observations of interacting phenomena had led her to this view. She identified a fragmentation of the nurse–patient relationship due to the practice of breaking the workload down into a series of tasks, and dividing each nurse's time between 30 patients.

She observed 'depersonalisation and categorisation' (such as referring to a patient as 'the liver in bed 10' rather than by name), and detachment from, and denial of, feelings. She noted attempts to eliminate difficult decisions by ritual task performance, and to reduce the weight of responsibility in decision-making through checks and counter-checks. She found 'purposeful obscurity' in the formal redistribution of responsibility, and avoidance of change. She found both idealisation and underestimation of personal development possibilities. Many of these phenomena persist to this day of course, and can be easily observed across health and social care services.

Importantly, she saw that 'the social defences prevent the individual from realising to the full her capacity for concern, compassion and sympathy, and for action based on these feelings that would strengthen her belief in the good aspects of herself and her capacity to use them' (Menzies Lyth, 1959; 1988, p. 75).

Menzies Lyth proposed that the success and viability of a social institution are intimately connected with the techniques it uses to contain anxiety. These ideas have been developed over time, with account being taken of the goodness of fit between organisational structures on the one hand, and the emotional demands of the work on the other. There is a need for healthy defences that protect the workforce, rather than alienate, detach or disempower it. If the institutional defences undermine a person's initial motivation for taking up the work, then they may decide to leave.

Unconscious Drivers of Change

Menzies Lyth's idea that the organisation of a hospital is defensive, with the unconscious purpose of stopping those who work in it – particularly those in charge – from feeling the emotional pain and anxiety associated with the work, is important for all care systems.

She had noted a marked resistance to change in the NHS of the 1950s and saw it as part of the social defence system of the time. Progressing into the next century, the pendulum has swung, and the uncritical acceptance and promotion of constant change across the welfare sector may have taken the place of inertia as a primary defence. Could it be that the constant restructuring of the services fulfils a similar function to those nursing practices observed in the Menzies Lyth study? That the unremitting process of reform is in part a social defence system that distracts from the existential anxiety associated with the uncertainty of sickness, risk, vulnerability, pain and death, and the enormity of the task of dealing with it? The compulsive nature of repeated reform, regardless of the inevitable costs and consequences of the disruption involved, suggests that this might be so. There is certainly ample evidence that major structural change keeps senior managers and board members detached from the front-line of healthcare (Healthcare Commission, 2007; Francis, 2010).

Often the approach to reorganisation appears simplistic, high on ideology, and low on detail. There is little, if any, attempt to evaluate the 'goodness of fit' between the new structure and the emotional task of caring for ill patients or vulnerable people. Risk assessments considering the true impact on the whole system are almost non-existent. Negative consequences then proliferate, with little readiness to address or pre-empt them – indeed, with a high degree of denial. There is a lack of understanding, a lack of thoughtful connection – a lack of kindness in the way the organisation as a whole is treated.

Thanks to the work of people like Goodall and Chance, anyone who intends to play around with the banana economy in a group of chimpanzees should be aware of the far-reaching damage that may be done. Less scientifically, most of us are aware of the likely effects of approaching a hive of bees quietly getting on with its peaceful cooperative task, and prodding it with a stick. The apparently ingrained lack of caution about repeated reform of our 'welfare' institutions does more than just disregard the immediate difficulties and limits of the implementation of the change itself. It fails to attend to the wider destructive potential of change for change's sake. It suggests a spiralling process of subjecting crucial national institutions to unacknowledged (and often unvoiceable) anxiety, failure to face up to negative effects, and a constantly growing recourse to 'omnipotent' manipulation.

Concern about the financial cost of the Welfare State, and about its weaknesses, is inevitable and right. However, the destructive spiral is set to continue, unless the powerful anxieties evoked in society and government, by virtue of the nature and limitations of the 'front-line work', are acknowledged and better contained. Therapeutic, caring and facilitative culture needs to be prioritised, and to be allowed to develop. The conditions that grow a hedonic culture need to be attended to, if such a culture is to put down roots and bear fruit.

Divided Loyalties, Fragmented Leadership

A side-effect of inexorable structural change has been the proliferation of project managers, governance, performance and improvement leads, initiative coordinators, 'champions' ... the designations change as rapidly as the initiatives that drive them. The result is a confused and fragmented set of relationships and accountabilities. Hierarchies are complicated by many masters, all requiring satisfaction from front-line staff. Multiple different paths of apparent accountability paradoxically allow endless displacement of responsibility. Leaders and managers find their sense of authority diluted and blurred, as they attempt to answer to, and exercise their judgement in, this web of fragmented accountability.

Menzies Lyth talked about the 'purposeful obscurity in the distribution of responsibility' (1959; 1988, p. 58) as a social defence against anxiety. In the modern Welfare State, this phenomenon is as bad as, or worse than, ever despite the rhetoric of 'flattened hierarchies', 'lean organisations' and a preoccupation with performance management. A consequence is that problems in the way things are done can become everybody's and nobody's business. As a result, crucial ethical norms, and the relationships required to express them in action, are hard to build and be trusted.

This situation might improve if the role of operational manager, actually running a service, was more valued and strengthened. There is a danger that an 'up to the minute' focus on business efficiency leads to managers of business and improvement processes being more valued than the leaders of the actual services the organisation is there to provide. Added to this, rapid promotions mean operational managers move on quickly, before they have accrued enough experience 'on the ground', or developed necessary skills. These trends reflect a serious underestimation of the complexity of supporting good-quality care. It is worth considering whether more operational managers, all equipped with a wider range of skills, including business, psychosocial and 'improvement' skills, might not provide a more integrated and coherent leadership than the current mix.

The Cost of Overloading the System

Whatever the underlying driving forces, it is clear that the constant changes have taken their toll on the workforce. There is anger that organisational change usually lacks an adequate evidence base (Oxman et al, 2005), and that commitments to huge upheavals are often rashly made, at huge cost, in what are no more than experiments, with no-one sure that innovation is going to result in something better. For staff trained in evidence-based disciplines this is particularly galling. Their trust in, and commitment to, the work of the service is consequently undermined.

The Health and Social Care Act of 2012, arising as we have seen without public mandate, and counter to assurances given in 2010, has spawned an ever-evolving set of changes in the NHS, from CCGs ('Clinical Commissioning Groups') through STPs ('Sustainability and Transformation Partnerships'), to ACOs ('Accountable Care Organisations'). Often it seems that as soon as anyone understands what one set of changes has entailed, or even what its acronyms convey, it gives way to the next. These changes not only confuse and disrupt healthcare services, but they make attempts by Local Authorities and the voluntary sector to work in partnership with the NHS difficult and frustrating.

The consequent 'lack of ownership' by so many professionals, along with the fast pace of change regardless of their underlying anxieties, feeds into their experience of the culture as unsafe and unreflective. Change is experienced as being dogmatic, imposed from the top, poorly researched, understood and justified. There are attempts at resistance from some quarters, such as with the High Court challenges to the introduction of Accountable Care Organisations (Dyer, 2018), but for the most part these come to nothing. As with the introduction of the 2012 Act itself, despite all the apparent objections, enough staff can usually be found to dutifully administer the implantation of the next change, out of deep-rooted diligence and loyalty to the institution and the people they care for.

Throughout the system there is a perception of rushed, clumsy implementation of policy without the mediation of intelligence and skill. There is anxiety that care will suffer. Add to this the history of the requirement for year-on-year 'efficiency savings', the reality of limited resources ensuing from the financial crisis of 2008 leading to wide public sector cuts, and the stage is set for a messy process characterised by ugly conflict, with power battles and scapegoating. Ongoing high turnover of NHS trust chief executive officers is likely to continue. The average time in the job was long quoted as two-to-three years: by 2014 a report by the King's Fund using the Freedom of Information Act (Janjua, 2014) found this to be just 18 months. Almost one third of all NHS trusts had at least one board-level vacancy, or an interim member. It was thus hard for staff to look to their trust boards or chief executives for any 'buffering' of the turmoil of change.

The Healthcare Commission has highlighted how frequent changes at the top are detrimental to the functioning of trusts. It has also observed that senior leaders are more likely to fail in organisations that are subject to particular external threats, such as forced mergers and reconfiguration of services, forced reorganisations, and responsibility for substantial capital projects. After outbreaks of *Clostridium difficile* that killed 33 people in Stoke Mandeville Hospital and 90 at the Maidstone and Tunbridge NHS Trust, it was noted:

> *Both Trusts had undergone difficult mergers, were preoccupied with finance, and had a demanding agenda for reconfiguration and PFI [Private Finance Initiative], all of which consumed the time and effort of senior managers.* (Healthcare Commission, 2007)

The conclusions of the inquiry into what happened in the Mid-Staffordshire NHS Trust challenged these same priorities:

> *While structures are an important and necessary part of governance, what is really important is that they deliver the desired outcome, namely safe and good quality care. There is evidence that setting up systems predominated over improving actual outcomes for patients.* (Francis, 2010, p. 398)

Much senior service management time has been focussed on implementing structural change rather than on improving services. This is often cited as a reason for disappointing rates of progress in some clinical areas. In Mid-Staffordshire, for example, the emergency admissions unit at the centre of the inquiry had been moved to different directorates three times between 2002 and 2007, and had had four different managers.

In social care the situation is at least as fragile. Radically reduced local authority social work services sit within, and are responsible for holding together, a complex web of outsourced, commissioned services. These are provided by fragmented, frequently financially vulnerable, private or voluntary organisations. Financial pressures, and the over-simplified commodification of care tasks, often mean that unrealistic economies are sought. Competition within a cash-poor economy can mean that organisations price their tenders for contracts unrealistically, leading to frequent failures, and collapse of services.

Constant re-tendering, with new providers replacing previous 'winners', and frequent transfer of staff contracts from one organisation to another, also means disruption to the embedding of services in the system. Service development and learning over time, vital to effective care services, is also compromised. This all leads to insecurity and lack of continuity for staff, and disruption to the care of vulnerable people. It causes turmoil in the networks of relationships across the system that are so vital to the timely response to changes in need, to the management of risk, and to the integration of the complex care some people require.

A study for the Voluntary Sector Social Services Workforce Unit in Scotland in 2009 explored the effect of these factors on staff (Cunningham and Nickson, 2009). A summary of the findings in their report 'A Gathering Storm' is offered in Box 9.2 below.

For decades, most services have been preparing for, going through, or recovering from major change – and frequently all three at the same time. Sometimes change offers an opportunity to refocus on patients' and service-users' experiences and needs, and be kinder. Sometimes a shake-up of a team will bring unspoken conflicts and differences out into the open, in a way that promotes kinder thinking on the part of staff members. But change, by its very nature, upsets the status quo; and even when it is well managed and

Box 9.2 Findings from 'A Gathering Storm'

- Re-tendering is becoming a major challenge to the financial stability of voluntary sector organisations for the foreseeable future.
- There are significant organisational impacts from re-tendering including:
  - Increased organisational resources devoted to such exercises;
  - Breakdown of cooperative relations between providers;
  - Concerns over service quality;
  - Difficulties in interpreting TUPE regulations [the rules relating to transfer of employment from one organisation to another];
  - Losing highly motivated staff;
  - Continued undermining of terms and conditions of employment.
- Evidence of a highly motivated workforce present in the sector prepared to undertake work over and above their contracted responsibilities to meet service-user needs.
- Workers expressed shock, disappointment and dismay at news that their services were being put out for re-tender.
- Significant violation of the psychological contract of some workers as a consequence of re-tendering, with some looking for alternative employment.
- Employees expressed dual concerns regarding their own employment security and the wellbeing of service-users.
- Employees received inconsistent information regarding their rights under TUPE.
- Feelings of violation among those whose employment was transferred were offset by protection of terms and conditions of employment under TUPE and continuity of service.
- Management and unions also contributed to the continued commitment of employees transferring to a new employer by dealing promptly with specific issues arising out of the transfer.
- Employees who retained employment with their original employer expressed significant relief.
- Employees who had been transferred or remained with their original employer continue to express high levels of commitment to service-users.
- Employees expressed significant concern regarding their employment security and continuity of employment if re-tendering became the norm.
- There was general satisfaction with the information and support provided by unions to their members, and re-tendering could provide opportunities for union membership growth.
- Service users and their families received little information about re-tendering and had no say in whether services should be re-tendered.

(Cunningham and Nickson, 2009)

welcomed by staff it can distract from the primary task of caring for others. While disruption can be mitigated to a degree by good operational leadership focussed on helping staff to be mindful of the task in hand, it is an uphill struggle when change is so frequent that the longed for period of stability never comes.

If healthy and effective cultures are to be re-grown, there is an urgent need for integrated and stable leadership throughout the system. Developing the understanding and resources needed to address the forces tipping towards agonic or agonistic cultures requires relationships to be built, trust to be developed, and confidence to grow. Repeatedly reapplying for your own job is not a ritual of affiliation, reconciliation or reassurance.

Difficulties in implementation of and/or achieving outcomes need to be faced as problems requiring thought and work, rather than as failures requiring further structural or personnel changes. Above all, leaders are required who can manage their own anxiety – about performance, even survival – sufficiently to connect with and understand the experience of their staff, to face and acknowledge reality openly, and to support those affected by change intelligently and sympathetically.

The Importance of Local Ownership

Lip service is often paid to the idea of 'distributed leadership', but with little effort to involve front-line staff in planned change. At worst, this means there is poor understanding of the rationale for change, let alone opportunity for teams to work through their feelings, and to adapt a centrally driven innovation to their local situation. Without the chance to develop a sense of ownership, staff are unlikely to commit themselves and their goodwill. Often the well-intentioned idea driving one initiative does not coordinate with the well-intentioned idea driving another initiative emanating from a different part of the organisation. Front-line staff feel caught up in conflict. They may also feel, with some justification, that they have been left accountable for keeping the service going whatever the disruptive effects of the changes afoot.

One form of change common across the public sector is that of 'replication'. When a particular model of care is seen as innovative and successful, the obvious question is how to roll it out to other areas across the country. This is not as straightforward as it might seem. Even when the model is highly technical, it will often require new ways of working and there are usually a proportion of staff resistant to changing their ways. When it involves a fundamental change in approach such as some of the new wave of social work initiatives or new therapeutic approaches in mental health, resistance can be a real barrier. It can be exciting being part of a pioneering project, where the innovative ideas emerge from extensive discussions in the team or the team is specially selected and attracts special funding. It is not so energising to be part of an industrial-scale roll-out programme, where one has to follow guidelines set by other people, over which you have little say. Outcomes can be correspondingly different.

The public sector has a tendency to approach psychosocial models of care in the same way as it might approach a new drug, as if, for example, a model successfully pioneered in a multicultural urban area will be equally successful in a largely white coastal town or sparsely populated rural area. Even where the demographics are roughly similar, it is important to approach such a move cautiously, with sufficient time spent thinking through how to adapt the model to a new context. Often the new model is compared to 'standard care' in an over-determined way that doesn't reflect reality. Within the 'standard care' group, there is likely to be a huge range of teams, some of them quietly getting on with the work, functioning well and proud of what they are achieving. Too often, the approach to change is determinedly evangelical, insensitive to how much has been invested in the existing way of working, and uninterested in incorporating established good practice.

This is not to argue that good models of working should not be replicated; but a plea to take an intelligently kind approach to the change management involved. This is not just about 'being nice' to everyone and making them feel better: the evidence is clear that nurturing a sense of ownership and a sense of agency is far more likely to lead to successful adoption of the new approach. Taking a 'must do' approach is doomed.

The 'Reclaiming Social Work' model (described in Chapter 14) was successful in Hackney where it was pioneered, but had problems being rolled out into other areas. This seems to have been dependent on how much the model was understood and championed by the particular host local authority. Models involving a private, charitable or social enterprise organisation such as 'Frontline' working with a local authority with joint responsibility for a service, have not always been straightforward or well thought out. The relationship between the two organisations is key and does not always receive the attention it needs (Bostock et al, 2017).

The success of a new initiative is also very much dependent on the relationship it has with the higher system. Here is how one leader of such a project described it.

> *New work is 'allowed' while the numbers are small and we appear to be amateurs. Innovation that does not encroach on the existing system and can be contained as an interesting pilot, or published as an inspirational case study, is usually celebrated. In the beginning, everyone involved is patted on the head, invited to talk about the work in important places and roundly praised. Later, as the work becomes more successful and therefore more challenging, the system reasserts itself.* (Cottam, 2018, p. 248)

In the English NHS, new initiatives have often been funded centrally for the first three years, but then the responsibility moves to local commissioners, who do not have the same investment or understanding. A 'specialist' service might well depend on a number of commissioning bodies if it is to remain viable and it is difficult and time-consuming to build the sort of alliances that will facilitate support and understanding of the purpose.

In her book about the need to revolutionise the Welfare State, *Radical Help*, Hilary Cottam describes 'Life', a project her team led that intervened with troubled families in Swindon. As with 'Reclaiming Social Work', there was a strong focus on team cohesiveness and one of the principles was an inversion of time: 80 per cent of the team's time was spent by the side of families and only 20 per cent on administration. 'Life' was radical and successful (Cottam, 2018, pp. 49–80).

In a later section of her book, Cottam tells how 'Life' was visited by David Cameron, the Prime Minister at the time, and his Minister for Communities and Local Government, Eric Pickles. They were impressed, and civil servants from the cabinet office soon followed with a plan to offer financial incentives to copy the project, on a competitive basis. This, and other developments, became known as the 'Troubled Families Initiative'. There would be financial rewards for each family that was 'turned around' – financial incentives that Cottam scathingly describes as a modern version of command and control: '*An approach based on horizontal relationships and a shift in power towards the families was translated back into a linear programme with outputs that could be measured and controlled*' (p. 250). In the process of supposed replication, the essence of the service was lost. Cottam says she tried in vain to explain that what was needed was *permission to free those at the front line to work in new ways* (p. 249).

Instead, the Troubled Families Initiative went on to demonstrate the problems that can arise from over-specified contracts and payment by results – ironic given that the task force had been set up to 'clear away the red tape to improve the lives of the country's most troubled families'. Central to the problem was the fact that two programmes had been separately assigned and implemented by two different Government departments (the Department of Work and Pensions and the Department of Communities and Local Government), anxiously and mistrustfully working in partnership with local government. Lessons have been learnt and the project is ongoing but the National Audit Office review (NAO, 2016) advised that payment by results is a challenging form of contracting, has attendant costs that government has often underestimated and is not suited to all public services. It suggested that a better way of partnership-working between central and local government would be to identify shared goals and ambition, rather than concentrate on a contractual relationship. Cottam observes:

> *Of course we want population-level change and we need to find ways to make these small-scale experiments work nationally, but the question is better positioned as: how do we create the conditions for growth? Scale is a linear process, but growth is modular: it will look more like the evolution of a honeycomb or the replication of cells than a process of distribution from the centre to the margins.* (Cottam, 2018, p. 242)

A more successful example of rolling out a small-scale local initiative more widely, and with central government involvement, has been the 'Pause' project (www.pause.org.uk). Pause was started-up in Hackney in 2013 and taken up and funded in other pilot sites by the Department of Education Innovation programme in 2015. It was a voluntary programme for women who had experienced, or were at risk of, repeated removal of children from their care. The women received an 18-month intensive package of emotional, psychological, practical and behavioural support. At the heart of the project was the relationship with the dedicated Pause practitioners, who were given a budget to spend on the women, and were encouraged to use their professional judgement in tailoring their approach to meet the unique needs of individuals. Despite this lack of uniformity, an evaluation report commissioned by the Department of Education was able to show a positive and significant impact on the women that engaged with it, a significant reduction in the number of pregnancies and a cost-offset to the local authority within two-to-three years (Department of Education, 2017). Pause continued to grow across the country, lessons being learnt and shared all the time. The key to this was the empowerment of individual practitioners to form a relationship and use their expertise flexibly.

Change and Grief

It is often the workers who are blamed if a new project does not succeed. Staff members' emotional response to change is frequently perceived and labelled as resistance, reaction, or self-interest – an inconvenience. Such reactions to change often have much in common with the effects of bereavement – shock, denial, anger and despair. However, a bereaved person is not regarded as willfully obstructive in quite the same way.

Any change, especially when imposed 'from outside', is emotionally disruptive and can affect the way staff think about their patients or clients, their colleagues, and themselves. Most staff are attached to their job, and also to particular ways of carrying it out. They invest valued parts of themselves, often at high personal cost, and take pride in what their service offers. They have found ways of managing their difficult feelings; ways that have become entwined with the way things have hitherto been done. A culture where the focus is always on novelty or change leaves people feeling insecure, undervalued and sometimes abandoned. If their service is redesigned, or closed down, they will feel bereaved, even if they can understand the rationale for what has been done.

Sometimes service changes have come piling in so quickly on top of each other that staff involved in opening a new service have been required to close it only a few years – or even, in extreme cases, months – later. This can feel devastating, particularly for those who had responsibility for getting the service up and running. New services, like new babies, demand intense attention, especially where the quality of the service relies less on technology and more on people and the development of a supportive psychosocial milieu. A service being cut dead before it has had a chance to mature and fulfil its promise can arouse feelings of loss akin to traumatic bereavement. A relentless rate of change allows no time for staff to work through appropriate grief for what has been lost. Indeed, the anxious drive towards change makes it hard to conceive of such feelings being natural, and grieving people will very likely be expected to move on immediately, and to put in the extra effort required to start up a different role in another newly designed service. Carrying such unresolved emotional preoccupations into their new roles is hardly a promising basis for confident, attentive and caring work.

Teams and organisations struggle with the same type of tensions as individuals. Change is always destabilising. Although it offers a chance to take a fresh look at habits that might have become uncritically ingrained, or to explore new ways of working and implement improvements, it risks stirring up tensions and interfering with good practice in the process.

In an ideal situation, the ideas for the changes being implemented would have emerged from staff teams themselves, or at least chime well with changes they have been thinking about. Indeed, a well-run, well-functioning, service will constantly be on the look-out for ways of improving its practice on the basis of its ongoing experience, aided by constructive feedback from users of the service and the absorption of new guidelines and examples of best practice.

Even in this situation, though, the inevitable ambivalence about, and loss involved in, change will be played out in the organisation and its constituent teams in some way, and needs attention. Most individuals have mixed feelings about change and are able to see advantages and disadvantages, particularly when the issue is something as complicated as working with the needs of others. But it is surprisingly difficult to hold on to mixed feelings in groups. There is always a tendency to polarise around a difficult issue, rather than accommodate the uncertain middle ground. The result is often a team comprising an unproductive mix of: 'gung-ho' optimists, who proceed clumsily, without clarity about complexity or risk; die-hard conservatives, who resist without opening themselves to new thinking; and the disengaged, whose energy and intelligence are wasted. If such polarisation is not addressed, change may be more of an appearance than a reality, with old ways simply being packaged in new forms, and results not reflecting the intentions behind the change. Problems of implementation may then become personalised, with scapegoating and blame undermining group wellbeing and effectiveness.

People will be able to develop more nuanced positions, and to find better ways of coping with and managing change, if leaders can resist the tendency to idealise the new and denigrate the past. Allowing that there are good reasons for grief, because something valuable is being lost, and good reasons for scepticism about the new, because nothing is perfect, enables staff better to manage the group process involved in change. Sensitive attention to the experience of staff will often require acknowledgement of the disillusionment they feel. To face the reality that a previous way of working may have had shortcomings is difficult, but people are more likely to commit to improving things once they have done so. If they see a cherished plan simply aborted, they may well become disillusioned with the leaders who have instigated or allow its termination.

In grief, a person has to work through a range of emotions over what may be a long period of time – exhortations to 'get over it' are well recognised as thoughtless, unproductive and even damaging. In change management, straightforward acknowledgement of feelings is much more effective than evangelical or coercive 'positive thinking' – a management attitude that is distressingly common and guaranteed to lower morale even further. However, a mature approach to the feelings of staff by senior management requires the capacity on their part, too, to manage anxiety – the anxiety that the staff will not cooperate, are incompetent or destructive, the anxiety that the organisation (and its managers) will fail.

It is perhaps not surprising that the loss involved in change tends to be denied and neglected. We are not a society that is particularly good at processing grief. Death itself is a modern taboo with many of us evading the reality and finding that death strikes or creeps up on us unrehearsed. We have a paucity of ritual to help us grieve. It is as if modern culture has created a sort of collective 'manic defence' against both the inevitability and uncertainty of death. Anton Obholzer, a medical psychoanalyst and consultant to organisations, suggested that the health service should more accurately be called a 'keep-death-at-bay' service:

> *In the unconscious, there is no such concept as 'health'. There is, however, a concept of 'death' and in our constant attempt to keep this anxiety repressed, we use various unconscious defensive mechanisms, including the creation of social systems to serve the defensive function.* (Obholzer, 2019, p. 176)

The Economist has argued that the uncontrollable costs of US healthcare are driven by fear of death (cited by Smith et al, 2001). Could it be that some of our addiction to 'recidivist change' is ultimately driven by fear; that our discomfort thinking and talking about death is fuelling the existential anxiety Menzies Lyth described?

Disillusion

Underneath the inevitable loss and disillusionment involved in change is a more disturbing disillusionment with the entire system. Connection with the enterprise of kinship, with the social solidarity and commitment that the Welfare State represents, is undermined. It is as if the basic contract that underpins the expectation of commitment and generosity is at risk. The organisation depends on its staff taking on difficult responsibilities with commitment and skill, while individuals depend on the organisation to recognise their needs and support them with goodwill, compassion and intelligence.

In the NHS the rhetoric of 'Patients First' (NHS England, 2013) was a complicated communication: was there an implication that previously staff had been putting themselves first? Should staff now be put second? Does it have to be one or the other – was it not possible that all parties could be respected and supported?

The capacity to 'hold' the anxiety of the work, to buffer the strain of continued effort and to support staff accordingly is crucial. If distrust of the organisation predominates, the ability of staff to face the realities and complexities of other people's needs, and to make difficult decisions whilst acting humanely, inevitably suffers.

This is not an argument for complacency, or for harking back to some 'heyday' when staff could expect a job for life, whilst being protected from the inconvenient complaints of patients. It is to stress the importance of people being able to trust each other to carry their share of responsibility, and to exercise their imagination for problem solving. This is a scenario of collective interdependence, of mature relationships within which mature individuals can depend on each other to work together to manage their tasks within a challenging and disrupted world. Such interdependent relationships are important within and between professions, and across hierarchies. In *Managing Vulnerability*, Tim Dartington, writer and social scientist, puts it as follows:

> *A mature dependency is not . . . about the simple gratification of needs, passively demanded of an often absent leader. It is an interactive process, requiring both thought and action, where there is a recognition of difference and a use of difference to achieve mutually agreed ends. An aspect of dependency is therefore a capacity for followership, for responding to the leadership being offered in a purposeful way.* (Dartington, 2010, p. 44)

If the basic contract to work together in this way is at risk, especially in the way in which the processes and human costs of externally driven change are managed, the capacity for mutuality and kindness is fatally eroded. Andrew Cooper, Professor of Social Work at the Tavistock Clinic, writing with Dartington, has considered the emotional life of organisations, commenting on the weakening and increasing permeability of boundaries around organisations, and what this means for the people involved (Cooper and Dartington, 2004). As the work organisation becomes increasingly unstable, it ceases to be experienced psychologically as a safe place, and there is a consequent withdrawal of psychological investment. Cooper and Dartington describe a trend where employment becomes increasingly about survival only, and 'environmentally blind individualism' is encouraged (p. 135). How can we minimise this risk?

Threats to Belonging and Continuity

In Chapter 6, in the context of team dynamics, we talked about the importance of creating a culture of stability that fosters a sense of attachment for staff, the sense of belonging on which safe and effective practice must be based. In a setting where the new is routinely prioritised at the expense of the established, very little feels permanent; and insecure services will find it hard to make staff members feel safe. Even well-functioning organisations need a vigilant attitude and ongoing attention to group relationships if they are to function as a secure base for the work.

The many employees providing social care for elderly people in the community are at particularly risk. Although local authorities have statutory duties, their financial situation became increasingly critical from 2010 onwards. By 2018, most social care was commissioned, rather than provided directly as was once the case, with 90 per cent of it supplied by up to 19,000 different organisations. The unprecedented financial pressure on these organisations meant closures and take-overs were common. Some carers reported not even knowing who employed them, with little sense of belonging to a team, let alone being supported. Some even worried about whether they would be paid (Humphries et al, 2016). The term 'precariat' emerged in about 2014 as a term to describe the bottom 15 per cent of society, living without job security or predictability in a manner that effects their material and psychological wellbeing. Many of the 1.5 million employees in social care in 2018 came into this category, lacking job security, sometimes with 'zero hours' contracts, worried about rent increases, often going into debt and sometimes relying on food-banks.

Those who rely on the services are just as in need of sensitive management, especially those with longer-term problems. Often, of course, practitioners are only too aware of the risks of letting them down, and make efforts not to do so. However, the sense of inadequacy and imminent failure can become part of their emotional struggle.

Compounding this, there is an unhelpful tendency on the part of leaders of change, particularly in the NHS, to try to persuade concerned service-users, to reassure them, from an 'expert' perspective. Often such behaviour is based on belief in the benefits of change. Too frequently, it involves denial – of financial pressures behind change, of uncertainties about models of care, and, vitally, of the anxiety and loss service-users will feel. This is particularly true when change disrupts long-term relationships between practitioners and those they are caring for.

Paradoxically, some very successful projects have encountered problems with sustainability. One local authority that was quick to take on the 'Reclaiming Social Work' model was Cambridge. It was so successful that OFSTED deemed it 'outstanding' in 2014, and described it as the best performing authority in the field of children's services. A year later, it had imploded. One reason was that as a result of the success, the leaders were recruited to other positions with higher salaries. Fields such as social work and mental health, which rely more on human factors than technology, are particularly vulnerable to change of personnel, as so much is down to the people who carry the culture, particularly the leaders.

Another public sector difficulty is that successful services are often expected to take the worst financial cuts within an organisation, in order to protect services that are on the brink of failing. For example, a mental health trust worried about the state of its inpatient wards might transfer money from a successful psychotherapy department. It might even move the staff, not realising that the psychotherapy department's success has been in large part due to the team spirit, shared ethos and positive culture that has been built up over many years.

A further danger is the watering-down of successful services, even when they are supported by research evidence. Again, 'Reclaiming Social Work' provides examples (Bostock et al, 2017). Some local authorities watered the model down before it was even fully established, assuming they could manage without the clinical member of the group and reducing the weekly reflective meetings – both aspects of the model that have been shown to directly affect outcome. Small teams were particularly vulnerable if more than one post was lost – a scenario that is common across the Welfare State with redundancies, 'freezes' on vacant posts, and people on long-term sick leave.

In the NHS, despite frequent invocations of 'evidence-based practice' in provision of clinical services, there is little sense of such a critical, informed approach being applied to organisational structure, team functioning and staff development. There is also little commitment in mental health and social care to set up research projects with a long enough time scale to show the benefits of organisational interventions. Introducing a new drug or technology is relatively simple compared to the change management that is needed to reform attitudes and organisational dynamics: yet often the same approaches are used with both, if at all.

What is certain is that patients and clients value continuity as much as staff value a sense of belonging. Continuity in general practice, for example, is much valued by doctors and patients (Tammes, 2017). A 2018 literature review on continuity of care in general practice concluded that consulting with the same doctor over a sustained period halves risk of premature death and results in fewer appointments (Pereira, Gray et al, 2018). It may not be possible for individual staff members to guarantee continuity, as they might need to go on leave or move jobs. But it should be possible for people to have an ongoing relationship with a well-functioning, stable service.

Professor Ray Jones described the importance of stability in social work:

> *Good practice means building a continuity of knowledge and relationship with children and families, trust and respect with other professionals and agencies, and an awareness developed over time about community networks, strengths and weaknesses. None of this is assisted by organisational churn and too excitable leadership. Calm continuity builds stability and security and is more likely to give space for reflective practice . . .* (Jones, 2016)

A GP, Dr Phil Whitaker, wrote angrily about the *unexamined changes* proposed to general practice in England:

> *The government is determinedly pushing GPs to 'work at scale' creating 'super-practices' serving anywhere between 30,000 and 100,000 patients. We are sleepwalking into a world of GP services being provided by huge health centres where your next appointment is with Dr AN Other, who you've never seen before and will probably never see again.* (Whitaker, 2018)

Whatever the advantages the Department of Health and NHS England think 'super-practices' will bring, there will be much lost – and also a detrimental effect on outcome – if continuity for patients is not taken seriously. Just as important, the organisational structure and change process needs to take into account staff's needs for stable relationships, a prerequisite for them to sustain themselves and work to the best of their ability.

Considering trends in modern corporations, Susan Long, Professor of Creative and Sustainable Organisations at the Royal Melbourne Institute of Technology University, Australia, warns:

> *During times of rapid change, alongside the breakdown of many institutional values comes an increase in uncertainty and anxiety, a questioning of identity, disenchantment and pain. In recent years, this has led to a narcissistic defence against these feelings, evidenced through isolation, withdrawal, instrumental attitudes to work and a sense of beating the system before it beats you.* (Long, 2008, p. 157)

These trends contain a tilt towards the agonic mode, and the roots of something worse – an agonistic world of conflict and brutality.

The nature of the problem goes further than simply the way in which people and change are managed. The attempts to improve and reform public services reflect and embody ideologies and attitudes that profoundly colour the 'organisation in the mind'

(Armstrong, 2005). In themselves – and especially when they are poorly managed – these tend to pull the work away from applied kinship, from attentive kindness to the people we work with, towards instrumentality, towards mechanical behaviour, and even towards neglect and active abuse.

References

Armstrong, D. (2005) *Organisation in the Mind: Psychoanalysis, Group Relations and Organizational Consultancy*. Karnac.

Bostock, L., Forrester, D., Patrizo, L., Godfrey, T., Zanouzish, M., Antonopoupou, V., Bird, M., Moreslesing, T. and Goldberg, T. (2017) Scaling and developing the Reclaiming Social Work model. Department of Education Children's Social Care Innovation Programme Evaluation Report, 45.

BBC (2018) *Dynasties*, broadcast 11 November, 2018.

Chamberlain, A. (1936) Lesson of the Crisis: Sir A. Chamberlain's Review of Events. *The Yorkshire Post*, 21 March, 1936, p. 11, column 7 (British Newspaper Archive).

Chance, M. R. A. (1988) *Social Fabrics of the Mind*. Lawrence Erlbaum Associates.

Cooper, A. and Dartington, T. (2004) The vanishing organisation. In *Working Below the Surface* (eds C. Huffington, D. Armstrong, W. Halton, et al), pp. 127–50. Karnac.

Cottam, H. (2018) *Radical Help: How We Can Remake Relationships Between Us and Revolutionise the Welfare State*. Virago.

Cunningham, I. and Nickson D. P. (2009) A Gathering Storm? Procurement, re-tendering and the voluntary sector social care workforce: a report for the voluntary social services workforce unit. University of Strathclyde, Glasgow. Available at: www.scvo.org.uk/policy-research/evidence-library/2009-a-gathering-storm-procurement-re-tendering-and-the-voluntary-sector-social-care-workforce [last accessed 11 August, 2019].

Dartington, T. (2010) *Managing Vulnerability: The Underlying Dynamics of Systems of Care*. Karnac.

Department of Education (2017) Children's Social Care Innovation Programme Evaluation Report, 49. Available at: https://assets.publishing.service.gov.uk/government/uploads/system/uploads/attachment_data/file/625374/Evaluation_of_Pause.pdf [last accessed 11 August, 2019].

Department of Health (2000) The NHS Plan. HMSO.

Department of Health (2010) Equity and Excellence: Liberating the NHS. Available at: www.gov.uk/government/publications/liberating-the-nhs-white-paper [last accessed 11 August, 2019].

Dyer, C. (2018) NHS accountable care organisations would be unlawful, campaigners tell High Court. British Medical Journal. 361: k1827.

Feldblum, J., Manfredi, S., Gilby, I. A., Pusey, A. (2018) The timing and causes of a unique chimpanzee community fission preceding Gombe's 'four-year war'. American Journal of Physical Anthropology. 22 March, 2018. Available at: www.doi.org/10.1002/ajpa.23462 [last accessed 11 August, 2019].

Francis, R. (2010) The Independent Inquiry into Care Provided by Mid-Staffordshire NHS Foundation Trust, January 2005–March 2009. HMSO.

Goodall, J. (1965) Chimpanzees of the Gombe Stream Reserve. In *Primate Behaviour* (ed. I. DeVore), pp. 425–73. Holt, Rinehart and Winston.

Ham, C. (2009) Lessons from the past decade for future health reforms. British Medical Journal. 339: b4372.

Healthcare Commission (2007) The Investigation Report into Clostridium Difficile at Maidstone and Tunbridge Wells NHS Trust. HMSO.

Hirschhorn, L. (1988) *The Workplace Within: Psychodynamics of Organisational Life*. MIT Press.

HM Government (2010) The Coalition: Our Programme for Government. Cabinet Office. Available at: www.cabinetoffice.gov.uk/media/409088/pfg_coalition.pdf [last accessed 11 August, 2019].

Humphries, R., Thorlby, R., Holder, H., Hall, P., and Charles, A. (2016) Social Care for

Older People. Home Truths. The King's Fund. Available at: www.kingsfund.org.uk/sites/default/files/field/field_publication_file/Social_care_older_people_Kings_Fund_Sep_2016.pdf [last accessed 11 August, 2019].

Janjua, A. (2014) Leadership Vacancies in the NHS: What Can Be Done About Them? The King's Fund.

Jones, R. (2016) 'I've seen the reclaiming social-work model cause serious implosion.' Available at: www.communitycare.co.uk/. . ./ive-seen-local-authorities-reclaiming-social-work-mode [last accessed 11 August, 2019].

Long, S. (2008) *The Perverse Organisation and Its Deadly Sins.* Karnac.

Menzies Lyth, I. (1959) The functions of social systems as a defence against anxiety: a report on a study of the nursing service of a general hospital. Human Relations. 13: 95–121. Reprinted in I. Menzies Lyth (1988) *Containing Anxiety in Institutions: Selected Essays*, Vol. I, pp. 43–88. Free Association Books.

Moberly, T. (2018) Scrap NHS competition rules, BMA says. British Medical Journal. 361: k2791.

National Audit Office (2010) Reorganising Central Government. HMSO.

National Audit Office (2016) The Troubled Families Programme Update Review. HMSO.

NHS England (2013) Putting Patients First: NHS England Business Plan 2013/2014–2015/2016. Available at: www.england.nhs.uk/wp-content/uploads/2013/04/ppf-1314-1516.pdf [last accessed 26 August, 2019].

Obholzer, A. (2019) Managing social anxieties in public sector organisations. In *The Unconscious at Work* 2nd edn. (eds A. Obhlzer and V. Zagier Roberts), pp. 174–83. Routledge.

Oxman, A., Sackett, D., Chalmers, I., et al (2005) A surrealistic meta-analysis of redisorganisation theories. Journal of the Royal Society of Medicine. 98: 563–8.

Peedell, C. (2011) Further privatisation is inevitable under the proposed NHS reforms. (Editorial.) British Medical Journal. 342: d2996.

Pereira Gray, D. J., Sidaway-Lee, K., White, E., Thorne, A., Evans, P. (2018) Continuity of care with doctors – a matter of life and death? A systematic review of continuity of care and mortality. British Medical Journal Open. **8**: e021161.doi:10.1136.

Power, M. D. (1988) The cohesive foragers: human and chimpanzee. In *Social Fabrics of the Mind* (ed. M. R. A. Chance), pp. 75–104. Lawrence Erlbaum Associates.

Smith, J., Walshe, K. and Hunter, D. (2001) The redisorganisation of the NHS. (Editorial.) British Medical Journal. 323: 1262–3.

Tammes, P. (2017) Continuity of primary care matters and should be protected. (Editorial.) British Medical Journal. 356: j373.

Walshe, K. (2010) Reorganisation of the NHS in England. (Editorial.) British Medical Journal. 341: c3843.

Whitaker, P. (2018) Finally, the NHS has realised: patient-doctor relationships should be partnerships, In *Health Matters. New Statesman*, 13–19 July, 2018, p. 60.

Chapter

10 Free to Serve the Public?

Ordered to be kind, we are likely to be cruel; wanting to be kind, we are likely to discover our generosity.

(Philips and Taylor, 2009)

Two Ways of Seeing

We probably all know the story. It may be apocryphal, but it sets our scene, and there are many similar examples. A mother sees her child run over by a car. Driven by her love, and her visceral drive to protect the infant, she rushes to the scene and, exercising strength far beyond what we should expect, seizes the bumper and lifts the vehicle off her child, thereby saving her from death or permanent disability. It's a high bar to reach, but it symbolises the power of action driven by concern for those closest to us. Graphically, it demonstrates the extra dimension that the 'kindness' inherent in kinship and the willingness and ability to apply oneself to the service of the other can bring to a situation of risk and vulnerability. It says that kindness moves mountains.

Now look at it another way. The mother made no risk assessment. She had no training in handling and lifting. She ignored the evidence that a car was unliftable. She intervened in a way that encroached upon the responsibilities of other services – the police, the fire brigade, the ambulance service. She almost certainly left other things unattended to – perhaps another child in the kitchen with a boiling pan on the stove, perhaps another made late for school. She didn't record the incident to enable later evaluation. She gave herself a back injury requiring care over the years, culminating in absence from work and several expensive operations. She was over-involved. She was irresponsible and out of control. The story surely illustrates the need for systems, skills, evidence, evaluation and regulation, and the cost of ill-managed care.

How do we read this contradictory picture? Almost certainly, we all feel that the remarkable act was the right one, and we would hope to be so transformed if it was our own child. Again, almost certainly, we would hope that we were always ready to 'go the extra mile' for our friends, our neighbours, our clients or our patients, although the bond, the sense of import and responsibility, and the actions we are ready and able to take, may diminish as we consider these groups. As our roles and responsibilities become more sophisticated or professional, we become aware of the need to ration our commitment, to distance and preserve ourselves sufficiently so we can offer the most to the many.

Accountable for working with the many, however much we pride ourselves on attending to the individual, we naturally look to evidence, to trends, to statistically analysed choices to help us decide what to do. Working with the many, we are exposed to risk and anxiety day after day. We know we get tired, we know we might make mistakes. We know problems are complex, and require, in turn, the deployment of a range of sophisticated, evidence-based professional skills and interventions. We know that skills and resources are limited and need organising for the best benefit. We want to share the responsibility; we want things to be managed.

At the heart of the issue is a tension between the types of thinking and feeling required to focus on kind, person-centred care on the one hand, and the thinking required to provide standardised, risk managed, and well-regulated care on the other. We need to understand this tension if we are to maximise the potential for improvements in effectiveness, efficiency and patient satisfaction. Reading our story above, most readers will be able to imagine the feelings of the mother if anyone were to interrupt her in full flight to require her to follow 'procedures' – and perhaps what would happen to her child should she delay. The example is emotive and extreme: and it is of course a 'story', but it does draw attention to the predicament of every staff member who must work within the tension between being free to act as an individual in response to the needs of the person in their care, whilst being accountable and following rules.

For many years society has, to a large extent, placed its hopes for better health and social care in the realm of structural and regulatory reform. The narrative has been one of standardisation and target setting, regulation, and performance management: doing things efficiently, applying evidence, inspecting and being inspected. Much less has been thought and said about how these processes influence the mind-set and culture of organisations and their staff, or about their effects on the conditions for effective and efficient kindness.

Free to Serve the Public

Hilary Cottam, already introduced, writes despairingly about the management culture across the Welfare State.

> *The welfare state was the foundation stone of post-war society: it gave us both practical support and a sense of who we could be. But today this once life-changing project is out of kilter. It has become a management state: an elaborate and expensive system of managing needs and their accompanying risks. Those of us who need care, who can't find work, who are sick or less able are moved around as if in a game of pass the parcel: assessed, referred and then assessed again. Everyone suffers in a system where 80 per cent of the resource available must be spent on gatekeeping, on managing the queue, on referring individuals from service to service, on recording every interaction to ensure that no one is responsible for those who inevitably fall through the gaps.* (Cottam, 2018, pp. 12–13)

Cottam may be guilty of exaggeration and over-generalisation, but most of us will be able to recognise the truth in what she describes. How has this state of affairs come about and, most importantly, how do we free-up staff to better help the vulnerable people in their care?

The American psychologist Barry Schwartz tells the following story:

> *When a group of psychologists interviewed hospital janitors to get a sense of what they thought their jobs were like, they encountered Mike, who told them about how he stopped mopping the floor because Mr Jones was out of his bed getting a little exercise, trying to build up his strength, walking slowly up and down the hall. And Charlene told them about how she ignored her supervisor's admonition and didn't vacuum the visitors' lounge, because there were some family members who were there all day, every day who, at this moment, happened to be taking a nap. And then there was Luke, who washed the floor in a comatose young man's room twice because the man's father, who had been keeping a vigil for six months, didn't see Luke do it the first time, and was angry.* (Schwartz, 2009)

Schwartz concludes:

> *Behaviour like this . . . doesn't just make people feel a little better, it actually improves the quality of patient care and enables hospitals to run well.* (Schwartz video presentation available at: www.ted.com/talks/barry_schwartz_on_our_loss_of_wisdom.html)

None of the job descriptions for these people, and none of the specifications for their tasks, described such behaviour. Although the hospital cleaners' job description no doubt listed tasks that would minimise the risk of hospital-acquired infections, of slips and falls, and so on, nowhere was there a reference, says Schwartz, to people. It is also clear that an inspection 'against specification' would have found shortcomings in performance and, in at least Charlene's case, may have resulted in disciplinary action.

Cleaners may have a lot to teach us. There is a tale about Bill Clinton making a visit to NASA. He encountered a janitor in an anteroom and, being a sociable sort of president, asked him what he did. 'I help people get to the moon', replied the clearly very focused and motivated 'ancillary' worker. The janitor showed clear focus on the primary task, the overall purpose, of the enterprise, and knew what – and how – his work contributed. He sounds proud, and the sort of person who would clean rather thoroughly.

The direct acts of kindness so appreciated by patients and service-users do not come about either from unfocused goodwill, or from the carrying out of prescribed 'kind' tasks: they emerge from a state of ongoing openness to, and empathy for, other people and their experiences, attentiveness to what is happening, and a readiness to respond with intelligent, kind action. They are less dramatic than the actions of the mother in our story, but are driven by similar kinship and connectedness. This is also true for Schwartz's cleaners – whose actions, driven by empathy and generosity, were indirect and may not even have been noticed by anyone looking at how people were interacting with the patients. Somehow, they were keeping the person and their ill-being in mind, and retaining the capacity to act as persons themselves, while carrying out an officially delineated task. They saw what mattered to the patient and those around them and shaped their actions accordingly. They also seemed clear about how their actions might affect the overall task of the ward, and were confident enough to act accordingly. However much Clinton's janitor friend might walk past 'vision statements' reminding everyone that they are there to get to the moon, it is only if he understands the links between his task and the team goal, only if he believes he is valued, only if he is treated in a way that accords with the team vision, that he will genuinely feel that his contribution is vital, and pay attention to the environment and his fellows accordingly.

In considering how to promote kindness we are talking, in essence, about four things:

- how to promote and sustain compassionate bearing in mind of the other;
- how to generate imaginative understanding of the contribution a person's actions can make to others' wellbeing;
- how to instil and support a confident belief in a person's own value and freedom to act;
- how to ensure that individuals have the knowledge and repertoire to act skilfully and compassionately according to circumstances.

However important the framework of policy, regulation and performance management for services, there are difficult questions to be faced about whether they are creating these conditions for kindness. These questions require response and management.

Industrialisation

A key feature of the modern organisation of services is their 'industrialisation'. Steve Iliffe, a Professor of General Practice in London, has considered this trend in relation to medicine (Iliffe, 2008). He likens the pattern of change in the late twentieth and early twenty-first century to the transformation of manufacturing from a set of craft disciplines to industrial process in the late nineteenth and early twentieth century. Concentrating particularly on general practice, he writes:

> *Medicine is changing from a craft concerned with the uniqueness of each encounter with an ill person to a mass-manufacturing industry preoccupied with the throughput of the sick.* (p. 3)

These changes have been driven in part by the increase in complexity of medical care. It is useful to remember that the vast majority of therapeutic interventions and diagnostic technologies have been invented since the middle of the last century. Before this, medical professionals used their clinical acumen to make diagnoses, but had few therapeutic interventions at their disposal, apart from some basic medication and surgery. Less dramatic but still significant, the diversity of vulnerability and sheer scale of modern cities bring increasing complexity and demand a broader skill set from those offering social interventions. In the public sector, having so much more on offer brings the need to manage resources and demand in a way that ensures an equitable and efficient service for all. A necessary focus on the improvement of the health and wellbeing of the whole population can lead to a loss of focus on the care of individuals and their families.

It is worth looking in more detail at the processes of industrialisation as they affect professional care. Iliffe describes how industrial approaches to ensure efficient working practice and manage the organisation of production processes are characterised by six activities summarised in Box 10.1 below (Iliffe, 2008, p. 41). Practitioners throughout the 'Welfare State' will recognise some, if not all, of these as active in their workplace.

Iliffe's view in 2008 was that we were undergoing a qualitative change in the delivery of services, a change that had its own internal logic and dynamics. There is heated debate about such things as targets and financial incentives, but a failure to recognise these as

Box 10.1 The Characteristics of Industrialisation

1. The central codification of knowledge: an increasing tendency to replace a range of professional opinion and individual experience with the development of 'evidence-based' protocols.
2. The standardisation of tools that direct the activities undertaken by practitioners.
3. The subdivision of labour: usually driven by cost-savings.
4. Machines replace human skills.
5. Incentive payments that reward certain activities rather than others.
6. Faster, time-limited work processes.

Summarised from Iliffe (2008)

symptoms of change on a much larger scale. While Iliffe saw the logic and some advantages of this change – and indeed concludes his book by appealing to GPs to engage with and influence the process – he did worry that it could lead to a constricted, impersonal work style, with limited responsiveness to individuals:

> *The process of change is not a mere reorganisation, but a transformation of an activity from a loosely organised enterprise with a poorly defined remit and wide scope for individual initiative, interpretation and innovation, into a predictable and prescribed series of tasks in the management of the public's health. It is creating anxieties among professionals about power, autonomy, and patient-centredness as well as concern among citizens about the motivation of professionals.* (p. 7)

Iliffe illustrates a central problem. If people need to be 'free to serve' for effective kindness to be achieved, how can the consequences of industrialisation – the danger of pulling their attention in quite the opposite direction – be minimised?

Drivers for Mediocrity

Iliffe is not the only author to draw attention – or, indeed, to mourn – the move from craftsmanship to mass industrialisation. Richard Sennett, Professor of Sociology at the London School of Economics and former University Professor of the Humanities at New York University, draws on pre-industrial models of craftsmanship to suggest that good work must include a degree of autonomy, the chance to develop skills and exercise judgements. He argues that doing something well for its own sake with an integral technique of constant improvement is a capacity most human beings possess, but the skill is not honoured in modern society as it should be: '*The Craftsman in all of us needs to be freed*' (Sennett, 2012, p. ix).

There is a great deal of evidence that individual improvement is more reliably nurtured in an environment that encourages inherent reward rather than a system of external reward and punishment. Despite this, our public services continue to develop systems of external measurement, reward and punishment. Whatever improvements such systems bring, they can discourage that drive to do our very best.

'Benchmarking' is an (industrially sourced) approach to systematising, ensuring equity and improving practice. The premise is that, to support standardisation, one can compare specific parts of wider systems of care.

Of course, systems vary from area to area – in cost and process, the skills deployed and the 'tools' made available, often in response to factors such as differences in geography and demography. Thus, comparison of simple 'benchmarks' may misrepresent a complex situation. This is a familiar argument to anyone who has considered the early-twenty-first-century vogue for 'ratings' and 'league tables', be it of schools, social services or hospitals: despite the dangers of the approach, such measures have become prevalent in many sectors of public life.

There is an inevitable distortion once an enterprise becomes valued primarily in terms of specific, concrete outcomes. Energy and attention becomes focussed on these to the exclusion of other important things. Such 'collateral damage' to all that is unmeasured may deplete other systems and services, on top of the cost of the benchmarking process itself.

As well as the dangers of undermining wider local systems in this way, there is a risk of 'benchmarking to mediocrity'. Benchmarks cannot be set at the level of the highest: or most services would fail them. They need to be achievable, given the variable and relatively low levels of investment in some services nationally. Once achieved, however, there is no further incentive to progress in that area, and attention can be diverted elsewhere, or, more likely, cuts may be proposed by higher tiers of management because it is felt that over-performing services can 'absorb' them.

Rigid thinking, and the absence of genuine understanding of the system into which a new idea is to be introduced, has damaging effects on services and people. It is perhaps inevitable that a large-scale health and social care system needs to industrialise and standardise, but this requires careful handling to mitigate the risks of turning people into objects or numbers. Moreover, it is far worse when the industrialising process is idealised, misunderstood and misapplied in ways that would dismay an expert industrialist or manufacturer.

If techno-centric industrial processes are allowed to create an impersonal, deskilled, rule-driven environment, staff may readily feel like tools and machines, and users of services may feel objectified. The roll-out of such an environment risks reducing choice and agency, and de-personalising the work of the staff member.

Paradoxically, it was just as this movement towards standardised industrial process was first gathering force, under the 'New Labour' administration in 2005, that a parallel emphasis was being put, in the NHS, on 'choice' and personalisation for the patient, through such initiatives as 'Choose and Book', where people were offered an apparent choice of hospitals for referral. Such choice appeared rather hollow in subsequent years, as significant financial pressures were placed on GPs not to refer at all. Such contradictions, which are often all too apparent to patients as well as staff, can undermine trust in NHS staff and services. Some sections of the public then begin to see a choice between impersonal public healthcare, explicitly systematised, governed by industrial measures, and rationed, and the privileged customer transactions of private medicine. Of course, private health services have their own clear vulnerability to poor practice and abuse, with the inevitable colouring of the relationship when the patient is a paying customer, who is both 'always right' and susceptible to persuasion and misinformation.

There is clearly also the potential for industrialisation to undermine a professional's autonomy and sense of freedom to attend to the person in front of them, with a consequent breakdown in trust between them. Undertaken with a limited and fragmentary understanding of the complexity of health and social care systems, and with insufficient flexibility, industrialisation can become destructive.

Accompanying all these changes, there has been one over-riding, and largely unquestioned idea – that welfare-related work in our public sector is a set of specific processes requiring regulation and performance management. Like industrialisation itself, regulation is seen as inevitable and largely desirable. However, it is not a neutral process: how it is constructed and managed, how it influences the behaviour of what is being regulated, and the general culture of regulation, all have profound effects. Essentially, this is a question of how staff are enabled to manage a balance between the demands of accountability, and attentive response to the people they are caring for. Unless this is understood, and borne in mind, the effects of regulation on people's capacity for intelligent kindness can be devastating.

The Culture of Suspicion

Trust is integral to the culture of kindness. How much we feel we are trusted, and how much we trust others, affects our capacity to trust ourselves and act compassionately. Social attitude surveys have shown that trust has been steadily on the decline in the UK since it was first measured in 1983 (Park et al, 2013). In 2009 the prominent British head teacher and author Anthony Seldon described a move from a presumption of trust to a presumption of mistrust (Seldon, 2009): distrust becoming the default position. He linked this to the move from seeing ourselves as citizens to seeing ourselves as consumers, a shift encouraged by the rhetoric of our public institutions at the time.

The philosopher Onora O'Neill discussed trust in the 2002 BBC Reith Lectures. Her view was that despite frequent news stories about (sometimes genuinely) scandalous cases involving public servants, in fact there was surprisingly little systematic evidence of growing untrustworthiness. Nonetheless, the culture of insatiable accountability and regulation was promoted as the way to reduce untrustworthiness and to secure ever more perfect control of institutional and professional performance. O'Neill concluded that such 'accountability' did not in fact reduce attitudes of mistrust. Rather, it has reinforced a culture of suspicion:

> *We have misdiagnosed what ails British society and we are now busy prescribing copious draughts of the wrong medicine . . . requiring those in the public sector and the professions to account in excessive and sometimes irrelevant detail to regulators and inspectors, auditors and examiners.* (O'Neill, 2002, p. 16)

O'Neill points to the need to give up 'childish fantasies that we can have total guarantees of others' performances' and urges us 'to free professionals and their public services to serve the public' (p. 59).

Staff feel this societal mistrust and suspicion both at a general level and in their encounter with the complex systems of control within which they work. This experience, of the need to allay suspicion, to fend off criticism, constantly threatens to undermine the conditions for 'freedom to serve'. It falls to leaders, managers and those governing health and social care organisations to develop strategies for 'buffering' this culture of suspicion, for creating an optimistic, trusting milieu within which staff can work creatively. This does not mean abandoning accountability: it means working to minimise the toxic effects of the suspicion implicit in it, and the ever-present fear of blame and shame, to be discussed in the next chapter.

Obscure Accountability

Clearly, the many shortcomings that inspection has revealed do not inspire confidence, and reinforce the case for standards and accountability. However, the question that follows is where accountability lies, and to whom. Onora O'Neill recognised the importance of this:

> *. . . underlying the ostensible aim of accountability to the* ***public****, the real requirements are for accountability* ***to regulators, to departments of government, to funders, to legal standards****. The new forms of accountability impose forms of central control – quite often indeed a range of different and mutually inconsistent forms of central control.*
> (O'Neill, 2002, p. 53, original emphasis)

Consider the predicament that confronted one of the authors when she was working as a consultant psychiatrist and clinical director (Box 10.2):

Box 10.2 Confused Accountability

There is a new requirement that all out-patients as well as in-patients should have an ICD-10 diagnostic code entered into the data system from the first appointment onwards. The message from my managers is that there is no option on this one. Now this might seem a reasonable enough demand, and indeed for many medical specialties would pose no problem at all, but the issue of diagnosis in some areas of psychiatry is a tricky one. Colleagues who run the drug and alcohol service, for example, are reluctant to have to stick such sensitive information on computerised medical records (increasingly available for scrutiny by employers and insurance companies). Reasonably enough they have asked for reassurance that it is possible to have a diagnosis removed once it no longer applies, but have received no response.

In the personality disorder service, we have always been wary of labelling our patients with a diagnosis many see as stigmatising. The diagnosis is based on the presence of a collection of behavioural symptoms such as self-harm, rather vague relationship patterns such as fear of abandonment and inner feelings such as identity confusion. Many of our patients manage to develop better ways of coping and no longer fulfil the criteria by the time they are discharged. It is generally considered poor professional practice to label people below the age of 21 with such a diagnosis, as their personalities are still forming and who would want to be stuck with a diagnosis based on their behaviour as an adolescent? Even with patients where the diagnosis is appropriate, I would usually take my time to get to know the person, wanting to assure myself that the symptoms were enduring rather than a reaction to recent trauma and wanting to rule out other diagnoses. Forging a trusting relationship with our patients is all important and a clumsily imposed diagnosis could easily make it a non-starter.

So what to do? Stick to my ground, risk financial penalties and perhaps attract suspicion to the service? Swallow my professional judgement and, if challenged by an understandably angry patient, wipe my hands of the decision and blame 'the system'? Distract the patients from therapy and encourage them to protest?

Personal reflection – Penny Campling, 2011

This story illustrates how central demands to specify and count can actually put pressure on a practitioner to behave unprofessionally – to place accountability to regulators before responsibility to the client or patient. The incompatible requirement invites compromise and evasion. The rationale for the requirement includes greater accountability and transparency. Funders want to know more about what they are paying for, and whether resources are going to the right people, so they can make decisions about future commissioning. There is nothing so wrong with that. But it is difficult to see how this will benefit the individual in need. They have certainly not asked for the information or been consulted on the requirement, and are, we know, concerned about confidentiality.

Detailed, concrete regulatory frameworks are not only problematic in themselves. Their requirements 'outrank' professional judgement, and divide loyalties for the worker between service-user and funder, between public and government. This risks undermining personalised care, and paradoxically makes personal accountability more elusive. A further complication is that the source and authority for the demand can be hard to locate, making discussion and debate difficult, if not impossible. The 'source' is often actually a tangled web of professional, policy, commissioning, contracting and information technology bodies and interests.

Thus regulation may create, and then occur within, a mistrustful culture. The demands of regulators can be at odds with the care actually needed, and the system frequently makes it hard for staff to negotiate these problems. Regulation also involves competition – through league tables, outcome comparisons, performance rankings and so on. In organisations infused with anxiety about competition within a market, this mix of driving forces can strengthen a 'pull towards perversion', which will be looked at in more detail in Chapter 12.

The Dangers of Performance Targets

Extreme cases tell an obvious story. There are performance-driven activities that can cause significant harm, and even lead to death, especially when they operate within a culture of mistrust. The drive to cut costs while meeting targets for waiting times in accident and emergency departments was apparently translated in the Mid-Staffordshire Trust into actions that included delegating, albeit unofficially, complex triage responsibilities to unqualified reception staff. The trust reduced ward staffing catastrophically, despite staff protest. Some are likely to have died as a consequence, and many suffered indignities that verged on the barbaric (Francis, 2010).

There are other activities that increase risk, obscure and mislead. As O'Neill pointed out, the real enemy of trust is deception. The most vivid examples of such deception have been evident in healthcare. In the face of waiting time targets, some hospitals reduced 'trolley waits' by such measures as re-designating hitherto non-clinical areas, so that they could (meaninglessly) take 'admissions'. Some introduced 'hello nurses' – who did little more than greet the patient – to obscure the fact that people still waited for genuine assessment. Ambulances waited to bring patients into the emergency department to avoid 'starting the clock', and having them recorded as waiting too long after arrival. In other places, people simply cheated, and figures relating to targets were 'massaged'. Hospital managers deliberately misrepresented records to make their performance look better. Such practices appear to have been widespread:

> *More than 6,000 patients suffered when hospital managers deliberately massaged waiting list data to hide the fact that they were missing government targets for shorter queues. Some patients were forced to wait much longer than they should have done and Nigel Crisp, the chief executive of the NHS, has accepted that the health of some may have deteriorated.*
> (House of Commons Public Accounts Committee, 2002)

Such stories demonstrate behaviour that damages the enterprise of improving – at times even delivering – care. The stories involve many people's participation. They illustrate the danger of approaches driven by concrete target or performance indicators, unmitigated by ethics, disconnected from the reality of the service-user's need and experience. Some showed the effects of high anxiety and panic, scarcely contained and leaking out into desperate unconsidered action. Some were just unreflective, unsubtle and unhelpful.

Extreme examples are not the norm, although there were probably more cases than have come to light. However, they are extremes of a spectrum: the dynamics they illustrate are present wherever governance, performance and quality management are less dramatically, but no less clumsily, (mis)handled.

Unintended Consequences

There is evidence that, besides supporting improvement, target- or indicator-driven activities can have a range of unhelpful unintended effects. This is hardly a new insight. Researchers from the University of York and the University of St Andrews reported a range of possible consequences in 2000, which are helpful to bear in mind (Box 10.3).

Steve Iliffe covered similar ground in *From General Practice to Primary Care*, describing the risks of a system where economic factors outweigh professional imperatives in shaping GPs' behaviour. He describes three main risks: poor performance in domains where performance is not measured; hitting the target but missing the point; and

Box 10.3 Adverse Effects of a Target Culture

- **'tunnel vision'** – concentration on areas that are included in the performance indicator scheme, to the exclusion of other important areas;
- **'suboptimisation'** – the pursuit of narrow local objectives by managers, at the expense of the objectives of the organisation as a whole;
- **'myopia'** – concentration on short-term issues, to the exclusion of long-term change that may show up in performance measures only in many years' time;
- **'measure fixation'** – focusing on what is measured rather than the outcomes intended;
- **'complacency'** – a lack of motivation for improvement when comparative performance is deemed adequate;
- **'ossification'** – the organisational paralysis that can arise from an excessively rigid system of measurement;
- **'misrepresentation'** – the deliberate manipulation of data, including 'creative' accounting and fraud, so that reported behaviour differs from actual behaviour;
- **'gaming'** – altering behaviour so as to obtain strategic advantage.

(Goddard et al, 2000)

discrepancies in data recording (Iliffe, 2008, p. 112). Even Professor Chris Ham, health policy academic, head of the King's Fund from 2010 to 2018, and a strong advocate of performance targets, acknowledged the dangers of disempowering front-line staff, stifling innovation and overloading the organisations providing care to patients (Ham, 2009). To this list of dangers we might add cynicism, disengagement and low morale in staff, and anxiety and mistrust in patients.

The systems thinker John Seddon comprehensively savaged the public sector target-driven 'system reform' approach in his book *Systems Thinking in the Public Sector* (Seddon, 2008). He is a proponent of a 'pure systems' approach, centring on constant attempts to understand and improve the process of delivering 'consumer value', rather than on externally imposed performance standards. Seddon warned that a focus on standardisation means services cannot meet the inevitably varied circumstances and needs of the individual 'customer'. This plants the seeds of longer-term failure while making short-term, small 'improvements' in performance. Seddon, echoing many of the York findings above, identified a number of problems, detailed in Box 10.4. These are not conditions likely to promote the perceptive, generous, autonomous and person-focused behaviour demonstrated by Schwartz's cleaners.

Box 10.4 Pathologies of Target Cultures

- Cheating;
- Placing the interests of the (political and regulatory) regime before those of the people who need the service;
- A focus on transactions and activity – in terms of quantity, timing and cost – instead of upon understanding what is of value to the 'customer' and examining the effectiveness of how the organisation delivers it or fails to do so;
- Fragmentation of the way in which a service works to meet user need;
- Added cost, in that attention to fragmented activity misses paying attention to fundamental wasted or misdirected effort;
- A command-and-control approach to management;
- A culture that sees people as requiring rules, direction, even coercion, rather than being motivated and intelligent about their work, identifying and solving problems, and being flexible in the variety of ways they need to work to deliver what service-users need;
- Diminished initiative and imagination, empty conformism and rote behaviour.

Seddon, 2008

An alternative approach would pass the responsibility and power of inspection into the hands of those delivering the service, and reduce the split between them and a scrutinising and regulatory management. Management would focus on intelligent intervention within the system to address problems and opportunities identified by, but beyond the control of, individual staff or functions. Seddon proposed a culture wherein the commitment, intelligence and goodwill of front-line staff are recognised and fostered, and where attention and resources are constantly focused on how successful the service is in meeting user need, and on solving problems. If there are to be measures, they should derive from the work towards offering value, not from a form of top-down engineering.

Such a culture is more likely to sustain and promote attentive, kind work than one which mistrusts and reduces the autonomy of staff, and which overwhelms them with excessive demands to count and measure activity for the sake of fragmented targets or standards. Such a culture does not over-specify a list of things that should be done – though it fosters the use of effective methods of audit. This is not a model that sees the delivery of, say, a written care plan, an offer of choice, a review meeting or the giving of a personalised budget as in itself evidence of quality and value. They may all be valuable in any one of many cases, but the emphasis is not on illustrating quality by counting such inputs, nor promoting value by focussing staff on delivering a list of them.

As O'Neill (2002) advises, intelligent accountability requires paying more attention to good governance, and the obligation to tell the truth. It is important to distinguish here between two extremes in the culture of governance. One, increasingly dominant, absorbs time, work, money and attention in the process of developing more and more policies and procedures – that demonstrate how (though not automatically that) the organisation will meet a dizzying range of external demands. The other creates the space for reflective critical attention to the work of delivering value to the service-user – and enables front-line staff genuinely and directly to regulate their own work.

Good governance is only possible if institutions, and their staff, are allowed some margin for self-governance, of a form appropriate to their particular task. There should certainly be a place for professionals and institutions to be called to account, but this must not be at the cost of their not being free, and feeling discouraged from addressing the quality of their services directly.

A More Facilitative Model

One standardisation project that tried hard to avoid some of the unintended consequences described above was the Quality Improvement Network of Therapeutic Communities (Haigh and Tucker, 2004). Importantly, this was a collaborative partnership, in this case between the Royal College of Psychiatrists' Research Unit (RCPRU) and the Association of Therapeutic Communities. The RCPRU has since rolled out the approach with other partner organisations to include residential facilities for people with intellectual disabilities, care homes for elderly people and psychiatric intensive-care units. Two nurses involved in the project described their experience as follows:

> *The first year was really difficult. We'd had quality monitoring visits before, organised by the Trust and the Health Authority, but they tended to be a bit irritating with lots of questions that seemed irrelevant and sometimes the reports just showed how little they'd understood about therapeutic communities and the patients we work with. So signing up to be part of this new quality network seemed an awful lot of extra work and we were all a bit defensive and worried about explaining what we do to outsiders. Because everyone was anxious, it was very much left up to senior staff to present things. But if your therapeutic community is involved in the project, you also get to send two staff members and two service-users (along with someone working for the Network) to visit another unit and that was really interesting because you get to see how others do things and realise there are some things we could improve but other things we do really well. In general, we find we always miss out the achievements and have a tendency to mark ourselves down. It's hard when you're working day-in, day-out, to see the progress.*
>
> *Each year it comes round, we feel more confident and it sort of frees us up to think afresh about things. After the first year, we made the decision to involve everyone at*

every stage of the process – that's all the staff and all the members [service-users]. It's nice to have the chance to welcome people and show them what we do and getting the feedback at the end of the day, usually leaves us in a real buzz! Despite the exhaustion! It's not that all the feedback is positive, but the criticism is usually about things we know we're not so good at and it often comes with helpful suggestions.

It's so useful to take time out to struggle with the big questions: why do we do it like that? Who has authority to make decisions? What do we want to do different next year? What are we proud of? And to be honest, we probably wouldn't do that in the same way without a bit of a push! It's really helpful to have the members involved. It seems really important that we step back and look at what we do with the people we do it for. It also makes them [the service-users] question things and often they come up with really useful suggestions. Sometimes it helps them get things in perspective, specially when they meet patients from other units and compare notes! And the visits to other units with them are a really good shared experience. We also send a few staff and patient reps to the annual Quality Network event in London which is a chance to talk about our experience and influence the process for the following year. (Sara Moore and Juanna York, Francis Dixon Lodge, Leicester, in personal communication)

Box 10.5 **Principles of the 'Quality Improvement Network' of Therapeutic Communities**

- It is an organic process, sensitive to feedback from front-line staff and users of services.
- Collaboration is reflected upon throughout the system.
- Extensive consultation occurs from the start of the project, with the original set of standards suggested by front-line staff and service-users and a lengthy piloting stage.
- Standards reflect aspirations of staff and the people they serve, who are encouraged to develop them further.
- Areas of excellence are encouraged and cascaded through the network.
- Standards are tailored to a particular client group.
- The emphasis is on encouraging development of the particular service and learning from each other.
- All standards are written in accessible, jargon-free language.
- Ownership of the system is encouraged by the holding of regular stakeholder events and the involvement of staff and service-users in visiting other units.

(Haigh and Tucker, 2004)

Some of the factors that define this particular project and contribute to it being a positive experience are highlighted in Box 10.5. While the processes described demanded a lot of staff time, the effort was clearly felt to be worthwhile and relevant, and the investment is dwarfed by what goes into funding the staff who administer 'top-down' governance.

Refining the Approach

The coalition government that came to power in 2010 made much of its aim of reducing bureaucracy within the English NHS, retaining only 'valuable' targets and moving to specifying and measuring 'outcomes' that embed quality and patient experience at the heart of regulation (Department of Health, 2010). There was a lot to commend in these proposals, but everything depended on whether they could be translated into a radical change in the culture. For a long time, the mind-set among regulators, commissioners and managers had appeared coloured by mistrust and the quest to control, expressed through the invasive and fragmented specification, measurement and policing behaviour that we have described. These attitudes were not simply going to go away. It was telling that, in the face of what had happened in Mid-Staffordshire, the headline government response in 2013 was to propose 'A new, rigorous inspection regime . . . for hospitals, GPs and adult social care' (we will explore the implications of this choice of focus as part of a wider argument in Chapter 13).

So, the culture was not going to change readily. The temptation to measure, and thus drive, disconnected processes persisted. The imbalance towards a certain type of concrete 'accountability', and away from responsiveness, remained uncorrected.

If there can be a genuine move to capture outcomes that have meaning for people and the staff who care for them, then the space to change may open up. However, it would still require a cultural paradigm shift, in order to transform governance to facilitate reflective ownership of quality and performance management by the staff involved, driven by the needs of service-users. Attention would need to be paid to understanding and addressing the workload pressure, the distractions from task, and the emotions and attitudes evoked by an overwhelming regulatory agenda at the front-line of service delivery. This would also require a considerable shift in resources.

There are a range of active discourses in health and social care services – and in the approach to their improvement. Some are derived from industrial thinking, some from engineering, some from the natural sciences, and some from complexity theory. Some are professional discourses, and some are simply political or personal styles and preferences. Some are in conflict. Many, if not mitigated by some form of humanising and value-based process, will skew and damage the art of care-giving. Such dangers will always be present, and it would be unrealistic to expect the conflict between regulatory approaches and good practice entirely to disappear. Careful attention to the balance between regulation and autonomy is needed.

There is nothing inherently wrong, for example, with having to 'tick boxes'. In defence of checklists – often seen as an irritation and an interference – Atul Gawande, the American surgeon, writer and public health researcher, points out that *'our stupendous know-how has outstripped our individual ability to deliver its benefits correctly'* (Gawande, 2009). He emphasises the fallibility of human memory and attention, and the difficulties of consistently and correctly applying the vast knowledge we have accrued. In the face of this much information, it is hard to argue against some attempt to distil what is likely to be important into the form of guidelines – and checklists if necessary. But Gawande's checklist message comes with a simple warning:

> *An inherent tension exists between brevity and effectiveness. Cut too much and you won't have enough checks to improve care. Leave too much in and the list becomes too long to use.*

Gawande also stresses the importance of teamwork (*'hand-overs should be a team huddle'*) and places the checklist clearly in this context: *'Just ticking boxes is not the ultimate goal here – embracing a culture of teamwork and discipline is'.*

This simple discussion of one aspect of regulation captures some important principles:

- there is a fine balance between steadying autonomy with some form of external reference point, and overwhelming the system with too many demands and too much information;
- it is important to keep the larger picture in mind, and how the part fits with the whole;
- any form of regulation will affect important relationships, either positively or negatively;
- open, honest and disciplined teamwork should be central, making use of, rather than accountable to, regulation.

Perverse, destructive or ineffectual attitudes and behaviours clearly do not derive only, or even mainly, from standardisation, targets, inspection and regulation. Individuals, teams and organisations vary. Many people, after all, are not corrupted by having to measure performance, or by having to compete. Many can keep a reasonable eye open for the wood when they are being forced to count the trees. Many organisations have managed to address targets and minimise the risk of distortion of the wider system. Until a worrying downward trend driven by 'austerity', thousands of people were relieved and grateful that they were able to receive the interventions they needed more speedily.

There has been evidence of well-set targets working: the incentives for GPs to actively monitor and treat blood pressure, for example, seemed to reduce the incidence of strokes (Iliffe, 2008, pp. 114–15). However, a pattern emerged of rapid improvement followed by a plateau in achievement, together with evidence of 'crowding out' of non-incentivised aspects of care (NHS England, 2018): so as we have discussed, the effects were not as straightforward as initially thought.

More encouragingly, the Reclaiming Social Work project set the explicit target of reducing the number of children being taken into care. The project supported this aim with the associated target of reducing the time spent by practitioners on administrative, bureaucratic work and instead increasing time spent working with clients and their families. Their efforts bore fruit (Munro, 2011). Such successes should not be forgotten; however, we need always to be vigilant as to whether the focus on any single target does not undermine other aspects of care. A balance must be found.

Finding the Balance

With the exponential growth of information technology since the 1990s, we can now collect and analyse detailed data on a scale hitherto impossible. Unless seismic cultural change takes place, such data will remain available, inviting analysis and in many cases bringing progress in its wake. We may look back nostalgically to a time that ran at a different pace, when the technical and administrative demands were not in any way so intense, and when staff did not feel constantly vulnerable to measurement and criticism. But the task for leaders is to attend to the adverse effects of the modern environment, whilst retaining the benefits. We do not need 'another swing of the pendulum', which will not occur in any case, however long we wait: the IT genie is out of the bottle. Whatever its costs and benefits, staff will remain under pressure to record and account for their activities.

The challenge is to find ways to promote the intelligent kindness required to mitigate the potential damage of a simplistic, concrete approach to data and to prevent 'cherry-picking' for political purposes. This challenge involves recognising the uncomfortable reality that the industrialisation of services, and associated monitoring and regulatory processes, however expertly applied, will always tend to draw staff attention away from here-and-now possibilities for effective kindness. Better to develop ways of helping staff manage the tension, than to wait for it to go away.

The individual worker, indeed the team or organisation, is pulled between responding and attending to specific, present, need or difficulty, and paying attention to standardisation and regulation. On the one hand, staff must recognise the personhood, vulnerability and ill-being of the unique people with whom they are working, and the anxieties and resonances evoked for them as human beings in their roles. On the other, workers must bear in mind, attend to and serve the needs of the data-gathering regime. Recognition of this tension is vital if we are to find intelligent ways of working that allow us to minimise the pull away from the people with whom we work. We must not let the pressure to produce impressive data over-define the creative choices of staff as they respond to their services-users' circumstances. The climate of 'reward and punishment', that the monitoring of such data brings in its wake, should not be allowed to lead us to lose touch with the inherent satisfaction of doing our best for another person.

References

Cottam, H. (2018) *Radical Help: How We Can Remake Relationships Between Us and Revolutionise the Welfare State*. Virago.

Department of Health (2010) Liberating the NHS: Transparency in Outcomes – A Framework for the NHS. Department of Health.

Francis, R. (2010) The Independent Inquiry into Care Provided by Mid-Staffordshire NHS Foundation Trust, January 2005–March 2009. HMSO.

Gawande, A. (2009) *The Checklist Manifesto: How to Get Things Right*. Profile Books. See also review by J. Quinn (2010) British Medical Journal. 340: c514.

Goddard, M., Mannion, R. and Smith, P. C. (2000) Enhancing performance in healthcare: a theoretical perspective on agency and the role of information. Health Economics. 9: 95–107.

Haigh, R. and Tucker, S. (2004) Democratic development of standards: the communities of communities – a quality network of therapeutic communities. Psychiatric Quarterly. 75; 263–77.

Ham, C. (2009) Lessons from the past decade for future health reforms. British Medical Journal. 339: b4372.

House of Commons Public Accounts Committee (2002) Inappropriate Adjustments to NHS Waiting Lists. 46th Report 2001–2002. HMSO.

Iliffe, S. (2008) *From General Practice to Primary Care: The Industrialization of Family Medicine*. Oxford University Press.

Munro, E. (2011) The Munro Review of Child Support: a Child Centred System. Department of Education. HMSO.

NHS England (2018) Report of the Review of the Quality and Outcomes Framework in England. Available at: www.england.nhs.uk/wp-content/uploads/2018/07/05-a-i-pb-04-07-2018-qof-report.pdf pp. 26–7 [last accessed 11 August, 2019].

O'Neill, O. (2002) *A Question of Trust*. The BBC Reith Lectures. Cambridge University Press.

Park, A., Bryson, C., Clery, E., Curtice, J. and Phillips, M. (2013) British Social Attitudes 30. Natcen Social Research.

Phillips, A. and Taylor, B. (2009) *On Kindness*. Penguin.

Schwartz, B. (2009) Our Loss of Wisdom. Video presentation at www.ted.com/talks/barry_schwartz_on_our_loss_of_wisdom.html) [last accessed 11 August, 2019].

Seddon, J. (2008) *Systems Thinking in the Public Sector*. Triarchy Press.

Seldon, A. (2009) *Trust: How We Lost It And How To Get It Back*. Biteback Publishing.

Sennett, R. (2012) *Together. The Rituals, Pleasures and Politics of Co-operation*. Allen Lane, Penguin.

Chapter

11 Blame

When you plant lettuce, if it does not grow well, you don't blame the lettuce. You look for reasons it is not doing well.

(Thich Nhat Hanh, 1991)

The 'Blame Culture'

Blaming comes naturally to us all. If something goes wrong we readily blame others, or ourselves, depending upon our character. This has some uses, and can be a meaningful way of analysing a situation. In its most neutral form, blame is a matter of attributing responsibility for a fault, or wrong. This might be positive if it leads to learning from experience: but blaming is usually more than a simple causal analysis. It allows retribution, the meting out of punishment, and it also has emotional consequences, which are punitive in their own right. Blaming is also sometimes termed 'naming and shaming', and shame is a powerful and distressing thing to feel.

Punishment might make sure the same thing does not happen again: a primitive form of education. There is, however, another powerful driver for blame, related to revenge: it allows the discharge of painful and powerful emotion by those who have been, or feel, injured. This may not only be by those who have directly suffered the injury or loss. Other people may be horrified by what has occurred, and feel empathically indignant. They might also have found an opportunity to vent feelings related to other grievances, or an outlet for some self-righteous sadism.

There is another very practical reason for blame, particularly in healthcare. We have a fault-based compensation system whereby, if you suffer a disabling injury, you may only get the wherewithal to deal with it by holding a person or organisation to account. If no-one is to blame, you could be pretty well on your own. This is not as stark in the UK as in the USA, as ongoing medical care from the NHS is free of charge, and we have other forms of 'social security' that are not available there: but as this social security has diminished over the years, fault-based compensation has been needed more.

Whereas legal aid was once available to medical negligence claimants in the UK, changes in 1995 substituted 'conditional fee arrangements', more popularly known as 'no win no fee'. This was headlined as saving costs, and widening access to justice for those who could not pay expensive legal fees. In the event it appears to have encouraged speculative claims. Modern communications have enabled wide reaching and persistent 'touting' for business by compensation lawyers, bringing cases against a wide range of public bodies and individuals. People have begun to claim compensation for a range of injuries, large and small, which they might otherwise have accepted philosophically.

Sensational reporting in the press, and other media, may also compound the situation. Such stories emphasise 'wrongdoing', and narratives that divide and demonise individuals, often from implicit positions of self-righteousness. Sometimes these stories have covert political agendas; sometimes they are just 'for the hell of it'. Naming, shaming and blaming are portrayed as self-evident civic virtues, with little concern or compassion for the consequences. There are many examples: some are cited within this book.

In this chapter we examine some of the manifestations of blame from the 'legalistic' to the 'angry pack' mentality, and its impact on health and social care. We are particularly concerned with its effect on staff and the culture within which they work. Nothing we say, however, should be read as ignoring the pain, loss and outrage that disappointed, damaged or bereaved people quite legitimately feel when things appear to have, or have actually, gone wrong.

Uncertainty and Self-Blame

Before exploring what happens when mistakes are suspected, and formal investigative processes come into play, it is worth digressing and reminding ourselves of the nature of the work: the uncertainty, the complexity of the problems, and the 'impossible' dilemmas faced by those working in health and social care. Inevitably, decisions are sometimes made that can be seen, in retrospect, to have made matters worse. Even when the situation is rapidly remedied, and does not require formal investigation, staff still struggle with feelings of self-doubt and self-blame. Such feelings may also be aroused (albeit irrationally) by distressing, but unavoidable, 'failures' of care – despite one's best efforts, someone suffers or dies. Some people may also feel responsible when staffing shortages mean that it is impossible to do the best for someone, because one is simply spread too thinly.

It can be an almost unbearably heavy burden to make intricate, uncertain interventions in high-risk situations, some of them 'life or death', whether mistakes are made or not. Inevitably, of course, mistakes do occur in such complex and high-pressure work. Often matters can be readily put right, or consequences are relatively minor. More rarely, but significantly, there may be terrible consequences, which can haunt the individuals involved for years.

Social workers have to engage with the sheer weight of forces in the system pitted against their clients: the corrosive effect of poverty, the complicated dynamics in dysfunctional families and failing communities, against a background of declining resources. All this requires sophisticated decision-making, and living with the reality of uncertain outcomes. It can leave a person feeling that they are working in a swamp, desperately jumping from one bit of solid land to another, and often missing.

In healthcare too, given the complexity of the human body and mind, uncertainty is the rule rather than the exception. On a day-by-day basis, clinicians are sifting evidence and experience, signs and symptoms in the patient and making similar crucial decisions based on best probabilities. Add to this the inevitable reality that such decisions often have to be made quickly, under pressure, and it is not difficult to understand why staff are often worn down and preoccupied by nagging doubts and a sense of failure.

Struggling with the limits of our responsibility is an ongoing psychological task and an important part of the work itself, particularly at the start of a career. Many from the caring professions are inclined to exercise harsh judgement on themselves. There is evidence, for example, that doctors and nurses tend to have more obsessional traits than the normal population and tend towards the self-critical (Firth-Cozens, 1999; Firth-Cozens and Harrison, 2010).

The following description by Raymond Tallis will resonate with many, not just doctors:

> *Medical life is dogged by a sense of inadequacy, by guilt and self-blame. When a patient dies and one believes, rightly or wrongly, that he might have been saved had things been managed differently, one is put into the role of a guilty survivor. The usual reassurances . . . seem obscenely inadequate to such a despair. A death cannot be glossed over by Christmas-cracker aphorisms. Doctors who make mistakes feel frightened, guilty and alone.* (Tallis, 2005, p. 213)

Many health and social care staff would say the feelings Tallis describes, and particularly the loneliness, have become worse over the years since 2005, for reasons this chapter will make clear.

In an ideal set-up the organisation would readily understand such emotions and reactions. 'Culture trumps everything', as the joint founder of Reclaiming Social Work, Steve Goodman, said. He went on to describe an environment 'where there is support and good humour and mistakes are accepted and put right as quickly as possible' (Rix, 2011). Such a culture would be reflective about, and supportive of, both a staff member who has a neurotic tendency to self-blame and one who has actually made a mistake that needs to be sensitively managed with the patient or client. Most importantly, there would be an understanding of the complex nature of the work across much of the Welfare State, and how vulnerable this leaves those doing it.

Instead, the fear (and likelihood) of litigation is such that much of the workforce live in fear of being publicly humiliated. This is compounded by the fact that local authorities and healthcare trusts, as corporate structures, have to preserve their reputations as businesses and service providers; there is an incentive to blame 'bad' employees for things that go wrong.

The Legal Paradigm and Its Cost

A legalistic way of thinking has increasingly influenced the culture across health and social care in the UK, shifting the focus to the moral failing of the individual. As one consultant anaesthetist described the legal paradigm, 'Bad things happen because individuals make mistakes, so by dealing with the wrong-doer the error is dealt with. The error can be dressed up by the legal system to look like a punishable offence . . . It does not understand that the professionals are trapped in a complex system that from time to time is prone to error' (Ramakrishna, 2015).

There is a poor fit between this way of thinking and the reality of health and social care work. Martin Elliott, a children's cardiothoracic surgeon at Great Ormond Street Hospital, was 'Gresham Professor of Physic' from 2014–2018. He gave a public lecture on the scandal, and the court case, arising from the numbers of children who died from heart surgery in Bristol in the 1990s. He noted:

> *It takes a remarkable amount of confidence to operate on a child, and one does the procedure within a team that is watching every aspect of your work and performance . . . I was horrified that other members of the team were not called to the GMC hearing and that a culture of blame was evident with almost a witch-hunt being evident, focussed on the surgeons. Where were the cardiologists? Where were the other anaesthetists? I asked Mr Roger Henderson, QC to the GMC hearing, where these people were. His answer was telling; pragmatic and procedural "the reason that no cardiologist and no anaesthetist was in the frame was that the case which was unwieldy enough as it was would have become wholly unmanageable and hopelessly prolonged had any of them been charged. It took long enough as it was but would have taken even longer had others been charged" . . . I heard at the time that the cardiologists had also been advised by their defence societies not to make statements.* (Elliott, 2015)

On some occasions, and in some fields of practice, an error may be clear (even though its causes may be complex): giving the wrong injection, removing the wrong kidney. In other fields, such as the care of people with multiple morbidity, mental health, or child protection, things may not be so clear-cut. Staff caught up in serious adverse events may only have made the type of decision that others make every day, but due to a combination of circumstances, and with hindsight, the outcome has been catastrophic.

The legal system in the UK attempts to preside over professional care delivery by applying rules that determine malpractice, or negligence. One of the problems with this is that a fault-based compensation system channels resources into those cases where blame can be established, to the neglect of the remainder. There are some benefits to the detailed scrutiny that occurs in an adversarial approach, and from the point of view of the service, it does allow for financial liability to be avoided if no fault is found; though sometimes this may be on technicalities that do not feel like 'natural justice'; particularly if injury has been severe.

Various 'no-fault' compensation systems have been considered over the years, such as the one in operation in New Zealand. However, the risk of taking on responsibility for everything that goes wrong, regardless of whether 'negligence' can be proven, means such systems can end up costing even more money (Elliott, 2016).

As things stand, the financial cost of 'medical accidents' has steadily increased. A National Audit Office (NAO) report in 2017 revealed that between 2006–2007 and 2016–2017 the number of clinical negligence claims registered each year with the NHS doubled from 5,300 to 10,600. The annual cash spend on these claims went from £0.4 billion in 2006–2007 to £1.6 billion in 2016–2017, with the cost of clinical negligence claims rising faster than NHS funding year-on-year, thus making increasing inroads into scarce resources.

The NAO report noted the lack of a coherent cross-government strategy, underpinned by policy, to support measures to tackle these rising costs. The authors analysed the factors contributing to the rise, and identified some possible remedies such as alternative dispute resolution teams, settling more cases before court proceedings, introducing fixed-claimant legal costs, and challenging excessive legal costs.

A less confrontational approach may reduce legal costs, but the range and complexity of the issues involved means that the necessary change will need to arise from a number of cultural shifts. It will be important that any changes that occur do not prejudice patients' interests and sense of inherent justice: and, as with any change, it will be important to be alert to unintended adverse consequences, such as have arisen from the shift to conditional fee arrangements.

The costs of the current system, of course, are not only financial, and this is where moving away from confrontation and blame may help most. Legal processes can be slow, obscure and frustrating for patients. They inevitably produce a defensive, legalistic response from the carers accused. Professionals are placed under intense stress, shamed, distracted from their work, and may have their careers ended. Teams become anxious and dysfunctional, and practice as a whole may become defensive and anxiety-ridden. All of this is well-recognised: for example it was noted in a Chief Medical Officer's paper 'Making Amends' (Donaldson, 2003). There are various types of victim when things go wrong, as will be considered later.

Child Protection – Learning from Experience?

In parallel with the ever-prevalent drivers for blame, and the rise of 'compensation culture' in the UK, there have been ongoing attempts to understand and counter the causes of accident and injury, to critically and undefensively examine and learn from our mistakes. The two perspectives have long been in tension.

Child protection procedures have evolved in response to a series of high-profile tragedies. Box 11.1 below gives an account of this.

This can all be read as a story of adverse events leading to learning from experience: but there are other possible narratives. One is of a series of tragic failures, with the system letting down the most vulnerable in its care. Another is that of officials being named, blamed, shamed and sometimes sacked for systemic failures: or indeed for the misdeeds of those who perpetrated the abuse.

The narrative of progress in developing enlightened regulation is countered by one of increasingly defensive 'tick-box' practice, of an 'industrial' nature as has been discussed in the last chapter, and of disproportionate, overly burdensome, scrutiny deterring recruitment of people to work with children or vulnerable adults – particularly in places like Haringey, tainted by its reputation.

There was a political preoccupation in the early twenty-first century with making failings in health and social care into 'a criminal offence'. This gathered pace in the wake of such cases as that of 'Baby P': as if it had been insufficient fear of the penalties that led to failures in care. In any case, would increasing the punishment for 'failures' be a reliably effective stimulus to improvement? Or would it simply ensure that people made more strenuous efforts not to be 'caught' and blamed? If it were to become a criminal offence to notice something about a child and not 'report' it, is there not a perverse pressure, if in doubt, not to notice, to turn that blind eye – the end of so-called 'soft' information, where people might record a vague concern, that they think, in itself, may amount to nothing?

In May 2010 the incoming Conservative/Liberal Democrat coalition government asked Eileen Munro, then Professor of Social Policy at the London School of Economics, to review all child protection procedures in England. This was a response to concern that successive changes had made the system too bureaucratic and anxiety provoking, and stifled social worker initiative in making difficult decisions. Professor Munro published her first report analysing the problems in October 2010. She identified

Box 11.1 **Child Protection: How Tragedy Changed Law and Practice**

The Children Act 1989 systematically codified the child protection structures and principles in use since. Prior to this, legal protection was largely piecemeal, through a variety of other legislation. Principles of the 1989 Act were that the needs and safety of a child are always put first, that professionals should initially attempt to work with parents to keep the child safe, and that children should always be placed with their own family rather than in care unless it would put them at risk of significant harm to do so.

A number of cases since have prompted procedural overhauls:

Victoria Climbié, 'Every Child Matters' and The Children Act 2004: eight-year-old Victoria Climbié died in February 2000, with 128 separate injuries on her body from months of abuse by her aunt Marie Therese Kouao, and Kouao's boyfriend Carl Manning. Despite Victoria's contact with health professionals, police and social services, and having twice been taken to hospital, the abuse was not recognised until after her death.

The ensuing public inquiry, headed by the former chief inspector of social services, Lord Herbert Laming, was the most extensive investigation into the child protection system in British history. In response the government published a green paper entitled 'Every Child Matters' and subsequently passed the Children Act 2004.

Changes introduced included abolition of child protection registers in favour of 'child protection plans', and creating an integrated children's computer system (ICS) to ensure information was more routinely and robustly collected. A post of 'Director of Children's Services' was created in each council, ultimately accountable for the safety of all children in their area. A common assessment framework was created, so practitioners within health, education and the police could instigate better support for families not deemed to reach child protection thresholds. Local 'Safeguarding Children Boards' were set up with responsibility for multi-agency child protection training, and for the investigation of the causes of deaths and serious harm which may have been preventable in their area.

Jessica Chapman, Holly Wells, and 'Vetting and Barring': in August 2002 two ten-year-old girls, Jessica Chapman and Holly Wells, went missing from their home in Soham, Cambridgeshire. Less than two weeks later their bodies were found in a ditch at Lakenheath, Suffolk. In December 2003 Ian Huntley, a school caretaker in the village who had befriended the girls, was found guilty of the murders. After Huntley was convicted, it was revealed that he had been investigated in the past for sexual offences and burglary, but had still been allowed to work in a school as none of these investigations had resulted in a conviction.

Sir Michael Birchard, a retired civil servant, conducted an independent inquiry into the events, questioning how employers recruited people to work with vulnerable groups, particularly the way background checks were carried out. One of his recommendations was for a single agency to vet all individuals who want to work or volunteer to work with children or vulnerable adults. Early 'roll-outs' evolved into the 'Disclosure and Barring Service' established in the UK in 2012.

Baby P, the Second Laming Report, and 'Working Together to Safeguard Children': in 2008 a 17-month-old toddler Peter Connelly (originally and often still referred to as 'Baby P') died after suffering extensive internal and external injuries over a nine-month period. Despite having been seen numerous times by a range of professionals, and been the subject of a child protection plan, social services were never aware the mother had a new boyfriend who, along with a friend, was largely responsible for the injuries and the child's death. Because Connelly died in Haringey, the same borough where Victoria Climbié had also died, it prompted a media frenzy, which resulted in major scrutiny of child protection procedures in England.

Lord Laming was instructed to conduct a review of child protection procedures. As a result of his recommendations the government's official child protection guidance 'Working Together to Safeguard Children' was strengthened and the ICS system guidance was relaxed. Many of the issues identified lay in failures of practice rather than policy. As part of his review, Laming recommended the recruitment, training and supervision of social workers as a key issue to be tackled.

Adapted from 'Child Protection' on the website 'Community Care' www.communitycare.co.uk/2005/03/15/child-protection-3/

problems due to poor IT systems, high caseloads, limited supervision and not enough emphasis on reflective practice and decision-making. She also highlighted the need to take a 'systems approach' that would allow feedback on any unintended consequences of recommendations.

Her final report in 2011 called for a review of statutory guidance, an inclusive inspection framework to examine the effectiveness of all local services, and a new benchmarking system of performance data. By this point 'Working Together to Safeguard Children', the statutory guidance on inter-agency working, was 55 times longer than it had been in 1974. Munro's report emphasised the importance of developing the right skills and competencies for social workers, stressing the need for social work students to receive training in child development, and for a system of high quality continuing professional development. Amongst her final recommendations she again stressed the importance of supervision, and protected time for reflection, in order to help keep a clear focus on the child, and not be manipulated by any disturbed parental figures involved (Munro, 2011).

The Duty of Candour

There is no doubt that mistakes are not always managed well within our caring institutions. Many policy initiatives have attempted to address this, including revamping the 'duty of candour', the principles of which are openness and transparency (GMC, 2015).

Staff have an ethical and professional duty to be honest about mistakes they have made, as spelled out in various policy documents. In practice though, 'cover-ups' continue to come to light, that have left patients and their loved ones in the dark, without access to the relevant information, let alone an apology. Duty of candour was enshrined in law in the 2008 Health and Social Care Act, but its application to practice was left vague. A more significant legal step was taken in 2015 in response to the recommendations of Robert Francis after the failings of Mid-Staffordshire NHS Trust: in an attempt to reverse the culture of individual blame and focus instead on systemic failures of responsibility, all health and social care providers were bound by duty of candour, including large organisations.

This seems right in theory, but in practice it has led to new levels of administration, more bureaucracy, and a variety of local interpretations. The result has been to over-simplify an issue that is actually very complex, in an attempt to make the ruling workable, and measurable – to provide a box that can be readily ticked. In one mental health trust, for example, it became policy in 2018 that consultant psychiatrists had to apologise in person and within 72 hours, to the family of anyone who had committed suicide. Many mental health staff suffer terribly at the thought that they have failed to predict or curtail a suicide; but can we seriously expect one person to take on the responsibility for the suicide of any of the 600 patients on their list? There is also something infantilising and counterproductive about being forced to apologise. It kills the spirit of authentically asking for forgiveness; and the person on the receiving end is surely wise enough to see through someone who is just obediently (and perhaps reluctantly) following protocol.

Having a policy that risks allotting blame to an individual, simply by virtue of their professional position, is certainly not what Robert Francis or the CQC intended when it expanded duty of candour to all provider organisations. And it is unlikely to be what is generally understood by 'candour'. It is common, too, to hear staff cynically comparing the new duty of candour expected of them with the lack of candour from the Government about decisions affecting the NHS and social care.

Guilt, Shame and 'Second Victims'

There is another phenomenon, intimately related to blame: shame. Guilt is the sense of having done something wrong, violating some established standard – often an internalised one, or a social norm or a law. Shame is a more painful and pervasive feeling of humiliation and distress caused by the consciousness of wrong or foolish behaviour. It is about feeling inadequate, unworthy and dishonoured. Shame often has a physical dimension – from embarrassing blushing to an overwhelming sense of over-arousal – so called 'burning shame'.

Guilt and shame overlap, but differ in their intensity, and their absoluteness. Guilt may relate to a particular action, and in a healthy context it may be a spur to reparation. Shame is more personally undermining, with impulses to hide, disappear, or be dead. It is the difference between 'I've done something wrong' and 'I'm all wrong'.

For all the caring professions, there is a risk that being blamed for a mistake is not viewed as just having made one specific misjudgement or mistake: it is a moral and ethical failure – and so leading not just to guilt, but profound shame.

Eileen Munro made a pertinent observation in an opinion piece in *The Guardian*, the year before her review of child protection procedures was commissioned. She wrote:

> *When a plane crashes, the starting point is that the pilot didn't want the plane to crash, and would have done everything in their power to prevent it . . . Serious case reviews . . . make no such assumptions about the professionals involved – doctors, police officers, and social workers . . . Both public opinion and formal investigations conclude that children are harmed or killed because people working in child protection are stupid, malicious, lazy or incompetent . . . Why is this assumed? Surely it is reasonable to believe that people who choose to work in this demanding field want to help children, rather than allow them to be hurt? . . . If we make this small leap of faith, we might consider if there is any point in repeatedly asking why staff do not follow procedures, and ask instead what hampers them from doing so. We need a way of conducting serious case reviews that treats people and procedures as integral parts of the same system.* (Munro, 2009)

The concept of the 'second victim' of error has become well-recognised. Martin Elliott, already quoted above, puts it this way:

> *A blame culture increases the pressure on the so-called 'second victims'... the healthcare givers who themselves have been traumatised by the event, and who experience many of the same emotions as the victims and their families, up to and including severe post-traumatic stress disorder. The signs and symptoms these second victims show are similar to those in acute stress disorder, including initial numbness, detachment, and even de-personalisation, confusion, anxiety, grief and depression, withdrawal or agitation, and re-experiencing of the event. They may also suffer shame, guilt, anger and self-doubt. Some healthcare workers leave their profession and a few even commit suicide because of the experience, and the whole can be compounded if the case goes to litigation.* (Elliott, 2016)

There are too many such victims. Moreover, across health and social care, there is huge variation in access for staff, not just to emotional, but legal support. This can depend on your profession or your organisation and the particular local circumstances – for example, the type of relationship your trust has with the local coroner's office, or the relationship between the social services department and local media organisations. Within the NHS, trusts vary widely in the amount they invest in legal support and it is increasingly common to hear of health and social care professionals facing legal proceedings without proper legal support, or understanding of their position. In addition, the support of trades union representatives is becoming less dependable, and delivered with less expertise. In 2008, a survey of Unison members found that only 24 per cent agreed, or strongly agreed, that 'unions make a difference to what it is like to work round here' (Upchurch et al, 2008, p. 129). Thus, already anxious, often deeply distressed staff, as well as being forced into a difficult adversarial position, find themselves ill prepared to face the ordeal – whether they have made an error or not. Box 11.2 below tells the story of the protracted suffering of social workers involved in the Haringey child deaths.

After describing the effects of serious adverse events on individual staff members, Martin Elliott went on to describe the effects on the healthcare organisation as a whole.

> *Some have even suggested that there is a 'third victim', namely the healthcare organisation in which the event took place. It may suffer bad publicity, deterioration in morale and become unable to work with its staff to make necessary changes. As we have seen, the organisation may demonstrate knee-jerk reactions to incidents resulting for example in suspension, which end up amplifying the problem. Both the second and third victims may be so severely affected that they cease to be able to carry out their work, wasting years of training or organisational development.* (Elliott, 2016)

Ultimately of course, it is service-users who suffer most from these types of scenarios. In mental health services, for example, it sometimes happens that inpatient suicides cluster on one particular ward. One way of understanding this is that staff, frightened by the first suicide and its consequences, are emotionally disabled: managers are overwhelmed by anxiety about the reputation of the ward and paradoxically distracted from what's happening within it, and traumatised front-line staff are unable to be as open and attentive to the emotional needs of their patients.

Haringey Social Services, traumatised, first by the death of Victoria Climbié, then eight years later, by the death of Peter Connolly ('Baby P'), appears to be a classic 'third victim'. Ten years on from Peter's death, Haringey Council were still

Box 11.2 The Long Shadow of Blame in Haringey

In 2009 Liz Davies, at that point a senior lecturer in children and families social work at London Metropolitan University, spoke with Lisa Arthurworrey, social worker for Victoria Climbié.

Nearly ten years on from Victoria's death and having presented evidence at the criminal trial of the murderers, the serious case review, the Haringey disciplinary hearings, employment tribunals and appeal, the appeal against the General Social Care Council (GSCC) for refusing her social worker registration, and the appeal to the Care Standards Tribunal against her name being placed on the Protection of Children Act list, Lisa is also mainly confined to her house. She is also ten years older and still awaits GSCC registration three years after a judge said she was fit for practice 'as of today' (Davies, 2009).

Davies also visited Maria Ward and Gillie Christou, the social worker and team manager respectively for Baby P, who had been murdered the previous year. Although their names had not been put on the Protection of Children list, they had been dismissed from their employment along with the director and deputy director of Children's Services and the head of safeguarding in Haringey. Their cases had been reopened in reaction to the media frenzy including the Sun's 'call for justice' which started over a year after Baby P had died. At this time they were also waiting for the GSCC's verdict concerning their registration. The GSCC had looked at their cases in 2008 and decided to take no action, but then reopened them after the media coverage erupted.

The GSCC hearing eventually reported in 2010, having decided to suspend, but not remove, the two social workers from the register. They listed a number of mitigating factors such as Maria Ward's case load having almost doubled in the six months prior to Baby P's death making it 50 per cent above that recommended by the first Laming Report. Ward was described as having an unblemished record of professional conduct both before and after the events in question (Jones, 2014).

struggling to recruit social workers. In an era where staff vacancies are common across the whole of the Welfare State, the link between a publicised serious adverse event and future recruitment problems is highly pertinent. A vicious circle is created that is hard to reverse.

Desperate to prevent this scenario after the tragic death of four-year-old Daniel Pelka, killed by his mother and her partner in 2012, Coventry Social Services launched a successful, albeit controversial, recruitment drive with the strap-line 'Do it for Daniel'. They were trying to avoid becoming a Haringey-like 'third victim', publicly acknowledging their problems and showing their determination to learn from mistakes. Chief Executive, Martin Reeves, explained:

> *We've always been absolutely clear that we would never use Daniel's death as a PR tool. What we are saying is that it has changed us. It has changed our attitude to social-care reform and how we support our staff.* (Reeves, 2014)

Of course, in so difficult an area, where major tragedies occur, recent years have seen something of a 'backlash' against the concept of 'second' and 'third' victims.

Criticisms of the terms have drawn attention to the risks of equating the suffering of the professional and that of the person that is actually injured – and the possibility that if the professional, or the system, involved also takes up a 'victim' position, it can be an avoidance of responsibility, condoning complacency and avoidance of necessary change (Clarkson et al, 2019). This is of course a risk, but the importance of the terms lie in the recognition that the professionals involved do indeed suffer a form of injury, albeit different in nature from the person who is directly subject to a catastrophic error: and that it is both inhumane and counterproductive to ignore this. Perhaps the terms 'secondary' and 'tertiary' victims would better convey the distance from direct, possibly life-changing or fatal physical damage?

Jack Adcock, Hadiza Bawa-Garba and the General Medical Council

The issue of the failings of the individual versus those of the system moved centre stage in the NHS in 2017/2018. In 2015 a trainee paediatrician, Dr Hadiza Bawa-Garba, had been criminally tried for the death of Jack Adcock, a child in her care some years earlier. The jury convicted her of gross negligence manslaughter. Like the social worker Maria Ward, Dr Bawa-Garba had an unblemished record both before and after the death of Jack Adcock. On the day the child died, Bawa-Garba had been on her first shift back from maternity leave after a 14-month break. She had been rostered to be the most senior doctor in the children's assessment unit, the consultant being absent. Two of the three duty nurses were from an agency. The unit was full of other sick children, on six wards spread over four floors. The computer system was down, so the results of blood tests were delayed. The legal findings, and the General Medical Council's (GMC) subsequent role in the case, are summarised in Box 11.3 below.

Dr Bawa-Garba's treatment by the GMC caused distress and indignation throughout the medical profession. Junior doctors were already feeling humiliated and undervalued following the imposition of a new contract in October 2016. Amongst other things this extended their 'normal' working hours well into the evenings and weekends. Their industrial action in protest had been energetic but unsuccessful, and had attracted unfamiliar opprobrium in sections of the press and social media. Whilst working in progressively more difficult and under-resourced circumstances, the message now received from the GMC was that individuals would be held personally responsible for any mistakes made, regardless of context.

There was another concern. After Jack Adcock's death Dr Bawa-Garba had written undefensive 'personal reflections' upon events, trying to understand what might have gone wrong, in keeping with the GMC's own 'Good Medical Practice' requirements. These reflections were required by the court, and were available to the prosecution QC to assist his cross-examination (Nicholl, 2018). Now it seemed that critical self-examination for the greater good, a key requirement for progress through medical training, and a mainstay of medical revalidation, could be used in court against you.

In the event, the Court of Appeal overturned the High Court's judgement, allaying some of the fears, but leaving open the concerns about written reflections, and also the broader issue of the criminalisation of healthcare workers who make mistakes. Should Bawa-Garba have been charged in the first place? What were the drivers that took her to court, when similar tragedies, in other circumstances, might have been handled differently?

Box 11.3 Jack Adcock, Hadiza Bawa-Garba and the General Medical Council

Jack Adcock, a six-year-old child with Downs syndrome and a known heart condition, was admitted to Leicester Royal Infirmary on 18 February, 2011. He died of sepsis later that day, in part because of failings in his treatment. Dr Hadiza Bawa-Garba, the doctor-in-training who treated him, and a nurse, Isabel Amaro, were found guilty of manslaughter on the grounds of gross negligence on 4 November, 2015. Dr Bawa-Garba had continued to practise until her conviction. There were no concerns about her practice during these four years.

She was given a 24-month suspended sentence, and could no longer work. In February 2017 her fitness to practise was reviewed by a Medical Practitioners Tribunal, the statutory body adjudicating such cases on behalf of the medical regulator, the GMC.

The GMC made the case to the tribunal that she should be erased from the medical register (or 'struck off'), in large part on the basis that *'. . . the wholesale collapse of the standard of care provided by you came out of the blue and for no apparent reason . . . it [is] therefore impossible to have any confidence that this would not happen again'* (MPTS, 2017, p. 7 para 20).

Instead, the tribunal took the view that Dr Bawa-Garba's fitness to practise was impaired, as demonstrated by her conviction, but after careful consideration deemed that she should be suspended from practice for one year, but not removed from the medical register. It noted that a trust investigation had been carried out which highlighted multiple systemic failures at the time of, and contributing to, Jack's death. These included failings on the part of the nurses and consultants, medical and nursing staff shortages, IT system failures which led to abnormal laboratory test results not being highlighted, deficiencies in handover, lack of access to data at the bedside, and the absence of automatic consultant review. The tribunal therefore determined that *'whilst your actions fell far short of the standards expected and were a causative factor in the early death of Patient A, they took place in the context of wider failings'*.

The GMC challenged this decision in the High Court, on the basis that the tribunal was wrong to think that public confidence in the profession could be maintained by any sanction short of erasure: and that the tribunal had 'effectively over-ruled' the criminal conviction.

In a High Court judgement of January 2018 Lord Justice Ouseley said: *'I come firmly to the conclusion that the decision of the [Medical Practitioners] Tribunal on sanction was wrong . . . The Tribunal did not respect the verdict of the jury as it should have. In fact, it reached its own and less severe view of the degree of Dr Bawa-Garba's personal culpability . . . It did so as a result of considering the systemic failings and failings of others, and then came to its own, albeit unstated, view that she was less culpable than the verdict of the jury established'* (General Medical Council v Bawa-Garba, EWHC, 2018).

Doctors were outraged and afraid: the message received was that they would be personally blamed if things went wrong, regardless of circumstances. Dr Bawa-Garba was encouraged to appeal, and her costs were contributed to by colleagues through the 'crowd-funding' organisation Crowd Justice.

In August 2018 the Court of Appeal stated that *'the present case is unusual. No concerns had ever been raised about the clinical competence of Bawa-Garba, other than in relation to Jack's death'*. The Court recognised that the MPTS had not attempted to undermine the verdict of the jury in November 2015, which found Bawa-Garba guilty of manslaughter, and that it was entitled to conduct an 'evaluative exercise' to determine what sanction was most appropriate. They stated that *'there is no presumption of erasure in the case of serious harm and that the MPTS was right to draw attention to the systemic failings on the part of the hospital'.* It was noted that Dr Bawa-Garba's suspended sentence had been at the lightest end of the sentencing range, and that she presented no greater risk of falling standards than *'any other reasonably competent doctor'* (Bawa-Garba and The General Medical Council etc., EWCA, 2018).

In April 2019 Dr Bawa-Garba was granted permission to return to practice under close supervision.

An overarching hostile environment of 'crime and punishment', and trying to make problems go away by 'criminalising' them inevitably plays a part.

The 'No-Blame' Cultures

The need for a 'no-blame cultures' has long been recognised. In 2000 The Chief Medical Officer's paper 'An Organisation with a Memory' spelt it out clearly, as it heralded the introduction of 'significant event analysis' into the NHS (Department of Health, 2000).

Following the events in Mid-Staffordshire, and the subsequent Francis reports, the Government asked Professor Don Berwick, from the US Institute for Healthcare Improvement, to advise on how to improve the quality and safety of care in the NHS. Berwick set up an advisory committee of experts in organisational theory, quality improvement, and safety and systems to distil the lessons from Mid-Staffordshire into the changes that were needed.

Key messages from the report, published in 2013, are summarised in Box 11.4 below: the conclusions are largely in keeping with the themes of this book.

Sarah Wollaston, an ex-GP, and at that time a Conservative MP and member of the Commons Health Select Committee, commented as follows:

> *The Berwick review into patient safety opens with a reminder that 'at its core the NHS remains a world-leading example of commitment to health and healthcare as a human right'... One phrase stands out from the list of problems identified: 'fear is toxic to both safety and improvement'. It is further emphasised in the recommendation that we should abandon blame as a tool and instead make sure pride and joy in work, not fear, infuse the NHS.*
>
> *That is not to say that staff should not take responsibility for their actions, just that recourse to criminal sanctions should be extremely rare and primarily to deter wilful or reckless neglect or mistreatment.*
>
> *The best way to make the NHS safer is to trust the goodwill of staff and help to bring out the best in them at every level of the organisation by supporting a commitment to lifelong learning and openness. Rules and regulators have a place but cannot replace professional development.* (Wollaston, 2013)

In the event, although the need for a 'no-blame' or 'just culture' is most pressing in organisations such as the NHS and in Child Protection teams, where small errors can have catastrophic consequences, other sectors of society, where the consequences of mistakes are perhaps not so tragic, may have gone further in thinking about and addressing the issues (Box 11.5 below). A key element in any 'no-blame cultures' is that speaking up about errors is a fundamental duty of every employee: and that mistakes are seen as part of human nature, not a shameful indication of general inadequacy.

Box 11.4 Key Learning from the Berwick Report 2013

Problems identified	Required change from the system to address these problems
Patient safety problems exist throughout the NHS as with every other healthcare system in the world.	Recognise with clarity and courage the need for wide systemic change.
NHS staff are not to blame – in the vast majority of cases it is the systems, procedures, conditions, environment and constraints they face that lead to patient safety problems.	Abandon blame as a tool and trust the goodwill and good intentions of staff. Reassert the primacy of working with patients and carers to achieve healthcare goals.
Incorrect priorities do damage: other goals are important, but the central focus must always be on patients.	Use quantitative targets with caution. Such goals do have an important role en route to progress, but should never displace the primary goal of better care.
In some instances, clear warning signals abounded and were not heeded, especially the voices of patients and carers.	Recognise that transparency is essential and expect and insist on it.
When responsibility is diffused, it is not clearly owned: with too many in charge, no-one is.	Ensure that responsibility for functions related to safety and improvement are vested clearly and simply.
Improvement needs a system of support: the NHS needs a considered, resourced and driven agenda of capability-building in order to deliver continuous improvement.	Give the people of the NHS career-long help to learn, master and apply modern methods for quality control, quality improvement and quality planning.
Fear is toxic to both safety and improvement.	Make sure pride and joy in work, not fear, infuse the NHS.

From: Key Learning from the Berwick Report. East London NHS Foundation Trust www.qi.elft.nhs.uk/wp-content/uploads/2013/12/key-learning-from-the-berwick-report.pdf

Reflective Practice

Berwick's conclusions about safety in the NHS clearly echo Eileen Munro's findings in her review of child protection procedures; and similar principles have underpinned developments in professional education since the 1990s, with varying degrees of success in the face of other pressures such as those discussed above. The case for change might appear self-evident, but the forces conspiring against it are powerful.

Despite this, there have been determined efforts to change the culture. Many professional bodies have adopted the idea of 'reflective practice' already referred to, albeit to a mixed reception. In 1983, Donald Schon, a philosopher and Professor of Urban Planning at the Massachusetts Institute of Technology, published his book *The Reflective Practitioner*. This introduced concepts of 'reflection-on-action' and 'reflection-in-action' to explain how professionals meet the challenges of their work with a form of informed improvisation that is improved through feedback from practice (Schon, 1983).

Box 11.5 What Are the Characteristics of No-Blame Cultures?

No-blame cultures tend to be driven by specific organisational characteristics, including:

- **A shared understanding of complexity:** unfortunately humans are biased to attribute errors to people, even if the cause is systemic. No-blame cultures spend time and energy ensuring employees understand how complex organisations are, so they can better attribute errors to systemic factors.
- **An appreciation for others:** air traffic control organisations expose employees to the stresses and problems that arise in their colleagues' jobs so that, if things go wrong, everyone is more likely to understand why it went wrong, rather than blame poor performance.
- **Belief in honesty:** honesty is an oil that lubricates the functioning of high reliability organisations. Without honesty, organisations don't have a true overview of where they are and therefore aren't able to make effective and informed decisions. No-blame cultures therefore value and incentivise honesty.
- **The regular use of debriefs:** critique is fundamental to the success of no-blame cultures because it allows processes to be effectively understood, deconstructed and put back together in better ways. Debriefs help ascertain what went wrong and what should be changed in future and ensure everyone is on the same page.
- **Deference to expertise:** operational decision-making in normal organisations tends to follow the organisational chart, despite subject-matter experts often in a better position to make informed decisions. In no-blame cultures, the hierarchy is loose enough that experts are able to lead on operational issues where appropriate.
- **A focus on behavioural expectations:** in an increasingly complex world, achieving outcomes becomes more difficult because of the number of variables involved. Judging people on outcomes can therefore be unfair, while judging them on behaviours encourages alignment with organisational values.
- **Realistic understanding of human beings:** holding people to high standards can encourage performance, but organisations shouldn't ignore the realities of human beings (for example, that people can have 'off days'.) No-blame cultures are underpinned by the reality of being a human being and people are not expected to be superheroes. Instead, they are encouraged to see themselves as imperfect but valuable parts of a wider system.

From: Investors in People (2018). What Does A No-Blame Cultures Actually Look Like? www.investorsinpeople.com /what-does-a-no-blame-culture-actually-look-like/

The concepts were not new in themselves, but Schon's formulation and terminology rapidly gained ground, and have lasted well. This model is now integral to the professional development of the health, social care and teaching professions: and is a mainstay of their appraisal and revalidation systems. Schon describes a form of self-awareness linked to taking action in the world: a cycle of experience, reflection upon and learning from that experience, translation into action, and consequent new experience.

The approach, like any other, is open to criticism, and it has met some resistance in practice. As with any good idea, the reflective approach can suffer from being rendered concrete, and then deployed as a requirement imposed from above. Busy practitioners may then view it as demeaning, out of touch, and an imposition distracting them from their vital work, especially if they are of a personality type oriented to action rather than introspection. There may also be a healthy degree of scepticism about how self-critical it is possible to be 'on the record', despite one's organisation's protestations about confidentiality, and assertion of 'a no-blame' cultures.

For doctors, Dr Bawa-Garba's experience went to the heart of this – and must have provided other professions considerable food for thought. The fate of her written reflections, passed to the prosecution QC, was taken as a timely warning by a profession already viewing appraisal and revalidation procedures as irksome, and now possibly self-incriminating, bureaucratic requirements. It did not help that the regulator requiring such reflections from all doctors had relentlessly pursued Dr Bawa-Garba's erasure from the register, on the basis that clearly established systemic failings provided no mitigation for her errors.

Subsequently the GMC acknowledged the difficulty, stating that they do not ask for reflective notes from doctors in order to investigate a concern, and that they had 'publicly called for doctors' reflective notes to be given legal protection and will continue to press for this' (Nicholl, 2018).

The position was finessed in September 2018, in the guidance 'The Reflective Practitioner' (Academy of Medical Royal Colleges, etc., 2018). The importance of the reflective process was robustly restated, with some advice on how to document it: 'A reflective note does not need to capture full details of an experience. It should capture learning outcomes and future plans . . . the information should be anonymised as far as possible . . . Reflective notes should focus on the learning rather than a full discussion of the case or situation. Factual details should be recorded elsewhere'. Ultimately, however, and despite all this manoeuvring, notes would still have to be disclosed to the courts: and doctors were advised to seek legal advice if this was required. Given this position, all health and social care professionals may be forgiven for considering that their reflections after serious untoward incidents have two potentially conflicting functions. One is to provide a thoughtful and constructive analysis of what went wrong: the other is to support a defence in court.

How can we hold on to reflection in such a potentially hostile environment? We are up against a vicious circle here: the more the perceived threats, the more difficult (and dangerous) it is to reflect openly. But in turn, it is only through reflection and the opportunity it brings to learn from experience and gain self-knowledge, that there is any hope of moderating the hostile factors at work.

Is A 'No-blame Culture' Possible?

The case for a 'no-blame culture' is so compelling that it would have been in place years ago, were it simply a matter of deciding to have one. We have to infer that there are powerful forces acting against it. It will need care, attention, and determination, at all levels of society, to address these.

One of the difficulties with the blaming mind-set, seeking individuals and groups to hold responsible when things go wrong, is that it arises so readily and rapidly. The power of social media to whip-up often ill-informed emotion is an increasing worrying phenomenon. For example, the baby Alfie Evans died of an incurable degenerative neurological condition in Alder Hey Hospital in Liverpool in 2018. When the decision was finally made to turn off the ventilator, after numerous thoughtful deliberations in court, nursing staff arriving and leaving the hospital were accosted by an emotional crowd of protesters accusing them of murder. Yet Alder Hey's decision to cease medical intervention that they considered futile and inhumane had not been taken lightly.

The situation had arisen because of the parents' wish to prolong the life of their child despite evidence that almost the entirety of his brain had been eroded. Many clinical and legal professionals had been consulted, all bringing their considerable training and expertise to bear in weighing up the prognosis, and the suffering for the child involved in continuing to actively intervene and prolong a painful death. Alder Hey's decision not to continue to prolong his life resulted in a legal battle that ended up in the European Court of Human Rights, where the hospital's position was supported.

Whilst the situation was painful for everyone involved, it shocked many to see the rage on the faces of the protesters turned against the hospital staff. It is hard to practise in an environment where communal knee-jerk hatred can emerge so readily, and irrationally. Added to this, the media, with its readiness to churn out 'scare stories' about NHS and social services staff in an increasingly contemptuous tone, does nothing to help matters.

However, the situation is not a simple one. For example, the very high death rates at the Bristol Royal Infirmary Children's Heart Unit were only finally acted upon after what has become known as 'whistle-blowing', the tireless demands of the parents affected, and an appropriately critical and cynical media (Elliott, 2015). Blaming and shaming may possibly be destructive, unfair, and an opportunity to vent hostility: but equally people and systems must be accountable for their mistakes or misdeeds. Professions have long been viewed as 'closing ranks' at times of trouble, and have undoubtedly done so. It is this perception that the GMC is struggling against in its pursuit of 'public confidence' in the medical profession. The increasing use of the term 'just culture' rather than 'no-blame culture' reflects the concern to be clear that the aim of the 'no-blame' approach is not to absolve professionals of responsibility for their actions.

It is difficult, but essential, to maintain even-handedness when tragic events have occurred. Not all professional mistakes are major tragedies however: some are 'near misses' where tragedy is narrowly avoided, and some are simply of lesser magnitude. All offer an opportunity for learning, as has been discussed; but this can only be done if deliberate shaming is avoided, whilst maintaining accountability, and crucially, not lodging responsibility in an individual when it belongs to the system.

Our attitude to risk as a society, and the perception that anything that goes wrong – including death – must be someone's fault, affects everyone. Working at the front-line with the most vulnerable, where decisions routinely affect another person's autonomy, suffering and mortality, is a precarious place to be at the present time. This can make the ordinary but sometimes agonising feelings of guilt and self-blame that accompany the job particularly frightening and difficult to process, with obvious effects on subsequent practice.

In 2011, Sharon Shoesmith, director of Haringey's children's services when Peter Donnelly, 'Baby P', died, appealed against the High Court judicial review that had supported her dismissal. She won recognition that the process had been unlawful. In his final observations, Lord Justice Kay referred to another case regarding public servants being 'made a public sacrifice', then went on to comment specifically in relation to Sharon Shoesmith:

> *Those involved in areas such as social work and healthcare are particularly vulnerable to such treatment. Whatever her shortcomings may have been (and I repeat, I cannot say) she was entitled to be treated lawfully and fairly and not simply and summarily scapegoated.*
> (Court of Appeal, 2011)

Perhaps the essence of the shift required is contained in Munro's observation from 2009:

> *When a plane crashes, the starting point is that the pilot didn't want the plane to crash, and would have done everything in their power to prevent it . . .*

The 'Germanwings' airline tragedy of 2017, when a psychologically disturbed pilot flew his plane into a mountainside, showed that, extremely rarely, a pilot might crash deliberately (BBC, 2017): but this should not, and did not, become the starting point for subsequent air crash investigations. Instead, when such disasters occur, there continues to be a comprehensive exploration of all factors in the system – a quest to discover the range of real 'reasons for' the event. Only if the investigation reveals wrongdoing – for example, gross negligence or acts of sabotage – does the focus move to attributing blame. Rather than a compulsive hunt for a 'crime', this approach fosters an atmosphere of collective concern, solidarity and mutual regret, avoiding accusation, shaming, obfuscation, defensiveness and evasion. If such an approach were possible in health and social care, this would increase the chances of all involved being able to process their feelings, learn, and move on to work together, educated by their experience, and committed to improving practice.

References

Academy of Medical Royal Colleges, COPMED, GMC and MSC (2018) The Reflective Practitioner. Joint AoMRC, COPMED, GMC and MSC Guidance. Available at: www.copmed.org.uk/images/docs/reflective_practice/Summary_of_The_reflective_practitioner_guidance.pdf [last accessed 12 August, 2019].

BBC (2017) Germanwings crash leaves unanswered questions. BBC News website 23 March, 2017. Available at: www.bbc.co.uk/news/world-europe–32084956 [last accessed 12 August, 2019].

Berwick D. (2013)A promise to learn – a commitment to act: improving the safety of patients in England. Department of Health.

Clarkson, M. D., Haskell, H., Hemmelgarn, C. and Skolnik, P. J. (2019) Abandon the term 'second victim'. British Medical Journal. 2019;364:11233.

Court of Appeal (2011) Judgement approved by the Court, Neutral Citation Number: (2011) EWCA Civ 642 paragraphs 37–38.

Davies, L. (2009) Let's get rid of social work's blame culture. The Guardian Joe Public Social Care blog. Available at: www.theguardian.com/society/joepublic/2009/jun/25/social-work-baby-p-victoria-climbie [last accessed 12 August, 2019].

Department of Health (2000) An organisation with a memory. Report of an expert group on learning from adverse events in the NHS chaired by the Chief Medical Officer. HMSO.

Donaldson L. (2003) Making Amends: a consultation paper setting out proposals for reforming the approach to clinical negligence in the NHS. Department of Health.

Elliott, M. (2015) The Bristol Heart Scandal and its Consequences: Politics, Rationalisation and the Use and Abuse of Information. Gresham College. Available at: www.gresham.ac.uk/lectures-and-events/the-bristol-scandal-and-its-consequences-politics-rationalisation-and-the-use [last accessed 12 August, 2019].

Elliott, M. (2016) To Blame or Not to Blame? The Medical Profession and Blame Culture. Gresham College. Available at: www.gresham.ac.uk/lectures-and-events/to-blame-or-not-to-blame-the-medical-profession-and-blame-culture [last accessed 12 August, 2019].

Firth-Cozens, J. (1999) *Stress in Health Professionals: Psychological and Organisational Causes and Interventions.* Wiley-Blackwell.

Firth-Cozens, J. and Harrison, J. (2010) *How to Survive in Medicine: Personally and Professionally*. Wiley-Blackwell.

GMC (2015) Openness and honesty when things go wrong: the professional duty of candour. Available at: www.gmc-uk.org/ethical-guidance/ethical-guidance-for-doctors/candour—openness-and-honesty-when-things-go-wrong [last accessed 26 August, 2019].

Investors in People (2018) What does a no-blame culture actually look like? Available at: www.investorsinpeople.com/what-does-a-no-blame-culture-actually-look-like/ [last accessed 12 August, 2019].

Jones, R. (2014) The Story of Baby P. Polity Press.

Munro, E. (2009) Beyond the blame culture. *The Guardian*, 3 November, 2009. Available at: www.theguardian.com/commentisfree/2009/nov/03/serious-case-review-child-protection [last accessed 12 August, 2019].

Munro, E. (2011) The Munro review of child protection: final report, a child-centred system. CM, 8062. HMSO.

National Audit Office/Department of Health (2017) Managing the costs of clinical negligence in trusts. National Audit Office.

Nicholl, D. (2018) The role of reflection in the post Bawa-Garba era. Royal College of Physicians. Available at: www.rcplondon.ac.uk/news/role-reflection-post-bawa-garba-era [last accessed 12 August, 2019].

Radhakrishna, S. (2015) Culture of blame in the National Health Service: consequences and solutions. British Journal of Anaesthesia. 115 (5): 653–5.

Reeves, M. (2014) 'Do It For Daniel'; the story behind Coventry's social work recruitment campaign. *The Guardian*, 22 September, 2014. Available at: www.theguardian.com/social-care-network/2014/sep/22/do-it-for-daniel-coventry-social-work-recruitment [last accessed 26 August, 2019].

Rix, J. (2011) How Hackney Reclaimed Child Protection Work. *The Guardian*, 8 November, 2011. Available at: www.theguardian.com/society/2011/nov/08/reclaiming-social-work-hackney-breakaway-success [last accessed 26 August, 2019].

Schön, Donald A. (1983) *The Reflective Practitioner: How Professionals Think In Action*. Basic Books.

Tallis, R. (2005) *Hippocratic Oaths: Medicine and Its Discontents*. Atlantic Books.

Thich, N. H. (1991) *Peace Is Every Step*. Bantam Books, p. 78.

Upchurch, M., Danford, A., Richardson, M. and Tailby, S. (2008) *The Realities of Partnership at Work*. Palgrave Macmillan.

Wollaston, S., Member of the Health Select Committee (2013) Why a Culture of Fear and Blame Won't fix the NHS. *The Telegraph*, 7 August, 2013. Available at: www.telegraph.co.uk/news/politics/10228052/Why-a-culture-of-fear-and-blame-wont-fix-the-NHS.html [last accessed 12 August, 2019].

Chapter 12

The Hostile Environment

The aim is to create here in Britain a really hostile environment for illegal migration.

(The Rt Hon. Theresa May (Kirkup and Winnett, 2012))

So far we have considered how kindness can be compromised by various pressures: individual and group dynamics, the demands of the work, poorly managed organisational change, industrialised 'target cultures', and blame. Now we will look at when kindness itself is under direct attack; when as a matter of operational policy, or for political reasons, the explicit intention is to be unkind, shaming or confrontational. When this happens it is usually framed as some form of 'self-defence'.

The term 'hostile environment' gained popular recognition in the context of UK immigration policy from 2012 until its unravelling in 2018. The Home Office explicitly used unkindness as a tool of public policy, an approach that may also be finding its way into the 'Welfare State': and so requires careful consideration.

Theresa May, then Home Secretary, explained the approach in an interview in the *Daily Telegraph* newspaper in 2012: *'What we don't want is a situation where people think that they can come here and overstay because they're able to access everything they need . . . The aim is to create here in Britain a really hostile environment for illegal migration'.* The policy included immigration checks being required of the likes of landlords, banks and GP surgeries. An 'enforcement campaign' in the summer of 2013 involved billboard vans driving around London carrying the warning 'Go Home or Face Arrest'. Immigration enforcement vehicles were branded like police cars. All application processing became more rigid and demanding: even the most straightforward immigration and visa applications seemed to be being made as difficult as possible. Explicitly framed as a way of defending the UK against illegal immigration, it appears that the policy rapidly generalised: and all immigration matters were dealt with in a 'hostile' manner. Box 12.1 gives an example.

Reports accumulated of individuals being unfairly and inhumanely treated by the system. This was exemplified by the fate of members of the 'Windrush generation' of immigrants from the Caribbean (Box 12.2).

People who had come to the UK as children, and become part of British society, found they lacked certain documents demanded for them to continue working, get treatment from the NHS, or even to remain in the UK. Campaigning journalists such as Amelia Gentleman (Gentleman, 2018) publicised cases of devastatingly inhumane treatment of

Box 12.1 British High Commissioner's Baby Son Denied a UK Passport after Being Born in Trinidad

The baby son of a former British High Commissioner was denied a UK passport after he was born in a Caribbean state where his father was in post.

Former UK diplomat Arthur Snell, who served as British High Commissioner to Trinidad and Tobago from 2011 to 2014, said he was left feeling 'powerless and nervous' after the Home Office refused to grant his newborn son a passport in 2011.

While Mr Snell said he was able to 'quickly resolve' the issue, he said it illustrated a 'cultural priority within the Home Office to reject wherever possible' – highlighting that, as a white diplomat, he was easily able to resolve the problem where many others can't.

'What it showed me was that the Home Office tends to default to no as an answer because of the hostile policies. It seems they want to make it as difficult as possible for someone to be British – like that's almost the mission statement', Mr Snell told *The Independent* (Bulman, 2018).

Box 12.2 Undocumented Citizens: The 'Windrush Generation'

The 'Windrush generation' were British Commonwealth citizens who arrived in the UK between 1948 and 1971 – named after the ship MV Empire Windrush, which first brought workers from Jamaica, Trinidad and other islands, as a response to post-war labour shortages in the UK. Many of the arrivals became workers in vital roles, such as cleaners, drivers and nurses, and British institutions relied upon them.

Their free movement ended with the 1971 Immigration Act, after which a British passport-holder born overseas could no longer settle in the UK unless they both had a work permit and could prove that a parent or grandparent had been born in the UK. However, Commonwealth citizens already living in the UK were given indefinite leave to remain.

As there had been no restrictions on entry before 1971 many of those who arrived as children travelled on parents' passports and did not apply for travel documents. The Home Office did not keep a record of those granted leave to remain, or issue any paperwork confirming it. Subsequently, in 2010, landing cards belonging to Windrush migrants were destroyed by the Home Office. As a result of this, it became difficult, if not impossible, for 'Windrush' arrivals to prove they were in the UK legally, once official policy required documentary evidence of immigration status to receive many social and societal entitlements.

people who had lived in the UK for most of their lives. The Government, forced to defend itself, backtracked on its policies once they were subject to media and parliamentary scrutiny. Amidst the furore, the then Home Secretary, Amber Rudd, repeatedly denied claims that the Home Office was driven by deportation targets. When evidence emerged that she should have been aware that there was, in fact, just such a target culture, she duly resigned (BBC, 2018).

This all relates to the concerns of this book for a number of reasons. A policy supposedly designed to deal with a delinquent few generalised to being a response to everyone: proposals to deal with 'illegal immigrants' were applied throughout the organisation producing a 'hostile' response to all immigration applications and related matters. Crude and indiscriminate targets were put in place: and in meeting these,

Box 12.3 'Former Watchdog Chief Labels Disabled Benefits Process a "Hostile Environment"'

Andrew McDonald had his benefits stopped after assessors decided he was no longer ill enough to qualify for Personal Independence Payment (PIP). This benefit is intended to help with the additional costs of living with disability. It is not means-tested. McDonald was diagnosed with Parkinson's in 2007 and three years later was told he had incurable prostate cancer. He retired because of ill health in 2014 and qualified for PIP the following year, a decision reaffirmed on review in 2017. Each time assessors awarded him 11 points, comfortably over the eight-point threshold for lower level support.

At his third review in 2018 he was awarded two points – a decision that suggested his health was improving. 'I was flabbergasted: I had two degenerative conditions and my Parkinson's had become worse since the turn of the year – it's now described by my neurologist as 'very severe'.

(Butler, 2018)

a deportation was a deportation, and could be counted as a 'success' whatever the circumstances. Targets in such a complex area, where one person's whole future is pitted against another's periodic 'performance indicators', invite instrumental relationships of the worst type, where people are used as a means to an end, rather than seen as respected others.

Targets have also beset the UK benefits system. A 2018 media story with similar themes to that of the former High Commissioner's baby boy involved Andrew McDonald, once a senior civil servant. He described the disability benefits assessment system as a 'hostile environment' after being told he was ineligible for 'Personal Independence Payment' (PIP) support despite having Parkinson's disease and incurable prostate cancer (Butler, 2018: see Box 12.3).

In both Snell's and McDonald's stories, the decisions were not just erroneous, but absurd. Such experiences are common for those at the underprivileged end of society. Both the diplomat and the civil servant had the social advantages and influence to feel confident in protesting, and bring their case into public awareness. To quote Snell:

> *I felt powerless and nervous when it was initially rejected, but I had all the confidence that comes with the job and I had cultural confidence that my own heritage and the fact that my family history meant it was a fixable problem.*
>
> *But if you take someone faced with these obstacles who doesn't have the financial means and is made to think their right to British citizenship is questionable, and who doesn't have the network resources, in many cases they will end up just thinking well maybe this can't be done and just give up.* (Bulman, 2018)

When McDonald asked the Department of Work and Pensions (DWP) to review the decision against him, they responded that it was up to him to supply evidence to prove that his condition had not improved – effectively suggesting that the withdrawal of his benefit was no responsibility of theirs. McDonald was shocked by the figures at the time showing that 71 per cent of PIP decisions were overturned on appeal: a worrying statistic, which indicated the unreliability of the decisions made. How many others with equally valid cases had given up before the appeal stage? McDonald told the press:

> *I was shocked by the way this was being administered against the interests of some of the most disadvantaged people in the country . . . I thought this was a system to give people a hand up; in practice they encounter a sleight of hand that is completely out of kilter with the best traditions of British public service.*

Unkindness had explicitly been made a tool of public policy, with stated aims of deterring people from wanting to be in the UK by means of deliberate, calculated hostility, and of preventing benefit fraud by making all claims difficult, and throwing the burden of proof on the applicant. Is this a justified and proportionate approach – and, indeed, is it even effective? Can, and should, this substitute for efficient, effective and humane 'due process'?

Zero Tolerance

In 1999 the NHS began concerted action to deal with violence, abuse and harassment of staff by patients or their relatives, in response to a rise in reported incidents. In Chapter 5 we considered this from the point of view of an individual staff member's emotional experience. In this chapter, we explore it in relation to the wider political environment.

The 'Counter Fraud and Security Management Service' (CFSMS, also known as 'NHS Protect') was set up in 2003, lasting until it was reorganised out of existence in 2017. This produced a significant increase in the numbers of offenders being prosecuted (NHS Employers, 2008). Even so, a staff survey in 2008 by the Healthcare Commission showed that 12 per cent of staff across all trusts reported being physically assaulted by patients over the previous 12 months.

In this context, mindful of the risks to staff, and the legal requirements to protect their safety, trusts have attended to the issue with a range of thoughtful measures, and appropriate education of their employees. However, in tandem with this, a 'zero tolerance' approach to violence and abuse was declared, and publicised widely through a range of channels, including prominent notices on display in all NHS settings. Potential offenders (apparently everyone) were notified of the policy, and the forceful way they could expect to be treated if they were abusive. Posters showed a variety of grim-looking security personnel or police, and used an iconography of alert. One example, from Northern Ireland, showed two stick figures against a bright yellow 'hazard alert' background, one punching the other to the ground. The caption was 'ZERO TOLERANCE on abuse of healthcare staff'. It begged the question of who exactly was punching who (Northern Ireland Health and Social Care Board, 2017).

The evidence base for such material preventing violence and abuse is not clear. By their nature, violence and abuse are likely to be impulsive, irritable reactions to frustration or perceived slight. Whether the risk of this is reduced by someone reading a threatening notice, and deciding on an alternative course of action as a result, is debatable.

What is more evident is that the proliferation of communications about violence and abuse creates a sense of imminent danger and societal decline. One such notice was published on Flickr in 2008 with a comment:

> *I was rather surprised to see the need for this sign in the Radiology department of the hospital. I was taking my mother in for a CT scan. What is the world coming to?*
> www.flickr.com/photos/nikonsnapper/2300873528

The situation is, of course, a difficult one, and responses have to be judged carefully. As an example, a manager having to respond somehow to staff distress about high levels of aggression and sporadic violence on an acute mental health ward may opt to declare 'zero tolerance', and involve (or at least inform) the police in all such incidents. Whereas in the short-term staff might feel supported, and that their difficulties are being recognised, the actual causes of the problems may not be being addressed. Responsibility for developing authority and control through the ward culture is abdicated. It might be that such authority is hard to maintain, due (for example) to chronic understaffing, or high rates of 'bank' nurse usage: but unless such issues are addressed, problems are likely to recur. Most police forces, in any case, are unlikely to take on routine responsibility for maintaining order in such settings. Criminal sanctions, if they are to be deployed, are more powerful as a last resort than as a routine response, particularly as the decision to be aggressive or hostile is not often a rational one, particularly in the presence of mental disorder. This is not necessarily about absolving the person from responsibility, but rather about a recognition that systemic factors are also at play, and that modifying these may be more effective than threatening the individual with sanctions.

The 'Zero Tolerance' approach is more than a simple communication of intent to address a difficulty: it adopts a rhetoric of confrontation explicitly at odds with the reduction of violence by means of calming situations and preventing 'flashpoints'. It also carries historical baggage. The term came into widespread use in the USA in the 1970s, to describe a politically driven approach to law enforcement based on the idea that fiercely prohibiting minor crimes could in turn prevent wider public disorder. It evolved to describe a policy of severe penalties without allowance for extenuating circumstances. Successes were claimed for the approach – such as the 'cleaning up' of New York City in the 1990s – but largely by the parties responsible for the policies. Critics maintained that the changes had arisen from social improvements, not the 'tough' approach of certain politicians.

Those who have deployed the term so widely across UK health and social care settings may have been unaware of this baggage: and so possibly also unaware of the implicit attitudes of severity, inflexibility and lack of compromise, seeing it simply as a way of 'talking tough'. It might be asked whether such 'tough talk' does any harm, so long as the actual action taken is thoughtful and flexible, and recognises that many of the 'perpetrators' may be unwell, disadvantaged or even confused? A paper on 'Violence against Staff' issued by 'NHS Employers' in 2008 recognises many contributory factors to abusive behaviour and violence against staff, and provides thoughtful advice on how to modify them (NHS Employers, 2008) (Box 12.4). However, this was 'behind the scenes'. The public narrative at the time was one of 'toughness', inflexibility and self-righteousness. This can 'up the ante' and may in fact fuel confrontation: for example, where a staff member rapidly takes up a 'zero tolerance' position in the face of legitimate criticism or complaint, especially if this comes from someone who is relatively inarticulate or unsophisticated.

This is not to say that action should not be taken against those who are abusive or violent in making their complaints. This should be done swiftly and effectively, whilst at the same time thinking about the systemic issues that may bring about such behaviours,

Box 12.4 Ways to Reduce the Risk of Violence

NHS Employers, 2008

There are many ways to reduce the risk of violence. The Health and Safety Executive suggests:

Providing suitable training and information to staff;
Improving the design of the working environment;
Making changes to aspects of staff roles;
Recording incidents of physical assault or verbal abuse so that patterns can be discerned. Any employer must notify their health and safety enforcing authority if an act of violence at work results in death, serious injury on incapacity for normal work for three or more days;
Looking at the way departments' work could help to address some of the factors which prompt individuals to commit abusive or violent behaviour. This could include looking at the way patients are given information on waiting times and what will happen to them, especially in areas such as A&E.

Violence against Staff, NHSemployers.org
www.nhsemployers.org/~/media/Employers/Publications/Violence%20against%20staff.pdf

and modifying them. Such thinking is present in the 'Violence against Staff' paper, and the actions of NHS England. The accompanying rhetoric matters, however, because even though thoughtful due process is being deployed, it is subsumed in, and implicitly denigrated by, an overarching narrative of threat and confrontation.

Another example will further illustrate how narratives of abuse and confrontation can be active in the everyday running of the NHS.

'This New Fight against NHS Fraudsters'

Certain groups of people are entitled to free prescriptions in the NHS. Some documentary evidence of entitlement may be required, but often the system falls back on a 'self-declaration' – you can tick a box on the back of the prescription form stating, for example, that you have a valid exemption certificate – and this may not be checked. Perhaps inevitably, some people misrepresent or misunderstand their circumstances, and thus some of those who should have paid get their medicines without doing so.

In the mid- to late-twentieth century the issue of prescription charges was a contentious one. Many people believed that charges negated the principle of healthcare 'free at the point of need' – what was the point of free diagnosis if you had to pay for the treatment? These objections were countered by an argument that those in 'real' need could have their prescriptions free, or take advantage of other schemes such as pre-payment certificates. To make sure that the needy were not put off seeking treatment, if you attended a pharmacy in the 1980s you were subjected to a range of publicity telling you how you might get free prescriptions, or limit the cost.

By 2010 onwards the arguments about payment had largely subsided, and the focus had switched to those who were not paying who should have done so – anxieties had arisen about 'fraud'. If you attended a pharmacy in 2018, the publicity predominantly warned you not to claim free prescriptions if not entitled, with threats of penalty charges should you be 'caught'. A range of posters and leaflets threatened a '£100 Penalty Charge', and a 'Facebook' campaign was also mounted to this effect (NHSBSA, 2018). Estimates of the money at stake varied; one estimate in 2018 was that 'prescription fraud' of all types within the NHS cost £256 million a year (Legraien, 2018). The budget for the Department of Health in England was approximately £124.7 billion in 2017/2018, so this was approximately 0.2 per cent of the annual spend.

In October 2018 Matt Hancock, newly appointed as Health Secretary, and with a reputation to build, announced the establishment of a new database listing those entitled to free NHS prescriptions nationally, for pharmacists to cross-check when issuing drugs. Leaving aside the (considerable) issues of how accurate the database would be, and how potential discrepancies would be dealt with, this can be easily seen as 'good housekeeping' – if a system is in place it should be administered efficiently. However, the accompanying narrative was somewhat more melodramatic:

> *Mr Hancock said: 'Those who abuse the NHS and choose to line their own pockets with money that should be spent on patients and frontline care will no longer have anywhere to hide.*
>
> *The new technology and analysis, combined with intel and experience of counter-fraud specialists will form the starting point of this new fight against NHS fraudsters. The message is clear: the NHS is no longer an easy target, and if you try to steal from it you will face the consequences.* (Legraien, 2018)

This story was widely, and largely uncritically, reported. Newspaper headlines heralded a 'crackdown on prescription cheats' (*Daily Mail*, 2018).

Was this not simply an accurate description of delinquent behaviour, with abusive individuals depleting our national healthcare of vital resources, at a time of great need? Again we have to think of the nature and purpose of the narrative: but first we should consider how accurate it is. In March 2018 *The Observer* had reported a statement by the Patients Association, a UK advocacy group that aims to improve patients' experience of healthcare.

> *Data released under the Freedom of Information Act shows that 1,052,430 penalty notices were issued to patients in England in 2017 – about double the level in the previous year ... 342,882 penalty notices were subsequently withdrawn because the patient was entitled to the free prescription.*
>
> *'These Freedom of Information requests appear to show a penalty system that is dysfunctional' said Lucy Watson, chair of the Patients Association. 'Any organisation issuing penalty notices and then having to withdraw nearly one in three because they were issued in error is not operating as it should. This compounds the unjust and haphazard nature of prescription charging in England, with some patients facing substantial costs to manage their conditions, and others being entitled to free prescriptions'.*
>
> *Peter Burt, a patient who was wrongly issued with one of the penalty notices, said he worried about how certain patients would react to receiving one.*
>
> *'Some of the people who received these notices will certainly be in vulnerable situations and some will be receiving prescription medication for anxiety and mental health issues', Burt said. 'They should not be receiving letters threatening court action just because the NHS can't be bothered to check the records to see whether they have a prepayment card – especially if there is no intention of carrying out the threat'.* (Doward, 2018)

Be this as it may, if a system of selective fee paying is in place, it needs to be implemented, and the two out of three cases of wrongful claims of exemption need to be dealt with somehow.

This brings us back to how the non-payment is portrayed. In a scenario in which those who do not pay are cynical abusers, lining their pockets at the expense of an easy target, it's only right that they should be 'caught', confronted and punished. This would leave pharmacy staff 'policing' the system, to ensure that punishment is meted out. Unsurprisingly, these staff have little appetite for this. In any case, people who are confronted, and threatened with a penalty that they may not even be able to pay, might be being justly chastised: but equally they might have made an innocent oversight. In either case they are likely to feel shamed – embarrassed and humiliated, particularly if confronted in a public place in their own community.

Might an alternative narrative improve matters, whilst the same rules are enforced? Could people's behaviour still be changed, without 'demonising' it? If you want to teach people a lesson, educational methods are often best. A system of simply checking a person's exemption, and if necessary regretfully explaining to them that they are not on the database, might go some way to detoxifying the issue – especially if there was a readily activated process of 'appeal' and restitution if someone had been wrongly missed out, perhaps allowing them a month's medication whilst the matter was addressed. This might be dismissed as a naïve suggestion, neglecting the complex realities of the situation – but it is no less naive than the story of a 'war against fraudsters'. It is also what was probably occurring on many occasions throughout the country, regardless of the rhetoric.

Hancock's narrative in 2018 was not unique to him: it has been employed by a succession of Health Secretaries, and it is endemic in the service. He did, however, miss an opportunity to challenge the 'received wisdom' of demonisation at a point when he was introducing a system with potential to settle the matter neutrally and efficiently. An effective routine method of checking prescription exemption, coupled with calm but persistent enquiries if discrepancies appear, might ensure due payment without threatening everyone taking a prescription to their pharmacist with action against 'abusers', and creating the suspicion that, even if not you, the next person in the queue might be a fraud or a cheat.

Inflammatory Arguments, Soothing Rituals

A hostile environment arises for a range of synergistic reasons. Many of the dynamics feeding into it have been considered in earlier chapters. The 'fight-flight' basic assumption plays a part, as does projection of aspects of ourselves we do not want to acknowledge. We are inclined to scapegoat and blame other people, and other groups. The hostile environment also feeds upon itself. As anxiety rises, primitive emotional responses escalate in order to deal with it. Society starts to become over-aroused. Hostility is seen as a form of 'strength', almost as a civic virtue.

The idea of 'mentalisation' is valuable here, as it clarifies the link between thinking and feeling, and the conditions needed for them to be held in balance. The concept is grounded in psychological, philosophical, neuroscientific and developmental theory and research (Allen and Fonagy, 2006).

Box 12.5 Mentalisation

- 'Holding mind in mind'.
- Aspiring to understand each other as autonomous thinking and feeling persons.
- Seeing oneself from the outside and others from the inside.
- 'Feeling clearly' i.e. thinking about feelings in ourselves and others.
- It is both conscious and unconscious/automatic.
- It is active – something we do or fail to do.
- It is impaired by intense emotion.

Mentalisation is essentially the ability to think about our own emotional reactions, and those of others, and how these underlie our behaviour. We make sense of each other and ourselves, implicitly and explicitly, in terms of how we can understand subjective states and mental processes. This requires the capacity to 'hold mind in mind' (Allen and Fonagy, 2006). Box 12.5 summarises the important features.

Crucially, in a hostile environment, hyper-arousal can lead to a collapse of mentalisation. Stress interferes with the ability to be mindful of our own minds and the minds of others. A vicious circle then links hostility, stress and our capacity to be mindful, in opposition to the virtuous circle described in Chapter 4. This is illustrated in Figure 12.1.

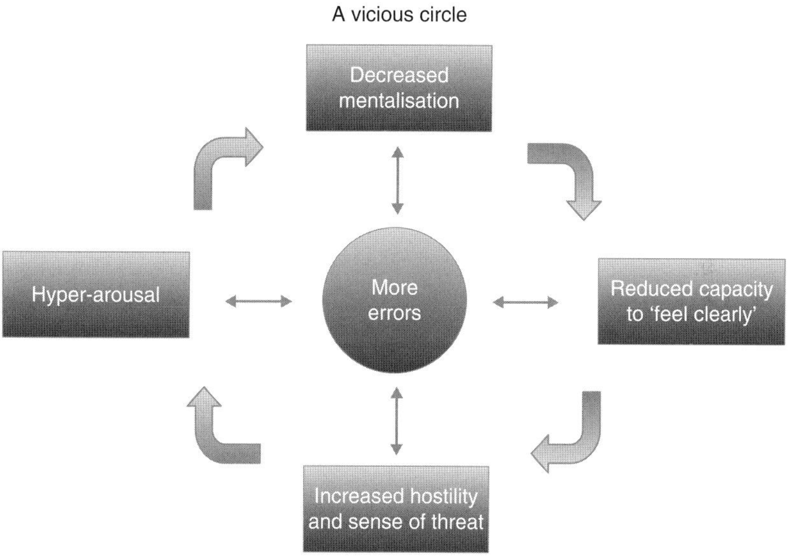

Figure 12.1 A Vicious Circle

Of course, circumstances play a significant part in the development of a hostile culture. There may indeed be high rates of illegal immigration, with competition for scarce resources. People do behave abusively to those who are trying to help them, and some people do commit fraud and theft. How then does the 'hostile environment' differ in practice from the necessary rational, effective protection of one's resources, and of one's kith and kin?

There are a number of ways. Perhaps most importantly, the hostile environment is pervasive, generalising beyond attention to the specific misdemeanours of a few. A culture arises wherein we are all potential fraudsters, or abusers, and may be treated as such 'just in case'. As the Windrush generation discovered, we may discover we do not even have a right to be in the country at all.

In some times and places this goes to extremes, giving rise to regimes of suspicion and surveillance. Alexander Solzhenitsyn wrote vividly about Stalin's Russia in his monumental work *The Gulag Archipelago* (Solzhenitsyn, 1973). Many people then ended up in prison camps, after being arrested in the night on a variety of trumped-up charges. In the first chapter Solzhenitsyn discusses, amongst other things, how many arrests took place simply for operatives to meet their targets, and thus not come under suspicion themselves.

Although we may avow that 'this would never happen' in the UK, there is clear evidence that it happens frequently elsewhere. If the UK is different, then why? Is it simply that we have not, to date, suffered sufficient depletion of resources and social upheaval? Or is there something inherently protective in British society, or the British psyche? It is comforting to think so, but if this is the case, we need to identify and nurture it – as this book is attempting to do.

One vital antidote, in any society, is a sense of affiliation and fellow feeling (and indeed a capacity for kindness), whilst still dealing with the real threats that confront us. In recent years, some organisations have tried to protect staff from abuse by appealing to just such fellow-feeling, to people's common humanity. The non-confrontational approach is perhaps better able to make people think about their own behaviour more critically, and the behaviour of others more kindly. In 2014 'Transport for London' (TFL) addressed the abuse of their staff by means of a simple poster, with childlike handwriting on a plain white background: 'My mum works on the tube. Last night someone shouted at her again. I thought she was crying. But she said it was just something in her eye' (TFL, 2014).

This poster captured the popular imagination in London, and was photographed and posted on social media repeatedly: people seemed to find it emotionally touching, and none of those responding asked 'What's the world coming to?' It promotes mentalisation, communicating the idea that abused staff have thoughts, feelings, and indeed children. Whereas the self-righteous narrative of 'zero tolerance' risks ratcheting up a climate of abuse and intolerance, conflict reduction may actually be more likely if other means are used: encouraging mentalisation, reducing tension and promoting a sense of the common good. By 2018 the same approach was being used in a poster campaign by at least one NHS trust, in North Tees and Hartlepool. A little girl in a nurse's uniform was pictured with the caption 'MY MUMMY is a nurse. PLEASE keep her SAFE at work'. Children of other staff members were also pictured in variations on this theme (images can be found at Bodell, 2018). Oddly, but perhaps inevitably given the prevailing rhetoric, press coverage of the campaign seems to have unanimously described it as 'hard-hitting', somewhat missing the central point.

Be all this as it may, even by 2018 it did not appear that 'zero tolerance' in the NHS was going away any time soon. The annual NHS staff survey had reported that 'while 15 per cent said they had experienced physical violence from patients, relatives or the public in 2013, that increased slightly to 15.2 per cent in 2017'. Despite such a minimal change, of no statistical significance, this was billed alarmingly in the press as 'Violence against NHS staff in England reaches five-year high', and the new Health Secretary announced 'A partnership between the NHS, Crown Prosecution Service and police forces is being set up to try to bring perpetrators in England to court more speedily, as part of a tough new 'zero tolerance' approach to such crimes' (Campbell, 2018).

This relaunch of the policy included important initiatives. Key action points included better collaborative working between the NHS and the Crown Prosecution Service to seek prosecutions and assist victims in giving evidence, improved training in dealing with workplace violence, and improved psychological support for staff who are victims of work-related violence (MDDUS, 2018). Despite this the 'zero tolerance' rhetoric reared its head once more.

Each time such stories are retold, the initiative is billed as 'new', yet as we have seen, the 'tough new zero-tolerance approach' story had already been around for almost two decades: the same story of 'toughness' being repeated once more, with even a tiny variation in incidence being billed as a clear and present danger.

In terms of the discussion of the two modes of primate functioning in Chapter 9, this type of story-telling, inciting fear and offering a 'hard line' response by 'the authorities' is characteristic of the agonic mode. By contrast, the TFL and North Tees and Hartlepool poster campaigns offered a more hedonic approach. Hedonic societies rely upon active maintenance of a range of affiliative and soothing rituals. However, as has been noted, the danger is that if hedonic societies are distracted, and cease paying attention to their affiliative needs, they can collapse.

It is also important that values of affiliation and commonality are asserted in a way that does not simply rely upon a common enemy – that they are not founded on projection and evacuation of negative feelings as discussed in Chapter 6, but upon the real assimilation of our complex emotions, and the necessity of continuing to be in relationship with one another. This may be more difficult in the short-term, but is likely to lead to more stability in the long-run.

In Chapters 5 and 6 we considered how complex feelings can be responded to either in a way that narrows our attention (using defence mechanisms) or in a way that deepens our insight, empathy and rapport. Thinking and emotional experience are intimately related. Mentalisation is a recognition of this, and the capacity to mentalise may well be a precondition for learning how to function effectively with others, and return to the hedonic mode after a rift in relationships. Effective mentalisation may reduce the stress of being with others, and can thus increase the ability, in turn, to learn what are viewed as more 'technical' skills.

Developing this further, a person in a difficult or unfamiliar situation may experience anxiety and distress that resolves if it can be linked to thought, freeing up the ability to think and learn. If a person does not manage the uncertainty, and instead resorts to primitive defences as discussed in Chapter 5, the emotional experience is unavailable for conscious reflection, making it hard both to learn, and to practise with understanding and effectiveness.

So, at times of trouble and difficulty, our initial emotional responses may be primitive and unproductive. If we recognise and understand this we can move on; if unprocessed or evacuated such responses unconsciously determine policy or action. Solutions that appear logical may in fact be expressions of primitive fears or impulses, with a veneer of post-hoc rationalisation. Because of this, we need to take great care in how we establish policies, 'drives' and initiatives that appear to be solving problems, but are in fact enacting dramas with a cast of abusers, fraudsters and illegal aliens.

A defining characteristic of the 'hostile environment' is an ever-present suspicion and mistrust of others, which closes down on the reflection and open discussion so necessary to establish a creative group life. How can we hold on to reflection? We are up against a vicious circle here: the more hostile the environment, the more difficult (and dangerous) it is to reflect. But, in turn, it is only through reflection and the opportunity it brings to learn from experience, and gain self-knowledge, that there is any hope of moderating the hostile environment, and of practising with intelligent kindness.

Is the Hostile Environment Fit for Purpose?

The 'Welfare State' is intrinsically hedonic, rooted in affiliation and mutual care. However, it is no coincidence that it emerged after an all-consuming, highly destructive war, when most people longed for peace and calm. Even so, people being what they are, boundary issues soon arose, as a consequence of competition for, and exploitation of, the resources being dispensed, and as a way of transacting issues of status and priority. Rules were required, which then needed to be enforced.

It is, however, quite possible to maintain and enforce rules whilst still functioning in the hedonic mode: any action necessary can be accompanied by 'soothing rituals' (i.e. carried out with kindness) and appeals to fellow-feeling, in order to de-escalate hostility. The alternative, involving threat and denigration, is more likely to promote confrontation. Does such unkindness even fulfil its supposed objectives?

In 2012 the 'hostile environment' was promoted as a deterrent to illegal immigration. Despite this, many asylum seekers, and others, continued to try and reach the UK, held back by physical barriers rather than a change of heart due to the policy. People still wanted to be here because, despite the bureaucratically 'hostile' and inhumane environment, our settled civic society and material wellbeing had great appeal for those fleeing civil disorder, war, terror and poverty. The environment would have to be *very* hostile to be worse than what they had left behind. Thus the changes introduced, rather than deterring those supposedly being targeted, just potentially made life worse for everyone.

People cannot be let into the country at will, nor should a permissive attitude be taken to fraud, exploitation or violence in our civic institutions. It may, however, be that boundaries and codes of behaviour could be enforced kindly: and indeed enforcement may be more effective under such conditions, with people more readily brought 'on side' into what we regard as good behaviour. There is clear evidence that violence and abuse can be reduced by attention to calming environments, keeping people informed of what to expect, and by personal interactions that are soothing and respectful rather than confrontational. Policy recommendations by employers are in line with this. Gently inducing private shame and fellow feeling in someone may be a far more effective way of moderating their behaviour than publicly humiliating, threatening or denigrating them.

Of course, expressions of hostility and unkindness may fulfil functions other than the technical ones they purport to address. They can be ways of venting emotion, perhaps frustration at difficult circumstances, feelings of being overwhelmed or exploited, or even primary sadistic impulses. There is a widely-perceived political need to sound 'tough' in times of difficulty – or even create apparent difficulty in order to consolidate one's grip on power.

We need to take care, because the rhetoric of the hostile environment sets the stage for conflict: with the lines of 'right and wrong' drawn absolutely. These are the preconditions for war: which is readily used as a metaphor amongst the language of 'vows' and 'crack-downs' so often used by the press. It bears repeating that the moves towards kinship described in Chapter 1 were immediately post-war: the population was chastened, and the appalling destructiveness and waste inherent in conflict was apparent to everyone. There was an appetite for solving problems by other means. By the dawn of the 2020s that appetite seemed to be waning.

There is ample evidence from other disciplines that use of kindness and appeals to fellow-feeling can fulfil the same objectives as confrontation, threat and attack. Perhaps the ultimate 'hostile environment', in popular imagination, is the interrogation room. The scenario readily evokes images of coercion, intimidation, deliberate demoralisation and torture. Since the Al-Qaeda attack on the World Trade Centre in Manhattan in 2001, some Western nations' attitudes to torture have changed, and, particularly in the USA, various interrogation techniques previously shunned have been embraced for reasons of 'national security'. If 'terrorists' are being interrogated, it is apparently self-evident that all is justifiable for the common good. A President of the United States has asserted that 'waterboarding works' and 'we have to fight fire with fire' (BBC, 2017). Waterboarding is an interrogation technique that simulates drowning.

A paper in the journal Psychology, Public Policy and Law in 2014 examined the impact of 'rapport-based interview techniques' on suspects' resistance to interrogation, using a sample of 181 interrogations with international (Al-Qaeda and Al-Qaeda-inspired), paramilitary and right-wing terrorists. Findings clearly indicated the effectiveness of rapport-based interrogation styles in which suspects are treated with respect, dignity and integrity. The lead authors, Laurence and Emily Alison, based in the Psychology Department at Liverpool University, have explored these issues over many years, and developed their model on the basis of detailed observations of over 2,000 hours of field interrogations with 'high value' detainees and terrorist subjects. They have concluded that these 'rapport-based' interpersonal methods, whilst by no means a guarantee, are an interviewer's best chance of securing 'accurate, expedient and potentially lifesaving information and intelligence'. An interesting and accessible account of their work, and that of others in the same field, has been written by the journalist Ian Leslie (Leslie, 2017).

Treating other people with respect, dignity, integrity – in other words, with kindness – is not 'soft' or ineffectual. It is often the most effective way forward in difficult circumstances. Also, if this works when interrogating terror suspects, indeed actual terrorists, then surely it bears similar consideration in dealing with fallible, but largely well-meaning and skilled practitioners and the vulnerable people they care for. We need to bear this in mind as we take a final look at how things can go very wrong, before returning to intelligent kindness itself.

References

Allen, J. P. and Fonagy P. (2006) *Handbook of Mentalisation-Based Treatment.* John Wiley & Sons.

BBC (2017) Donald Trump says he believes waterboarding works. BBC News website, 26 January 2017. Available at: www.bbc.co.uk/news/world-us-canada-38753000 [last accessed 13 August, 2019].

BBC (2018) Amber Rudd resigns as home secretary. BBC News website, 30 April, 2018. Available at: www.bbc.co.uk/news/uk-politics-43944988 [last accessed 13 August, 2019].

Bodell, M. (2018) Children of NHS staff call on the public to 'keep mummy safe at work' Nursing Notes. Available at: www.nursingnotes.co.uk/children-of-nhs-staff-call-on-the-public-to-keep-mummy-safe-at-work/ [last accessed 13 August, 2019].

Bulman, M. (2018) British High Commissioner's baby son denied a UK passport after being born in Trinidad. *The Independent*, 25 April, 2018. Available at: www.independent.co.uk/news/uk/home-news/windrush-latest-british-high-commissioner-arthur-snell-son-uk-passport-denied-citizen-a8321056.html [last accessed 13 August, 2019].

Butler, P. (2018) Former watchdog chief labels disabled benefits process a 'hostile environment'. *The Guardian*, 6 October, 2018. Available at: www.theguardian.com/society/2018/oct/06/former-watchdog-chief-labels-disabled-benefits-process-a-hostile-environment [last accessed 26 August, 2019].

Campbell, D. (2018) Violence against NHS staff in England reaches five-year high. *The Guardian*, 31 October, 2018. Available at: www.theguardian.com/society/2018/oct/31/violence-against-nhs-staff-in-england-reaches-five-year-high [last accessed 26 August, 2019].

Daily Mail (2018) NHS launches crackdown on prescription cheats who dishonestly claim free medication in bid to save £300million. *Daily Mail*, 13 October, 2018. Available at: www.dailymail.co.uk/news/article-6273427/NHS-launches-crackdown-prescription-cheats-bid-save-300million.html [last accessed 13 August, 2019].

Doward, J. (2018) NHS agency falsely accuses more than 340,000 of prescription fraud. *The Observer*, 10 March, 2018. Available at: www.theguardian.com/society/2018/mar/10/nhs-falsely-accuses-thousands-patients-prescription-fraud [last accessed 26 August, 2019].

Gentleman, A. (2018) Amelia Gentleman on Windrush: 'I've felt like an immigration case worker'. *The Guardian*, 20 April, 2018. Available at: www.theguardian.com/membership/2018/apr/20/amelia-gentleman-windrush-immigration [last accessed 13 August, 2019].

Kirkup, J. and Winnett, R. (2012).Theresa May interview: 'We're going to give illegal migrants a really hostile reception'. *Daily Telegraph*, 25 May, 2012. Available at: www.telegraph.co.uk/news/uknews/immigration/9291483/Theresa-May-interview-Were-going-to-give-illegal-migrants-a-really-hostile-reception.html [last accessed 13 August, 2019].

Legraien, L. (2018) Prescription exemptions to be digitised to help Government tackle fraud. *The Pharmacist*, 15 October, 2018.

Leslie, I. (2017) The scientists persuading terrorists to spill their secrets. *The Guardian*, 13 October, 2017. Available at: www.theguardian.com/news/2017/oct/13/the-scientists-persuading-terrorists-to-spill-their-secrets [last accessed 26 August, 2019].

MDDUS (Medical and Dental Defence Union of Scotland) (2018) Zero tolerance – can it work? Available at: www.mddus.com/resources/resource-library/risk-alerts/2018/november/zero-tolerance—can-it-work [last accessed 26 August, 2019].

NHSBSA (2018) Leaflet 'Over 1 million people received a penalty charge notice . . . don't assume you're entitled'. Available at: www.facebook.com/NHSBSAHelpWithHealthCosts/photos/a.566661800089187/1822842477804440/?type=3 [last accessed 13 August, 2019].

NHS Employers (2008) Violence against staff. Available at: www.nhsemployers.org/~/media/Employers/Publications/Violence%20against%20staff.pdf [last accessed 14 November, 2019].

Northern Ireland Health and Social Care Board (2017) Poster: Warning: Zero tolerance on abuse of healthcare staff. Available at: www.bda.org/news-centre/blog/abuse-from-patients-whilst-at-work-what-can-you-do [last accessed 13 August, 2019].

Solzhenitsyn, A. I. (1973) *The Gulag Archipelago 1918–1956*. Harper & Row.

TFL (2014). Poster: My mum works on the tube. Available at: www.wearewhatwedo.gr.com/en/2017/02/kindness-and-other-demons/ [last accessed 13 August, 2019].

Chapter

13 The Pull towards Perversion

Enantiodromia: The tendency of things to change into their opposites, especially as a supposed governing principle of natural cycles and of psychological development.

(Oxford dictionary online)

Perverse Dynamics

The organisations that make up our 'Welfare State' sit within a broader society that shapes their rules and arrangements, and the conscious and unconscious social pacts that allow them to function. In Chapter 1, we noted the spirit of cooperation that was around in the immediate aftermath of the Second World War, and how this provided a value base and a fertile ground for implementing the Welfare State. Since then this communalism has been steadily encroached upon by individualism, consumerism and a shift towards 'the market'. Living standards have risen, vastly more material goods are available, and the trauma of the War has receded: yet at the same time we are preoccupied with financial constraints, and the limitations of what may be provided. What type of changes have these shifts brought about in our civic institutions? What have the negative consequences been, and are these safely outweighed by the positive?

'Perversion' is a strong word, with vivid negative connotations. It is commonly used with two different, albeit related, meanings. One is in referring to sexual behaviour considered strange and unpleasant. The other involves something being changed so that it is not what it was, or should be, as in 'perversion of justice', or 'perverse incentives'. Here, we are concerned with this second strand of meaning, and specifically how care can become not-caring, or even sadism. In this usage it is closely linked to the concept of 'enantiodromia', which may sound forbidding, but describes a frequently recurring pattern in human life: there is a natural tendency for things to turn into their opposites. Young radicals become old conservatives, or a revolution inspired by equality, freedom and brotherhood turns into the 'the terror'. Slightly differently, but on the same principle, micro-managing 'accountability' may produce suspicion and obfuscation, not openness and transparency. A legal duty of candour might worry people into covering their tracks.

There is a perverse tendency in many of our care-giving organisations that will be recognised readily by those who work in, or depend upon them. On an immediate level, this might appear as ostensible attempts to keep the system functioning, to prevent abuse or waste, in a broader context of limited resources and pressures towards 'efficiency'.

Across the Welfare State there are daily concerns with such matters as gate-keeping and risk, wastage, and people missing appointments. Frequent 'assessments' take place to manage 'risk' or 'eligibility', but commonly the outcome is that nothing more is offered and people are sent away, often after telling their story and exposing their vulnerability. If you miss a hospital appointment, you have to persuade your GP to refer you again, an administrative deterrent with undertones of humiliation. Assessors driven by 'payment by results' have all-too-frequently (and wrongly) concluded that seriously disabled or sick people do not qualify for benefits, with consequences ranging from inconvenience to tragedy.

Such petty, and not so petty, cruelties, familiar across all 'welfare' settings, mean that parts of our systems have become, in practice, unkind: a perversion of the explicit aims of the organisation arising from its procedures. Individual staff members may then attempt to mitigate their effects, or relish them, dependent upon character.

There are, of course, even more serious examples of perversion of the explicit aims of health and welfare organisations, and we have considered a variety of them in this book. Research conducted by researchers at University College London (UCL) and the Camden and Islington NHS Foundation Trust in 2018 found that what they termed 'abuse' was taking place in 99 per cent of UK care homes. Such inhumanity ranged from making people in need of care wait unnecessarily for help, to deliberately neglecting people with challenging behaviours, with a few more serious misdeeds. Highly stretched staff resources were identified as a central cause of such neglect and abuse (Cooper et al, 2018).

In previous chapters we have explored a variety of themes that shed light on how good intentions can have bad outcomes. Key examples are:

- How good staff can become bad;
- How well-meaning teams can become dysfunctional and invest precious time and energy enacting divisive dramas;
- How services that need to cooperate around a patient or client can end up fragmented, even fighting amongst themselves;
- How, despite apparent commitment to them, the most vulnerable in our society can end up being neglected and excluded from care;
- How change agendas and their management, while aiming for improvement, can make things worse;
- How industrialisation, designed to ensure uniform, high quality services, can undermine care;
- How attempts to regulate services and staff and hold them to account can promote mistrust and defensiveness, raise anxiety and distract from the task.

Our focus in this chapter is the pervasive political and economic discourse promoting the market and how this can amplify all the factors above. In doing so, we will be considering recent history, but we are not suggesting that there was a previous, unproblematic 'golden age' without perverse dynamics.

Unkindness and hostility will always be present in our relationships with each other. They are part of human nature. We all have it in us to be unkind, consciously or unconsciously, deliberately or accidentally, and to varying degrees. Against this background, systemic pressures may make us more or less likely to be so. Individuals working in health and social care are probably no more (or less) perverse than those in other sectors. However, an organisation and its members are intertwined: the decisions and actions of individuals are influenced by organisational culture, and, in turn, reinforce it, for good or ill. The nature of work in the welfare sector, and the way it is being managed, produces particular difficulties for the staff and the system. The concept of perversion sheds light on frankly exploitative behaviour, helping explain how many people in positions of trust end up abusing those positions and how people may be collectively perverse despite individual attempts to be otherwise.

Psychoanalysts have long concerned themselves with perversion, using the term with a variety of precise definitions and theoretical underpinnings. Detailed consideration of these perspectives is beyond the scope of the current argument, but at their heart is a pathology of personal relatedness. Instrumental relations have dominance – in other words, people are used as a means to an end, as tools and commodities, rather than seen as respected others. In this way, something that purports to be one thing may become something quite different, and much less straightforward.

Perversion, however, is more than just something being different from what it claims to be, or being about relating to others instrumentally. There is an additional dimension, which involves a particular form of gratification, which is why the term is used so often about certain forms of sexual behaviour. The American psychoanalyst, Robert Stoller, offers one compelling formulation of this. In his book *Perversion: The Erotic Form of Hatred* (Stoller, 1986) he suggests that the main clinical factor in sexual perversions is hostility, which combines with sexual desire to produce a variety of abnormal sexual behaviours. The idea of hostility contaminating the caring task may also be helpful in considering the perversion of care-giving.

To examine the systemic pressures involved we will first consider the nature of 'perverse organisations'. We will then look at the way that market forces have taken hold across the NHS and Welfare State with the potential to create a culture that can skew, even actively pervert, the delivery of care.

Knowing and Not Knowing

In 2018 the public became aware of malignant practice in Gosport Memorial Hospital in Hampshire. The hospital had, it appeared, hastened the deaths of many patients over a number of years. Some staff had expressed concerns, but these had not been attended to. In his foreword to the report of the independent enquiry, James Jones, the retired Bishop of Liverpool, stated alarming conclusions that illustrate perverse dynamics. He is quoted in Box 13.1 below.

Susan Long, an Australian organisational consultant and academic, explores such issues in her book *The Perverse Organisation and Its Deadly Sins*. Her argument is that the behaviour of modern large corporations is becoming increasingly perverse. Although these systems differ from the Welfare State in many respects, her observations are pertinent. She identifies some key features of a 'perverse state of [organisational] mind'. Essential to these is the failure to acknowledge the existence of others or their rights. She states:

Box 13.1 From the Report on Deaths at Gosport Memorial Hospital

The documents that the Panel has found reveal that . . . during a certain period at Gosport War Memorial Hospital, there was a disregard for human life and a culture of shortening the lives of a large number of patients by prescribing and administering 'dangerous doses' of a hazardous combination of medication not clinically indicated or justified. They show too that, whereas a large number of patients and their relatives understood that their admission to the hospital was for either rehabilitation or respite care, they were, in effect, put on a terminal care pathway. They show that, when relatives complained about the safety of patients and the appropriateness of their care, they were consistently let down by those in authority – both individuals and institutions. These included the senior management of the hospital, healthcare organisations, Hampshire Constabulary, local politicians, the coronial system, the Crown Prosecution Service, the General Medical Council and the Nursing and Midwifery Council. All failed to act in ways that would have better protected patients and relatives, whose interests some subordinated to the reputation of the hospital and the professions involved.

(Gosport Independent Panel, 2018)

> *Consumerism, greed, and changing values worldwide are increasingly leading interactions between individuals in societies to become almost exclusively transactions motivated. This, in turn, promotes the emergence of a perverse state of mind. The perverse state of mind, a product of group unconscious dynamics, is one for which the existence of 'others' and their rights becomes denied. The perverse state of mind in groups is the most important mechanism behind abusive and corrupt behaviours.* (Long, 2008)

Long describes another key aspect of the perverse state of mind: it 'acknowledges reality but at the same time, denies it' in the pursuit of its own aims. It thus 'turns a blind eye' to the consequences of abusive behaviour. She argues that organisations can function in this way, just as much as individuals.

The phrase 'turning a blind eye' originates in a story about the eighteenth century English naval hero, Horatio Nelson, blind in one eye. Nelson was given a signal to retreat in a sea battle with the Danes. Judging that this would be an error, but unable to directly disobey orders, he purportedly raised his telescope to his blind eye and said 'I do not see the signal'. 'Turning a blind eye' as a clinical concept originates in the work of John Steiner (Steiner, 1985), who details the dynamic of knowingly deciding not to know something, usually to avoid psychic pain.

'Knowing and not knowing' at one and the same time is central to the concept of perversion. There may be powerful forces working against recognition of the negative aspects of our caring institutions, despite an undercurrent of complaint 'on the ground'. Such forces often seem to be striving actively to prevent acknowledgement of problems. This is what the Gosport Independent Panel, as cited above, described. It was also evident in the way the UK Government struggled for years to ignore the evidence of the human cost of rolling out its Universal Credit programme – a programme whose expressed intentions were benign. Forces encouraging 'turning a blind eye' may be particularly strong when problems arise from an urgency to implement key elements of the 'reform agenda' of whatever government is in power.

Some of this non-recognition may be relatively straightforward. Managers and leaders, convinced about the benefits of, or reputationally dependent upon, one change or another, may simply minimise the evidence of problems or of unintended consequences. They may try to persuade staff who see problems that they are being negative, and that they should overlook the costs to them and those they are caring for.

However, there are more serious – and quite explicitly perverse and corrupting – manifestations of this turning of the 'blind eye'. In Mid-Staffordshire NHS Foundation Trust between 2005 and 2009, a culture of cost-cutting, target-driven behaviour, and poor management led to significant deficiencies in the quality of care in some parts of the hospital, with neglect of patients, and concerns about avoidable deaths. A report by the Healthcare Commission concluded:

> *In the Trust's drive to become a foundation trust, it appears to have lost sight of its real priorities. The Trust was galvanised into radical action by the imperative to save money and did not properly consider the effect of reductions in staff on the quality of care. It took a decision to significantly reduce staff without adequately assessing the consequences. Its strategic focus was on financial and business matters at a time when the quality of care of its patients admitted as an emergency was well below acceptable standards.*
> (Healthcare Commission, 2009, p. 11)

Although describing the danger of unmitigated financial efficiency drives, this formulation overlooks a key component of the process. The trust knew about these dangers and of their increasingly obvious effects. Managers and leaders appear to have ignored, or even silenced, feedback from staff at all levels that would have alerted them to the problem. Staff did try – more than a third of the 515 safety incident reports submitted by ward staff attributed the problem to inadequate staffing. Consultants found their incident reports downgraded to being 'minor events' without consultation or investigation. One senior consultant actually used parliamentary privilege to expose this climate to the Parliamentary Health Select Committee.

Thus, despite the considerable attention given to clinical governance systems over the preceding decade, the process of reporting concerns, far from being used to help the trust manage the quality of its services, lost credibility completely. A senior manager in the trust even called for a specialist independent investigator to remove any statements in his report suggesting that people had died because of poor care, because it would distress people and bring bad publicity for the trust (Francis, 2010, p. 23).

Events in Mid-Staffordshire were part of a wider landscape in which this 'knowing and not knowing' was gaining ground. In 2010 Tony Delamothe, Deputy Editor of the British Medical Journal at the time, contrasted the attention and public awareness relating to a range of NHS scandals in the 1990s with more recent inquiries, such as those into deaths through hospital infection in several trusts, and the Mid-Staffordshire case itself (Delamothe, 2010). He argued that there appeared to be a determination to regard recent scandals as rare exceptions, and to fail to note patterns – despite the apparent consistency and frequency of examples of similar concerns. He commented that there 'should be enough material for a meta-inquiry into English medical scandals of the twenty-first century'. It appeared that there was at best avoidance of, and at worst active resistance to, what was 'known' being directly acknowledged and made properly available for understanding and action.

Robert Francis's final report into what happened in Mid-Staffordshire contained a bewildering 290 detailed recommendations. Given that few people would be able to hold all of these in mind at any one time, this was essentially an invitation for interested parties to 'pick and mix' a few that suited their own perspective. Jeremy Hunt, then Health Secretary, made a statement to Parliament in March 2013, shortly after the report was released. He flagged up a number of changes, summarised in the *Daily Mail* newspaper thus: *'A new chief inspector of hospitals . . . A statutory 'duty of candour' on hospitals and GP surgeries to stop them concealing mistakes . . . A ban on gagging clauses . . . A new criminal offence to prevent managers fiddling figures . . . '* (*Daily Mail*, 2013). As if the 290 recommendations weren't enough, the *Daily Mail* seemed particularly impressed with Mr Hunt's additional proposal that students seeking funding for nursing degrees would first have to serve a year as a healthcare assistant. This gave it its headline: *'Nurses told, "you're not too posh to wash a patient": Minister orders student nurses back to basics to improve compassion in NHS'.*

The Government's eventual formal response (Department of Health, 2015) had a headline promise of *'A new, rigorous inspection regime . . . for hospitals, GPs and adult social care'*, and reiterated Mr Hunt's other suggestions. Such an emphasis on command and control carried an implicit message that failings were due to crimes, misdemeanours and vanities that should be policed, meanwhile turning a blind eye to the 'culture of fear and blame' identified by Francis. So what had not been noticed and learnt? We outline some of the factors contributing to a perverse climate in Box 13.2.

Box 13.2 A Perverse Climate

Perversion flourishes where:

- People are related to instrumentally: controlled, manipulated or treated as a means to an end;
- Individual gratification outweighs responding to the needs of others;
- The rights of others are not recognised;
- Levels of hostility are high and contaminate interpersonal relationships;
- There are high levels of cognitive dissonance owing to the difficulty of reconciling conflicting imperatives and demands whilst trying to hold to basic values;
- There is avoidance of, or refusal to acknowledge, the negative consequences of some actions.

A Perverting Force?

Our particular concern is the way a competitive market economy has been actively promoted without proper democratic debate or proper understanding of its impact on society. A neoliberal consensus that competition for market dominance is the best driver for quality, profit and shareholder value has been carelessly applied to public services. The value of public services lies in what they contribute to collective and individual wellbeing; not in stock market placement, extracted profit and shareholder dividends. The fact that such a market, by definition, involves many business failures and collapses of services has been largely ignored, despite the calamitous results for people in need. The associated priced and commodified view of need, skills and service has transformed our civic institutions and is at odds with the idea of an integrated service that prioritises the needs of the vulnerable. Perhaps most worrying, is the way prioritising the market viewpoint can insidiously affect the attitudes, feelings and actions of staff.

Uncritical acceptance of the market paradigm can be a growth medium for a range of perverse attitudes and behaviours that pull attention and commitment away from kinship and kindness at best, and lead to a range of active abuses at worst. This is not a simple matter of debating whether delivery of services should be through a 'mixed economy' of public, third-sector and private organisations. A market-based approach influences how every part of the system – client, staff member, task, service location and so on – is valued, defined and treated. It is based in a worldview of commodities, competing technologies and providers, with a pervasive discourse of 'customers' and 'prices'.

Crowding Out Altruism

If people become commodities, they matter by virtue of their market value, rather than as individual citizens with internal lives and legitimate personal concerns. In tandem with this, a pervasive economic rationalism sets the making, or saving, of money as what gives work its value, rather than any intrinsic personal or interpersonal quality of the task.

In the 2009 BBC Reith Lectures, considering 'A New Citizenship', Michael Sandel, the Harvard political philosopher, argued the importance of a politics orientated less to the pursuit of individual self-interest and more to the pursuit of the common good (Sandel, 2009a,b). He was critical of the market triumphalism of the preceding three decades, particularly the expansion of markets into social problem areas such as prisons and healthcare. In a pertinent and important turn of phrase, he said we were *'drifting from having a market economy to becoming a market society'*.

In other words, rather than holding on to a sense that we have collectively constructed a market so as to better organise aspects of our creative, entrepreneurial, trading and economic life, we have now begun to think and define ourselves, and everything else, in terms of market values.

Sandel's critique is that markets are neither neutral nor inert. The move of markets and market thinking into social areas previously governed by non-market norms actually shifts these norms in a way that may be undesirable. A classic study in this field by Richard Titmuss, the first Professor of Social Administration at the London School of Economics, looked at different systems of blood donation (Titmuss, 1971). It compared the US system, which permitted the buying and selling of blood for transfusion, with the UK system, which relied wholly on voluntarily donated blood and banned financial incentives.

To the surprise of some, the commercialisation of blood in the USA led to shortages, inefficiencies and a greater incidence of contaminated blood. This contamination contributed to the scandalous use of infected blood products in the UK in the 1970s and 1980s, another chastening example of 'turning a blind eye' (Wise, 2015, inter alia). Titmuss concluded that putting a price on blood had turned what had been a gift into a commodity: once blood is bought and sold in the marketplace, people are less likely to feel a moral obligation to donate out of altruism. Introducing a market value eroded the non-market norms – the norms of kinship and kindness – associated with blood donation, with serious effects.

As further evidence that markets leave their mark on social values, Sandel described a child care centre where the parents were routinely turning up late at the end of the day, with the result that centre staff had to stay on longer than they wished. They decided to start charging fees for lateness expecting this to act as a disincentive, with the hope that staff could then go home on time. To their surprise, it had the opposite effect, and the number of late pick-ups increased. Attaching a financial tariff to lateness seemed to have changed it into something else, and altered the thinking and behaviour of the parents. They now seemed to find that paying for the extra time removed any anxiety and guilt and entitled them to be late. In this example, what was intended as a fine for 'bad' parents became a fee for a commodity. Parents stopped worrying about being late for their children and decided it was a service worth paying for (Sandel, 2009a, p. 7).

Attaching a cost to something, and the resultant commodification, can, then, have consequences very different to those intended. However important it is to be able to relate cost to task in health and social care, this danger requires careful attention.

An Economy of Kindness?

Some economists propose that ascribing a monetary value to everything is helpful, and that attributing a market price to something like 'happiness' enables us to measure social progress in ways that do not simply rely on crude measures of production and consumption (Powdthavee and Stutzer, 2014). The intention is that by putting market prices on a variety of different things, one has a way of comparing their relative value, and weighing one against the other.

This is the theory behind the area of health service research that tries to evaluate and compare the quality (and quantity) of life achieved by various interventions, rather than just technically specified 'success' rates. There are, for example, measures of quality-adjusted life years (QALYs) and disability-adjusted life years (DALYs). These have been developed to help balance the benefits of particular treatments for various conditions, and ascertain the relative 'value' or 'cost effectiveness' of keeping someone with a terminal or severe chronic condition alive.

Although very necessary, given that resources are limited, placing a 'value' on life in its various manifestations is a problematic and bold enterprise. Highly technical cost–benefit analyses have been developed, each with their own internal logic, but these are controversial and may at times appear somewhat random, as an example cited in a British Medical Journal editorial illustrates:

> *The National Institute for Health and Clinical Excellence (NICE) requires strong reasons for supporting an intervention that costs more than £30,000 ($49,200) to deliver a year of good quality life. The Department of Transport generally puts a much higher value on life when deciding on measures to reduce the risk of road and rail deaths. This implies that lives could be saved with no extra overall expenditure by diverting resources from spending on road and rail safety to spending on medical interventions.* (Weale, 2009)

Needless to say, the author was not proposing this as a policy, but drawing attention to the difficulties inherent in attributing a monetary value to life, and the discrepancy between models used in different government departments. This highlights how any such value should be viewed circumspectly as an imperfect tool to inform decision-making, not as a 'bottom line' upon which a decision is based.

In his final Reith Lecture, Sandel showed the absurdity of what he called 'market mimicking governance'. He gave the example of a cost–benefit analysis of new air pollution standards undertaken by the US Environmental Protection Agency, where it assigned a monetary value to human life: $3.7 million per life saved, except for people over the age of 70, whose lives were valued at $2.3 million. Sandel went on to say:

> *Lying behind the different valuations, was a market-mimicking assumption: younger people, with more years still to live, would presumably pay more to save their lives than older people would pay to save theirs. Advocates for the elderly didn't see it that way. They bitterly protested the 'senior citizen discount!'* (Sandel, 2009b)

Sandel sees the idea that everything can be captured in monetary terms as seductive because it offers a way of making political choices without making hard and controversial moral decisions. Problems start when cost–benefit analysis is treated as if it were a science, rather than a subjective conceptual model. Monetary valuations, and the rationales by which they are determined, become imbued with more significance than is sensible. This shifts decision-making from the realm of a democratic politics concerned with the common good, to 'experts' responsible for a technical tool – what Sandel describes as an 'ultimately spurious science'. This spurious science appears to have found rather too many uncritical students among commissioners and contract managers.

If economic measures become idealised as 'objective', and prioritised over other equally valid measures, this may be used to duck bigger social and ethical decisions. Commissioning, research, and even clinical or practice protocols, then get skewed. For example, recovery from depression may be equated to, and assessed, in terms of economic recovery, and thus services that prioritise (or claim to prioritise) such recovery are themselves prioritised. This ignores how 'depression' arises from a complex set of conditions affecting our mood, thoughts and relationships. Many people would view improvement in these as more important than the capacity to function at work.

This progression – from a useful economic model, to an essential criterion for social transactions, determining how we think about ourselves and each other – is what Sandel means when he talks about moving from 'having' a market economy to 'being' a market society. We find ourselves thinking in terms of the monetary cost or value of things in a way that crowds out other meanings. An uncritical substitution of economic measures for political, moral and ethical judgement risks fracturing the bonds between us, as human beings sharing a difficult world. It removes the person from the picture – and without the person it is hard to stay connected to kinship and kindness.

The Commodification of Vocation

'Vocation' literally means 'calling'. The implication is that one has been called to follow a certain life path by some destiny, or, in the original religious use of the word, by God. The idea of vocation – religious or secular – has been a source of energy for many generations of professionals. Although most people today would interpret the word 'vocation' in a secular way, it continues to convey a sense that one's chosen profession is more than 'just' a job. It suggests that one is deeply privileged to have the opportunity and the expertise to be involved in one's chosen work, with an active welcoming of the responsibilities and duties involved that goes beyond the detail of a job plan or financial reward. Motivated by vocation, people will readily work over and above their contracted hours. This may seem old fashioned, not to mention open to abuse. Despite this, many, perhaps most, of the staff working in our public services, from receptionists to directors, have this attitude, and commit themselves to their work on this basis. Such a sense of vocation contributes greatly to humane, attentive practice. Undermining it is destructive, for staff and service-users alike.

Micro-management of the work of these professionals, with curtailment of their autonomy, is too often part and parcel of a more commercial paradigm. This undermines the values of vocation, with the person less able to feel that their commitment and compassion is freely given and self-determined. For the people who receive care, often highly sensitive to the personal relationships involved, the disappearance of this attitude is bad news.

The 1980s brought 'a new public management' (Hood, 1991) to public service institutions and agencies in both the USA and UK. Approaches were developed to make public services more 'business-like' and to improve their efficiency by using private sector management models. In the UK this led to the introduction of the 'internal market'. It also began a shift in attitudes towards the relationships between the management, the staff and those they served – who became 'customers'.

The shift in organisational ethos had effects on the nature of staff roles, particularly with the 'contracting out' of support services, so that in the NHS cleaners, porters and people in similar roles were split off managerially, and subject to a much more industrial management style. As local authorities contracted out more and more services, care work became specified as specific fragmented 'activities', individually costed. The sense of spontaneous relational activity for the public good became hard to sustain. By the early 1990s the role of 'care coordinator' was predominant in social work. A sensible wish to organise the variety of supports a client needed turned into a culture within which a generation of social workers found themselves forced into roles more like travel agents than professionals skilled in relational practice.

Lessons from the NHS

The years 1997–2010 saw further profound changes in our public institutions, billed as being driven by 'rational management'. A few examples relating to changes in staff contracts in the NHS will illustrate the no doubt unintended negative effects on the culture of vocation. The changes were all, in part, attempts to make expectations more explicit and equitable, and to make payment more transparent and fair. But intertwined with such rational aims were barely hidden implications of mistrust, and an apparent wish to specify, commodify, command and control. Further, the process significantly monetarised clinical and caring tasks: a powerful force against the sense of vocation.

The new consultant contract of 2003 introduced a breakdown of senior doctors' working weeks into a number of contractually specified 'programmed activities', each of which had to be agreed with their line manager. The new 'General Medical Services' contract for GPs in 2004 introduced a 'Quality and Outcomes Framework' with income tied firmly to specific and prescribed clinical activities. For most other NHS staff, 'Agenda for Change', also rolled out from 2004, introduced a complex scoring system as a means of grading and remunerating their roles.

Prior to the new consultant contract, the informal understanding was that senior doctors were paid to do their appointed job with a degree of autonomy and flexibility. In return the consultant put in whatever extra hours were required 'pro bono'. However, there was mistrust of a highly autonomous, partly unaccountable workforce, and awareness of a long history of consultants holding NHS posts, and receiving NHS salaries, whilst simultaneously undertaking lucrative private work. In fact, much of this had already changed by the time the new contract was introduced, with a new generation of doctors, many of them women, holding senior posts. In some specialties and some geographical locations, there were virtually no doctors practising privately.

In the event there had been an underestimation of what the new scheme would actually cost – consultants had generally been doing unpaid work for the NHS in their own time, rather than doing private work in NHS time. Trusts, now obliged to pay for this work, were forced to look for opportunities to save money and limit the number of consultant sessions it would allow people to do – or, indeed, to cut back on other services to fund the gap.

Incentive packages for GPs had been around since 1990, when the first new contract sought to incentivise health promotion by linking payments to identification of patients at risk of various conditions. The 2004 contract implemented a fresh approach to this through the 'Quality and Outcomes Framework', or 'QOF', micro-managing consultations through a complex system of targets. Specific clinical activities had to take place, such as taking a blood pressure, doing a particular blood test, or offering health advice – and for each activity a computer code had to be entered into the patient's record. At standard intervals the practice's patient records would be 'interrogated' by external software to check what codes had been added, and whether targets for these had been met. A resultant multitude of small payments would add up to provide a significant proportion of a practice's income.

Many GPs were concerned about the consequences that focussing on such specific, concrete, areas of clinical need had for their ability to think about the whole person and their families. Any agenda for the consultation over and above the presenting problem had now been set by the practice's targets. Anecdotally, many patients began to complain about the amount of time their GP spent 'looking at the computer'.

'Agenda for Change', a new national pay system for all NHS staff other than doctors, dentists and senior managers, was finally introduced in 2005. The aim was for pay scales to be tied into a 'knowledge and skills framework', rather than 'simple' seniority (i.e. experience and commitment). Staff moving onto this system had to fill in a long form giving details of their work, which was then scored under various domains such as 'physical strain', 'emotional pressure', 'concentration' and 'responsibility'.

As with the consultant contract, the new system was more problematic than anticipated by policy makers, and ended up costing far more money. At the time, there was a strong sense of the process of commodification that Sandel considers. Staff were explicitly being encouraged to emphasise the burdensome and demanding nature of their job, in order to be banded and paid as highly as possible. This promoted a negative way of thinking about their work, which focussed on its onerous nature rather than the rewards of working with patients. Both individuals and professions were drawn into 'haggling' over the burdens and demands of their roles. Staff were encouraged to dwell upon trading their skills rather than valuing them in terms of how they serve others. Such an approach to defining healthcare tasks, and differentially remunerating work, was in fact a driver towards competitiveness and envy: toxic components of any care system.

In 2016 there was a bitter dispute between the training-grade doctors and the Department of Health, headed up by the Health Secretary Jeremy Hunt. There was a political agenda: moving the NHS to being a 'seven day service fully functioning over weekends', as promised in the election manifesto. Doctors were concerned that this was impractical, and would (perversely) compromise services during the week, given that it was proposed on the basis of existing, and already stretched, staff and resources.

A crucial part of the dispute related to working hours, and the loss of 'overtime' for evening (up to 10pm) and weekend work, which was re-designated 'routine'. In much of the press this was depicted as being about money. Denigrating and dismissive things were said about the greed, privilege and sense of entitlement of these young doctors. They were not used to being described in such ways, having previously been sustained in difficult jobs by a sense of public appreciation.

A junior doctor working weekends, and well into the evening on weekdays, was no longer to be viewed as worthy of 'special' appreciation or reward, with overtime payments as a symbolic acknowledgement of 'going above and beyond' what might normally be expected of an employee in most walks of life. Instead, these working hours, already so antisocial in terms of an ability to pursue a life outside work, became simply poor working conditions, preventing a fulfilling work-life balance: a far cry from a vocation.

Recruitment faltered, and many young doctors moved to work elsewhere, or left the profession. As a result, Mr Hunt proposed that newly qualified doctors should be compelled to work for five years for the NHS after qualification (Donnelly, 2017): further removal of their autonomy, and a policy almost designed to perversely bring about the opposite of what was purportedly intended. Previous generations of doctors trained in the NHS had unthinkingly expected to spend their working lives there, even if a minority of consultants had developed a parallel private practice. Instead, a policy involving 'serving time' for five years looked likely to lead naturally to a feeling that, at that point, you had 'paid your dues', and you could look around for alternatives. Instead of having a vocation, you would have adverse working conditions to endure, a debt to pay, and a date by which it might be viewed as 'paid' (the actual financial debt, accrued by paying for five years as a medical student, would probably take considerably longer to pay back).

Each of these examples illustrates key aspects of the ways in which vocation, a sense of agency, commitment and goodwill can be undermined. These are summarised in Box 13.3 below. This is especially evident when ill thought through, mistrustful and over-intrusive management shapes organisational culture and turns the work into a tightly controlled market. The consequences for work directed by intelligent kindness can be serious.

Although we have used recent contractual changes in the NHS to illustrate our point, readers with more interest in social care do not have to look far for their own examples. Domiciliary care workers are, in the main, employed by private sector organisations, receiving around the minimum wage. They are expected to deliver specified, timed and costed interventions to some of the most vulnerable people in our communities. Their contracts frequently specify that they will not be paid for time travelling between tasks, or for extensions to the duration of their visit on the basis of need. They rarely meet with

Box 13.3 Threats to Vocation

- Failing to recognise and value the sense of agency, responsibility and personal initiative in the work;
- Failing to recognise and undermining the values that motivate the worker;
- Failing to recognise the complexity and necessary choices involved in the task;
- Skewing the focus away from the whole person by over-prescribing fragmented tasks;
- Pulling the worker's attention away from the care task towards bureaucratic accountability;
- Putting a monetary value on the burden of the work creating competition and envy;
- Over-specifying and micro-managing the work of staff.

colleagues, so there is no sense of a community of care. This is a life like an Uber driver, but with even less sense of autonomy, much more anxiety, and a great deal more emotional and physical effort. A senior local authority commissioner said to us, with weary sarcasm, *'you have to be hard, tough and preferably cynical to do that kind of work: just the sort of attitudes you want from people providing such intimate care!'*

The Marketisation of Public Services

From the 'new public management' of the 1980s onwards, there have been steady, incremental steps towards the application of market philosophy to all public services, especially health and social care. Margaret Thatcher commissioned a review of the NHS by Roy Griffiths, previously a director of Monsanto Europe, and deputy chairman of the Sainsbury's supermarket chain. The 'Griffiths Report' of 1983 set in motion the development of the 'purchaser–provider' split within the NHS and social care. The management and clinical functions of services were divided, with new bodies of internal 'commissioners' specifying and 'purchasing' care from 'provider' bodies, both inside public sector organisations and in the independent sector.

This was intended to build more accountability into the work of service providers, both for what they did and for how they spent money. It was intended to enable changes for the better in systems that might otherwise be rigid and resistant, through the application of financial incentives and imperatives. In the longer term, promotion of a variety of different providers was seen as a way of fostering innovation, getting value for money and bolstering the capacity of existing services through a competitive market.

In the event, following devolution within the UK, Scotland and Wales moved away from these market-orientated models. Scotland abandoned the purchaser–provider split in 2004, and Wales in 2009. The two countries instituted 'health boards' as an alternative, both holding the budgets and providing services. The divergent systems in the years since will no doubt provide a fascinating 'natural experiment' as to the effects of the differing administrative frameworks; sadly this is beyond the scope of this book.

Whatever the merits of the new market driven ideas, they were ideal vehicles for the steady importation of the ideology of a primitive kind of competition, even of 'survival of the cheapest', into health and social care services. In the NHS, many non-clinical services, such as cleaning or catering, were rapidly transferred to the private sector: and by the beginning of the twenty-first century clinical services such as pathology or physiotherapy were going the same way. In social care, the great majority of previously public sector services were contracted out.

This process has been in accord with explicit policy, but has also gained traction as an unintended consequence of other NHS and local authority funding, evaluation and management changes. Management focus shifted to the cost of defined processes and transactions, albeit with a relatively undeveloped 'quality' component. The theory was that commissioners ('the purchasers') would develop detailed specifications for services, build them into contracts and 'tender them out' to find someone to do them well at the cheapest price. Providers were exhorted to become 'innovative', 'lean' and efficient in order to compete amongst themselves.

This system was predicated on the idea that the purchasers could accurately specify what was needed, and also make accurate comparisons between offerings, with an assumption of ready equivalence between potential providers, regardless of their nature and experience. Market-driven changes predicated upon the idea that competition always promotes improvement were, of course, reliant upon good subsequent management, and successful resolution of any difficulties that might arise: conditions that in the event could not be taken for granted.

Whether or not these necessary pre-conditions were ever in place, the competitive dimension was problematic. To cite some possible pitfalls: different providers might apportion cost differently to the same processes, or claim, in ways that specifications are too blunt to catch, that they can do the same things at a lower price. If an NHS provider, such as a small hospital, lost the contract for a specific service (whether because of purported poorer quality or higher cost), its ability to continue with its wider remit and services would be undermined. The concept, and the reality, of an integrated, universal service then suffers. A successful bidder for one component of care, of course, takes on no responsibility for integrating that into the wider picture, also undermining service integration.

Operators 'entering the market' from outside the public service framework are not guaranteed to have an investment in the functioning of the system as a whole. The surrounding infrastructure of care services represents competition, not 'kin' in need of collaboration and support. If market competition is the name of the game there is nothing wrong with the common practice of large private companies running a new project at an initial loss, outbidding, and thus destabilising, other providers, only to put up their costs to a commercial rate once the new service is established and the commissioners (and service-users) are committed. Similarly, if investors, such as venture capitalists or large conglomerates, acquire a portfolio of care homes for the elderly, and then sell off properties when real estate prices in the neighbourhood go up, this is simply 'good business practice', despite the detrimental effect on the elderly residents in their care (Pollock, 2004, p. 180).

These are examples of how attempts to bring in the private sector as 'partners' to support and revitalise public sector provision may in fact, perversely undermine and dismantle it. However, by the second decade of the twenty-first century the idea of healthcare as a marketed and purchased commodity appeared politically unassailable. The controversial 2012 Health and Social Care Act had facilitated widespread NHS contracted provision by commercial companies with no previous expertise or experience in healthcare by opening all services to 'any willing provider'. The NHS had explicitly (and unashamedly) become a market for businesses to enter, whatever their ethic, whatever their view of what was justified by profit. To compound this, by a perverse legal technicality, such businesses were free from scrutiny under the Freedom of Information Act. Information about their activities was deemed 'commercially sensitive' and exempt from the Act, whereas NHS providers, as part of a 'public authority', had a duty of disclosure.

Even without perverse activity as such, the private and independent sector tends to take on quite specific, well-delineated activities and treatments, as opposed to holistic care. Whereas this might work well for certain procedures, such as a cataract operation, for other more complex difficulties, such as diabetes or mental health problems, overall care risks becoming fragmented. In this context, the dismantling and privatisation of the probation service in England and Wales is a sad and salutary tale.

There is conflicting evidence as to the effectiveness of competition in driving up quality, with views held passionately on both sides. Much has to do with how one defines and measures both competition and quality, with some evidence of both positive and negative links (Propper et al, 2003, 2005; Cooper et al, 2010). Researchers place caveats on the proposition that competition has a positive effect on the development of institutions. They also point out that payer-driven competition (commissioning) is not the same as competition promoted by patient choice. Commissioners looking for cost savings may well be at odds with patients (however poorly or well informed) looking for choice.

Most importantly, Carol Propper and her colleagues at the University of Bristol observed in 2005 that a fixed-price system and a competitive market 'gives hospitals incentives not to accept more severely ill patients ('dumping'), to undertreat such patients ('skimping') and to attract the less severely ill and over-treat these ('creaming'). These incentives are present whether or not competition exists, but are intensified when hospitals are subject to actual competition, or competition based on league tables' (Propper et al, 2005, p. 15).

By 2018 Carol Propper was Professor of Economics at Imperial College, London, and published a further paper on competition in healthcare, drawing upon studies of over 30 years of such reforms in England. Her view at this point was that these policies:

> *... have broadly had positive effects ... patients and hospitals have responded in a manner that suggests patients care about quality and hospitals, in turn, respond to demand. Better hospitals have attracted more patients, the quality of some services has risen, there do not appear to have been large equity issues, and policies that pursue the alternative tack of consolidation have not brought benefits in the medium term ...* (Propper, 2018)

However, her analysis is purely economic: the review at no point considers the effects of the changes upon staff and the culture in which they work. In addition, although she gives some consideration to how matters might otherwise have been organised, she does not do this extensively: and thus the question of whether matters would have improved in the last 30 years in any case remains largely unanswered. She also does not take the opportunity to compare outcomes in Scotland and Wales, where the internal market was dismantled, as a way of illuminating this, although noting implicitly that direct comparisons may be difficult, due to the different nature of their populations, and the smaller size of their hospital sector.

As we have already indicated, another alarming aspect of the competitive market is its instability. Over a six-month period in 2018, 58 councils reported the closure, or 'cessation of trading', of care homes in which they had invested nearly £60 million, and of home care services involving just under £50 million. The care of about 6,000 very vulnerable people was seriously disrupted (National Audit Office, 2018). Such statistics vividly illustrate the destabilising effects on care services of a mixture of unrealistic pressure, within scarce resources, to keep prices down, and the lack of fit between a competitive market of profit-driven providers and the neediness of vulnerable people.

The ongoing controversy – and a great deal of informed concern – about marketisation points to the need for caution, and much more understanding of the incentives and outcomes generated by competition. Without it, there may not be the vigour and ambition needed to address the challenges faced in care services. Creative competition may be required to produce excellence and innovation. However, the results of the Gombe experience reported in Chapter 9 should be borne firmly in mind: stimulating competition for bananas tipped a placid society over into brutality and murder. Institutional 'dumping', 'skimping' and 'creaming' may be a small step towards brutality. Simplistic or ill-considered mimicry of commodity markets is dangerous in health and social care, and a potential engine for perverting its delivery.

Internalising the Market

Both the research and the political debate about competition have largely been based on short-term to medium-term analyses, within a shifting frame of narrow and concrete measurements. They rarely consider the effects on the attitudes and work of staff within our public welfare organisations. Such consideration is urgently needed.

Over and above the effects of the 'competitive market' upon the management of services themselves, it appears to have entered into the minds of staff as a form of destabilising anxiety, whether or not actual competitive tendering is happening. It might be argued that a degree of anxiety is helpful in countering complacency and inertia. However, the anxiety is amplified in many cases by mistrust between commissioning staff and providers, and by poor management of the issue within organisations. High degrees of anxiety in the context of system dysfunction and internal conflict are not likely to promote innovation and imagination, especially when allied to the unmanaged invasion of people's thinking and language by the 'cost for commodity' aspect of the market. The quest to 'do more for less', in the context of competitive threats and severely limited resources, can have a corrosive effect.

Costing health and social care, in the quest for efficiency and improved performance, is unavoidable, of course. However, it is difficult to apply a model based upon costing specific procedures and activities as if they were 'stand-alone' in a universal service that carries ongoing responsibility for the complex care of ill, disturbed or disadvantaged people 'from the cradle to the grave'. Partly because of the poor 'fit' between costing models and the reality of care, and partly because of the unfiltered injection of preoccupation with cost, activity and competition into organisations and their staff, a dangerous shift has occurred. Instead of being technical tools deployed by management and business staff, market models pervade the daily work.

All public sector staff are now aware of the contracts that define, and sometimes restrict, the work they do. They know that if their service does not achieve the activity levels agreed (for good or bad reasons) or, indeed, if the commissioners simply choose to change the contract, there will be financial penalties and possible job losses. The consequent anxiety can skew practice, frequently invading the front-line relationship with patients and clients, and undermining cooperation with other services. The frequent disconnection between funding, contracting and specification, and the realities of providing care and treatment often amplifies the damage done.

Our public sector has faced 'efficiency savings' for decades. Although some of these measures were well thought through, with genuine examination of the most efficient ways of meeting need, many appeared to have been introduced relatively haphazardly, with any mitigating service remodelling only happening after the decision to cut funding. Goodwill on the part of staff has been undermined by the relentless, year-on-year, and frequently unconsidered nature of this process. Even if subjecting health and social care services to market forces were to be advisable, a financially driven, rather than value-driven, process risks undermining any belief that there is a rational and creative 'market' at work. Increasing efficiency within limited resources is hard enough: being required to continue to deliver to specification regardless of funding reduction, whilst setting out into a competitive market on unstable wheels, is dangerous.

Caught between attention to needy patients or clients, the contradictory and unpredictable demands of 'efficiency', and poorly specified activity, staff make decisions with varying degrees of awareness that the welfare of the person in front of them is not necessarily the priority. Many are distressed by their complicity with compromise. The nursing press, for example, has frequently carried articles and letters from nurses protesting about the poor quality of care they are involved in delivering (Maben et al, 2007). Other nurse authors have described colleagues as being 'deeply distressed at their perceived failure at meeting their patients' needs' (Chambers and Ryder, 2009, p. 53) or suffering 'moral distress' when their capacity to provide effective and compassionate care is limited by resources (Fournier et al, 2007, p. 262). It is common for staff to feel a deep sense of frustration arising from their diminishing power to influence the systems within which they work, whilst carrying increasingly personal responsibility for both 'productivity' and adverse outcomes.

Staff become prone to 'doublethink', having to hold contrary opinions or beliefs at the same time, and, rather than live in a state of exhausting cognitive dissonance, some may withdraw emotionally, becoming depressed or adopting a cynical approach to the work. Such ways of coping inevitably undermine their capacity for kindness. Of even more concern, though, is the pull into a perverse state of mind where the contradictions are denied, and the erosion of values is unacknowledged and largely unconscious.

The unmediated injection of competition and a preoccupation with money into care services is a dangerous threat to kindness. We urgently require ways of ensuring that the priority of serving and preserving the welfare of others can remain uppermost in the minds of staff. Whilst looking for new ways of working to improve both quality and efficiency is important, it is also vital to find a way of ensuring that a 'more for less' mentality does not ignore the limits of the finite and pressurised resource that is the workforce.

It was encouraging that, in January 2019, as a new ten-year plan for the NHS was announced, the Department of Health and Social Care voiced the need to wind back the competitive market in healthcare. It was accepted that such a market destabilises and fragments the system, as we and many others have argued. The absence of similar attention to the market in social care was, given their arguments, shocking, especially since this sector may have suffered even more than the NHS.

Removing aspects of competitive tendering will not, in itself, counter the commodification of the work, and preoccupation with cost. Re-constructing the system, and mitigating the long-term effects on staff and services of such a determined, extensive and deep-rooted ideological project, will require thoughtful and intelligent work. It will, without question, require more than a hasty, top-down, short-term 'change programme'.

Our use of the term 'perversion' has been intended to bring home the seriousness of the present risks to our caring institutions arising from the necessities of managing and funding them within limited resources, in an evolving 'free market' culture. Previous eras were neither risk nor problem free, but their risks and problems were different, and we need to attend to our own times, where there is a tendency to commodify human values, and 'turn a blind eye' to resultant difficulties.

We have repeatedly seen enantiodromia at play – things becoming quite different from how they were intended. Interventions meant to be helpful have had the opposite effect. To limit the risks of this, a form of 'binocular vision' is required, observing (and attending to) both the emotional and practical aspects of a complex reality at the same time. It is always difficult for those involved at the time to understand the 'macro-changes' in the culture of which they are part. For this reason we agree with Professor Steve Iliffe who, in his book *From General Practice to Primary Care*, appeals to his readers to engage with these issues and 'make social reality legible to ourselves and our communities' (Iliffe, 2008, p. 203).

We should also not forget the potential effects of hostility, growing out of resentment. It is easy to see how this aspect of perversion might rear its head in modern services, struggling with the inevitable frustrations of the daily working environment and all its various, conflicting demands. Hostility can readily contaminate the act of care. On a practical level, the potential for a market of commodified care to become a 'growth medium' for forces that fatally undermine kinship and kindness requires recognition. It requires intelligent management, not denial. We will consider what such intelligent management might involve in the next chapter.

References

Chambers, C. and Ryder, E. (2009) *Compassion and Caring in Nursing.* Radcliffe.

Cooper, C., Marston, L., Barber, J., Livingston, D., Rapaport, P., Higgs, P., Livingston, G. (2018) Do care homes deliver person-centred care? A cross-sectional survey of staff-reported abusive and positive behaviours towards residents from the MARQUE (Managing Agitation and Raising Quality of Life) English national care home survey. PLOS|ONE. Available at: www.journals.plos.org/plosone/article/metrics?id=10.1371/journal.pone.0193399 [last accessed 14 August, 2019].

Cooper, Z., Gibbons, S., Jones, S., et al (2010) Does Hospital Competition Save Lives? Evidence from the English Patient Choice Reforms. London School of Economics.

Daily Mail (2013) Nurses told, 'you're not too posh to wash a patient': Minister orders student nurses back to basics to improve compassion in NHS. *Daily Mail*, 25 March, 2013. Available at: www.dailymail.co.uk/news/article-2299085/Youre-posh-wash-patient-Minister-orders-student-nurses-basics-improve-compassion-NHS.html [last accessed 14 August, 2019].

Delamothe, T. (2010) Repeat after me: 'Mid-Staffordshire'. British Medical Journal. 340: c188.

Department of Health (2015) Culture change in the NHS: applying the lessons of the Francis enquiries. HMSO.

Donnelly, L. (2017). Doctors could be forced to work at least five years in NHS under plans for 'home-grown' expansion. *The Telegraph*, 14 March, 2017.

Fournier, B., Kipp, W. and Mill, J. (2007) The nursing care of AIDS patients in Uganda. Journal of Transcultural Nursing. 18: 257–64.

Francis, R. (2010) The Independent Inquiry into Care Provided by Mid-Staffordshire NHS

Foundation Trust, January 2005–March 2009. HMSO.

Gosport Independent Panel (2018) Gosport War Memorial Hospital: The Report of the Gosport Independent Panel. HMSO.

Griffiths, R. (1983) Report of the NHS Management Inquiry. HMSO.

Healthcare Commission (2009) The Investigation into Mid-Staffordshire NHS Foundation Trust. Healthcare Commission.

Hood, C. (1991) A public management for all seasons. Public Administration. 69 (1): 3–19.

Iliffe, S. (2008) *From General Practice to Primary Care: The Industrialization of Family Medicine*. Oxford University Press.

Long, S. (2008) *The Perverse Organisation and Its Deadly Sins*. Karnac.

Maben, J., Latter, S. and Macleod Clark, J. (2007) The sustainability of ideals, values and the nursing mandate: evidence from a longitudinal qualitative study. Nursing Enquiry. 14; 99–113.

National Audit Office (2018) Adult Social Care at a glance. Available at: www.nao.org.uk/wp-content/uploads/2018/07/Adult-social-care-at-a-glance.pdf [last accessed 14 August, 2019].

Pollock, A. (2004) *NHS plc: The Privatization of Health Care*. Verso.

Powdthavee, N. and Stutzer, A. (2014) Economic Approaches to Understanding Change in Happiness. Discussion Paper No. 8131, Institute for the Study of Labor, Bonn. Available at: http://repec.iza.org/dp8131.pdf [last accessed 14 August, 2019].

Propper, C., Burgess, S. and Gossage, D. (2003) Competition and Quality: Evidence from the NHS Internal Market 1991–1999. CMPO, University of Bristol.

Propper, C., Wilson, D. and Burgess, S. (2005) Extending Choice in English Health Care: The Implications of the Economic Evidence. CMPO, University of Bristol.

Propper, C. (2018) Competition in health care: lessons from the English experience. Health Economics, Policy and Law. 13: 492–508.

Sandel, M. (2009a) The Reith Lectures 2009, Lecture 1: 'Markets and morals', broadcast 9 June, 2009, BBC Radio 4.

Sandel, M. (2009b) The Reith Lectures 2009, Lecture 4: 'A new politics of the common good', broadcast 30 June 2009, BBC Radio 4.

Steiner, J. (1985) Turning a Blind Eye: The Cover-Up for Oedipus. International Review of Psycho-Analysis. 12: 161–71.

Stoller, R. (1986) *Perversion: The Erotic Form of Hatred*. Karnac.

Titmuss, R. (1971) *The Gift Relationship: From Human Blood to Social Policy*, (eds A. Oakley and J. Ashton, 1997). Reissued LSE Publications.

Weale, M. (2009) Economic progress and health improvement. British Medical Journal. 339: 1097.

Wise, J. (2015) UK government apologises for contaminated blood scandal. British Medical Journal. 350: h1673.

Chapter

14 Cultivating Intelligent Kindness

You Can't Grow Roses in Concrete

(Munro, Turnell and Murphy, 2014)

So far, we have argued that intelligent kindness should guide the design and organisation of health, social care and welfare services, and shown how the approach will sustain and bring the best out of their hard-working staff. Benefits will be large and small scale, affecting both the organisational culture, and the daily work.

This needs a change in mind-set, and the adoption of a new set of attitudes and beliefs, as we have discussed in detail in the preceding chapters. In summary:

- An unsentimental recognition that connection with kinship and kindness is a core, creative motivating factor in all forms of practice.
- If this is fostered, it will drive quality, effectiveness and efficiency, as outlined in the 'virtuous circle' explored in Chapter 4.
- It is essential to understand what promotes or inhibits kindness at an individual, team, organisational and inter-agency level.
- It is important to learn from, and apply, all that is known about how to address these dynamics, integrating this work with other necessary approaches to delivering and governing services.
- Processes such as industrialisation, performance management, regulation and competition have inimical 'side-effects' that need to be understood and mitigated.
- A sense of agency and of 'freedom to serve the public' is crucial to attentive, responsive and effective kindness. This needs to be fostered, not eroded.

Kindness and compassion cannot be promoted solely by a campaign of fine words, mission statements, and 'heart-warming' posters on the walls of our caring institutions, nor by moralistic demands that staff and managers 'just be kind'. The word 'intelligent' in our title emphasises how we must *understand what is involved* in turning intention into action, and then work cooperatively with this awareness, as we tackle all aspects of our daily routine.

Our previous chapters have drawn attention to many instances where things have gone wrong: with abuse, inhumanity, or simply organisational processes working against good practice. Of course, every day millions of people are being effectively and sensitively cared for. Many organisations are working to develop approaches that support staff and promote compassionate care. However, this work is vulnerable. It is increasingly difficult to do, and could be far more effectively encouraged and supported.

There needs to be coherent attention to *all* levels of the system, from the individual to the organisation, from practice to policy. It needs to be recognised that intervening at any one level will only be truly effective if it is supported by work at the other levels. We have already argued that individually focussed interventions like Mindfulness, or Compassionate Mind training, will be to no avail, and indeed can make matters worse, if attention is not paid to the wider culture in which staff work. We might add that this is just as true for other approaches such as 'resilience' training.

A Systemic Approach to Cultivating Intelligent Kindness

The word 'cultivating' is used advisedly. To employ a metaphor, in building a flourishing garden the attentive gardener chooses the best available plants or seedlings, to be placed in soil carefully prepared to host and nourish them. The environment is taken into account – rainfall, sunlight, pests and predators. Growth is monitored, intelligently and attentively, with action taken if things are not going well. A successful garden *emerges* from careful nurturing of the system *as a whole*. Concentrating too much on any one type of intervention, whether watering, feeding, weeding or pest control, will not secure the productivity or quality of that system. Investing in expensive garden tools may help but unless the growing environment is understood, and properly tended as a complex system, all that will be of limited avail.

A similar approach needs to be brought to bear in health and social care. We can choose the best people for the work (if candidates are not put off by the environment they will face). We can educate and train them, specify their roles, design and organise the services in which they work. We must, though, develop and act on the basis of a *systemic* understanding of the enterprise as a whole – its core nature, its determinants, enabling factors, the threats it faces and the environment in which it sits. We must attend to the conditions under which the culture and practice we want can best emerge. Eileen Munro and her colleagues entitled their report on Signs of Safety 'You Can't Grow Roses in Concrete' (Munro, Turnell and Murphy, 2014). Similarly, you can't build a culture with bricks (or initiatives, imperatives, rules and manuals): you *cultivate* it, so that the work we aspire to can grow out of it.

Just as the gardener understands the nature, the potential, and the needs and vulnerability of the seedling, so we must start from our understanding of the caring relationship between clinician or practitioner and those they are asked to help. We have argued that this is always relational – psychosocial – both in terms of the needs of the client or patient, and in terms of the work of those helping them. We have outlined the characteristics of a compassionate, attentive and effective relationship. We have drawn attention to the conscious and unconscious feelings and attitudes in the individual worker that can influence or undermine their relationship with sickness, ill-being, distress and risk. We have stressed the need for individual clinicians and practitioners to manage themselves in such relational practice, and for them to be helped to do so as fellow human beings.

The medium that grows and sustains effective relational practice must be constantly and consistently attended to. It is, before anything else, a *relational system*. The quality of the relationships between clinicians and practitioners in teams, between teams, and across systems, is the sustaining medium in which intelligent kindness can grow and in which its 'harvest' of effectiveness, satisfaction and efficiency is protected and nourished. We have outlined many of the factors at work in such relationships. We have argued for resources and attention to be paid to fostering their health, openness and supportiveness, and the quality of collaboration and communication in this human system.

This growing medium sits in a wider environment. Intelligent kindness has to be nurtured within a crowded landscape, and throughout inclement weather. The daily work in health and social care grows steadily more intensive, and more complex. Our population is growing in size, people are living longer, more interventions are possible, and expectations have risen. This is all happening within an evolving climate of regulation, industrialisation, commodification, and competition within a market economy. The anxiety inherent in the caring task, with its risks, challenges, uncertainties and pains, is intensified by all of this; and complicated by the twin blights of over-expectation and mistrust.

As in the garden, where healthy, well-rooted plants can endure bad weather, when individuals, teams and communities of practice are solidly grounded in intelligent kindness, health and social care systems can thrive during difficult times. However, this must involve attention to the challenges that are faced, and how they might promote growth, rather than prevent it.

Ways of Seeing the System

The wellbeing of all levels, and all components, of the system depends on how it is thought about and tended by the people in it, and in wider society.

Before discussing some examples of methods and initiatives that can help to achieve this, we will consider how the system may be represented, and so held in mind. There are two ways to view it: one is as a psychosocial system – a system of 'kinship' (Figure 14.1 below) – and the other is as an organised 'role and task' system (Figure 14.2 below).

The first figure brings together the relationships that need attention and support. The individual practitioner's relationships with the service-user, with colleagues in their team, and in the wider organisation and system are represented above the central horizontal line. The group and inter-group relationships that require healthy cultivation appear below that line. As we have argued throughout this book, all these relationships are interdependent, and need to be addressed systemically. The second figure offers a systemic representation of the functions and processes that need to be organised and delivered. Both images sit within the same environment: these political, social and ideological factors have a constant, powerful influence on the culture, organisation and work of the system, and need managing if intelligent kindness is to flourish. Attention to both perspectives is necessary for the health and effectiveness of services. The first is all too often neglected, to the detriment of work undertaken to address the second.

When we consider the system as one of roles and tasks, the main consideration is how to provide and align policies, service models, and information systems. Crucially, this requires sufficient resources, both human and financial. The design process must ensure that all parts of any proposed system of care are in place and ready to play their expected parts, whether in terms of interventions delivered, or their timeliness. Sufficient

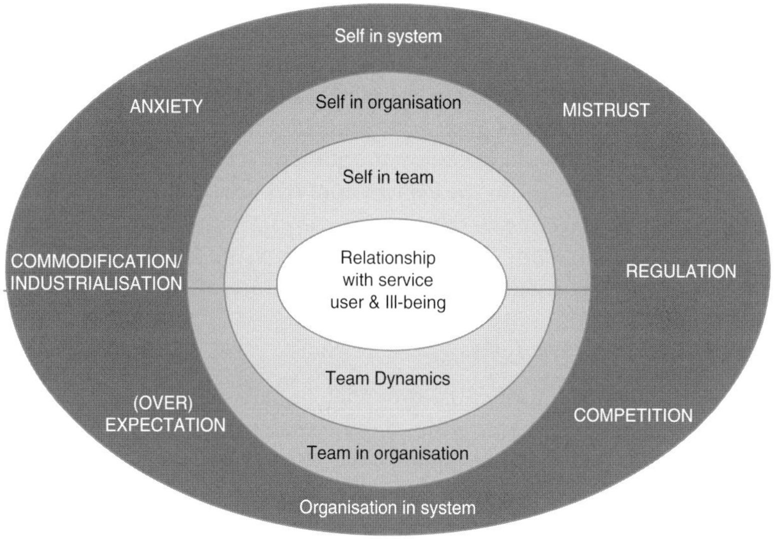

Figure 14.1 The Kinship System

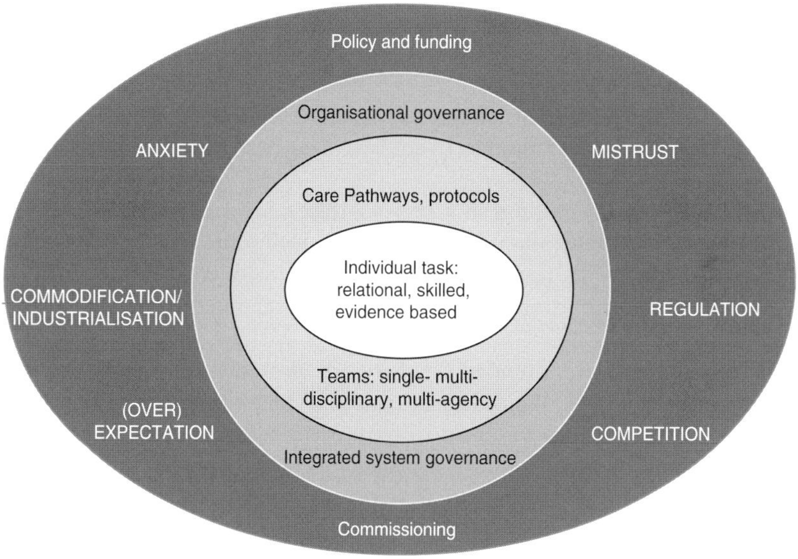

Figure 14.2 The Role and Task System

structure, clarity and consistency must be in place for staff to undertake their work. But it is the quality of the relationships, and how they are managed, at every level of the system, that will turn a 'wiring diagram' into a fully functional human enterprise.

Both practitioners and leaders may become entrenched in one or the other view of the system. When people are preoccupied with managing the demands, the consequent anxieties, and the frequent contradictions, of regulation, industrialisation, performance management, and competition, their attention can be distracted from building the relationships with each other and with service-users, through which effective and humane care is delivered. Equally, when people attend primarily to the 'kinship system' they may use this to justify an unproductive non-participation in necessary reflection upon quality, standardisation or efficiency. Rather than taking either view to the exclusion of the other, a 'binocular' or 'bifocal' view of the system needs to be developed.

Bearing such ideas in mind, and taking this view, we will now consider some approaches to promoting intelligent kindness in and across the Welfare State.

Cultivating a Healthy Culture

Staff who provide services need a culture that prioritises and promotes collective values and a common purpose. This should draw upon a 'kinship system' of attentive cooperation between colleagues, and foster a sense of agency, ownership and optimism. In turn, such a culture will offer a sense of safety and containment, allowing people to manage the inevitable anxiety and uncertainty of the work, and the distress it so often causes.

Practitioners need to be supported in remaining open to the lives of service-users, to the experience of colleagues and partner services, and to their own experience, as they encounter the possibilities, risks and problems in delivering care. As part of this, the value, and necessity, of reflective practice needs to be explicit within the culture in which staff work. Reflection should be supported and enabled, with sufficient time and space both for 'reflection in action' as work is undertaken, and for 'reflection on action' in dedicated time to think about it. If this can be done sensitively, and if the necessary 'mental space' is provided, morale, effectiveness, efficiency, and intelligently kind practice are all more likely to thrive.

This will only come about if the factors that can undermine a healthy relational system are carefully managed. Staff who feel routinely 'instrumentalised', unheard, or dumped with unrealistic expectations, will not build such a culture together. They will not be able to do it if they feel mistrusted, and in fear of blame.

Whilst these threats are attended to, there are also effective, positive approaches that can contribute to the conditions required. They need to begin at a 'whole system level' – organisation-wide, and across inter-agency networks. Unless staff across the system *know* that they are working together within a culture directed by common values, they are unlikely to develop the working relationships described above.

Dialogue

Dialogue lies at the heart of a healthy, reflective culture. A 'dialogical approach' invites staff to come together, not to hear their leaders' ideas or their visions – however deeply and sincerely held – but to hold conversations about the realities of practice, their experience of working together, and their ideas for improvement.

There is a long tradition of 'dialogic' organisational development (Bushe and Marshak, 2015). In this tradition, honesty, critical thinking, creativity and imagination are genuinely encouraged and invited to the table. Offering staff the opportunity to bring and discuss *narratives* about their work, and about the lives and experiences of service-users, enriches the dialogue, and helps build mutuality and common purpose. This is the most powerful way of developing common values: growing and sustaining them, rather than asserting them in 'mission statements'.

There are many ways to stimulate and organise such dialogues. They can range from open invitations to share experience, to conversations relating to a core question or challenge. Some are 'branded' techniques, some are simply intelligent, creative improvisation. We offer a few examples of both in Box 14.1 below, but encourage readers to explore, and indeed to create, further approaches.

Techniques like these can be helpful, and it should not be too expensive or too challenging to train enough staff to convene and facilitate such meetings. A properly funded, stable workforce will make involvement in such processes possible. But less formal approaches can be just as useful. Bringing staff together, as a matter of routine, in supported conversational mode to share their lived perspective on any aspect of their work will always help. For example, dialogue exploring themes such as the translation of values into action, collaboration, serious incidents or planning will contribute to the health of the collective culture. Different communities, such as first-line managers, receptionists, or members of a single discipline can be convened, as well as more diverse 'whole community' gatherings. The key is to make the invitation attractive, to be genuinely open to dialogue, and to promote wide and diverse involvement. Those convening such conversations need to have sufficient understanding of the dynamics of groups, expertise in hosting and facilitation, and readiness to demonstrate in action that people have been listened to.

As an example, the Economic and Social Research Council funded a collaborative research project between the Universities of Edinburgh, Strathclyde and Swansea, looking into social care in Wales and Scotland. Their report, 'Meaningful and Measurable' noted:

> *The quality and reach of dialogue within organisations needs to be sufficient for practitioners to feel valued and listened to, and for different parts of the organisation, including frontline practice and information people, to understand each other's contribution to achieving outcomes.* (Miller and Barrie, 2016)

There is limited value in any such work if the invitation to conversation between skilled colleagues is sporadic, episodic or simply a series of one off 'events', whilst 'business as usual' continues. Cultivation of a healthy relational culture requires clear and consistent commitment, authorisation, and, continuous, dependable, work. It requires a *strategy*, just as much, and just as importantly, as does financial management. Inclusive events or processes, such as those we have sketched out above, need to be part of the expression of such a strategy, not the strategy itself. In Box 14.2 below we offer some suggestions as to how one might create and develop such a strategy.

Box 14.1 Some Dialogic Approaches

Open Space Technology™ is a particularly helpful example of a formal 'technique', especially with large, diverse groups (www.openspaceworld.org/wp2/what-is/). Here, people are invited to come together to address a core question – for example 'How can we improve joint work with older people with complex needs?' Those attending are invited to convene conversations around issues, ideas or challenges that they *identify themselves*, and the outcomes of these discussions are captured and shared in 'real time'. Several phases of such convened discussions, each responsive to some degree to large group reflection on the previous one, are held. Agreements and plans for change can then be developed, and introduced into the wider system, with a significantly greater sense of ownership and agency amongst staff affected.

Another 'formal' approach to creating dialogue across the system is World Café methodology (www.theworldcafe.com/key-concepts-resources/world-cafe-method/). Like Open Space Technology, it brings people together to explore a core question. In the World Café approach those attending are organised into small groups to discuss different aspects of the question. In this model, the questions tend to be pre-set, with groups exploring them around tables, moving on from discussing one question to the next table, where they are briefed on the discussion so far and build on it, and so on. Again, the capture of thinking happens in real time – subsequent sharing and application of the thinking is important.

In the USA, multidisciplinary 'Schwartz Center Rounds' were introduced in 1997. They are now held in over 190 sites across the UK and Ireland thanks to work, initially by the King's Fund, and later by the Point of Care Foundation (www.pointofcarefoundation.org.uk). These are typically held in hospitals, but are readily transferable to any system of care. An hour a month is booked in, with an open invitation to anyone in the organisation to attend, and basic refreshments offered. The 'Round' begins with personal sharing by a small panel who tell stories about their work and how they have experienced it, followed by large group discussion. The 'task' is to engage with and think about the narratives, and each other, not to evaluate, extract implications, or 'recommendations'. As Jill Maben, Professor of Health Services Research and Nursing at the University of Surrey has blogged:

> *The healthcare environment is a busy, hierarchical, outcome-orientated environment where stoicism is valued and where staff are exhorted to put patients first, but Rounds offer a 'counter-cultural space' where staff experience is the priority, emotional disclosure is encouraged, and staff support and listen to each other without judgement.*
>
> (nihr.ac.uk, 2018)

Sharing such experiences brings people together and promotes empathy for each other. It cultivates a community, a sense of belonging to the larger organisation. Research has identified persuasive evidence for the effectiveness of Schwartz Rounds (Maben et al, 2018). Psychological wellbeing, empathy and (re-)connection with a sense of vocation seem to be improved in those who attend, with some evidence of a 'trickle effect' into the wider organisation.

Box 14.2 A Strategic Approach to a Healthy Culture

- **Authorise from the very top** of the organisation or system, especially engaging commissioners in developing, sustaining and strengthening it.
- **Cost the work** into organisational budgets, costs of contracts, etc.
- **Ensure time** for involvement is budgeted for and authorised.
- **Ensure proper training** and freeing up of skilled staff to facilitate dialogic work.
- **Engage widely** – practitioners, leaders and managers, administrative and technical staff. Avoid relying simply on the attendance of the 'immediately willing', the very vocal, or the seniors.
- **Ensure service-users and patients are included**, in settings where they are properly supported, and able to bring their stories and take 'centre stage' should they wish to. **Avoid** turning them into spectators at professional dialogue.
- **Employ approaches** like revolving representation by teams across the system. Everyone in the system will never get into the room at any one time. For example, having two representatives at one event, with one of them at the next, with a new representative, can work well.
- **Ensure feedback and reflection** in 'home' teams: their leaders must be fully engaged with the spirit and detail of the process.
- **Authorise and facilitate 'co-creation'** of ideas or proposals for development by sub-groups mandated by the community of staff, but always tie their work back into wider system engagement to ensure critical review, understanding, ownership and trust.
- **Collective ownership** means quicker and smoother implementation of any idea than when un-engaged staff are asked or told to change what they do.
- **Don't despair** if the process seems slow: developing and sustaining culture is a long-term project with real benefits.
- **Don't be afraid of the cost**: the benefits in performance, staff morale and retention, effective collaboration and even sickness levels are likely to repay it.
- **Use external facilitators** where neutrality may be vital, but don't rely on them to be the motive force.
- **Ensure continuity**, as a strategic, coherent and sustained programme of attention to the relational health of the system; not just a series of sporadic events.

Design and Development

Dialogic approaches to strengthening the culture of kinship illustrate how engaged, reality-based and practice-based conversation can contribute to highly effective, practical, service planning and design. Not only *can* it contribute, it *should* do. Commissioners and service planners will be more effective if they convene a community to build a shared understanding of need, experience and what works. If they invite and explore narratives, rather than simply examining models, numbers or achievement of targets, their thinking, planning and outcomes will be improved. Their plans, service models and contracts will be underpinned by the intelligence of service-users, citizens, practitioners and managers from across the system, in the real world, within its local circumstances. Such plans are likely to be more feasible and effective, and there will be much greater ownership of the process of implementation, than if change is planned behind closed doors by 'experts'. The process will have strengthened the relationships across the system that are so crucial to its functioning.

Services, of course, have to be affordable, so those bringing together such communities need to be honest about the limitations to what is possible, whilst acknowledging any consequent weaknesses in what is developed. Such honesty is key to building trust in the process. Even where the aim is to introduce 'proven' models from elsewhere, it is vital to give communities of staff and service-users the time and space to understand and evaluate them.

No model of care is perfect, and though some services may be deemed to be 'failing', many parts of their local system will be doing relatively well. Under-performance may be the product of failure to address challenges about which practitioners are only too aware. There may be difficult relationships that have not been addressed, or other local factors, quite separate from the model of care involved. There may be poor alignment with colleague services, or competing priorities, often amplified by under-resourcing of a particular service or its partners.

Introducing a new approach without attention to such issues will neither inspire confidence, nor achieve avowed aims. Any such project needs also to recognise that staff and service-users will often be anxious about breaking continuity of relationship as a result of service changes. Critically, a new model may have been trialled in an environment very different from that in which they live and work: a classic error is to see a model that has worked in a relatively tight urban environment as simply transferable to a dispersed rural community.

No-one will trust the piloting of a new approach, and no such innovation will be successful, unless practitioners are confident that such factors have been recognised and taken on board. A community of staff that has genuinely been invited to commit to trying something new, and helped to understand it, will be much more likely to try to make it work. If staff are confident that the limitations and risks involved are being faced, and that their experience of testing it out will be listened to, real commitment becomes possible.

Of course, this collaborative approach to service design and development requires attention to the realities of relationships in the system, especially those generated by the competitive market. Competition can, in itself, inhibit openness, creativity, confidence and commitment in all who take part in joint planning forums. This may be manifest in the ways different professions, specialisms or services participate in service review, design and planning.

Competition between large external organisations – which are able to manage financial risk, and have teams of expert bid writers – and smaller, more cash strapped local providers, can seriously skew collaborative action and thought. This is not simply a power imbalance due to size. Larger organisations may be more prone to 'gaming': they are frequently ready and able to take on services at unrealistically low prices in order to enter, or stay in, a market, usually with the intention to re-negotiate prices over time. This can often be linked to 'over-promising', minimising real world limitations as to what may be provided: which has credibility due to their apparent breadth of operations compared, for example, with a small local provider.

The management of financial risk will always affect the positions that organisations and their staff take in discussions, and perhaps even their participation in such discussions. For example, when 'payment by results' is involved, those carrying the consequent risk are likely to contribute very differently from partners with the security of 'up-front funding'. It should be stressed that it is not just 'negotiating' positions that are affected, but also the actual thinking of the staff involved. Anxiety about job security, uncertainty about what can be said, self-interest, 'tribalism', hierarchical, defensive or dismissive attitudes and behaviours can all colour the conversation.

Another perspective on dialogic work suggests how best to manage such dynamics. Richard Sennett was introduced in Chapter 10. In his book *Together: The Rituals, Pleasures and Politics of Cooperation*, Sennett stresses that the dialogic approach avoids 'win-lose' discussion, where people are invited to put forward views, and debate them, in order to persuade each other and settle on the 'right' course of action. He recognises that such 'dialectical' conversation will always have its place. However, he emphasises the creative value and cooperation-promoting power of inviting participants in dialogue to express their *diversity and differences*, to listen to each other and develop mutual understanding (Sennett, 2012). Such an approach to dialogue will, of course, leave the hard decisions about courses of action to those with the responsibility for finalising plans, or issuing contracts. But, if they have asked the right questions in an open way, listened to the diversity of real experience, and understood the factors involved in enabling effective services, their plans' credibility amongst practitioners and service-users, and their likely success, will be greatly strengthened.

Key to such an approach is what a social care commissioner in Wales, in conversation with us, called 'changing language'. She welcomed the way in which Welsh legislation supported much more emphasis on collaboration towards 'desired outcomes' for service-users than on 'inputs', tasks or 'outputs'. She felt that this change in language and preoccupation enabled the relationship between commissioners and providers to become more collaborative, at organisational and, especially, at practitioner levels. Instead of arguing their positions, they could ask questions together, 'lift the lid' on the reality of service-user need, and consider how services are working, by paying attention to each other's perspectives. Interestingly, this commissioner stressed the importance of the heads of organisations being fully committed to such an approach, and of the need for them to have strong relationships with each other, relationships which model and give permission for working in this way.

Our correspondent also highlighted the need to provide space and time for reflection, meeting, and 'socialisation' at team and wider levels, recognising that this contributes to the intelligence and value of what practitioners will bring to reviewing and planning, as well as supporting good practice. We will discuss this more directly later; here we will simply celebrate the fact that our contact, a commissioner, was explicitly recognising the importance of building such reflective space into service delivery and practice. She recognised the 'up-front' cost of including it in specifications and contracts, but enthusiastically asserted its longer-term value for service-users, staff and the wider 'economy of care'.

The need for improved collaboration was recognised in a 2018 Government Policy Paper 'The Public Sector: ensuring collaborative commissioning' (DDCMS and OCS, 2018). This paper addressed the commissioning of a wide range of public services in England. More sanguine than we are about the benefits of competition and a market economy, it nonetheless made clear that attention to relationships and collaboration is vital:

> *The key to effective public services is the relationships between staff, volunteers, and the users of the service. In instances where this is working well, the accountability arrangement — the relationship — between the service provider and its commissioner is built on a shared mission.*
>
> *To this end, the government's vision for public services in the modern era is one of 'collaborative commissioning'. This means that in the future, local stakeholders will be involved in an equal and meaningful way in commissioning and all the resources of a community, including but not confined to public funding, will be deployed to tackle the community's challenges. People will be trusted to co-design the services they use. Rather than being seen as a place of distinct policy priorities — health or crime or educational under-achievement — a community will be seen as a 'system' of interconnected parts, each of which impacts the others.* (DDCMS and OCS Policy Paper No: 5, 2018)

The final sentence of this extract points to another key concern. Commissioners and planners need to shift from narrow, 'sector-' or 'service-' specific design, planning and contracting. They need to consider whole systems, in order to work out how collaborative efforts can lead to a range of desired outcomes for communities as a whole. Citizens and current users of services have key perspectives to bring to such planning. The Policy Paper recommends such an approach, based on work in places such as the London Borough of Sutton, to introduce 'Citizen Commissioners' (https://vcsutton.org.uk/citizens-commissioners/).

Of course, involving representatives of communities, or people with specific needs, does not in itself guarantee the productive and effective dialogue we have been recommending. It is how it is done that makes the difference, especially what work is done to learn about and understand the situations, aspirations and resources of real communities. It is vital to see patients or service-users in their social context – in their families, in their potential local networks – rather than simply as individuals in need.

In the small town of Frome in Somerset, a GP practice, supported by local commissioners, took the lead in mapping the range of services and community groups offering support to local people. They then worked to identify gaps in what was available to help people with challenging needs – making no distinction between health and social care, but simply working out what would help them manage their difficulties and improve the quality of their lives. This might be looking after someone's physical and/or emotional needs, help with shopping, walking the dog, or helping someone reduce their loneliness and increase their confidence by joining a local choir. Work to fill these gaps was then supported by professional and voluntary 'connectors' to build relationships with and help people get the support they needed. The project was a genuine collaboration between community and professionals. It recognised and valued the roles of carers and neighbours. Over three years, from 2014 to 2017, while emergency hospital admissions across Somerset rose by 29 per cent, with a 21 per cent increase in costs, in Frome they fell by 17 per cent, with a 21 per cent reduction in costs (Brown, 2018).

As well as attesting to the value of rooting planning and commissioning in its social context, the Frome project underlines other truths. First, 'bottom-up' planning, owned locally by, and strengthening the relationships within, self-identifying, real communities, is very powerful. Secondly, it is helpful to 'broaden the frame' around need, not just to work with the strengths and resources of clients or patients, but also to include an understanding of the social resources, indeed the potential social capital, of a community. To do so is in the interests both of people in need, *and* of the public services that help to support them.

Important themes run through this discussion of the design, planning and commissioning of services. Behind all of them is the notion that both the psychosocial 'kinship' system, and the task and role system, need to be held in mind. Key points are summarised in Box 14.3.

Box 14.3 Key Principles for Commissioning, Planning and Service Change

- **Prioritise the quality of relationships**, from the front-line to top management, within services and between organisations. This promotes effectiveness and efficiency as much as the models and systems developed.
- **Narrow the gap** between commissioners and providers, between managers and their practitioners: promote collaboration and co-creation.
- **Avoid top-down planning**, and trust the value of promoting dialogue about, critique of, and ideas about services, by communities of practitioners, service-users and citizens. Make the required time available.
- **Seek narratives about lived experience** from clients or patients in their social context: this will help understand their needs, but also identify resources that can be brought to bear, or developed, alongside service interventions.
- **Actively attend to the experience of practitioners.** Not only will this provide vital information, but the ensuing dialogue will build collective ownership of and commitment to any eventual change.
- **Manage the 'politics'** of this dialogue, facilitating commitment to common values, and a diversity of perspectives, without promoting premature debate about, or negotiation of, options.
- **Be aware of skewed thinking** arising from contracting relationships and models, especially 'payment by results'.
- **Plan for whole systems and outcomes**, not fragmented duties, inputs or outputs.
- **Aim for 'community rootedness' and local relevance** of any plans.
- **Recognise the diversity of desired outcomes** for communities of people with particular needs, and for ordinary local communities.
- **Allow agency and creativity** by designing-in flexibility, and avoiding over-specification.
- **Be honest about resource limitations:** if money has to be saved, be clear about this and involve people in finding solutions, but never pretend that 'more for less' is inevitably possible.
- **Value, build and strengthen relationships between leaders** of collaborating organisations, within a common commitment to leading co-creation and cooperation at every level in the system.
- **Recognise the cultural impact** of commissioning, service planning and change implementation: and also how a healthy culture will improve both planning and implementation.

Cultivating Effective Teamwork and Inter-team Collaboration

Chapters 6 and 7 explored the dynamics active within teams, and in their collaboration as parts of systems of care. We argued that the quality of relationships within, and between, teams supports sensitive and effective work by practitioners. Healthy teams help members to process their experience, and to manage both their anxiety and the personal costs of their work. This facilitates bearing the service-user in mind, and intelligent assessment of need, risk, and the services required. Well-functioning teams promote open and imaginative dialogue, decision-making, and cooperation; both internally, and with colleagues in partner services. Teams can help buffer the unhelpful, distracting effects of anxious performance management, and other potentially intrusive factors originating elsewhere in the system. The team can reflect upon how the whole system functions, and identify shortcomings or problems.

As a consequence, the needs, aspirations and circumstances of service-users will be better held in mind across the whole system, and the interventions of all involved are likely to be better tailored to need, better coordinated and more effective. It is probably no exaggeration to suggest that healthy teams are the key factor in securing the safety, humanity, wellbeing and effectiveness of staff, the responsiveness and quality of care of the system, and the interests of patients and service-users. They can be the main determinant of intelligent kindness in practice. This view has been recognised widely across all sectors.

The practical application of this understanding is dependent on a number of pre-conditions. First, staff must actually *be in a team*. For many social care practitioners, such as domiciliary care workers, their working lives are characterised by isolation, travelling from one client to another throughout the working day. Their paid time is for 'client contact' only, with their engagement with other staff reduced to 'clocking in', or 'logging in' remotely to a coordinating hub. Similarly, healthcare practitioners can be members of very large and widely spread groupings, or work across a number of services without any sense of any 'home team'. Hospital wards, so often dependent on agency staff, have inconsistent teams.

In such circumstances, it is close to inevitable that the awareness and activities of the worker will 'narrow down' to simply providing variously planned or unplanned, fragmented, interventions. What they find, what they learn and what they worry about when they engage with patient or client, is likely to stay with them, unconsidered by colleagues or the wider system. They miss out on the benefit that arises from a team's 'containment' of their experience, and its contribution to their thinking. Imaginative ways of building teams around the work of such practitioners, with strong links with colleague services, need to be found wherever possible.

Where the team *does* exist, there are of course still challenges to its functioning of the type we have already described. High caseloads, poor staffing levels, targets, time pressures and over-intrusive performance management can turn team meetings into crowded, mechanical, procedural, unreflective spaces. Underestimation or mishandling of the complexities of relationships and the alignment of roles and tasks in multi-disciplinary teams, discussed in Chapter 7, can undermine team functioning. Failure to value and assert the importance of reflective dialogue, considering the relationships and work of team members, and the functioning of the wider system, can lead to ambivalence about participation. Higher tiers of management may reinforce this ambivalence. Especially as they manage limited resources, they may utterly neglect the necessity of prioritising support for effective teamwork, and building reflective space into the system as a whole.

Attempts have been made to address some of these factors. For example, the Royal College of Surgeons, responding to the reported low morale of their trainees, piloted a modern version of the old, team-based, 'firm' structure in their Improving Surgical Training programme in 2018 (Royal College of Surgeons, 2015). Prior to recent reforms of medical staffing and education, hospital medical care was delivered by small and cohesive, albeit hierarchical, consultant-led teams of doctors in training. In the absence of such arrangements, a lack of support structures due to trainees having no consistent close work colleagues was a major source of unhappiness. It was hoped that this would be addressed by tightening up the team structure and sense of belonging.

A good example of strengthening teamwork and building reflection into everyday practice is the Reclaiming Social Work project. This approach was pioneered in Hackney in 2008, independently evaluated in 2011 (Munro, 2011), adopted by a number of other local authorities since then, and further evaluated in 2017 by the Department of Education (Bostock et al, 2017).

Central to this whole system approach to change is the formation of multi-disciplinary workforce units of five to seven people, each with specialist roles, and a weekly reflective team meeting. The project delivered benefits for clients, the staff and the organisation (see Box 14.4).

An organisation's commitment to cultivating healthy, effective, reflective teams is helped if commissioners and planners, like our correspondent in Wales quoted above, recognise their value and importance. Realistic staffing levels, and the costing in of time, can then be better guaranteed. Senior managers within services need to have a similar attitude. For teams to function healthily, offer productive reflective environments, and relate well with other services, their leaders need to be given the responsibility, the authority, and the skills, to lead them well. The conditions for such leadership are, at best, fragile, but will be improved if there is an educated awareness at all levels of the system that being able to manage the dynamics of a team is a core competence for people whose role is to assure the quality and effectiveness of services, as well as staff wellbeing.

Box 14.4 The Reclaiming Social Work Model

Units of five to seven are led by a consultant social worker who is both manager and practitioner, and who holds cases collectively with the team, i.e. there are no individual case-loads. There are weekly meetings where families are discussed, offering intensive reflective time to consider and decide what happens next. All staff are trained in systemic family therapy and this model underpins the work. Amongst other positive outcomes, workers reported higher levels of satisfaction, lower levels of stress and there was a reduction in sick leave (Munro, 2011).

One of the aims of this approach is to free practitioners to do direct work with children and families and reverse the usual split where social workers spend 80 per cent of their time doing admin tasks and only 20 per cent in direct contact with clients. A unit co-ordinator makes this possible by freeing the rest of the team from admin tasks. In this model, children and families see two to three times more of their workers compared to comparative authorities, parents' ratings of the work are higher, the number of 'looked-after' children is lower, and where children are put into care, there is better placement stability (Munro, 2011; Bostock et al, 2017).

It will help if professional education and training explicitly includes preparing trainees to work in teams, emphasising that the understanding required, and the skills involved, are central, essential components of practice. It is not enough to simply allocate someone the task of leading a team, and leave them to it: the complexity of the task must be recognised, and support for the development of the skills required is essential. Too often, training for leaders narrows down to such issues as 'chairing meetings', 'managing conflict' and 'dealing with difficult people'. While such issues are important, they can reinforce a simplistic 'managerialist' approach, rather than supporting the sophisticated understanding and skills that will promote truly creative teamwork.

Many leaders of teams and organisations have found it helpful to explore group dynamics more directly than in general leadership training programmes. They have committed time, and been supported, to develop their understanding of how groups work, and to consider the implications for how they manage themselves in groups and in their roles as leaders. Learning events covering experiential group relations have been held for decades, with various approaches involved. The investment can be well worth it for the individuals involved, their colleagues and the people they lead. Helpful trainings, of various depth and length, are provided by many organisations, such as the Tavistock Institute for Human Relations, the Institute of Group Analysis and the Association of Therapeutic Communities.

There is also a wide range of approaches to 'team-building' that can be employed, and tools that teams can use to help them develop their effectiveness. There are countless guides to team-building in all sectors, from business, sports and the military, to health and social care – too many to survey or recommend here. But it is important to ensure that when such techniques are used, facilitators balance developmental 'exercises' with a clear invitation to members to bring their experience into the room and reflect upon it.

One way in which team leaders can be offered reliable support in their roles, including their management of the boundaries of their teams and their relationships with other services, is through regular, facilitated, reflective forums. These bring team leaders together across the system to share their experiences of leadership and of working together. They can be within a single organisation or across wider collaborative systems of services. Such forums not only strengthen individual skills, but also go a long way to improving relationships, communication and cooperation.

Outside facilitation can also be helpful, at relatively modest cost. If such events are properly organised – not simply as annual 'away days' with ill-defined aims – they allow the team to consider how they are working together, including how the leader is working, and being worked with. Such intervention should not be seen solely as remedial for troubled teams, or as vaguely well-meaning but ill-defined 'staff support', but as a valuable foundation for skilled practice, for the benefit of service-users, practitioners and the organisations within which they work. An organisation employing one or two skilled group facilitators/consultants could offer such support routinely to a multitude of teams.

We are proposing a strategic approach to cultivating reflective, dialogical and cooperative teamwork within organisations and across systems. Such a strategy should be comprehensive, paying attention to *all* teams in the system, not simply those that are new or 'malfunctioning'. The approach should make clear that support for team wellbeing is a requirement, not something voluntarily 'opted into' according to the preference or whim or character style of team members or leaders.

Box 14.5 Cultivating Healthy and Effective Teams

- **Recognise the central task** of cultivating the team as both a healthy psychosocial, and 'task and role' system.
- **Develop a comprehensive strategy** for supporting this work, and engaging senior leaders in it.
- **Adopt tools** to evaluate the climate and effectiveness of teams. These can be used by teams themselves, and/or for monitoring.
- **Make time for**, and invest resources in, developing and sustaining teams and inter-team relationships.
- **Train and educate** staff in what being part of a team means, both as people, and as skilled and effective practitioners.
- **Recognise, and develop** approaches to managing the complex politics of multi-disciplinary teams.
- **Value and allocate resources to reflective dialogue** about team experience – of practice, and of working together and with colleague services.
- **Understand and value the role of the team leader**, providing the appropriate breadth and depth of training, supervision and support.
- **Provide external facilitation and support** to augment the role of team leader in convening reflective dialogue and cooperation, and to allow reflection upon how leader and team are working together.
- **Create a community of dialogue and reflection** for the leaders of teams across systems.
- **Make all of this a routine requirement** of everyone's role, with senior leaders explicitly responsible for supporting it.

The strategy should be sustained and monitored over time, with recognition that the promotion and support of healthy teams is a continuous process. There are many tools that can be used to evaluate the culture and functioning of a team, some described in Chapter 6. Such tools can be employed by teams and their leaders themselves, or as methods of collecting information about how an overall strategy is progressing. It may be helpful to give senior leaders explicit responsibility for developing and monitoring the effectiveness of the strategy, perhaps with a named person with overall responsibility.

A summary of our thoughts on such a strategic approach to developing and sustaining effective teamwork appears above in Box 14.5.

'Growing' and Supporting Practitioners

In Chapter 10, we drew out some central issues in supporting and enabling good practice. There are four basic questions that need to be thought through and acted upon:

- How to promote and sustain compassionate bearing in mind of the other;
- How to generate imaginative understanding of the contribution a person's actions can make to others' wellbeing;
- How to instil and support a confident belief in a person's own value and freedom to act;

- How to ensure that individuals have the knowledge and repertoire to act skilfully and compassionately according to circumstances.

If individuals practise in the relational, dialogical and participative culture we have discussed, answers to these questions will emerge and be sustained as part of the process. When staff are invited to consider their, and their service-users' experience, in reflection upon, critique of, and development of the services in which they work, this promotes the attentiveness, imagination and ownership, required. When they work in teams where relationships *and* task are properly managed, they will experience day-to-day encouragement and support in sustaining these qualities in their everyday practice. If commissioners and leaders apply what they have learned from practitioners and service-users to the design, organisation and alignment of services, staff will find themselves cooperating within a system that better supports such practice.

Much, though, depends on the kind of people they are. It will be of little avail to create the conditions that promote and sustain intelligent kindness if there is a clash between such values and those of individual practitioners. How they see their work and what it means to them, their professional identities, their attitudes to each other and to patients and service-users, are central factors.

Education and Training

What do young people considering training as practitioners in health, social care and wider welfare systems think they are embarking upon? What messages are conveyed by the recruitment processes? How are candidates assessed and selected? What does their training then involve, and how much are the relational and humane aspects of practice valued and integrated into their education? Does the education clearly recognise intelligent kindness, by this or any other name, as the 'psychosocial heart' of both skilled practice and the 'duty of care'? Do the educators and trainers recognise it themselves?

Selection processes will contribute if they invite candidates into dialogue with patients and service-users, and into interactive exercises with others, and assess applicants on their relational skills: on what kind of people they reveal themselves to be. If such information is valued in decisions about selection there is a better chance of recruiting the right people. Such an approach will convey, from the very beginning, the clear message that professional excellence is about the qualities of the person, as well as their technical capabilities.

Courses themselves must similarly integrate values, attitudes and relational skills into all aspects of training: not simply offer them as supplementary to, and distinct from, 'more important' technical competencies. Whilst there are many examples of innovative courses with psychosocial and ethical components, too often such initiatives are one-off modules or discussions, rather than integral to the whole course. As such, they risk being viewed by trainees as irrelevant (Wear and Zarconi, 2008), or even optional, particularly when there are many more concrete skills and a knowledge base that can be more easily learnt, and tested. Communications skills, for example, are not something that can be taught over a few afternoons; systemic thinking cannot be covered in a one-off lecture course if the aim is for its values to be internalised; teaching student nurses about compassion, then placing them on wards that are understaffed and offer no time for them to practise it, will engender confusion and resentment.

The capacity to make and sustain attentive, compassionate, relationships should be at the heart of all training and should be *modelled* in the relationships between trainers, supervisors, mentors, and their trainees (Firth-Cozens and Cornwell, 2009, p. 10). Like all complex social skills, this involves understanding both oneself and others, and needs to be learned through experience. Exposure to service-users' stories, and placements with families or individuals with complex needs can promote understanding and empathy in the trainee.

The ability to pay attention to, to empathise with, and to make sense of another's need and experience requires self-management and commitment, and needs to be practised in an ongoing way if it is to be sustained under pressure. To create an effective medium for nurturing intelligent kindness, educators in health and social care need to build a culture of reflection and enquiry and provide a living–learning experience that promotes self-awareness and learning from mistakes. Receiving sensitive and continuous feedback – some of it directly from patients and clients – is an important aspect of such training, and should form part of a reflective dialogue throughout the process. Lectures on how to practise with kindness, or indeed instructions to do so, will have little value, unless they are complemented by such forms of learning.

Continuing Professional Development

A mixture of financial pressures, demand, and the sheer problems of releasing staff, have made continuing professional training and development a challenge for health and social care organisations. At the same time, the twin drivers of regulation and risk aversion (associated with a fear of financial penalties) have led to a proliferation of 'statutory' and 'mandatory' training. This training is frequently indiscriminate. It is common for a business planner and a nurse both to do the same 'handling and lifting' course – every year! An expert on child protection and domestic violence sits alongside her secretary for the same annual whistle-stop tour of child protection. No one questions whether annually is right – it just is. And if you come in from another organisation you must do most of it again so that 'regulations' can be satisfied. There is an enormous opportunity to rethink this kind of training – to ensure the right people get the right training at the right level, to remove duplication, and to re-consider frequency. There might then be a chance to make space and free-up resources for continuous learning about relational practice.

Such education may consider general themes, or more specialist approaches. It may be about teamwork, leadership or broader systemic perspectives. It may be undertaken in taught courses, or through experiential learning supported by reflective dialogue. Regular, well facilitated, reflective training groups, or action learning sets, to which staff working in particular roles, or with specific methods or needs, can bring their experience and learn together, can be very helpful.

Whatever the forms of learning involved, whether at entry level, or for experienced practitioners, there is always the danger of a lack of 'fit' between what people learn, how they aspire to practise, and the culture and preoccupations of the working environment they return to. Frequently, it's just not possible to practise their newly learned skills. Not only does this mean wasted resources: it can breed disillusionment, frustration and disengagement. Leaders, trainers and trainees need the opportunity to recognise, learn from and squarely face such dissonance together, if the value of training and development is to be realised.

Supervision, Reflection and Support

Staff working across the Welfare State have always had to struggle with situations that take them to the brink of their humanity, and present-day pressures may exacerbate this. The culture of the modern health service, and conventional social care, is frequently poorly suited to the emotional labour involved in containing the work's attendant anxiety. The importance of such labour can go unrecognised, and the skills and attention of leaders are rarely directed to addressing this need.

The importance of reflective, sometimes called reflexive, supervision is widely acknowledged. Despite lip service being paid to its importance, it is not yet sufficiently valued and prioritised in practice.

The current bias towards monitoring performance, implementing procedures and developing competencies through 'supervision' requires a clear shift. A typical supervision session, if it actually happens, can end up being little more than an update on progress on every one of a massive caseload, or an anxious exploration of one case that has gone wrong. It would be more productive if supervision were to give sufficient priority to helping staff to manage themselves in their roles, process difficult feelings, sustain compassionate attention and develop the responsiveness and confidence to work cooperatively with others. Of course, properly skilled supervisors are essential. They need to be well-supported themselves, to help manage their own anxieties about performance, risk, and outputs, so that they can attend to this work. A helpful outline of what is involved appears in *Supervision in the Helping Professions* (Hawkins and Shohet, 2012).

It is also helpful to consider models other than traditional one-to-one supervision. The Reclaiming Social Work model, for example, includes a half-day of group supervision each week where staff are encouraged to talk in depth about their experience of one family with whom they work. One of the results, alongside better outcomes for service-users, was a 55 per cent drop in staff days lost in sickness (Munro, 2011). Group supervision can be useful not just because it's cheaper, but also as a way of creating a wider team and social milieu which nourishes kindness and creativity in practice.

Everybody working in the system would benefit from being supported in this way, including leaders and managers at the top of the organisation, and 'support staff' such as receptionists and porters. Imaginative use of mentoring and support groups can help, alongside participation in the dialogic settings discussed above. This is not a naïve argument for expensive and time-consuming self-indulgent or self-regarding space: as we have demonstrated throughout this book, the benefits, in terms of performance, staff wellbeing, and service-user experience, will more than outweigh the costs.

Making Relational Practice Possible

All work to care for and support people is relational by its very nature, from the short one-off encounter to longer-term engagement with a person in need. Even a staff member working at a distance, making an appointment, issuing a prescription or processing a benefit claim will be better motivated and more effective if directed by intelligent kindness. There is evidence that enabling genuine, longer-term relationships between practitioners and patients or service-users is of benefit to both. The benefits of continuity in primary care were referred to in Chapter 9. In Raglan, in Wales, a small domiciliary care project was set up in 2014, looking at how to replace task-based care for people with dementia with a high quality home-based relational approach. This had many strengths, including improved terms and conditions for staff, and development of supports in the local community, with more productive outcomes for service-users. At its core was enabling staff to build *relationships* with people suffering from dementia, in order to understand them and their situations before any decisions were made about what services to offer. Staff then worked with the clients as a small team, covering for each other, and, working out as they went along what work was necessary; doing what seemed helpful as situations changed. Remarkably, in this small team there was a 0 per cent sickness rate over 18 months! The project has been recommended for attention by SCIE in its examples of Commissioning Home Care for Older People (www.scie.org.uk/publications/guides/guide54/practice-examples.asp).

The relatively simple Raglan approach demonstrates that there are ways of enabling relational practice, and that they have benefits. A range of other proposals and models have emerged over the years, especially for work with people with severe and complex needs.

In 2013, the 'Future Hospital Commission', set up by the Royal College of Physicians, published a report, 'The Future Hospital: Caring for Medical Patients' (Future Hospital Commission and RCP, 2013). This was in response to a growing awareness of the dangers of fragmented care when in-patients require input from several specialities. Among many recommendations that would make care coherent and ensure the patient would be borne in mind as a 'whole' person, the report proposed more general physicians who should play a key part in the coordination of care in hospital for patients with complex needs. It recommended the establishment of 'new, senior, operational roles prioritising the coordination of medical care' (recommendation 4).

In 2014, a joint report by the Royal College of General Practitioners and the College of Social Work, 'GPs and Social Workers: Partners for Better Care', proposed close collaboration between these professions to coordinate and integrate care for the most vulnerable patients and clients in their communities.

The Innovation Unit was set up as a not-for-profit social enterprise with the aim of using innovation to create different, higher-quality, lower cost public services that better meet social challenges. In 2018, they published a report which evaluated a two-year programme, run by the Unit and the Social Care Institute for Excellence, to 'develop, implement and evaluate' a Named Social Worker approach (Innovation Unit, 2018).

> *A Named Social Worker is a dedicated social worker who has an ongoing responsibility for an individual with a learning disability, autism or mental health need. They are the primary point of contact who are responsible for challenging decisions and advocating on behalf of the young person, across the system.*

All such initiatives have the potential to enable attentive relational care. The danger, though, is that the new roles proposed will pay less attention to building a meaningful relationship with the patient or the service-user than to trying to organise the system of care they receive. The latter is, of course, important, but will be less than productive if that work is not grounded in relationship. The experience, over many years, of trying to

Box 14.6 Promoting Relational Practice by Individual Practitioners

- **Radically refocus education and training,** integrating sensitive relational practice into the core attitudes, skill-sets and professional identity, of trainees.
- **Make space for continuous learning about relational practice,** supported by reflective practice in post-qualification training and continuing professional development.
- **Provide skilled reflective supervision, in protected time,** for individuals and groups of practitioners.
- **Organise roles and practice to enable deeper relationships** between staff and service-users or patients, especially those with continuing and complex needs.

introduce roles like this, whether in the voluntary or statutory sectors, is that it can be problematic. Factors such as preoccupation with bureaucracy, lack of cooperation with the role by colleague services, and, especially, lack of time for face-to-face contact with the service-user, can seriously undermine the relational element of this way of working. Research into care coordination in mental health introduced as part of the Care Programme Approach following the 1991 Health and Social Care Act identified and described these problems in more detail (Simpson et al, 2003). Managers and leaders will need to undertake concerted strategic activity, and make significant shifts in resources, if they are to facilitate more longer-term relational work.

There are, then, many dimensions to the task of promoting a system in which individual practitioners build intelligent kindness into their practice. A short summary appears in Box 14.6 above.

Making It Possible

We should not underestimate the challenges involved in the systemic cultivation of intelligent kindness in public services. It will involve complex work, investment of time, money and – indeed – intelligence! Many readers will be wondering just how overwhelmed staff will actually find the time to participate in the range of processes we have recommended. Many more will ask where the money will come from. We are confident there will be significant improvements, in effectiveness, efficiency, in staff wellbeing and retention, and in outcomes for patients and service-users, if the work is undertaken. This will help reduce the net costs. But the reality is that the system is under-resourced as it is, and that must be honestly faced.

New money should not be tied to micro-management through measuring outcomes or markers of preferred, prescribed, process as it was in the early years of the century.

Whatever investment becomes available, what has to come first is a change in attitudes, especially amongst leaders. There has been encouraging attention to the kind of leadership that will help. Michael West, Head of Thought Leadership at the King's Fund, has done much work on 'compassionate leadership', including its place in innovation and collaboration (www.kingsfund.org.uk/audio-video/michael-west-collaborative-compassionate-leadership). It is important, though, not to underestimate the degree to which the culture of leadership in the public sector needs radical change, especially given the financial and performance pressures, and regulatory preoccupations, that predominate.

It is a strong and wise senior manager who recognises that a large part of the job is to manage their own anxiety, and restrain any impulse to pass it on to staff below them. The effective leader understands what their staff's work involves and can listen well enough to identify the barriers that make it difficult to do. The mature leader can ask, rather than tell, staff how to achieve difficult targets. An intelligent and honest leader recognises that saying that something is so ('we are a people-centred organisation', for example) does not make it so: resources, attitudes and skilled behaviour do. It is a principled and brave leader who is honest enough to accept and defend the real limits to what staff can do within the resources they have. A leader acting as a principled representative of a society concerned about its wellbeing will remain open enough to acknowledge problems, errors or abuses in the services they lead. Leaders with intelligence will hold in mind *both* their identity and responsibilities as members of an organisation or service *and* their equally important responsibility to collaborate as part of a wider community. Above all, a courageous leader will resist the lure of the role of hero or ruler of an organisation and instead strive to be the convenor of its community, the guardian of its conscience and the servant of its purpose.

References

Bostock, L., Forrester, D., Patrizo, L., Godfrey, T., Zanouzish, M., Antonopoupou, V., Bird, M., Moreslesing, T., Goldberg, T. (2017) Scaling and developing the Reclaiming Social Work model. Department of Education. Children's Social Care Innovation Programme Evaluation Report 45.

Brown, M. (2018) Compassionate Community Project. Resurgence and Ecologist Issue 307, March/April 2018.

Bushe, G. and Marshak, R. (2015) *Dialogic Organisational Development: The Theory and Practice of Transformational Change*. Berrett-Koehler.

College of Social Work and Royal College of GPs (2014) GPs and Social Workers: Partners for Better Care. Available at: www.basw.co.uk/system/files/resources/basw_104434-7_0.pdf [last accessed 26 August, 2019].

Firth-Cozens, J. and Cornwell, J. (2009) Enabling Compassion in Acute Hospital Settings. The King's Fund.

Future Hospitals Commission and Royal College of Physicians (2013) Future hospital: Caring for medical patients. RCP.

Hawkins, P. and Shohet, R. (2012) *Supervision in the Helping Professions*. Oxford University Press.

Miller, E. and Barrie, K. (2016) Learning from the Meaningful and Measurable project: strengthening links between identity, action and decision-making. Health Improvement Scotland.

Munro, E. (2011) The Munro Review of Child Support: a Child Centred System. Department of Education, HMSO.

Munro, E., Turnell, A. and Murphy, T. (2014) 'You Can't Grow Roses In Concrete.' Organisational reform to support high quality Signs of Safety practice.

Royal College of Surgeons (2015) Improving Surgical Training. RCS Professional Standards.

Sennett, R. (2012) *Together: the Rituals, Pleasures and Politics of Cooperation*. Allen Lane.

Simpson, A., Bowers, L. and Miller, C. (2003) The History of the Care Programme Approach in England: Where did it go wrong? Journal of Mental Health. 12(5): 489–504.

Social Care Institute of Excellence (2014) Commissioning Home Care for Older People. Available at: www.scie.org.uk/publications/guides/guide54/practice-examples.asp [last accessed 14 August, 2019].

Social Care Institute for Excellence (2016) Named Social Worker. Available at: www

.innovationunit.org/projects/named-social-worker/ [last accessed 14 August, 2019].

Wear, D. and Zarconi, J. (2008) Can compassion be taught? Journal of General International Medicine. 23(7): 948–53.

West, M. (2017) Collaborative and Compassionate Leadership. King's Fund. Available at: www.kingsfund.org.uk/audio-video/michael-west-collaborative-compassionate-leadership [last accessed 14 August, 2019].

Chapter

15 Rehabilitating the Welfare State

Most human beings have an almost infinite capacity for taking things for granted.

(Aldous Huxley, Themes and Variations (1950))

We British have had our Welfare State since 1948. We take it for granted that we have free healthcare according to need; that we have social care to fall back upon if all else fails, and to protect us from ourselves; and that we have a system of benefits to save us from penury.

Several million of us also have secure jobs in health, social care, and the benefits system. Each day, families are supported, children's safety is attended to, illness is diagnosed and treated, and financial support is given to those who would otherwise be destitute. Often this goes well, if not very well indeed – and we don't really know what we'd have done if the support wasn't available.

All these services are, in their own way, imperfect, but we start from a position of expecting that they are there for us. Of course, once a 'Welfare State' has been put in place, we can examine its failings in detail. It may seem intrusive, or prescriptive, or rigid. It might undermine our motivation or sense of responsibility. We might be able to 'game it' for personal gain. It may not give us what we want, just when we want it. It may just not be up to the job it claims to be doing. It is readily available to be criticised or critiqued, and we can easily forget what happened before it was put into place, or what life might be like if it wasn't there.

'Welfare' has become a pejorative term over the years. In one reading, the 'Welfare State' has much in common with the idea of the 'nanny state', so often negatively invoked by both those who have had, and haven't had, nannies of their own. This is an objection to the state taking the place of a parent, and telling us how to run our lives, when we should be 'grown-up' and independent; or perhaps more often, 'mollycoddling' *others* when *they* should be fending for themselves.

Most, if not all, of us use the NHS at some stage in our life (mostly towards the end), so most of us would assert its value. Few of us have to rely on social services, or the benefits system, so it's easier to be dismissive of them and question their value. As we have discussed in earlier chapters, both idealisation and denigration run through all of these attitudes. Such polarisations offer easy, emotionally determined positions that ignore the complexity of the daily work, caring for and supporting our kin.

During its '70th birthday' celebrations (a curious anthropomorphism) it was frequently said that the NHS was 'our national religion'. Psychologically difficult to integrate with such supposed celebrations were the revelations, around the same time, that at the Gosport Veterans Hospital people's lives were shortened by inappropriate and excessive prescription of opiates (twice as many as were killed by Dr Harold Shipman, according to the *Sun*). Some years earlier, the opening ceremony of the 2012 Olympic games had paid tribute to the service with a tableau of Mary Poppins visiting pyjama-clad children in old-style metal-railed hospital beds – whither the objections then to the nanny state?

At the other extreme of public esteem, the benefits system, and those who rely on it, have long been ready vessels for discontent. Observations of its failings abound: populist views of it as being ready prey for 'scroungers' have been circulating since its inception. Imagined scenarios such as 'boatloads of immigrants' arriving in the country and collecting their social security payments on arrival have, in one form or another, perplexed the popular imagination for years, as have the 'workshy'. At the same time, the inflexibility and injustices of the system have troubled those of a different political persuasion. Amongst these different narratives, the system has had to walk the difficult line of scrutinising claims appropriately, whilst remaining flexible and accessible, trying somehow to make fair and supportive judgements in difficult funding environments.

Our book has not been able to consider the realities and specific dynamics of the benefits system in anywhere the same depth as health and social care: others are better qualified to do this. However, there are some similar dynamics and pressures at work to those we have discussed relating to the areas of work we know well, and there are reputational issues in common.

As we noted at the outset, 'rehabilitation' has two complementary meanings: 'restoring to health' and 'restoring privilege or reputation after a period of disfavour'. Starting with the second of these, 'the Welfare State' as a concept has slipped into disfavour, despite the fact it embodies much that most of us hold dear. We have already noted the difficulties in acknowledging and addressing our own vulnerability, and the vulnerability of others, and the tangled, ambivalent or contradictory feelings that are evoked. Both idealisation and denigration may come to the fore. It is difficult to see something clearly whilst it is being denigrated: but equally difficult if it is idealised. The task is to be able to consider what happens, and how things are done, as both good and bad at times, and good and bad in parts.

If it is to be an ongoing project, our Welfare State needs both forms of rehabilitation. First we have to restore the concept to favour, so we can value all its institutions for what they are, or at least for what they are striving towards. Only then will we have the grounds for helping it back to health, rather than letting it 'wither on the vine'.

We began, back in Chapter 1, by noting how little recent attention has been given to understanding and promoting the Welfare State's central embodiment of kinship. There seems to have been a failure to understand and value this, a paucity of positive rhetoric, a lack of pride, a loss of historical narrative. This becomes more pressing as the generation who are old enough to remember the hardships and anxiety before the Welfare State was part of our landscape are no longer with us. Programmes of reform are more likely to be effective if we are able, as a society, to reconnect to, and so rehabilitate, the idea that pooling resources and sharing responsibility for each other can be good for everyone.

We can only think about how to restore the system to health and vitality if its central premise is valued. Even so, some have argued that it is beyond repair. Is rehabilitation realistic or do we need a 'revolution' as some (on both 'left' and 'right') have suggested? Can we envisage a restorative process, and enthuse others to return this great project to health? Or do the fault-lines run so deep that it would be better to dismantle the whole enterprise and start from scratch?

We are where we are. We have a massive, well-organised, well-funded (by the standard of most societies in other times and places), well-staffed (by the same standard) and high functioning system already in place. Every day there are millions of interactions, between millions of people, in pursuit of its aims. Most of what it does is of high quality, and for the most part kindly delivered. It can't just be broken up, and something swiftly and efficiently put in its place: but equally we cannot afford to be complacent. There are undoubtedly good reasons to worry about its health; and we have explored these in detail. There are also good reasons to be concerned about its 'fit' for modern life: particularly in the delivery of social care and social support, and in the provision of material benefits. The world we live in now is very different from that within which the systems were designed.

This book has discussed deep-seated problems and vulnerabilities that will always be present as we go about our business of giving and receiving care, because humans – both staff and those in need of their care – *are* human. The project of looking after each other is inherently challenging. It is costly, in human terms, and in terms of the financial investment required. It will stir up ambivalence, or even negative, hostile feelings, in practitioners and in society at large. It will always present dilemmas, stretch resources and sometimes fail. But this will be less likely if the nature and dynamics of the work are well understood and the project is properly managed. Alongside a consideration of all these problems, we have offered some pointers to potential remedies. Some of these remedies involve supporting and strengthening capability, while others aim to mitigate the difficult dynamics evoked by the work, and its organisation and management.

Although there is much ill-being, damage and worrying vulnerability in the system, there is plenty of evidence of success, and potential for recovery. The foundations for rebuilding the enterprise are there: the basic vision, the underlying values and the, admittedly vulnerable, social contract behind it. Enough of the system is in good enough condition to enable restoration, refreshment and sensitive modernisation. Above all, there are the millions of staff committed to contributing to the health and wellbeing of those they serve. Despite the many frustrations and even the potential personal harms inherent in their work, they are still ready to invest their efforts in public services.

Any plan for restoring the Welfare State needs to recognise, value and encourage the hard work, creativity and commitment of its staff. The intelligence of patients and service-users, and of communities in general, is also of tremendous value, if only they are properly involved. The prospects for rehabilitation are good, if these living resources can be actively and intelligently nurtured and engaged.

Such rehabilitation will take determination and nerve. Leaders – who may variously be politicians and policy makers, educators, managers and senior professionals – need to elicit a *mandate* from society to undertake the project. This means unambiguous promotion of the common good and the importance of collective investment through taxation in the services of the Welfare State. To have the most effect, the argument needs to be set within a wider expression of the importance to all of us of human connectedness, interdependency, and the urgent need to act to reduce inequality. Health and social care services, however well organised or well funded, cannot deal with social ills in isolation, without the availability of employment and housing, and education that aids the development of socially aware and secure young people.

Rehabilitation cannot be a matter of another 'reform' or restructuring. As we have repeatedly observed, such changes all too readily produce the opposite of what is needed. It is likely to be much better served by a fundamental shift in focus away from such 'managerialist', often politically motivated, interventions. A more constructive approach would involve *supporting and enabling* the work of practitioners at all levels in the system – including those in leadership roles. The test of the value of any governance or organisational process is whether it facilitates the attentive, imaginative and compassionate connections with service-users, and with colleagues, that will produce excellence. All who work in the system need to be enabled to manage the tension between the effects of industrialisation, regulation and task-related stress, and the need to care kindly and effectively for those who require services.

And here we should, once more, consider kindness. As we have discussed in Chapter 5, all our relationships with others, and even with ourselves, contain both kindness and unkindness (hostility), in varying measure, and in some sort of balance – albeit not always a healthy one. One or other (usually unkindness) may be unconscious, but it is present nonetheless. For practitioners, one's intrinsic unkindness may well be unconscious: but it can also be vaguely known about, just 'sitting in the back of the mind', perhaps coming to awareness at times of stress. What we need, when grappling with the characteristic stresses of the current daily work, the stresses we have considered in detail, is a way of knowing both, holding them in balance, and then striving to shift that balance, rather than deny our negative feelings, or that it *is* a balancing act.

We can't all suddenly become 'kind', whoever we are, and whatever role we have. But we can become *kinder* than we might otherwise be, and thus help the caring enterprise on its way. We can be more vigilant and wise about our own hostility, rather than simply enacting it unconsciously or unthinkingly. By so being, we might reduce the risk of behaving unkindly under pressure. We might do this for moral or ethical reasons, or simply because it works – for as we have shown, being kind is often the best way to get the 'job' of caring or healing done.

What might happen if everyone working in our Welfare State had an explicit understanding that the psychological climate and the dynamics of relationships require at least as much attention and skilled hard work as structure, 'pathways' and business processes? What might happen if all involved, not just those 'on the front-line', were able to be attentive to the emotional reality of care-giving, and apply their imagination to how to manage its potentially dangerous tensions and dynamics. This might take us a long way from a culture where, at worst, the provision of care can be secondary to organisational and personal success, where targets are achieved under duress, and 'blind eyes' are turned to inconvenient realities. Might it be one way of steering clear of a morass of punitive responses, confused accountability and unrealistic expectations?

As to accountability, a readiness at all levels to share collective responsibility, to collaborate in monitoring and working to improve the system, will help. This duty must be viewed as a lively, dialogic process, continuously sustained in our organisations, not a lonely, concrete and unsupported individual responsibility to 'report serious incidents', 'blow a whistle' or 'raise' a grievance.

Might it be possible for management bodies and professional organisations to move beyond agreements that staff can have 'committees' or union meetings, to a 'contract for collaboration'? Could professional bodies take their share of the responsibility for encouraging and entering dialogue about local services, including, but not restricted to, the experience of their members. Would they be ready to sit round the table as cooperative partners sharing the responsibility for organisational and service wellbeing? Could there even be formal structures, at the level of organisational governance, to help make such things happen. If the necessary changes of attitudes and growth of trust were possible, what might be achieved?

A society's social conditions and attitudes, and its political and economic models, influence the health, potential and wellbeing of its members. These factors also determine both the society's and the individual's readiness to take action to ameliorate problems, and their favoured models for how things should be managed. They affect people's feelings about fellow citizens, about people in various kinds of need, and about those who try to meet that need and their successes and failures. In this way, the culture and effectiveness of public services is very much determined by the socio-economic climate, and how these services are valued and experienced by society at large. In turn, the wellbeing of the enterprise is integral to the culture and general health of our society.

Having come into being when it did, and for the reasons it did, what will the 'Welfare State' look like as we progress further into the twenty-first century? Can we maintain the commitment to kinship inherent in its founding? The future is always uncertain, but at the time of writing it seems even more so than usual. Much that our society has relied upon is changing. Divisions and disagreement are deeper than many of us ever remember. Maybe there is, once more, a need to find ways to bind us all back together, and emphasise what we have in common, rather than what divides us? The Welfare State has immense potential symbolic value in this regard, if used carefully and cannily.

The prospects for its rehabilitation are, of course, highly dependent on sufficient funding. The resources needed by the system as a whole require honest consideration. In particular, the dangerously low funding of social care must be addressed. The required rehabilitation work cannot be done 'on the cheap', nor can the project somehow be used as yet another pretext for reducing expense.

For as long as we can remember, it has been difficult to make the case for adequate staffing: the central call upon funding. It is hard enough to argue for staffing levels that can respond adequately to people's needs. It becomes even more difficult if the proposal includes a view of adequacy that is wider than simply having enough staff for 'face-to-face' contact, to perform tasks, fill rotas or to manage case-loads. Broadening the terms of the argument to include staffing levels that allow adequate support, collaboration and time for reflection will require care and convincing articulation. But this will be necessary to improve effective cooperation and significantly shift the culture.

Whilst more 'front-line' staff are needed, even those posts that are funded and advertised have proved hard to fill in recent years. On top of the difficulties with recruitment, there has long been a steady flow of staff out of the system, often citing difficulties with working conditions, and the organisational culture, as reasons they have not stayed. Recruitment and retention may well be boosted if staff were part of a collaborative human enterprise such as we have described, rather than the intimidating and debilitating industry that many have begun to expect. The knock-on savings from not paying for agency workers, with the associated discontinuities and inefficiencies that are inevitable when there is no settled community of staff, will help. Sickness absence, under-functioning due to stress, resignations and premature retirement are highly likely to reduce. Errors, neglect, sub-standard outcomes, and the need for a 'zero-tolerance' approach to disturbance – and the legal costs these generate – are likely to lessen substantially in the presence of an adequately staffed, properly supported workforce.

We are well aware that to talk of 'the Welfare State' as a single entity, as we have done in this book, implicitly suggests that it is a unified system. It began with a unified vision, but in daily life, whilst working within it, or seeking care from it, people's experience is much more often one of fragmentation, lack of coordination, and even conflict between one part and another. At the time of writing, the structural integration of health and social care remains high on the strategic agenda, in recognition of its potential benefits. It has not proved easy to achieve. The project is ongoing – and the ideas we have put forward are pertinent. The task is to develop integrated, cooperative working, rather than simply drawing two systems into closer proximity, with the danger that they continue to project into each other, and more readily apportion blame for things that go wrong.

Whilst health and social care are being forced into some sort of rapprochement, a key focus for the reputational rehabilitation of the Welfare State as a whole will need to be the benefits system. The grudging, mistrustful and hostile attitudes that are so readily struck towards the provision of financial support for the vulnerable must be addressed; whilst at the same time acknowledging that systems of financial benefits for penury have been recognised as both essential, and problematic, for centuries. For centuries, too, the poor have suffered disproportionately when times are hard – and there is good evidence that this is still the case.

There will always be a potential for abuse – which is rarely 'big time' compared with other forms of financial fraud that are both much more lucrative, and (strangely) viewed more indulgently. But without systems of financial aid, or 'social security', poverty and distress will continue to ruin the lives of many, with consequent demands on the wider system of health and social care. An indiscriminate focus on what, of course, should be *part* of its aims – the 'return to work' – must be carefully tempered when it is the lives of the troubled, sick, disabled or dying that are involved. Such tempering is more likely to be possible if there can be more effective linking and appropriate sharing of knowledge and understanding between health, social care and benefits services.

We believe that there are considerable advantages to the language of 'rehabilitation' and 'restoration', rather than one of 'improvement', 'efficiency' or 'reform', all of which have too long been euphemisms for cost-cutting, and which now evoke weary cynicism rather than commitment.

Substantial rehabilitation of the Welfare State is both urgent *and* possible. Inevitably, it will be a complex undertaking, and will require investment of money, time and energy, attitude changes, and new ways of thinking about both management and professional practice. There will be risks and hazards along the way. All involved will need to develop shared understanding and fluency in asserting, justifying and communicating the values, concepts and language of the enterprise. Together, we have to grow the confidence, and the expertise, to design and implement strategy that integrates 'the human' with the technical and structural aspects of our public services. This is, as they say, 'a big ask'.

This book has drawn attention to recent events in the history of our Welfare State, and most particularly in its health and social care services. It bears repeating that, in considering the changes that have occurred over our professional lifetimes, we are not suggesting that there was a previous, unproblematic 'golden age'. We do however know that scrutinising recent history helps us to understand why things are as they are today and move forward more intelligently.

Our observations of human nature, and how we manage ourselves as individuals, and in groups and organisations, are timeless. They are grounded in the evidence and traditions that we have cited. We are offering a way of understanding, a way of thinking about the present day and its dynamics that may suggest ways forward for the future.

As our generation hands on to the next, the pace of change persists, and may well be accelerating. The exponential growth of the 'world-wide web' since 1989 has had a profound effect throughout society, including all aspects of the Welfare State. Social media have revolutionised how, and thus what, we communicate. This has made it all the more urgent that we consider carefully how we relate to others, and what primitive forces may shape our interactions. Such forces are of the kind we have considered extensively in earlier chapters and need to be discussed much more fully in society at large. Artificial Intelligence offers many opportunities, for re-thinking and redesigning how things are done, but there are many attendant risks. Within this context, 'jobs' are becoming more complex, but less secure, and those of us who have them now should expect to work longer than previous generations, who were unlikely to live as long, or be as healthy as they aged. These are some of the many new challenges that need to be addressed, whilst the old ones are still being wrestled with. They will need to be addressed with some new ideas and tools, and of course, many old ones. We offer you those that we have.

Index

Locators in **bold** refer to tables; those in *italic* to figures

About the Authors

John Ballatt

The interest in the first edition of our book gave me the chance to meet and think with a wide range of people, in a variety of roles and sectors, in the UK and beyond. In practitioners, leaders, educators and policy makers, I encountered weary resignation, painful despair and frustration, impressive determination and commitment, and a hunger for ideas and support that would make their work more effective and satisfying. These experiences have driven and shaped my work with Penny and Chris on this edition.

These days, I specialise in offering tailored support and development assistance to individuals, teams and organisations, mainly in health and social care. I lecture and facilitate workshops on systemic perspectives in the development of culture and organisation that promote humane, cooperative and effective practice. Before that, I worked in practice, training, management and commissioning roles at senior levels in the voluntary sector, local government and the NHS, for over 30 years. Bringing together my thoughts and feelings generated by this mixture of 'insider', 'outsider' and 'educator' experience has been a welcome, if often disturbing, experience.

I nowadays live in Leicester, UK, with my wife and co-author Penny Campling, spending my time keeping up with a lively and lovable group of step-offspring, listening to as much music as I can, and getting around a fair bit. My current project is learning to relax.

Penny Campling

I'm often asked what led me to write a book about kindness. Back in 2009, I was a clinical director and consultant psychiatrist working over-hard to cope with financial cuts that were starting to affect the lives of the people we were trying to help, as well as the service itself. I became aware that the combination of pressures was eroding the culture within the organisation. It seemed that anxiety and resentment increasingly coloured the way we related to each other, undermining the respect and ordinary kindness that make difficult tasks just that bit more manageable. Was it possible to reverse this trend? What would need to happen? My experience as a psychotherapist had taught me that it was important to confront directly the factors that denigrate and undermine an individual or organisation, whilst also focussing on positive values and a constructive way forward.

Writing has always been my way of struggling with complicated issues at work, so a new book project seemed in order. Once started, I realised it was a subject that would allow me to explore and share so much of what has excited me during my career. What makes people 'tick' and behave well – and, indeed, badly – towards each other? How do people cope with the emotionally demanding aspects of difficult inter-personal work? How do we organise ourselves in a way that brings out the best in all of us? Sparky conversations over the kitchen table with my partner, John, soon made me realise it would be a better book if it emerged through dialogue, making a strength of our differing backgrounds, perspectives and personalities. Expanding to include Chris as a third author for the second edition has increased the opportunity for creative argument and further enriched the process, and, hopefully, the outcome.

Chris Maloney

I've relied heavily on the NHS at significant times in my life, for my own problems, and with a very sick child. I also worked there for 30 years. Much personal and professional experience is tied up in this book. It's been helpful to get some of what I've seen, thought and felt out in the open, and to try to make helpful suggestions rather than just complain.

Kindness has always mattered to me, and much of my working life has been trying to remedy cruelty. After qualifying as a doctor I trained as a GP, and then as a psychiatrist and a psychotherapist. I set up a psychotherapy service in East Berkshire: often our patients had been traumatised and abused: often by those who were supposed to be caring for them. I was then a GP Partner in Hackney, East London, for 12 years: a chance to work with both 'mind' and 'body'. This was very different. Most people had had an easier start in life, although people rarely see a doctor because good things are happening to them.

Many patients in the practice were refugees, and gradually, because I asked, they would tell me what had happened to them. I started an expert witness practice with asylum seekers in 2003, making integrated psychiatric and physical assessments of their reported torture, and other injuries and experiences, mostly for their asylum claims.

I spent a lot of time with Penny and John when they were writing the first edition (mostly distracting them). They involved me in their thinking, in many enjoyable late-night conversations – and they were very tolerant of my 'two-pennorth' at various stages. The book did impressively well, and helped a lot of people think about what was happening to them. As time passed I nagged them to do a second edition, until they called my bluff by suggesting I did it with them. Then I called theirs by agreeing! It's been a privilege and a pleasure.

Acknowledgements

We want to thank everyone who gave such a warm welcome to the first edition of the book: it was heartening to know it struck a chord with so many people. We were taken aback by the enthusiasm and recognition with which people read the book, and invited us across the country to meet and talk with them. Conversations with readers, colleagues, mentors and friends have enriched our thinking, and stimulated new ideas. Much of the great success of the first edition depended on 'word of mouth', which nowadays so often means appreciative and encouraging blog posts and 'Twittering'.

There are too many of all these people to mention individually, but we hope they know who they are. We did, however, get particular encouragement from Iona Heath, Clare Gerada, Patrick Pietroni, and Tim Dartington. For this new edition, we have received helpful advice from many people. In particular, we would like to thank Rosie Thomas and Bob Carter for their generosity with their time and ideas.

Returning to our book after eight years was quite an experience. Thanks to our friends and families for their patience and support, and especially to Monica Petzal, for so much encouragement, dinner and practical advice.